FINANCIAL MANAGEMENT

in Agriculture

Third Edition

FINANCIAL

Peter J. Barry, Ph.D.

Professor of
  Agricultural Finance
University of Illinois
  at Urbana–Champaign

John A. Hopkin, Ph.D.

Stiles Professor of
  Agricultural Finance
Texas A&M University

Danville, Illinois:

MANAGEMENT

in Agriculture

C. B. Baker, Ph.D.

Professor of
  Agricultural Economics
University of Illinois
  at Urbana–Champaign

The Interstate Printers & Publishers, Inc.

Library of Congress Catalog Card No. 82-84347

ISBN 0-8134-2291-4

PREFACE

As in previous editions, the third edition of *Financial Management in Agriculture* applies the principles and tools of finance to managerial problems in agriculture. Many important problems of agricultural firms involve financial management: financing resource control, evaluating new investments, designing financially feasible business plans, reporting business performance, and managing risks and liquidity. Most agricultural firms differ greatly from large corporations in other industries. Farms and ranches are typically proprietorships, partnerships, or corporations of smaller size with special characteristics. The farm operator must manage financial activities as well as those in production, marketing, and personnel. Land, climate, and biological factors are especially important. Special financial institutions and lending programs are also available. All these factors make financial management in agriculture important and unique.

The central focus of *Financial Management in Agriculture* is on planning, analyzing, and controlling the business performance of agricultural firms. The book contains 19 chapters, organized into six sections. Section I introduces the nature and scope of financial management and establishes profitability, risk, and liquidity as the major performance criteria. The three chapters in Section II present the financial statements for measuring and analyzing business performance and show cash flow budgeting as the central coordinating tool for financial planning and analysis.

Section III develops the concepts of financial leverage, risk, and liquidity and their joint effects on business performance. Various strategies for managing business and financial risks are considered, with emphasis on managing credit and liquidity. Section IV develops the principles and tools of asset valuation and long-term financial decision making. Capital budgeting methods are identified under conditions of risk and inflation and under alternative financing arrangements for owning and leasing business assets.

Section V contains three chapters which treat the structure, performance, and policy issues of financial intermediaries serving agriculture. This section provides important information for understanding how financial markets influence the decision-making environment of agricultural firms. The final section considers legal forms of business organization and the management of equity capital in agriculture.

This edition differs from previous editions in the organizational flow of material, revisions in chapter content, and updating of empirical data and other information. The content reflects new information about the effects of inflation and risks on financial decisions. It also reflects changes in regulations during the 1980s affecting income taxation in the United States and the performance of financial institutions providing credit and related services to agriculture. New chapters are added that focus on risk management in farm businesses and leasing of non-real estate assets. Material on financial planning, cash flow budgeting, and feasibility analysis is consolidated and directly follows chapters on financial statements and financial analysis. In addition, cost of capital concepts are linked more directly to farm financial structure and to the effects of leverage on expected returns and risk. In our judgment these changes will benefit students, instructors, and others who use the book in the classroom or in independent study.

The principles and tools of financial management which are stressed in the book are applicable in most countries of the world, although the book's institutional setting reflects the financial and legal environment of the United States. Thus some of the content will need to be supplemented for users in countries whose financial markets, institutions, and instruments differ from those of the United States in organization or in degree of development.

The book is intended primarily for third- or fourth-year undergraduate students and beginning graduate students. The student is assumed to have brief exposure to micro economic principles, and some statistical measures are used in developing analytical techniques. Otherwise, the book represents a starting point in the study of agricultural finance. Some chapters have appendices which carry material to greater depth. Comprehensive reference lists and suggested topics for discussion are provided in each chapter.

We are indebted to persons and groups too numerous to include specifically. Special thanks are due to J. R. Brake, J. H. Clark, S. C. Gabriel, J. S. Holderness, J. M. Holcomb, L. J. Robison, and S. T. Sonka, for critiques and suggestions on parts or all of the manuscripts for the various editions. A large number of students and instructors have made useful suggestions and have raised critical questions that have furthered the book's development. Finally, we are grateful to the book reviewers of several journals whose comments and critiques have contributed to the revision process.

PETER J. BARRY
JOHN A. HOPKIN
C. B. BAKER

CONTENTS

SECTION III

Capital Structure, Liquidity, and Risk Management

SECTION IV

Capital Budgeting and Long-Term Decision Making

SECTION V

Financial Markets
for Agriculture

SECTION VI

Other Topics

SECTION I

Introduction

Chapter 1

NATURE AND SCOPE
OF FINANCIAL MANAGEMENT

Financial management involves the acquisition and use of resources by a business and the protection of its equity capital from various business and financial risks. The evaluation of new investments, financial planning, liquidity management, and relationships with financial intermediaries are also important. Financial management is closely related to the production and marketing activities of farm businesses and to cash management of farm households. In this chapter we introduce the firm's organizational areas and their relationships to the process of management. We also consider the special relevance of time and risk in financial management.

The Financial Function

Figure 1.1 portrays an organizational flow chart of a farm business that shows how finance is related to production, marketing, and consumption. The firm's beginning balance sheet is the source of current, intermediate, and fixed farm assets which are used to produce saleable commodities. These farm assets, along with new purchases, are financed by the firm's equity capital (its "savings") and by borrowed capital. Other assets may be leased or hired from off-farm sources. The availability of credit plays a central role in financing asset acquisitions and as a source of liquidity for meeting obligations and countering risks.

Produced commodities can be sold for cash or for "receivables" which can be liquidated during the year or carried forward to the ending balance sheet. In addition, some commodities may be stored in inventory for later sale. The income expectations from current sales, or anticipated sales from inventory, influence the amount and

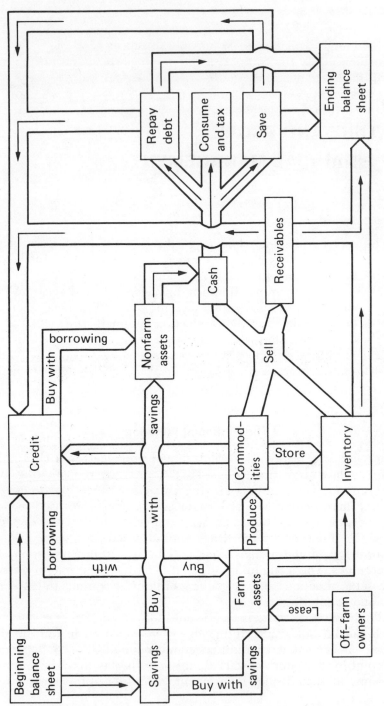

Figure 1.1. Organizational flow chart of the farm firm.

terms of credit available to the business from its lenders. Credit is also influenced by the composition of assets and past borrowing activities. These credit effects and other influences on cash flow determine the firm's liquidity position.

The cash from commodity sales is used to pay debt obligations and to meet outlays for taxes and family consumption. The remaining cash goes into savings and, along with other assets, enters the ending balance sheet. Effects of nonfarm activities on cash flow and balance sheets are also accounted for. These processes are then repeated as another year begins.

These activities occur in a farming environment characterized by high risk and uncertainty. The traditional business risks in agriculture come mostly from production activities and from resource and commodity markets. These business risks occur as unanticipated variations in farm production and in commodity and resource prices, uncertainties about personnel performance, technological change, and changes in the legal environment. These business risks combine with financial risks, attributed to borrowing and leasing, to bring strong challenges in risk management for farmers and their lenders.

The Firm's Organizational Areas

Managerial decisions are considered in three areas: production, marketing, and finance. In the past, farmers' managerial efforts mostly centered on production and marketing: what to produce; how to produce; what combinations of inputs and outputs; and when, where, and how to buy and sell. This focus reflected the non-corporate, small-scale structure of most farm businesses. Historically, agriculture was dominated by single proprietorships with ownership, labor, and management resting with one individual or family. In contrast, large corporations separate and specialize these functions so that owners hire managers who, in turn, hire the laborers.

More recently, financial management in agriculture has been recognized as a high payoff area requiring more strength and special skills. Farming and ranching have become commercial businesses with larger capital-intensive units that are increasingly dependent on commodity markets for acquiring inputs and selling products and on financial markets for financing transactions. Changes in technology have led to specialized farm production and greater capitalization. The combined effects of larger, more efficient machinery and equipment and the business expansion needed for full resource utilization have stimulated high rates of financial growth to preserve the economic viability of farm businesses. Thus financial management plays an important role in accumulating capital and responding to risks.

Efficiency in production and marketing is important. But highly efficient production systems may not assure adequate and reliable farm incomes. Financial management involves these types of questions: Is the farm business large enough to provide an adequate income? Is growth a business goal? What is required to achieve growth? How can I evaluate new investments? What type of financing is available? How is the lender involved? How can I increase my credit worthiness? Which lender is most appropriate? What loan terms will best fit repayment capacity? Despite reasonable farm incomes, why is cash always in short supply? How seasonal are cash flows? Do family living expenses compete with reinvestment of business earnings? How should business and financial risks be managed? Should cash or credit reserves be held? What type of insurance do I need? What are the alternatives for tax management?

The three areas of a business are not independent. Production and marketing decisions are influenced by lenders' actions affecting the size, cost, and other terms of loans, and by farmers' risk attitudes and other financial decisions. Similarly, alternative investments and financing programs affect cash flows, income expectations, and the firm's financial position.

The Management Process

The process of management can be ordered into a systematic set of steps, each having a unique focus. Table 1.1 identifies these procedural steps and illustrates their application to the firm's organizational areas. Even this simple classification scheme reflects the complexity and scope of management.

The steps of the management process are identified as follows:

1. Formulating Objectives

Objectives or goals guide the decision process. A manager must identify relevant and feasible objectives, their desired levels of attainment, and acceptable deviations from these levels.

Table 1.1. The Process of Management as Applied in Organizational Areas of the Firm

Procedural Steps in Management	Organizational Areas of the Firm		
	Production	Marketing	Finance
Objectives	Optimal resource use and organization	Optimal time, place, type of sales, and purchases	Optimal financial flows and structure
Problem Definition	Production opportunities and constraints	Market opportunities and constraints	Financial opportunities and constraints
Gathering Information	Production records and technical literature	Sales and purchase records and market reports	Observation and experience with lenders; cash flow budgets
Analysis	Production coefficients	Supply, demand, terms of trade	Leverage and liquidity coefficients
Synthesis	Production outcomes	Costs and returns estimates	Reserves and growth rate
Decision and Action	Commit resources to enterprise and resource organization plans	Buy and sell	Borrow, lease, pay debts, insure, expand the business
Accepting Consequences	Enterprise diversity and resource flexibility	Contract sales, hedges and government programs	Insurance, liquidity management, growth and decline
Evaluation	Compare output against expectations or production standards	Compare actual performance with budgeted expectations	Compare actual growth rates and financial structure with projections

2. Defining the Problem or Opportunity

The need for a decision must be identified, whether it is a favorable opportunity to exploit or a difficult problem to resolve. Separating the symptoms from the actual cause is crucial.

3. Gathering Information

Data, facts, and other information are needed to resolve the problem and achieve the desired objectives. Included are the manager's possible actions, the likelihood of the occurrence of certain events, a set of available resources, legal requirements, the firm's financial position, and information about relevant external factors.

4. Analysis

The information gathered in Step 3 must be analyzed to

evaluate the estimated contributions of all managerial actions to the firm's objectives.

5. *Synthesis*

Complete evaluation of managerial actions requires a synthesis of the estimates in Step 4 with previous knowledge about the firm and its environment. Combining the effects of production, marketing, and financing decisions is important too. Some form of budgeting is commonly used.

6. *The Decision and Action*

After considering all relevant alternatives, the manager must choose a course of action and administer the plan.

7. *Accepting Consequences*

The manager must be willing and able to accept both favorable and unfavorable outcomes. This involves effective risk management.

8. *Evaluation*

Prior decisions must be re-evaluated as changes occur in technology, laws, economic conditions, markets, and personal situations to determine new courses of action.

Managerial effectiveness depends in part on accurate problem definition and efficient use of the management process. Impediments arise throughout the steps of the process as a result of limits on human abilities to observe, order, and analyze large amounts of complex information. External changes can often create new problems or opportunities quickly enough to re-orient the decision process before current issues are resolved. Objectives must be feasible and realistic. The symptoms of a problem must be separated from the underlying cause. Searching for information and problem solutions is often time consuming, costly, and emotionally demanding. Decision making itself can be an anxiety-producing act. Superior managers generally show an orderly approach, strong analytical skills, decisiveness, and the capacity to accept consequences.

In Table 1.1 we apply the management process to the firm's organizational areas. During one day, a business manager applies the process to many problems, both large and small. Each decision situation may vary in size of potential gains or losses, frequency of occurrence, urgency of pending action, and flexibility or cost of change following the decision. Managers who effectively apply the decision process will usually achieve a greater managerial capacity and receive greater rewards.

Time and Risk

The impacts of time and risk are important factors in financial management. Long planning horizons are needed to properly analyze the payoffs from capital investments and their contributions to the firm's objectives. Moreover, the manager's expectations about future events and decision outcomes are mostly uncertain. Risk and uncertainty reduce the reliability of future plans and shorten planning horizons. Indeed, the very need for management largely arises from these uncertain expectations.

For some decisions, especially routine repetitive ones, the manager can accurately identify the possible outcomes and judge their likelihoods. Moreover, the losses may be offset by gains over time. In other cases the manager may have much difficulty delineating the possible outcomes, and even more their likelihood.

Business and financial risks complicate financial management. They may trigger substantial efforts to manage risks and protect cash flows and equity capital. Reducing the likelihood of risks, building risk-bearing capacity, and transferring risks to other economic units all warrant careful consideration.

It is also common to observe a "life cycle" effect in a farm business which reflects the life cycle of the firm's manager and influences his planning horizon. A farm business usually passes through four stages in its life cycle: establishment, growth, consolidation, and transfer. The results of the management process differ with each stage, as shown in the following chapter.

Tools of Financial Management

Concepts and tools of financial management are the central focus of this book. In this chapter we briefly introduce some of the basic tools under the headings of information flows, budgeting methods, and contributing disciplines.

Information Flows

Information about past, present, and expected business performance is essential for the financial manager. It is provided by an effective financial accounting system which reports the firm's profitability, liquidity, solvency, and risk positions. An information system aids in financial control, risk management, the meeting of legal requirements, and financial planning. The system also provides information about credit worthiness and management ability to lenders and other outside parties.

Other information comes from a firm's external environment as illustrated by colleges of agriculture, agricultural agencies in government, the communications media, farm organizations, agribusinesses, and investment and marketing services. Efficient access to external information provides a timely information base and stronger capability for responding to new conditions.

Budgeting Methods

Budgeting methods involve an orderly approach to assembling and analyzing information and choosing among financial alternatives. In financial management, the emphasis is on *cash flow budgets* and *capital budgeting*. Cash flow budgets are essential for establishing financing programs and managing liquidity in light of seasonal patterns for farm production and marketing.

Capital budgets enable the manager to compare new investments under different financing alternatives using various decision criteria. Sometimes budgeting can be computerized using simulation or mathematical programming techniques. Electronic data processing and recording systems provide much of the planning data. Use of the computer can greatly accelerate the budgeting process and increase analytical capacity.

No planning procedure is perfect; nor is budgeting error-free. The plans derived from empirical observations, logical deduction, pencil and paper analysis, or computerized techniques are subject to the quality of data and the careful application of the management process. Moreover, the best plans are still subject to substantial uncertainty.

Contributing Disciplines

When the study of finance originated, it largely emphasized a firm's acquisition of funds and described the structure and functions of lending institutions. During the growth periods of the 1950s and

1960s, however, business finance expanded to include investment analysis, financial planning, and re-investment decisions. Instabilities of financial and commodity markets in the 1970s and 1980s have given emphasis to sources of risk and risk management. Management of assets, liabilities, and liquidity have come to the forefront.

Financial management is essentially applied economics under conditions of time and uncertainty. Much of managerial behavior is explained or guided by the principles of economics. Production economics involves a firm's optimal allocation of limited resources among alternative uses. The technical areas of agriculture—soils, agronomy, animal science, and engineering—provide basic data about input-output relationships, production capacities, and technological factors. These are applied in production economics when cost and return data for farm enterprises are available. The principles of exchange in agricultural markets influence the terms of exchange for resources, farm products, and financial capital. These terms of exchange must be considered in resource allocation and enterprise planning. Finally, the principles of consumer choice outline the household's allocation of family income between consumption and saving.

Principles of finance modify but do not replace the principles of production economics, exchange, and consumption. In subsequent chapters, for example, we define credit as an individual's borrowing capacity. As such, credit is an "economic good" to be produced, managed, and marketed. We emphasize that the terms of exchange between the borrower and lender may influence a manager's resource allocation, rate of growth, and ability to manage risks. In this light, knowledge of principles and methods for marketing credit is essential to financial management.

Topics for Discussion

1. Identify the steps of a systematic management process. Where do impediments lie? How are risk and uncertainty involved?
2. Illustrate some of the financial decisions that farmers must make. How do they differ from production and marketing decisions?
3. Identify some of the interrelationships among decision making in finance, production, and marketing. Why are they important?
4. How are the effects of time and risk important to financial management? Illustrate some financial methods for managing risks.

5. Where does a farmer obtain information needed in production decisions? In marketing decisions? In financial decisions?
6. A farmer is considering taking his son and daughter, young college students, into the farm business. They are concerned with whether or not this is a wise decision. How would you address this situation using the management process? What questions arise? What alternatives are possible? What information is needed? What risks are involved, and how can they be managed?

References

1. Barry, P. J., and C. B. Baker, "Management of Financial Structure: Firm Level," *Agricultural Finance Review*, 37(February 1977):50-63.
2. Brake, J. R., and E. O. Melichar, "Agricultural Finance and Capital Markets," *A Survey of Agricultural Economics Literature*, University of Minnesota Press, Minneapolis, 1977.
3. Frey, T. L., and R. Behrens, *Lending to Agricultural Enterprises*, American Banking Institute, New York, 1982.
4. Lee, W. F., et al., *Agricultural Finance*, 7th ed., Iowa State University Press, Ames, 1980.
5. Lins, D. A., N. E. Harl, and T. L. Frey, *Farmland*, Century Communications, Inc., Skokie, Illinois, 1982.
6. Van Horne, J. C., *Financial Management and Policy*, 5th ed., Prentice-Hall, Inc., Englewood Cliffs, New Jersey, 1980.
7. Weston, J. F., *The Scope and Methodology of Finance*, Prentice-Hall, Inc., Englewood Cliffs, New Jersey, 1966.
8. Weston, J. F., and E. F. Brigham, *Managerial Finance*, 6th ed., Dryden Press, Hinsdale, Illinois, 1982.

Chapter 2

MANAGERIAL GOALS

Before developing the principles and tools of financial management, it is important to establish the goals which guide managerial behavior and which will be used in evaluating the financial performance and managerial decisions of agricultural businesses. These are expressed as a goal or utility function containing three elements: profitability, risk, and liquidity. We assume that these three criteria, taken together, determine the overall well-being or utility of the firm's decision makers.

Nearly all the material in the chapters to follow relates to these criteria. Information systems are designed to report business performance for analysis in terms of profitability, risk, and liquidity. Decisions on investments, financing, growth rates, and capital structure are also evaluated with these criteria. These criteria are important, and it is useful to consider their behavioral implications, origins, and interrelationships.

Goal Identification

It is nearly impossible to meaningfully evaluate business performance without knowledge of the goals or objectives which are associated with that performance. Goal *identification* leads, in turn, to the development of *measures* of goal attainment, of *targets* for these measures, and of *analytical procedures* for relating plans and expectations to the measures and to the targets. The results of goal identification are improved understanding of a business's past performance and better plans for its future.

These procedures sound very straightforward. However, goal identification is not an easy task. Much more than economics and finance is involved. Social scientists agree that individuals have many goals, both economic and social-psychological, which they are simultaneously striving to achieve. Many of these goals may be organized in hierarchies in which one goal must be achieved before attention turns to the next goal, and so on. As an example, one social scientist (Maslow) identifies five ordered goals. He identifies an individual's most basic need as providing for physical necessities such as food, clothing, and shelter. Then comes the need for security, followed by social belonging, recognition and esteem, and self-actualization. Clearly, individuals at different stages of this ordering exhibit different kinds of behavior.

Maslow's list seems remote from economics and financial management. But it helps to indicate the scope of individual goals and the difficulties an analyst has in designing performance measures which capture the unique characteristics and aspirations of every business and every financial manager. By the same token, these multiple hierarchies of goals also imply that using a single goal or measure (e.g., annual income) to evaluate the well-being of many individuals may not be satisfactory.

Instead, a middle ground is needed that portrays several meaningful financial characteristics of business performance and that is suited for measurement and analysis. For our purposes, this middle ground is reflected by the multiple goals of profitability, risk, and liquidity. The following sections discuss these criteria and their use in financial management.

Profitability

Economists generally analyze supply, demand, and prices by making precise assumptions about the objectives of consumers and business firms and by initially assuming away most of the problems of time and risk. Rational consumers are assumed to maximize the utility of consuming goods or services. Rational business persons are assumed to maximize the profits obtained from the production of goods and services. The consumers' search for utility maximization underlies the demand for goods and services, while the businesses' search for profits gives rise to supplies of goods and services. Taken together, demand and supply determine prices of goods and services.

The well-being of consumers can be evaluated by their utility attainment, and the well-being of businesses can be evaluated by their profits. Consider utility first. Why treat utility along with profits when evaluating business performance? One reason is that all business persons are also consumers, and if utility maximization explains their consumption behavior, then it may also influence their business behavior. This influence may be especially strong in agriculture due to the close relationship between the business and household for most farms and ranches. Another reason is that the framework for understanding the firm's risk responses is best developed in utility terms.

What is utility? It is not bankable, tradeable, or even easily measurable. It is simply a concept. Economists say that utility reflects the level of preference or enjoyment attached to a good or service. The higher the preference or enjoyment, the higher the utility. Profits have utility and more profits mean more utility. Similarly, the physical and financial assets that generate or protect profits have utility for their owners.

A business's quest for profits is a more tangible concept. Profits can indeed be measured. They are the difference between the value of goods and services produced by the firm and the costs of resources used in their production. However, there are numerous accounting approaches to measuring profits, and careful judgment is needed in choosing a particular measure.

In addition, the economic rules for organizing a business's inputs and enterprises so as to maximize profits are clear. A firm with a production function characterized by diminishing marginal productivity and operating in perfectly competitive markets will achieve profit-maximizing organizations of inputs and enterprises by producing so that marginal value products (the added value produced from added inputs) are equal in all enterprises and, in turn, are equal to marginal input costs. Or, when viewed from a cost-size standpoint, profit maximization guides the firm to a level of production where marginal revenue from added output equals marginal cost of added output. Moreover, in the long run, competition will cause this condition to occur at the firm's lowest point on its long-run average-cost curve.

These economic principles have served well in studies of economic behavior and in guiding decision making. But they assume away the principal effects of time and uncertainty, both of which are important determinants of real-world behavior.

Consider first how the effects of time modify profit maximization. Most firms plan to operate over long periods of time. They have long-planning horizons and are concerned with the level and timing of their profits during this planning horizon. Most firms prefer their profits and net worth to grow over time. A growth objective may mean sacrificing some profits in the near future in order to expand profits in the more distant future. How much sacrifice should occur to maximize the well-being or utility of the firm? Investments such as orchards, range improvement, herd expansion, and others also build up returns slowly over time and may therefore "pay off" more slowly. Yet, with more time, their total profits may exceed those from other investments. Financing terms on loans also influence the level and timing of returns.

These effects of time mean that static measures of profit are often inadequate. Instead, concepts and measures are needed to account for the level and timing of profits over a firm's planning horizon. We will show that the economic value of a firm is directly determined by the level and timing of the profits projected during its planning horizon. This economic value is called *present value*; and it is found by summing the annual projected profits, appropriately *discounted* for time.

The derivation of present-value models, their data requirements, and their uses will be developed in later chapters. For now we emphasize that our concept of "profits" is expressed by the value of the firm. In the absence of risk, we assume that investors desire to maximize the economic value of their claims on the firm's assets. More specifically, they are assumed to maximize the value of the firm's equity capital.

Risk

Profit maximization as it is portrayed in the preceding section ignores risks, yet, risks occurring as unanticipated changes are pervasive phenomena, and most individuals are averse to risks. Hence, the assumption of profit maximization must be modified to reflect the presence of risk and various attitudes toward risk.

Risk Aversion and Risk Premiums

Risk aversion does not mean that individuals are unwilling to take risks. Rather, risk aversion means that they must be compensated for taking risks and that the required compensation increases as the risks increase. In comparing a risky investment to a risk-free investment, the risk averter expresses the need for compensation by requiring a higher expected return on the risky investment than on the risk-free investment in order to be indifferent between them.

This difference in required returns is called a risk premium, or price of risk, that compensates the individual for bearing the risk.

As an example, consider an investment in a U.S. Government bond, which is essentially risk-free, and an investment in a beef-cow enterprise, which is known to be risky. Risk in this case means that declining cattle prices or death losses may result in economic losses for the investor. The bond is known to yield a 10 percent annual interest rate. In assessing the risk of the beef investment, the investor decides that a 15 percent annual rate of return will leave him indifferent between the two investments. The 5 percent difference is the risk premium required by the investor to make the two investments comparable. The risk premium compensates the investor for the added risk. Moreover, the risk premium increases as the level of risk or risk aversion increases.

The problems with using profit maximization to evaluate the behavior of a risk averter should now be clear. If the beef investment is expected to yield 15 percent while the bond yields 10 percent, then a profit maximizer would choose the beef investment. However, we have just seen that the investor's judgment of investment risk, together with the level of risk aversion, leads to indifference between the two investments. Moreover, if the expected profit rate of the beef investment were 14 percent instead of 15 percent, it would be unacceptable to the risk-averse investor, even though its expected profits would be greater than the bond investment. Market behavior produces the interesting and realistic observation that more profitable ventures are also more risky, with the differences in profits generally being just enough to compensate the average investor for the greater risk.

Risk Dominance

The trade-off between risk and expected profits is illustrated in Figure 2.1, where the risk of several investments is plotted against their expected profits. Higher risk is reflected by movement up the vertical axis, while higher profits are measured along the horizontal axis. Suppose that the investor is considering 10 investments with estimates of risk and expected profits reflected by points A through H in Figure 2.1. Even without knowing the investor's risk-return preference, some of these investment choices can be eliminated. For example, investments A and B both yield the same expected profit (E_{AB}); however, the risk of A (V_A) is lower than the risk of B (V_B).

Hence, B is eliminated as an inferior or dominated investment. In a similar fashion, C dominates D, F dominates G, and I dominates H.

Now compare investments A and C. Investment C has both higher expected profits and higher risk. The preferred investment is based on the risk premiums required by the investor. The same results occur for investments F, I, and J.

An important pattern is evident in Figure 2.1. Prospective investments are divided into two sets—a dominated set and a dominating set. The dominating set is also called the risk-efficient set. It has those investments or combinations of investments that provide minimum risk for alternative levels of expected profits. In Figure 2.1, the dominating set contains investments A, C, F, I, and J, which are aligned along the lower boundary of all the investment choices. The investor's optimal or expected utility maximizing choice will occur from among this dominating set.

Several characteristics of the dominating set are important. First, investments with higher-expected profits also have higher risk. Sec-

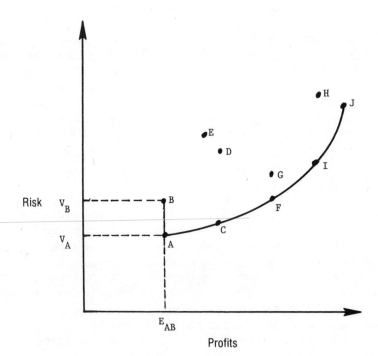

Figure 2.1. Trade-offs in risk and expected profits.

ond, the increase in risk is faster than the increase in profits. Third, the investment with maximum-expected profit is at the top of the dominating set (investment J in Figure 2.1). Fourth, the profit-maximizing investment is also the riskiest of the dominating investments. However, it is not necessarily the riskiest of all investments. Investment H, for example, has higher risk than J, but H is dominated by I. Fifth, if enough investments are considered, the dominating set becomes quite large and appears as a risk-profit curve or "frontier," like the dotted line, ACFIJ. Sixth, the optimal or expected utility maximizing choice cannot be predicted without knowing the investor's risk-return preferences.

Risk Measures

The next task is to establish procedures for measuring risk. To be meaningful, a risk measure should reflect how risks are perceived by an investor. While there is no sure way to model risk perceptions, most analysts assume that risk perception is expressed as the likelihood of several possible outcomes. Some of these outcomes may cause adversity or losses for the investor.

Hence, rather than use a single projection, it may be more realistic to describe outcomes from an investment in terms of a range of possible events, each associated with a probability. The probability distribution essentially reflects how an investor formulates expectations about the outcomes of risky events.

This concept of risk focuses on the random, or unanticipated, variability of outcomes, some of which are favorable for the investor, while others may cause losses or adversity. An alternative concept of risk focuses on the probability of loss or failure to meet a financial obligation. In the latter case, the probability distribution can be used to estimate the probability of loss.

The idea of a probability distribution is not difficult to grasp. Suppose that the beef-cow investor is also considering a hog investment. The investor believes that three possible profit rates could occur for each investment with the respective probabilities given in Table 2.1. The discrete probability distribution for the beef investment indicates a 30 percent probability of a 9 percent profit rate, a 40 percent probability of a 12 percent profit rate, and a 30 percent probability of a 15 percent profit rate. This probability distribution is graphed in Figure 2.2, with probabilities measured along the vertical axis and profit rates along the horizontal axis.

Table 2.1. Probability Distributions for Beef and Hog Investments

	Beef		Hogs	
Forecast	Profit Rate	Probability	Profit Rate	Probability
Optimistic	.15	.30	.21	.10
Most Likely	.12	.40	.15	.60
Pessimistic	.09	.30	.08	.30

These distributions are used to estimate three statistical measures which aid decision making: *the expected value, the standard deviation,* and *the coefficient of variation.* The expected value or mean of the probability distribution is a weighted average of the profit rates for the projected outcomes, using the probabilities as weights. Expected values are found by summing the products of each possible outcome times its probability. This process is expressed in a formula as:

$$E(\bar{V}) = \Sigma_i P_i V_i \qquad (2.1)$$

where $E(\bar{V})$ = expected value, Σ is a summation sign, P_i = the probability for each forecast i, and V_i = the profit projected for each forecast.

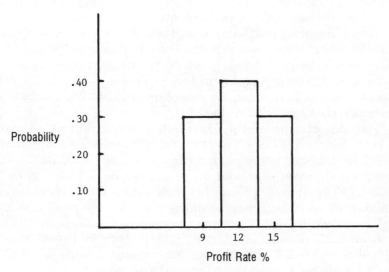

Figure 2.2. Probability distribution.

The expected values of the two investment choices in Table 2.1 are:

$$E(\bar{V})_1 = (.30)(.15) + (.40)(.12) + (.30)(.09) = .12, \text{ or } 12\%$$

$$E(\bar{V})_2 = (.10)(.21) + (.60)(.15) + (.30)(.08) = .135, \text{ or } 13.5\%.$$

The expected value of the hog investment (13.5 percent) is larger than the expected value of the beef investment (12 percent). Thus, its expected profitability is higher.

The standard deviation (σ) is a statistical measure of the amount of dispersion or variation of the projected outcomes about the expected value. Thus, it serves as a measure of the amount of risk. The standard deviation is found with this formula:

$$\sigma_T = \sqrt{\Sigma_i(P_i)(V_i - \bar{V})^2} = [\Sigma_i(P_i)(V_i - \bar{V})^2]^{\frac{1}{2}} \tag{2.2}$$

This formula indicates the following procedure for finding the standard deviation. First, find the difference between the expected value ($\bar{V}$) of the distribution and each projected outcome. Square each difference. Then multiply each squared difference by its probability. Add up these products (the sum is called the variance of the distribution). Finally, take the square root to find the standard deviation.

The standard deviation of the beef and hog investments are:

$$\sigma_1 = [(.30)(.15 - .12)^2 + (.40)(.12 - .12)^2 + (.30)$$

$$(.09 - .12)^2]^{\frac{1}{2}} = .023, \text{ or } 2.3\%$$

$$\sigma_2 = [(.10)(.21 - .135)^2 + (.60)(.15 - .135)^2 + (.30)$$

$$(.08 - .135)^2]^{\frac{1}{2}} = .040, \text{ or } 4.0\%.$$

Thus, investment 2 has the greater amount of risk.

Note that both the expected value and the standard deviation of investment 2 are greater than those of investment 1. How can these investments be compared? One useful statistical measure is the coefficient of variation (CV), which is the standard deviation divided by the expected value:

$$CV_1 = \frac{\sigma_1}{E(\bar{V})_1} = \frac{2.3\%}{12.0\%} = .192 \tag{2.3}$$

$$CV_2 = \frac{\sigma_2}{E(\bar{V})_2} = \frac{4.0\%}{13.5\%} = .296. \tag{2.4}$$

The coefficient of variation provides a relative measure of an investment's degree of risk. It shows the amount of risk relative to the amount of expected return. Since the CV for investment 2 is larger, we can conclude that it is the riskier venture. While its expected value is greater, the expected variation increases even more. An investor's choice between the two investments thus depends on his or her risk-return preferences.

Estimating Probabilities

Estimating probabilities is important in risk analysis. There are two schools of thought on this issue. The more traditional view contends that probabilities cannot be effectively used to describe the outcomes of specific investments or other events for several reasons. First, the classical view of probability theory holds that no statement can be made about the probability of a single event—only about the frequency of occurrence of events which are repeatedly observed under identical conditions. Second, historical data on costs, revenues, output, etc., needed to estimate probability distributions, either are not sufficiently available or are generated by conditions (technical, economic, managerial) that are likely to change in the future.

In recent years, another view of probability has gained widespread acceptance. This view holds that investors can formulate "subjective" probabilities of specific events which are based on, but not limited to, historical frequencies. Often these *subjective probabilities* may be based on historic data; however, if an investor feels that historic conditions are no longer relevant for future analyses, he or she may ignore them completely. In fact, future expectations based on combinations of historical data and subjective judgments may be the most effective approach.

Much theoretical work has studied the use of probability measures in decision making. Most of the techniques are still in an early state of development. Nonetheless, most individuals can express their expectations in probabilistic terms. As examples, consider the quantitative estimates of weather forecasters about the chance of rain, doctor's predictions of success in surgical procedures, and the odds on athletic events quoted by the sports media.

To illustrate further, consider a university student trying to estimate his likely grade from an agricultural finance course. He arrays the possible events as follows:

Grade	Probability (P_i)
A	_____
B	_____
C	_____
D	_____
F	_____

He must be sure that the probabilities are nonnegative $(P_i \geq 0)$ and sum to one $(\Sigma_i P_i = 1)$.

What sources of information might he use? He might conclude that the five events are equally likely and assign to each a 20 percent probability. Or he might observe the relative frequency of grades from a historic time series of similar classes taught by the same instructor, finding a distribution as follows: A = 25 percent, B = 35 percent, C = 20 percent, D = 8 percent, and F = 2 percent. Finally, he might take into account his own major, course background, grade performance, and interest in the course and determine that for him a probability distribution of A = 95 percent and B = 5 percent is best.

Try this procedure in evaluating your own grade expectations in probabilistic terms. Are the results realistic? The best possible? Do they help explain your actions? Is there a better way? Couldn't the same procedures work for farmers and other investors who must base plans on future prices, yields, costs of capital, etc.? Once the probability distribution is obtained, then the various statistical measures can be determined to show the amount of risk.

Liquidity

Besides profitability and risk, financial managers must also be concerned with liquidity. Hence, liquidity management contributes meaningfully to the manager's overall utility.

Liquidity refers to the ability to generate cash in order to meet cash demands as they occur and to provide for unanticipated events. Cash is needed to meet payments for the usual business and personal transactions: paying operating expenses, paying for capital items, meeting scheduled debt payments, and meeting family needs. Unanticipated events can include new investment opportunities or adversity that causes economic losses and makes it difficult to meet cash demands. Failure to meet these cash demands due to inadequate liquidity can seriously jeopardize business survival and credit worthiness.

The firm's need for liquidity is closely tied to its risk position;

the occurrence of risks cause the need for liquidity. Also, increased liquidity can lower the manager's risk premium. Hence, one way a risk-averse investor may display risk aversion is through effective liquidity management. The linkage between risk and liquidity becomes clearer when the firm's sources of liquidity are considered. Liquidity is generally provided by holding saleable assets or by having the capacity to borrow additional funds. However, the occurrence of serious risks may make it difficult to liquidate assets, especially if they have declined in value, and may make it difficult to borrow additional funds. For some kinds of events, commercial insurance provides another source of liquidity.

Life Cycle of the Firm

The close household-business relationship of most farms and ranches closely links the life cycle of the firm to the life cycle of the manager. Moreover, the manager's objectives may change over the life cycle. The life stages are indicated in Figure 2.3. The beginning manager focuses on establishment in agriculture with a viable organization and the control of sufficient resources for future growth. Wealth and liquidity are generally low; risk is high, because of unproven management ability. Family assistance has always been important, including parent-children business arrangements, gifts, marriage, and family loans or sales. Leasing of assets is also important. These strategies for entering agriculture may significantly influence cash flow, profits, and growth potential for many years.

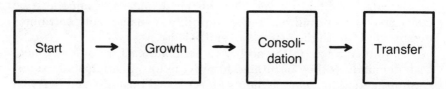

Figure 2.3. Stages of a firm's life cycle.

Once established in a business, the typical manager seeks to grow to more fully utilize management capacity, to gain economic security, or to maintain a competitive position in the industry. Beyond the growth stage, farm businesses enter stages of consolidation of gains and then transfer to new management. Objectives will change during these stages. In the consolidation stage, capital accumulation and growth may have lower value. The manager now has control of the business and has a stronger financial position. However, continued growth may be needed to maintain the financial position. Thus, growth may continue into the consolidation stage.

In the transfer stage, the manager is long on experience and capital but short on energy and length of planning horizon. The manager controls resources but may let others assume their use. Expansion of wealth and income-generating capacity may become less important, and investments with faster payback are preferred. Attention turns to assuring a stable source of retirement income that provides liquidity for emergencies and protection against inflation. Concerns turn to management continuity and production efficiency as the business is transferred to new management, and to minimizing the cost of transferring assets to heirs in an equitable fashion. In large firms with several specialized managers, the effects of the transfer stage are less noticeable.

These life stages will vary among individuals in length, in style, and even in behavior. Some beginners are highly risk-averse from the start. Others strive mightily for growth. Still others, who might benefit from an orderly transfer to new managers, struggle to retain their control well beyond the point of rational transfer.

Topics for Discussion

1. Why is goal identification important in explaining managerial behavior?
2. Explain the nature of utility and utility maximization. How do these concepts differ from profits and profit maximization?
3. Briefly explain how the profit concept is modified to account for the effects of time.
4. Define risk premium. What is it used for? Why are more profitable ventures also more risky? How is the risk premium related to risk aversion?
5. Suppose a risk-averse investor is choosing between two investments: Investment A promises a 10 percent expected rate of return with a standard deviation of 5 percent, while investment B also promises a 10 percent expected rate of return with a standard deviation of 3 percent. Which investment is preferred? What would be the investor's preference of a third investment, investment C, promising a standard deviation of 3 percent and an expected rate of return of 12 percent?
6. Explain the relationships between an investor's expectations and the use of probability distributions. How do probability distributions reflect investment risks? How can estimates of probability distributions be obtained?
7. Explain the meaning of liquidity, and indicate why it is an important element of a manager's goal function.

8. Explain the linkages between liquidity and investment risk.
9. Explain how the manager's goals may differ among the stages of their life cycle. How does the role of financial management change over the life cycle?

References

1. Anderson, J. R., J. L. Dillon, and J. B. Hardaker, *Agricultural Decision Analysis*, Iowa State University Press, Ames, 1977.
2. Boudreaux, K. J., and H. W. Long, *The Basic Theory of Corporate Finance*, Prentice-Hall, Inc., Englewood Cliffs, New Jersey, 1977.
3. Halter, A. N., and G. W. Dean, *Decisions Under Uncertainty with Research Application*, South-Western Publishing Company, Cincinnati, 1971.
4. Levy, H., and M. Sarnat, *Investment and Portfolio Analysis*, John Wiley & Sons, Inc., New York, 1972.
5. Luce, R. D., and Howard Raiffa, *Games and Decisions: Introduction and Critical Survey*, John Wiley & Sons, Inc., New York, 1957.
6. Maslow, A. H., "A Theory of Human Motivation," *Psychological Review*, 50(1943):370.

SECTION II

Financial Analysis,
Planning, and Control

Chapter 3

FINANCIAL STATEMENTS
AND INFORMATION FLOWS

An essential activity in financial management is the development of a timely, comprehensive information system that enables a manager to measure, evaluate, control, and improve the financial performance of a farm business. The information system is based on a coordinated set of financial statements that provide the data needed to analyze profitability, risk, liquidity, and other relevant performance criteria. The system may be designed to *report* business performance to managers, owners, lenders, and lessors, and to satisfy legal obligations, such as taxation or corporate disclosure. Or, the system may emphasize the data needed for *managerial decision making* in specific types of businesses. In practice, these reporting and decision-making orientations are closely related.

In this chapter we emphasize the design of an information system for financial reporting purposes. We will review the important financial statements used in measuring business performance and present convenient forms for their use in agriculture. These financial statements furnish the information needed for various types of financial analysis presented in later chapters. We also show the procedures followed in accounting for income tax obligations in the United States, since these obligations strongly influence accounting and financial management. As will be clear, financial and tax accounting are closely related, yet separate issues.

An Agricultural Accounting Perspective

The traditional practices in farm accounting have largely been informal, simplistic, and in many cases different from the Generally Accepted Accounting Principles of the accounting profession. This situation is in contrast with that of larger, corporate organizations who must have audited financial statements prepared by certified public accountants. Most farms are still relatively small operations, organized as proprietorships, partnerships, or family corporations. The manager must maintain the accounts, along with many other duties. Business and personal assets are generally closely associated in farming. In keeping records, farmers have mostly used "single entry" rather than "double entry" accounting. They rely heavily on cash accounting rather than accrual accounting, due in part to the privilege of reporting taxable farm income on a cash basis.

These accounting practices in agriculture are changing, however, as farms become more commercialized, relying more heavily on borrowed funds and leased capital to finance their operations. The needs for uniform methods of financial reporting have increased, as have the demands on farmers' financial management. Moreover, more sophisticated accounting services are being offered to farmers through commercial and public sources. Thus, the quality of financial information is improving significantly, as are the kinds of financial analyses permitted by a more comprehensive information base.

Coordinated Financial Statements

A set of coordinated financial statements includes (1) an *income statement*, which measures the value of a firm's production during a period of time; (2) a *balance sheet*, which measures the level and structure of a firm's asset and liabilities at a point in time; and (3) a *statement of changes in financial position*, which provides a linkage between the income statement and successive balance sheets. Each statement basically centers on the profitability of the equity (or ownership) capital invested by the firm's owners.

The income statement shows the change in the firm's equity capital due to a farm's economic performance during the accounting period, adjusted for the effects of nonfarm activities. In like fashion, the change in equity capital (or net worth) measured in balance sheets taken at the beginning and end of the accounting period should equal the change in equity capital reported on the income statement. The statement of changes in financial position completes the picture by showing in broad terms the various sources and uses of funds that are associated with the change in equity capital.

The following sections discuss some of the fundamental issues in designing a set of coordinated financial statements for use in agriculture. Since accounting is itself an important discipline in business administration, we only scratch the surface of this topic. Other literature considers accounting concepts and practices in much more detail (Frey and Klinefelter; Davidson, Stickney, and Weil).

The Income Statement

An income statement measures a firm's profits over a specified accounting period. The usual accounting period is one year; however, monthly, quarterly, and semiannual profit summaries are important in some types of businesses. The profit summary has various names: the income statement, the operating statement, or the profit and loss (P & L) statement. Its main purpose is to measure the net value of the firm's production during the accounting period. Most analysts are interested in the "bottom line" results. The bottom line measures the returns to the equity capital invested in the farm operation after all other resources used during that period have been accounted for.

One way to organize an income statement is shown in Table 3.1, for Farmer A. This statement has several distinct sections as we read from top to bottom. The top half of the statement accounts for the results of this year's operations, which are mostly cash transactions. Then changes in current inventories and capital items are accounted for. After nonbusiness transactions are considered, the bottom line measures additions to retained earnings. Retained earnings represent the growth in the firm's equity capital from income reinvested in the business.

Under operating receipts are listed the gross sales of farm products that are produced and held for sale in the normal course of business. Sales may be classified by enterprises or other meaningful categories. To obtain a true income measure for the period, the total value of all sales should be included, whether the goods were exchanged for cash or for an account receivable. Thus, a true income statement uses accrual accounting concepts. It may differ from the cash basis of income tax accounting allowed in the United States.

It is important to separate changes in the value of capital items (breeding livestock, machinery, etc.) from other products, because income from capital sales does not always reflect the proficiency of management nor the value of the firm's production. Moreover, income from capital sales may be taxed differently.

Other sources of farm income, such as government payments,

Table 3.1. Annual Income Statement, Farmer A

Operating Receipts

Cotton	$75,220	
Wheat	87,730	

Total Operating Receipts $162,950

Operating Expenses

Crop	$40,631
Machine Maintenance and Repair	16,544
Labor	12,050
Property Taxes	2,750
Insurance	400
Utilities	1,390
Miscellaneous	15,850
Interest	21,195

Total Operating Expenses $110,810

Net Income from Operations $ 52,140

Adjustments for Changes in Inventory

	Notes & Accounts Receivable	Crops	Market Livestock	Supplies	
Beginning	-0-	2,000	-0-	1,500	
Closing	-0-	2,000	-0-	1,500	
Net Change (±)	-0-	-0-	-0-	-0-	-0-

Adjustment for Changes in Capital Items

Gain or Loss from Sale of Capital Items	-0-
+Increment from Capitalization of Raised Animals	-0-
−Depreciation	−5,600

Total Adjustment for Changes in Capital Items −5,600

Profit (Loss)	46,540
Off-farm Income	-0-
Total Net Income Available	46,540
Proprietor Withdrawal	−19,760

Addition to Retained Earnings $ 26,780

custom work, and miscellaneous receipts, are usually treated separately to more precisely evaluate the manager's contribution to profits. Off-farm income is then added to farm profits to obtain the total net income available, as indicated in Table 3.1.

Operating expenses should include outlays for all inputs, purchased or hired, that are normally used up in production during the accounting period. Examples of operating expenses include the acquisition of feed, seed, fertilizer, machinery repairs, rent, taxes, hired labor, and so on. Interest paid or accrued on borrowed funds is also considered an operating expense. Operating expenses should also include the cost of feeder livestock, baby chicks, etc., which are chargeable against the current year's operation. Capital expenditures for machinery and equipment, breeding livestock, or dairy cattle are not listed under operating expenses. The costs of these items are charged against farm income over several accounting periods as depreciation.

Total operating expenses are subtracted from operating receipts to derive net income from operations. To this figure we must add or subtract any changes in the net value of various types of inventories and then adjust for changes in the value of capital items.

Table 3.1 identifies three types of capital change. The Gain or Loss from Sale of Capital Items shows receipts from the sale or transfer of a capital item in excess of or less than its book or depreciated value. The Increment from Capitalization of Raised Animals allows the farmer to recognize as income the value of home-produced animals added to the breeding herd. The cost of producing these animals is treated as an operating expense; thus, reporting their income in this fashion considers their effect on the farm's value of production. The Depreciation item under the capital adjustments section will be discussed later. The Adjustments for Changes in Capital Items section may be divided into various sub-accounts to show more specific changes. Examples might include sub-accounts for machinery, breeding livestock, buildings, range and pasture improvements, and others.

The figure labeled Profit (Loss) from operations in Table 3.1 indicates the net return to the farm operator for the resources—capital, labor, and management—which he or she has invested in the farm business. Off-farm income is added to this figure to indicate Total Net Income Available.

Unless operating expenses include an operator's salary or some form of family living allowance, the family's withdrawal must be subtracted from Total Net Income Available in order to determine the income retained in the business. If the business is a proprietorship or a partnership, income and social security taxes should be included with family withdrawals. If the business is incorporated, its income tax obligations should be listed in the summary.

Computing Depreciation

Depreciation is an accounting procedure by which the purchase cost of an asset with an economic life of more than one year is prorated over its projected economic life. Depreciation should reflect the actual decline in usefulness of an asset over time. Determining depreciation is complicated, however, because different assets may depreciate at different rates due to differences in use, care, and obsolescence. Moreover, the accepted methods of computing depreciation at best can only approximate the actual decline in an asset's value over time. It should be noted that land is an asset which never depreciates. This occurs because, theoretically, land is neither used up nor becomes obsolete. Buildings, fences, and other improvements which are attached to land may depreciate, but land does not.

Depreciation charges reflect cash needed from gross farm income to replace the depreciating asset. However, calculating depreciation is not a cash transaction. Hence, its effect is to reduce profits, but it does not reduce cash. In fact, because the allowable depreciation amount is tax deductible and reduces the cash outflow for taxes, charging depreciation increases the cash available to the firm.

The actual computation process is relatively simple. At the time a depreciable asset is purchased, the manager determines the length of its useful life and estimates its salvage value at the end of its life. A separate account is maintained for each asset showing its original cost, accumulated depreciation, and "book" value or depreciated value at any given time. At the end of each accounting period, the depreciation for the preceding period is calculated and recorded. This procedure reduces the book value and increases accumulated depreciation. Depreciation for all assets is totaled and entered under the Adjustment for Capital Items section of the income statement as Depreciation. An example of a depreciation record for a single machine is illustrated in Table 3.2.

Various methods of depreciation are used in accounting. Straight-line, double-declining balance, and sum-of-the-year's-digits are among the more common methods. The straight-line method provides the same amount of depreciation during each year of the asset's life. It is determined by

$$D_{sl} = \frac{OC - SV}{n}$$

where OC is the original cost of the asset, SV is the projected salvage value, and n is the asset's expected life. Consider, for example, a tractor costing $20,000, with a useful life of 10 years and a projected salvage value of $1,000. The annual depreciation charge would be

$1,900 = [(\$20,000 - \$1,000)/10]$.

Table 3.2. Record of Depreciation

Asset:	Tractor
Year Purchased:	January, 19—
Method of Depreciation Used:	Double-declining balance
Original Cost:	$20,000
Estimated Useful Life:	10 years
Estimated Salvage Value:	$1,000

Year	Depreciation Expense for Year	Accumulated Depreciation	Book Value End of Year
1	$4,000	$ 4,000	$16,000
2	3,200	7,200	12,800
3	2,560	9,760	10,240
4	2,048	11,808	8,192
5	1,638	13,446	6,554
6	1,311	14,757	5,243
7	1,049	15,806	4,194
8			
9			

The double-declining balance method provides an accelerated charge-off for depreciation. It is determined by

$$D_{ddb} = \frac{2}{n} R$$

where R is the remaining book value of the asset at the beginning of the year and n is the expected economic life. This procedure is followed until the book value reaches the salvage value. Using the $20,000 tractor as an example, the first year's depreciation is $4,000, or 20 percent of the tractor's book value. The second year's depreciation is 20 percent of the remaining $16,000, or $3,200. The salvage value is not quite reached in year 10. The operator could continue to depreciate the asset in subsequent years until the salvage value is reached, provided the machine is still used. If the machine is salvaged at the end of year 10, the unused depreciation could be added to the depreciation charge for the tenth year, as shown in Table 3.3.

The sum-of-the-year's-digits method adds the successive years of the depreciable life of the asset to determine the denominator. In the above case the denominator is

$$1 + 2 + 3 + 4 + 5 + 6 + 7 + 8 + 9 + 10 = 55.$$

The numerator for the first year is the remaining years of depreciable

Table 3.3. Depreciation Schedules for Three Methods of Computation[1]

Years	Straight-Line	Double-Declining Balance	Sum-of-the-Year's-Digits
1	$1,900	$4,000	$3,455
2	1,900	3,200	3,109
3	1,900	2,560	2,764
4	1,900	2,048	2,418
5	1,900	1,638	2,073
6	1,900	1,311	1,729
7	1,900	1,049	1,382
8	1,900	840	1,036
9	1,900	672	691
10	1,900	1,682[2]	345

[1]Original cost, $20,000; salvage value, $1,000; economic life, 10 years.
[2]Represents the difference between projected salvage value and book value at the beginning of the year, assuming the machine was salvaged at year end.

life for the asset, or in this case, 10. For each successive year the numerator is reduced by 1. Thus, depreciation for the first year is (10/55) of the total depreciable charge (original cost less salvage value). The first year's charge is 10/55 of $19,000, or $3,454; the second year's charge is 9/55 of $19,000, or $3,109; and so on.

As shown in Table 3.3, the method of computing depreciation strongly influences the level of depreciation in each year. Several features of U.S. tax laws also influence depreciation accounting, as will be shown below.

A difficult problem relating to depreciation is the impact of inflation on asset values over time. Appealing arguments can be made for charging depreciation according to the costs of replacing an asset, rather than according to its original cost, or otherwise adjusting the depreciation charge to reflect the effects of inflation. Accountants have adhered to the assumption of a stable monetary unit and to the principle of historic costs in preparing financial statements. The basic problem lies in changes in the purchasing power of the dollar and their effects on the amount of periodic income, when it is measured in the conventional manner. If the general price level has risen in the period between the incurrence of a cost (asset purchase) and its recognition as an expense (depreciation), the expense is reported in terms of dollars having greater purchasing power than current dollars. On the other hand, current revenue is reported in terms of dollars with current purchasing power. Thus, conventionally measured business income is overstated in periods of rising prices.

The Balance Sheet

In contrast to the income statement's summary of financial performance over an accounting period, the balance sheet shows the firm's financial condition at a specific point in time. The balance sheet is also called a financial statement, net worth statement, or statement of financial condition. It is a systematic listing of all assets and liabilities of the business, as shown in Table 3.4.

The balance sheet is divided into two parts with the value of each always equal to the other. The classic accounting equation underlying the balance sheet is Assets = Liabilities + Net Worth. As-

Table 3.4. The Balance Sheet

Name: Farmer A		Date: January 1	
Assets			
Current Assets			
Cash		$ 1,000	
Inventory		3,500	
Total current assets			$ 4,500
Intermediate Assets			
Machinery		48,000	
Original cost	$ 76,000		
Less depreciation	28,000		
Livestock		0	
Total intermediate assets			48,000
Fixed Assets			
Land		300,000	
Original cost	250,000		
Reappraisal increment	50,000		
Buildings and improvements		21,000	
Original cost	35,000		
Depreciation	14,000		
Total fixed assets			321,000
Total Assets			$373,500
Liabilities and Net Worth			
Current Liabilities			
Current portion of intermediate debt	$ 10,000		
Current portion of fixed debt	2,686		
Total current liabilities		$ 12,686	
Intermediate Liabilities		10,000	
Fixed Liabilities		227,874	
Total Liabilities		250,560	
Net Worth		122,940	
Total Liabilities and Net Worth		$373,500	

sets are those items of value which make up the firm. They include both physical assets and financial assets which represent claims on other economic units.

Liabilities represent claims on the firm's assets by lenders, lessors, and other creditors. Liabilities + Net Worth represent the total claims on the firm's assets. Liabilities are obligations owed to those who provide debt capital to the firm. Hence, we will use the terms *liabilities* and *debt* interchangeably. A debt obligation is characterized by a promise to pay the principal amount according to a specific time schedule with stipulated arrangements for paying interest. Net worth (or equity capital) represents the residual claims on assets held by the firm's proprietor, partners, or stockholders after debt claims are accounted for.

Classifying Assets and Liabilities

For analytical purposes, assets and liabilities are classified according to their liquidity. Liquidity refers to the firm's capacity to generate cash quickly and efficiently to meet its financial commitments as they fall due. Those assets which can be quickly converted to cash, with little or no loss in the net value of the firm, are considered highly liquid. In contrast, highly illiquid assets cannot be readily converted to cash without a substantial loss in value to the firm. Three broad classes of assets (and liabilities) are commonly used to express the degree of liquidity—current assets, intermediate assets, and fixed assets. Examples will show, however, that the time criterion only approximates the differences in liquidity among some types of assets.

Current assets are represented by cash and near-cash items whose values will likely be realized in cash or used up during the normal operating cycle of the business—usually one year. They also include assets whose conversion to cash would disrupt the normal business operation only minimally. Besides cash, current assets also include interest-bearing transactions accounts at financial institutions, other highly liquid financial assets, notes and accounts receivable, hedging accounts with commodity brokers, prepaid expenses, and inventories of supplies, livestock, crops, and feed which will be converted to cash during the year. The term *inventory* includes farm products awaiting sale, products in the process of production, or goods used in production. Examples of inventory include feed, seeds, farm supplies, livestock being readied for sale within the year or normal business cycle, and crop products being held for sale, whether in storage or growing in the field.

Intermediate assets are those yielding services to a business over several years; they eventually are fully depreciated and replaceable, or are liquidated within an intermediate period of time. There is no strict rule on the maximum life of intermediate assets, although 10 years is commonly used. Intermediate assets include machinery and equipment, automobiles, breeding livestock, notes receivable with maturities between 1 and 10 years, some types of financial leases, and household goods and personal effects. Other types of financial assets (stocks, bonds, life insurance cash value, equity in cooperatives, certificates of deposit, some retirement accounts) are also considered intermediate assets. Liquidation of intermediate assets is more disruptive and costly than liquidation of current assets; consequently, owners generally intend to hold intermediate assets for longer than one year.

Fixed assets have the longest expected life or maturity, usually exceeding 10 years. Real estate is the principal example of a fixed asset, including land, buildings, water-handling facilities (irrigation, tile), a residence, and various types of improvements, such as pasture establishment, brush control, fences, roads, and ponds. Mineral, building, and hunting rights associated with real estate may be accounted for separately, as well. Except for land, the other real estate assets depreciate over long periods of time. Other fixed assets include contracts and notes receivable with maturities exceeding 10 years and various types of long-term claims. Retirement accounts, remainder interests in trusts and life estates, royalties, and inheritances are examples.

Liabilities are also classified as current, intermediate, and fixed, using essentially the same time periods as the asset classification. Current liabilities are listed first. They include existing obligations that are payable within the next year. The main examples of current liabilities are notes payable to lending institutions and accounts payable to merchants and supply companies. Also included as current liabilities are accrued interest, taxes, and rent, as well as the current portions of intermediate and fixed liabilities which are payable during the next year.

Intermediate-term liabilities are obligations having a maturity of 1 to 10 years. They primarily involve notes payable over this range of maturity. These are usually called intermediate-term loans or installment loans. Obligations on some types of financial leases also constitute intermediate liabilities.

Fixed liabilities are characterized by maturity periods exceeding 10 years. Long-term loans, especially on real estate, constitute the main example of a fixed liability. These loans may involve mortgages on farm land; "purchase contracts" for land; and loans for buildings, structures, irrigation facilities, and other fixed assets.

It may also be important to account for any contingent tax liabilities associated with the sale of assets. If, for example, the fixed assets are sold at cost, less accumulated depreciation, then no tax liabilities should occur. But if assets are sold at current market values, involving substantial capital gains due to inflation, then tax obligations may arise if the assets are sold. Whether to include contingent tax liabilities on the balance sheet is based on the purpose of the accounts. If the accounts reflect a "going concern" without prospects for liquidation, then tax obligations are not usually included. If, however, the emphasis is more on the firm's security and collateral positions, in the event of possible default, then contingent taxes should be included. Considerable judgment and documentation are needed to determine the extent of the tax obligation.

Asset Valuation

The change in net worth between the beginning and end of the year in successive balance sheets should correspond to the Addition to Retained Earnings figure shown on the income statement. This identity provides an accounting check on the accuracy and completeness of the records and analysis. However, this check assumes that the effects of inflation and windfall events (gifts, inheritances) are treated consistently in the two financial statements. If, for example, asset values on the balance sheet change in response to inflation, then net worth will change accordingly. However, these unrealized capital gains are not reported on the income statement, thus yielding an inconsistency in these statements' formulation. Similarly, net worth may increase as a result of gifts and inheritances, although these sources of wealth are not considered sources of income.

Clearly, the principles for valuing assets may significantly influence the financial statements and resulting financial analysis. A generally accepted accounting principle has been that assets are valued at their historic cost and depreciated over time. Any gain or loss resulting from the asset's sale is entered in the adjustment for changes in capital items' section of the income statement. Under this approach, all intermediate and fixed farm assets are valued at their original costs, less accumulated depreciation. Consistency between the balance sheet and income statement is then assured.

However, farm land, machinery, and other farm assets have generally increased in market value in recent years due to the effects of inflation and other factors. Thus, for financial reporting purposes, ignoring these current market values may severely understate the firm's capital and net worth position for purposes of credit analysis, loan security, and other features of the financial performance. Thus, considerable care is needed in financial accounting to separate the effects of real business growth from the effects of inflation and unrealized capital gains, while still effectively coordinating the various financial statements.

The case of farm land is especially important. Farm land generally has increased in market value in recent decades. Moreover, farm land is frequently passed from one generation to another without being sold. Thus, the market value of much farm land is not explicitly established. Under these circumstances, the original purchase might have occurred several generations ago at prices which could be less than the current annual rent. How, then, can land valuation be handled in a farmer's balance sheet?

Several valuation approaches can be considered. One way is to ignore current market values completely and use only the land's original cost. This method has the disadvantage of showing land values that are far out of date, if the land was acquired many years ago and if its value has substantially increased. A second method, closely related to the first, is to use original costs of land in the balance sheet and provide estimates of current market values in footnotes to the balance sheet, so that an analyst can better estimate a firm's net worth and capital structure. This method still underestimates the firm's net worth, based on current market values. A third method is to update land values every year to reflect current market conditions. This approach makes it difficult to reconcile an annual income statement with beginning and end-of-year balance sheets, since unrealized capital gains would be included on the balance sheet but not on the income statement. Hence, additions to retained earnings on the income statement would not equal the change in net worth on successive balance sheets. A fourth method is to formulate a balance sheet with two asset columns, one showing original cost values for land and other capital assets and the other showing current market values. This approach has much merit, especially in more sophisticated accounting systems. It yields net worth figures for the cost concept and the current market value concept of valuation.

A fifth approach, utilized in the examples presented here, is to periodically reappraise values of capital assets, especially land, and also periodically revise the entries on the balance sheet to reflect the new values. Re-appraisal can occur at regular intervals (every 5 to 10 years) so that land values are reasonably current on the balance sheet, while still following an accounting procedure that yields consistency between the annual income statements and annual balance sheets. In Table 3.4, land values are indicated as original cost plus a *re-appraisal increment* which occurred five years earlier. Footnotes can be added to the financial statements that report estimates of current market values, if such information appears useful.

Other types of agricultural assets also present interesting valuation problems, especially when market prices are not readily available. Consider, for example, the valuation of growing crops or feeder livestock for a balance sheet being formulated at a time when the production processes are already underway. Generally, one of two approaches is used in valuing resources that are committed to production. One approach uses market values of finished products to estimate the value of products not yet in finished form. Hence, market prices for crops or livestock are applied to the growing crops or livestock with an appropriate discount to assure that the values of the growing commodities are not overstated. The discount reflects both the stage of production and the risk of loss of crops and livestock still in production.

The second approach uses costs of production as the basis of valuation and assumes that the values of items in production are reflected by the costs of inputs used in their production. This approach is more conservative than the market-value approach in that the accumulated costs of production are generally expected to be less than expected market value. The cost-of-production approach provides a reasonable safety margin against risk of yield loss and changes in product prices and, at least for crops, is more appropriate when producers use crop insurance to protect against weather loss and when crop prices are supported to the extent of production costs by federal government programs.

Statement of Changes in Financial Position

The statement of change in financial position provides a linkage between the income statement and balance sheets by showing the various flows of funds that are associated with the changes in equity capital. It basically is designed to show the magnitudes and specific sources of various funds that flow into and out of the business, under the condition that the total sources and uses of funds must be equal. Thus, this statement provides a mechanism for reporting more clearly how the firm's performance during the accounting period influenced and was influenced by the major funding activities.

In practice, the design of a statement of changes in financial position may vary among financial analysts, although its basic purpose remains the same. Moreover, the statement may be organized to show net changes in various accounts and funding sources, or gross flows of funds involving these items. Reports based on the net-change concept are more common, and likely convey sufficient information to most analysts. However, measures of gross flows are useful as well, especially as a basis for financial planning.

The net-change concept is intended to measure changes between beginning and end-of-period values for selected sources and uses of funds. It categorizes assets, liabilities, and income statement items in order to show how capital changes have occurred and how financing was provided. Under this approach a typical categorization of sources of funds is

1. Funds from farm operations
   a. Farm profit
   b. Depreciation
2. A net decrease in current assets
3. A gross decrease in non-current assets
4. A net increase in any liability
5. New equity from outside sources (stock sales, gifts, inheritances)
6. Total sources of funds

Depreciation is a non-cash item. However, it conceptually sets aside cash from gross income for replacing capital assets or for other uses. Thus, depreciation indirectly serves as a source of funds. Increases in liabilities are considered to provide funds to the business, as are decreases in the various asset categories. A gross change in a non-current asset is defined as: the asset value at the end of the period plus depreciation, minus the asset value at the beginning of the period.

In a similar fashion, a typical categorization of uses of funds is

1. A net increase in current assets
2. A gross increase in non-current assets
3. A net decrease in any liability
4. Fund withdrawals for family, dividends, income taxes, gifts, stock retirements, and so on
5. Total uses of funds

Table 3.5 shows the total sources and uses of funds for Farmer A, based on the net-change concept. Data for this statement come from Tables 3.1 and 3.4. Both beginning and ending balance sheets are needed. This statement indicates that net funds from farm operations totaled $52,140, including farm profit of $46,450 and depreciation of $5,600. Other sources were a decline in cash balance, an increase in current liabilities, and increased long-term debt.

Table 3.5. Sources and Uses of Funds, Farmer A (Based on the Net Change Concept)

Sources		Uses	
From farm operations	$52,140	Increase in real estate	$50,000
Farm profit 46,540		Decrease in intermediate	
Depreciation 5,600		debt	10,000
Decrease in cash	11,000	Proprietor withdrawal	19,760
Increase in current			
liabilities	888		
Increase in long-term debt	15,732		
Total sources	$79,760	Total uses	$79,760

Major uses of these funds were a $50,000 real estate purchase, debt reduction of $10,000, and proprietor withdrawals of $19,760 for family living and taxes. The totals of these sources and uses are each $79,760.

The gross-flow concept is similar to the cash flow budget approach to financial analysis (Chapter 5). It measures the total cash values of various sources and uses of funds that flow into and out of the business. It is more detailed, but more data-demanding too. Under this approach, a typical categorization of sources of funds is

1. Beginning cash
2. Farm operating receipts
3. Sales of capital items
4. Nonfarm income
5. Reduction in financial assets
6. New borrowings
7. Outside equity capital
8. Other sources
9. Total sources

Uses of funds are categorized as

1. Farm operating expenses
2. Capital expenditures: land, buildings, depreciable assets
3. Additions to financial assets
4. Payments on farm debt
5. Cash withdrawals: family living, corporate dividends, income taxes, non-business outlays
6. Equity capital withdrawals: stock retirement, gifts, inheritances paid
7. Ending cash
8. Total uses

A gross-flow statement for Farmer A is shown in Table 3.6. It shows that a total of $304,719 flowed through the business during the year, including operating expenses of $110,810, capital expenditures

Table 3.6. Sources and Uses of Funds, Farmer A (Based on Gross Cash Flows)

Sources		Uses	
Beginning cash	$ 12,000	Operating expenses	$110,810
Total farm receipts	162,950	Capital expenditures	50,000
Borrowed funds	129,769	Payments on debts	123,149
		Proprietor withdrawals	19,760
		Ending cash	1,000
Total sources	$304,719	Total uses	$304,719

of $50,000, debt repayments of $123,149, and proprietor withdrawals of $19,760. Ending cash totaled $1,000. These uses of cash were funded by $162,950 of farm receipts, new borrowings of $129,769, and the $12,000 beginning cash balance.

Accounting for Income Tax Obligations

Income tax obligations provide a strong incentive for farmers to maintain appropriate records and search for ways to maximize after-tax income. While tax accounting is in general similar to financial accounting, the rules are specified by law and by the guidelines of the U.S. Internal Revenue Service. In addition, some provisions apply specifically to farmers. Because taxes represent an important withdrawal of funds from a business, the taxpayer's principal objective is to make the tax obligation as low as possible, on average, from a given income level.

In this section we present some basic information about farmers' income tax obligations. The tax rules are voluminous, detailed, and subject to frequent change; thus, the tax issues cannot be treated in detail. Rather, we introduce the major types of tax obligations that will be considered in later chapters.

Tax obligations differ, depending on whether the income is "ordinary income" or "capital gains." First, we consider ordinary income. The amount of income tax owed by a taxpayer is determined by applying a schedule of progressive tax rates to the level of taxable income. "Progressive" means that the marginal rate of taxation increases as the level of taxable income increases. An example of a progressive tax schedule for a non-corporate taxpayer is shown in Table 3.7. Current tax rates for corporate taxpayers are shown in Table 3.8.

Taxable income is equal to "adjusted gross income" less deductions allowed for personal exemptions and selected other personal expenditures. Adjusted gross income is equal to gross income less allowable business expenses incurred in the production of gross income.

Cash and Accrual Accounting

In determining "gross income" and "business deductions," farmers may select either the cash or the accrual method of tax accounting. Under the cash method, all taxable income is included dur-

Table 3.7. Income Tax Rates for Non-Corporate U.S. Taxpayer[1]

Taxable Income	Pay	plus	Percent on Excess
0 - 3,400	0		0
3,400 - 5,500	0		11
5,500 - 7,600	231		12
7,600 - 11,900	483		14
11,900 - 16,000	1,085		16
16,000 - 20,200	1,741		18
20,200 - 24,600	2,497		22
24,600 - 29,900	3,465		25
29,900 - 35,200	4,790		28
35,200 - 45,800	6,274		33
45,800 - 60,000	9,772		38
60,000 - 85,600	15,168		42
85,600 - 109,400	25,920		45
109,400 - 162,400	36,630		49
162,400 - 215,400	62,600		50
215,400 and over	89,100		50

[1]These rates are effective for 1984 taxable income for married taxpayers filing joint tax returns.

Table 3.8. Corporation Income Tax Rates, United States, 1983

Taxable Income	Percentage Rate
0 - 25,000	15
25,000 - 50,000	18
50,000 - 75,000	30
75,000 - 100,000	40
100,000 and over	46

ing the tax year in which the payment is received. Similarly, farm business expenses are reported only in the tax year when they are paid. Under the accrual method, income is reported in the year when it is earned, and expenses are reported in the year when they are incurred, regardless of when the payments occur. Inventory changes are considered under the accrual method but are not considered under the cash method. Because of its flexibility and convenience, most farmers use the cash method in accounting for tax obligations. Cash accounting facilitates tax management by allowing farmers to shift sales and expenditures from one year to another in response to swings in farm income, and to defer tax obligations to later years in growing businesses.

Depreciation

The determination of depreciation charges allowable for tax accounting in the United States was simplified considerably in the

Economic Recovery Act of 1981. Taxpayers now figure depreciation charges according to an Accelerated Cost Recovery System (ACRS), which created five classes of capital assets with prescribed lives. A fixed recovery allowance, based on the double-declining balance method with a half-year convention for the first year, is applied to all assets (new or used) within specified recovery classes of tangible personal property. The assets are fully depreciable so that any realized salvage value is taxed as ordinary income to the extent of cost recovery deductions claimed. However, if a taxpayer claims investment tax credit (see below) on an asset, then the depreciable basis of the asset is reduced by half of the tax credit claimed, unless the taxpayer elects to decrease the regular investment credit percentage by two points. In the latter case, no basis adjustment occurs.

ACRS provides classes of 3, 5, 10, and 15 years for tangible personal property and real estate. Intangible assets are not included in the system. The three-year class consists of automobiles, light duty trucks, other small-ticket items, and breeding hogs. Most other machinery and equipment, including most farm machinery, falls in the five-year class. Also in the five-year class are farm storage facilities (corn cribs, grain bins, and silos), fences, tile lines, water systems, all other breeding livestock, feeding floors, petroleum facilities, and some public utility property. Most depreciable real estate falls in the 15-year class, although several exceptions are provided.

In addition, taxpayers are allowed several other elections in choosing depreciation methods, including use of the straight-line method. Taxpayers may also charge off as operating expenses a small amount of capital expenditures each year; the ceiling for the allowance began at $5,000 per year in 1981 and is scheduled to increase to $10,000 in 1985 and thereafter. However, no part of this "expensed" property is eligible for Investment Tax Credit (see below).

Table 3.9 indicates the capital recovery allowances under ACRS for the four investment classes. The percentages in the table are multiplied by the asset's original cost, or adjusted basis, to determine the level of depreciation allowed in each year.

Investment Tax Credit

An additional benefit from purchasing depreciable assets is the Investment Tax Credit (ITC)—a fiscal policy tool of the U.S. Government. Under the Economic Recovery Act of 1981, property in the

Table 3.9. Recovery Allowances for Accelerated Cost Recovery System

Ownership Year	Classes			
	3-year	5-year	10-year	15-year
	------------------------------ percent ------------------------------			
1	25	15	8	5
2	38	22	14	10
3	37	21	12	9
4		21	10	8
5		21	10	7
6			10	7
7			9	6
8			9	6
9			9	6
10			9	6
11				6
12				6
13				6
14				6
15				6

three-year class has a 6 percent ITC, meaning that 6 percent of the asset's cost can be credited directly against income tax obligations in the year of purchase. Property in the 5-year class and depreciable personal property in the 10- and 15-year classes are eligible for a full 10 percent ITC.

The investment tax credit applies against the first $25,000 of tax liability plus 85 percent of the tax liability exceeding $25,000. Used property is also eligible for ITC, although subject to a ceiling that increases from $125,000 of property value in 1982 to $150,000 in 1985. Other provisions assure that taxpayers may utilize ITC only to the extent of the amount the taxpayer has "at risk," that ITC is recaptured in part by the government if an asset is sold before its class life expires, and that unused ITC may be carried to other years.

Capital Gains Taxes

Ordinarily, a gain from the sale or exchange of property is included in income in its entirety and taxed at ordinary income tax rates (U.S. Master Tax Guide). But if the gain on the transaction is a long-term capital gain, it is subject to a lower tax. A long-term capital gain occurs if the capital asset has been held by the taxpayer for the required holding period—one year for most assets, one year for most livestock, and two years for horses and cattle. In determining the capital gain, a taxpayer must net all his long-term capital gains with his long-term capital losses and net his short-term capital gains with his short-term capital losses. The excess, if any, of net long-term capital gain over net short-term capital loss is subject to the capital gains tax.

The tax obligation is found for a non-corporate taxpayer by adding 40 percent of the net long-term capital gain to the taxpayer's other income and taxing the total at the ordinary income tax rate. Thus, 60 percent of the net long-term capital gain is excluded from taxation. To illustrate, a farmer who paid $200,000 for a tract of land and sold it 10 years later for $300,000 would pay ordinary income taxes on only $40,000 (40 percent) of the $100,000 long-term capital gain.

The calculations for corporate taxpayers who experienced net long-term capital gains are more tedious. First, corporate taxpayers must figure the ordinary income tax obligation on the total of ordinary income plus net long-term capital gain. Then, an alternative tax is determined by figuring the regular tax on ordinary income and adding to this tax 28 percent of the net long-term capital gain. The method producing the lower tax obligation is used.

The major point is that net long-term capital gains are taxed at lower rates than ordinary income. Thus, taxpayers have a strong incentive to convert ordinary income to capital gains, where possible, to reduce their tax obligations. An excellent example in agriculture is the hog farmer who produces his own gilts (young female pigs), charges their production expenses against ordinary income, retains them as sows (breeding livestock) in the herd for the required holding period, and then sells them as capital assets with only 40 percent of the gain in value subject to tax. Other possibilities for converting ordinary income to capital gains in agriculture include some types of soil and water conservation expenses, land-clearing expenses, and orchard development. Limits are imposed on all these possibilities, so the manager must carefully study the tax laws.

Topics for Discussion

1. Explain the concept of "coordinated" financial statements. In what ways are the income statement, balance sheet, and statement of changes in financial position coordinated?

2. Distinguish between operating receipts and capital sales. Would the sale of a tractor be an operating receipt or capital sale for a farmer? For a machinery dealer?

3. Explain the different methods of depreciation. What might influence the choice of depreciation method for a particular asset?
4. Discuss the accounting problems associated with rising values of farm land. What are some alternatives for dealing with these problems?
5. In formulating a statement of changes in financial position, is a net decrease in current liabilities considered a source of funds or a use of funds? Why?
6. A farmer reports the following financial information for last year's operation:

Current assets	100,000	Net worth, end of year	100,000
Depreciation	10,000	Operating expenses	30,000
Intermediate debt	50,000	Ratio of total liabilities to net worth	3
Proprietor withdrawals	5,000	Change in inventory	15,000
Capital purchases	20,000	Operating receipts	100,000
Fixed assets	200,000	Current liabilities	50,000

   a. Use this information to formulate an annual income statement.
   b. Complete the year-end balance sheet.

Assets		*Liabilities & net worth*	
Current	_____	Current	_____
Intermediate	_____	Intermediate	_____
Fixed	_____	Fixed	_____
		Net worth	_____
Total	_____	Total	_____

   c. Indicate the beginning-of-year net worth.

7. A farmer contends that the value of growing crops on his balance sheet should be $100,000 to reflect their anticipated market value. The lender argues for a $60,000 value to reflect the accumulated costs of production. Which is the proper figure to use? Why?
8. A farmer purchases a $100,000 combine for use in his operation. Indicate the investment tax credit and annual depreciation which the farmer may claim for income tax purposes.
9. A farmer sells a 40-acre tract of land for $120,000, compared to a value of $40,000 which he paid for the land 10 years earlier. Assuming a 20 percent tax rate, indicate the size of the tax obligation and the farmer's net gain from the sale.

References

1. Davidson, S., C. P. Stickney, and R. L. Weil, *Financial Accounting*, 2nd ed., Dryden Press, Hinsdale, Illinois, 1979.

2. Frey, T. L., and R. Behrens, *Lending to Agricultural Enterprises*, American Banking Insitute, New York, 1982.

3. Frey, T. L., and D. A. Klinefelter, *Coordinated Financial Statements for Agriculture*, Century Communications, Inc., Skokie, Illinois, 1978.

4. Helfert, E. A., *Techniques of Financial Analysis*, 5th ed., Richard D. Irwin, Inc., Homewood, Illinois, 1981.

5. James, S. C., and E. Stoneberg, *Farm Accounting and Business Analysis*, Iowa State University Press, Ames, 1975.

6. Lee, W. F., et al., *Agricultural Finance*, 7th ed., Iowa State University Press, Ames, 1980.

7. Meigs, W. D., et al., *Intermediate Accounting*, 3rd ed., McGraw-Hill Book Company, New York, 1974.

8. Penson, J. B., Jr., and D. A. Lins, *Agricultural Finance: An Introduction to Micro and Macro Concepts*, Prentice-Hall, Inc., Englewood Cliffs, New Jersey, 1980.

Chapter 4

FINANCIAL ANALYSIS
AND CONTROL

The financial accounting system established in the preceding chapter provides an information base for evaluating a farm business's profitability, liquidity, and risk. In this chapter we develop procedures for analysis and control according to these performance criteria. The emphasis here is on analyzing the firm's past performance in order to identify strengths and weaknesses and to develop feasible financial plans for the future. This chapter provides part of the analytical base for the methods of financial planning discussed in later chapters. In the following sections, we establish the steps of a systematic financial control process; identify various measures for evaluating profitability, liquidity, and risk; and apply them to a case situation.

The Financial Control Process

Financial control is facilitated by the process of measuring and monitoring the performance of a business over time in order to maintain desired standards of performance. The process is a dynamic one; it involves the passage of time and the use of new information that is fed back to the decision-making unit for processing, analysis, and response. The control process provides an orderly framework for responding to an uncertain environment, in which various shocks caused by unanticipated events trigger the need for control and response. Hence, an important part of the control process is the design of information systems and strategies for responding to risk.

The control process is systematically expressed by the following steps:

1. Identifying Goals

The identification of goals, or performance criteria, is the first step. The mix of goals, their ordering, and weights are important. Profitability, liquidity, and risk represent one set of goals for evaluating farm businesses.

2. Developing Measures for the Goals

Step 2 involves selection of indexes, indicators, or proxies to measure goal attainment.

3. Determining Norms for the Measures

The reality of goal attainment involves norms, targets, or standards for evaluating the degree of firm performance. Often "maximization" or "satisfaction" is too abstract or impractical. Moreover, some goals involve trade-offs in achievement levels; for example, attaining higher expected profits usually means accepting higher risk and lower liquidity. Specific norms provide a tangible basis for analyzing multiple-goal attainment.

4. Setting Tolerance Limits on Norms

Under risk and uncertainty, the norms for the various goal measures will seldom be exactly attained. Setting tolerance limits on norms allows for reasonable variations in performance measures before corrective actions are needed.

5. Developing an Information System

Periodic reports on the performance measures, based on a financial accounting system, keep the decision maker informed of the firm's progress and help to identify corrective actions when tolerance limits on norms are exceeded.

6. Identifying and Implementing Corrective Actions

Unanticipated events may cause one or more of the performance measures to exceed the tolerance limits for the respective norms. When this occcurs, appropriate actions are needed to restore performance to acceptable levels.

This fundamental process of control is essentially the same, whether it relates to the health and growth of organisms, an athletic contest, a space flight, an agricultural finance class, or management of a farm business. To illustrate, consider the task of controlling our health and comfort. A healthy human body must maintain a body temperature of about 98.6°F, maintain a pulse rate and blood pressure that are considered normal for the person's age, and achieve a specified metabolic process and chemical balance. The medical profession has developed measurements to determine deviations from established norms as indicators of health problems. Moreover, a sick body sends its own signals as well. Corrective actions are then prescribed and monitored to resolve the problem.

We follow a similar process in regulating our environment. One environmental goal is comfort. At work or at home, we specify a temperature norm or target on a thermostat, which controls the temperature. The designer of the thermostat specifies the tolerable ranges of deviation from the norm and devises a feedback system which keeps the mechanism informed of its present condition. When a tolerance limit is exceeded, a signal is sent to the decision-making center calling for corrective action. If the temperature is too hot, the air conditioner comes on until the temperature declines to the specified norm; if the room is too cold, the heater comes on to restore the desired temperature.

Clearly, technology can play a major role in the control process. Thermostats have engineering designs to automate temperature control. Computers may be involved in the information feedback activity. They may initiate corrective actions too, as in the case of space technology. Moreover, computers are playing an increasing role in information processing for managing farm businesses.

The process of business control in a farming operation follows the same steps just outlined. However, the process is less intense than its application in space flights, health, and other types of activities, and it involves substantial human input, especially in identifying and implementing corrective actions. In the discussion to follow we focus primarily on steps 2, 3, and 4 of the financial control process. The goals in step 1 are already established as profitability, risk, and liquidity. The information system in step 5 mainly involves the financial statements identified in Chapter 3, although sources of information external to the firm are important too. Corrective actions in step 6 are considered more fully in other chapters; they are usually unique to the particular decision situation.

Characteristics of Goal Measures

In selecting measures to reflect the firm's profitability, risk, and liquidity, it is important that the measures be meaningful and manageable. Meaningfulness refers to how well the measure actually reflects the stipulated goals. The match should be as close as possible. For example, if profitability is the goal, then crop yields per acre or milk production per cow would not be very meaningful, since other factors also influence profitability. A dollar measure of profitability would be preferred.

Manageability refers to the ease of computation, the ease of comprehension, and the number of measures involved. Measures that are easier to compute and comprehend are preferred. The number of measures should be numerous enough to provide for comprehensive analysis, but still few enough to work with efficiently. No set number is stipulated, although three or four measures for each goal is common in practice. Indeed, dozens of measures could be formulated from the various financial statements, although only a few are needed for effective analysis.

Measures may also be classified according to ratios or absolute measures. Ratios are relative measures that relate one item (in the numerator) to another (in the denominator). Ratios are easy to compute and usually easy to understand. They may be expressed as fractions, decimals, or percentages. They typically have greater generality in various types of comparisons than do absolute measures. As shown below, business analysts have developed a set of ratios which they compute and compare in determining business progress. Financial ratios for various industries are published by such firms as Dun and Bradstreet and Robert Morris Associates. Some trade associations and credit agencies compute ratios for their members. For financial analysis in agriculture, ratio measures of profitability are more widely available than measures of liquidity and risk, although this condition is changing as financial accounting in agriculture becomes more widespread. Moreover, some of the major farm lenders, especially the Farm Credit System, collect considerable financial information on farm customers and report some of it in summary form.

Absolute measures refer to dollar or physical levels of the measured item. Examples are levels of farm profits, total assets, net worth, working capital, crop acres, and volume of milk produced. Absolute measures have limited generality and are most useful for analyzing the performance of individual businesses. They also provide the data for developing the more general financial ratios.

Several types of comparisons can occur with the measures of business performance. Measures can be compared with norms and tolerance limits to evaluate the degree of goal attainment. Measures can be compared over time to identify important patterns or trends that may indicate possible corrective actions. Measures can be compared to budgeted projections to assess the quality of financial planning. Measures can also be compared with those of other firms to assess peer performance.

Finally, but of considerable importance, financial measures are only indicators, or signals, of a firm's performance. They may indicate the symptoms of a problem, but do not necessarily identify the underlying cause or the remedy. Further analysis is needed to identify why changes occur in measured performance. Moreover, the causal factors rather than the symptoms or indicators should be the object of corrective actions taken to resolve a properly defined problem. We will illustrate the relationship between the symptomatic role of financial measures and the underlying causes in later sections.

Profitability Measures

Profitability can be measured in several ways. One approach measures profitability as the relationship between the level of profits earned during an accounting period and the level of resources committed to earn those profits. Other approaches relate the level of profits to the volume of sales or to the efficiency with which various types of assets are managed. Profitability is also influenced by the margins between costs and returns per unit of production and the number of units sold. Hence, it is closely tied to efficiency and scale.

Information on profitability comes from both the income statement and the balance sheet. While only a few summary measures are used, it is important that the manager consider more than just prices and dollars. A successful firm must produce the kind and quality of products needed to meet its market commitments. Thus, a manager must monitor, evaluate, and control product quality throughout the production process. The degree of efficiency attained in converting inputs into outputs is also important.

The level of farm profits earned during an accounting period is an absolute measure of profitability. Changes in additions to retained earnings, or other profit measures should be studied closely. Even so, the change in profit position should be considered in relationship to other changes in the firm. For example, an annual increase in profits of 2 percent might be unsatisfactory if the firm's total assets are expanding by 20 percent per year. Under these types of circumstances, ratio measures of profitability provide more general performance indicators than absolute measures.

Returns on Assets, Equity, and Debt

Two commonly used profitability ratios are Returns on Assets (ROA) and Returns on Equity (ROE). In addition, we will also consider a third measure called Cost of Debt (COD) in order to show how these three measures are related to one another through the structure of the firm's debt and equity.

Return on assets is a percentage measure of the rate of return on the firm's investment in total assets during an accounting period. It is found by dividing a measure of the firm's returns to assets by a measure of the firm's total assets:

$$\text{ROA} = \frac{R}{A} \tag{4.1}$$

where R is the dollar returns to assets and A is the level of total assets.

The dollar returns to assets is independent of how the assets are financed. Thus, this earnings figure is calculated as the firm's income before deducting any interest, dividends, or other payments to suppliers of financial capital. For farm businesses, the returns to assets could be either the measure of Profit or Addition to Retained Earnings (see Table 3.1), plus the interest paid on borrowed funds. The differences between these two measures are off-farm income and proprietor withdrawals. A problem in agricultural accounting arises because the proprietor withdrawals may represent the payment to the farm manager's unpaid labor and management, as well as a return to the manager's investment of equity capital. In larger corporate firms the labor, management, and ownership functions are more easily separated and accounted for. In this analysis, we will assume that the dollar returns to assets are the sum of additions to retained earnings plus interest paid on debt.

The appropriate measure of total assets also involves a choice. Total assets could be measured at the beginning of the year, the end of the year, or as an average of the beginning and ending values. The average total asset measure is generally preferred, since it may be more consistent with the distribution of earnings throughout the year.

The Return on Equity measure is defined as:

$$ROE = \frac{I_e}{E} \tag{4.2}$$

where I_e is the dollar return to equity capital and E is the average equity capital invested during the accounting period.

The Cost of Debt measure is defined as:

$$COD = \frac{I_d}{D} \tag{4.3}$$

where I_d is the dollar cost (interest paid or accrued) on debt capital and D is the firm's average indebtedness during the accounting period. Note that the "Return on Equity" depicted here measures the realized return to equity during the accounting period. It is closely related to, yet distinct from, the concept of a "cost of equity" to be introduced in Chapter 6, which represents the firm's required return on equity capital.

To show the relationship among these three measures, it is important to recognize that the return to assets is the sum of the cost of debt plus the returns to equity:

$$R = I_d + I_e. \tag{4.4}$$

Moreover, the level of assets is the sum of the levels of debt and equity:

$$A = D + E. \tag{4.5}$$

Thus, we can express the Return on Assets (ROA) as a weighted average of the Return on Equity (ROE) and the Cost of Debt (COD) where the weights are the proportional claims of equity and debt on total assets:

$$ROA = (ROE)(E/A) + (COD)(D/A). \tag{4.6}$$

The weighted average concept is a useful one since it provides a consistency check on the profitability measures obtained from a set of coordinated financial statements. Moreover, a logical ordering of these three measures is based on the relative risk positions of the firm's debt and equity holders. The higher risk position of equity capital means that the returns (or costs) for equity should on average over time exceed the costs of debt. Returns to assets should fall between the returns to equity and debt due to the weighted average concept. Thus the logical ordering of these profitability measures is ROE > ROA > COD.

To illustrate, consider the performance measures for Farmer A during the previous year, as reported in Tables 3.1 and 3.2 of Chapter 3, and as summarized in Table 4.1 under the Year 3 heading.

$$R = \$\ 47{,}975$$

$$I_e = 26{,}780$$

$$I_d = 21{,}195$$

$$A = 357{,}800$$

$$E = 109{,}550$$

$$D = 248{,}250$$

where A, D, and E are averages of beginning and ending values.

$$ROA = \frac{47{,}975}{357{,}800} = .134, \text{ or } 13.4\%$$

$$ROE = \frac{26{,}780}{109{,}550} = .244, \text{ or } 24.4\%$$

$$COD = \frac{21{,}195}{248{,}250} = .085, \text{ or } 8.5\%$$

$$E/A = \frac{109{,}550}{357{,}800} = .306$$

$$D/A = \frac{248{,}250}{357{,}800} = .694.$$

To check ROA as a weighted average of ROE and COD, insert the appropriate values in equation (4.6).

$$ROA = (.244)(.306) + (.085)(.694)$$

$$= .134.$$

In summary, during the past year Farmer A achieved a return on assets of 13.4 percent, as well as a return on equity of 24.4 percent, and paid an average cost of debt of 8.5 percent, all consistent with an equity-to-asset ratio of .306 and a debt-to-asset ratio of .694.

Other Profitability Measures

There may be merit for comparative purposes in developing profitability ratios on a per unit basis, where the units represent the important enterprises in the business. In cash-crop farming areas, for example, profit per acre is often used in comparing one business with another or in evaluating performance over several years. In dairy regions, profit per cow is more applicable. Many other profitability ratios could be developed as well.

Efficiency ratios which help monitor profitability also vary with the type of farm and the nature of the business. Convenient ratios are needed to reflect the operating efficiency of various enterprises. For a cash-grain farmer, crop sales per acre or operating costs per acre are useful. For a swine farmer, the number of swine sold per litter, the feed cost per 100 pounds of hog, or the pounds of hogs sold per $100 of expenses are relevant indexes of operating efficiency.

Large commercial feedlot operators closely monitor feed conversion ratios. They also monitor daily non-feed costs per head. For some types of feeding programs, the cost per pound of gain is significant, while others analyze break-even margins. These types of ratios can be meaningfully compared with similar ratios for previous years or with peer group averages.

A more general ratio often used in business analysis is the *gross ratio*, defined as total operating expenses divided by gross operating receipts. This ratio indicates the proportion of returns that are absorbed by expenses. The income statement of Farmer A, as listed in Table 3.1, showed operating expenses of $110,810 and gross operating receipts of $162,950, for a gross ratio of .68.

Another useful ratio is the *fixed ratio*—total fixed expenses divided by gross profits. Gross profits are determined by subtracting costs of inputs from gross sales. This ratio is useful in analyzing feeder livestock operations. The costs of feeder cattle and feed, for example, are subtracted from cattle receipts to get gross profits. This figure is then divided into total fixed expenses for cattle feeding to determine the fixed ratio. Fixed expenses include interest, taxes, depreciation, contract payments under a lease, etc., which are beyond the manager's control. The fixed ratio reflects the proportion of the firm's gross profits represented by uncontrolled costs. The higher this ratio, the more limited is the manager's planning flexibility.

The *turnover ratio* is defined as the ratio of gross sales to total assets. The higher the ratio, the greater the turnover of assets. Thus the greater is the opportunity to produce profits, provided profit margins are positive.

Liquidity Measures

Liquidity relates to the firm's capacity to generate sufficient cash to meet its financial commitments as they become due. Whenever a firm cannot satisfy these financial claims, it is bankrupt even though the firm might be profitable and have a favorable net worth. The part of net worth comprised of claims on fixed assets is inaccessible without partially or wholly liquidating the firm.

The manager could evaluate the firm's liquidity by projecting the time patterns of cash inflows and outflows. However, the future cannot be projected with certainty; thus reserves are needed to provide flexibility in meeting cash outflows.

The liquid assets of the business are one important source of reserves. In Chapter 3, current assets were classified as those which would be converted to cash in the normal operation of the business without significant price discount and without interrupting normal business operations. Thus, current assets can be used to generate cash to meet current liabilities. They also contribute significantly to the firm's credit, another source of liquidity, based on the lender's appraisal of the firm's credit worthiness.

Information about liquidity comes primarily from the current section of the balance sheet—current assets relative to current liabilities. An important consideration is the time of the year when the balance sheet is taken. The balance sheet of a farm business is usually taken early in the year (January, February) when current assets and current liabilities are at a minimum for many types of farms. Most crop and livestock products have already been sold. Livestock feeders are a notable exception, as are crops stored subject to commodity loans. Even so, cash to be generated from sales of products produced later in the year usually far exceeds cash that can be generated from the sale of current inventory for most farms. Similarly, most of the firm's cash outflow will be incurred after the start of the year and is not reflected in current liabilities at the beginning of the year.

Thus, liquidity assessment based on balance sheet analysis should be combined with cash flow budgeting (Chapter 5), especially in support of financial planning.

The liquidity ratio most widely used by financial analysts is the *current ratio*—current assets divided by current liabilities. It specifies the dollars of current assets which are available for every dollar of current liabilities at the time the balance sheet is made. In the balance sheet for Farmer A, as shown in Table 3.4, the current assets are $4,500 and current liabilities are $12,686. Thus the current ratio is .35, indicating only 35¢ in current assets available for every $1 of current liabilities. Clearly, as of this date, the financial position is highly illiquid.

An absolute measure of liquidity that is closely related to the current ratio is *working capital*. Working capital is defined as the difference between current assets and current liabilities. It should be a positive value to signify a liquid situation, although the current ratio gives a more general measure. Farmer A's low liquidity is indicated by negative working capital of $8,186.

Several other ratios show selected aspects of liquidity for particular kinds of businesses. The *acid test ratio* is defined as cash plus government securities and other cash equivalents divided by current liabilities. It excludes such assets as inventory and accounts receivable when computing the liquidity ratio, assuming that neither of these assets could be immediately converted to cash to meet current obligations. The acid test ratio is not very useful in farm financial analysis. Accounts receivable are relatively unimportant to most farm businesses. Furthermore, livestock and crop inventories usually have a predictable time pattern for sale and well established markets. Consequently, their value for liquidity purposes need not be discounted below market value in the same manner that one might discount neckties in the inventory of a department store, for example. Thus, the current ratio is likely the best balance sheet ratio to use in measuring an agricultural firm's liquidity.

Another important ratio to farmers and farm lenders is the *intermediate ratio*. It measures the ratio of intermediate-term assets to intermediate-term debts. The intermediate ratio for Farmer A is 4.80 = $48,000/$10,000. This ratio signifies that Farmer A has $4.80 of intermediate-term assets for every $1.00 of intermediate-term debt. The intermediate-term ratio is not unique to either liquidity or solvency, but tends to bridge the gap between these two performance criteria.

Another meaningful ratio is the *current plus intermediate ratio*. This ratio is found by dividing the sum of current plus intermediate assets by the sum of current plus intermediate liabilities. The current plus intermediate ratio for Farmer A is 2.31 = ($4,500 + $48,000)/ ($12,686 + $10,000). This result indicates that Farmer A has $2.31 of current and intermediate assets available for every $1.00 of current and intermediate liabilities. Agricultural firms generally obtain most of their short- and intermediate-term financing from the same lender—either a commercial bank or a production credit association. These lenders generally utilize the farmer's current *and* intermediate assets as collateral to assure loan security. Hence, this ratio combines these assets and liabilities in a manner that provides meaningful information on loan security and repayability for both borrower and lender.

For completeness, the *fixed ratio* is also included as a liquidity measure. The fixed ratio is found by dividing fixed assets by fixed liabilities. For Farmer A, this ratio is 1.41 = $321,000/$250,560. This ratio indicates the margin of equity accumulated in fixed assets, and thus, reflects the capacity to refinance or restructure current or intermediate debt into longer-term debt. It is a less readily available source of liquidity than the current section of the balance sheet.

Measures of Financial Risk and Solvency

Financial risk relates to the firm's total structure. It deals primarily with the firm's ability to meet total claims and hence is closely related to solvency. A farm business is insolvent, in the final analysis, if the sale of all assets fails to generate sufficient cash to pay off all liabilities. Consider the following example:

Current Assets	$ 30,000	Current Liabilities	$ 10,000
Fixed Assets	200,000	Fixed Liabilities	190,000
		Net Worth	30,000
		Total Liabilities and	
Total Assets	$230,000	Net Worth	$230,000

Despite this firm's high liquidity, it is barely solvent, with only a narrow margin of equity ($30,000) relative to other liabilities. If a sudden emergency compelled the manager to quickly sell the fixed assets at "85 cents on the dollar," the business would be insolvent. From the lender's point of view, measures of solvency indicate loan recovery problems if the business fails. The smaller the safety margin of equity, the greater is the financial risk.

The financial analyst is concerned with trends in capital structure. Selected measures of solvency should indicate the firm's financial progress in generating new funds, making capital expenditures, retiring debt, and coping with business and financial risks. Information about solvency may come from both the balance sheet and the income statement. The balance sheet measures apply to a specific point in time, while income statement measures reflect an interval of time. The balance sheet measures are typically called "solvency ratios," while income statement measures are called "coverage ratios."

One important solvency measure is the ratio of total debt to equity. It is commonly called the leverage ratio and measures the firm's total obligations to creditors (lenders and lessors) as a percent of the equity capital provided by owners. Again, for Farmer A's balance sheet, outlined in Table 3.4, the leverage ratio is 2.04 = $250,560/$122,940. This ratio indicates that the firm is using $2.04 of debt capital for every dollar of equity capital. This farm business is highly leveraged. Moreover, nearly half of the equity is represented by a $50,000 unrealized increment in land values. If this increment is eliminated, the leverage ratio would be 3.44. Other ratios reflecting the same information are the ratio of net worth to total assets (low for Farmer A) and the ratio of total debt to total assets (high for Farmer A).

Many farm lenders prefer that borrowers have at least as much investment in their own business as the lender does. Therefore, a standard rule of thumb for the maximum leverage ratio is 1.0. However, this ratio varies substantially among farm businesses and from one type of business to another. Some financial intermediaries, for example, have leverage ratios ranging from 10 to 20. Even within agriculture, a farmer might attain high leverage by acquiring land and even depreciable assets through purchase contracts and by obtaining the usual margins of finance on annual operating inputs. Leverage is usually higher for larger operations with younger operators.

Solvency ratios do not indicate an optimal level of leverage for a firm. Each manager must decide this crucial question based on a careful analysis of projected profitability, risk, and liquidity. Clearly, selecting a leverage target is a complex decision. Once the decision is made, however, progress toward that goal is indicated by changes in the leverage ratio.

Coverage ratios taken from the income statement account for the relative claims of debt and equity holders on the returns to farm assets during a period of time. Thus, coverage ratios essentially relate a firm's financial charges to its ability to serve them. They serve as a counterpart to the solvency ratios that hold for a specific point in time.

The *interest coverage ratio* expresses the ratio of a firm's returns to assets (R) to the amount of interest charges (I_d) for a period:

$$\text{Coverage Ratio} = \frac{R}{I_d}. \tag{4.7}$$

For Farmer A, this ratio is 2.26 = \$47,975/\$21,195, indicating that \$2.26 of asset returns are available for every dollar of interest commitment. Or, one can say that 44 percent of asset returns are required to meet interest commitments. Notice that the interest coverage is analogous to an asset to debt ratio taken from a firm's balance sheet. The coverage ratio relates asset return to debt obligations for a period of time; the solvency ratio (A/D) relates total assets to total debt at a point in time. Generally, however, a coverage ratio is subject to greater volatility than solvency ratios, due to year-to-year swings in farm income.

A shortcoming of the coverage ratio defined above is that a firm's ability to service debt is related to both interest and principal payments. Moreover, these payments must come from the firm's cash flow rather than from the accrual concept of income. Thus, an alternative formulation of the coverage ratio is *cash flow coverage*. It is defined as gross business receipts divided by the sum of interest paid plus principal payments. It indicates the cash flow margin for meeting principal and interest payments.

For Farmer A, Table 3.1 indicates farm operating receipts of \$162,950 and interest paid of \$21,195. In addition, the Statement of Changes in Financial Position, based on the gross flow concept in Table 3.6, indicates total debt repayments of \$123,149. Thus Farmer A's cash flow coverage ratio is 1.13 = \$162,950/(\$21,195 + \$123,149). Thus more than 88 percent of the cash flow is required to meet debt service commitments. Clearly, this relatively low measure of cash flow coverage indicates a weaker financial position than do the other measures.

The *interest expense* ratio, defined as interest paid divided by total operating expenses, is another useful measure that reflects the proportion of operating expenses attributed to interest paid on borrowed funds. Greater leverage and higher interest rates have increased the importance of this ratio in farm financial analysis. For Farmer A, the interest expense ratio is .19 = $21,195/110,810.

Explaining Changes in Ratios

As indicated earlier, financial ratios and other performance measures are only indicators or signals of a firm's performance. Judgment and experience of analysts, as well as theoretical relationships and more detailed analysis, play important roles in explaining changes in ratios and identifying problems calling for corrective actions. Setting reasonable tolerance limits to allow for anticipated variation in ratios due to random events is an important part of the control process. Moreover, the norms that are established for the important performance measures may themselves change as changes occur in farm business conditions, government policy, the national economy, and international markets.

We will illustrate the issues involved in diagnosing changes in several key performance measures that represent a farm business's profitability, liquidity, and solvency. Consider first a business that has experienced an increase in its ratio of operating costs per dollar of sales from .60 to .70. On the surface, this change suggests a decline in profitability. It should alert the manager to the possibility that production costs are getting out of control. But several other factors could be involved too. The ratio could have increased because product prices or production levels declined so that the value of total sales also declined, while total costs remained about the same.

The higher ratio of costs to sales could also reflect the firm's adjustment in output levels toward greater productivity and higher profits. Profit maximization occurs at an output level where marginal returns equal marginal costs. This condition may differ from the level of output that results in minimum average costs of production. This situation indicates a fundamental limitation of ratio analysis; that is, its emphasis on average relationships rather than marginal relationships. Marginal analysis is preferred in planning and decision making; but in financial analysis, the available data are usually best suited for deriving ratios based on average relationships.

Next, consider the possible reasons for an observed decrease in a firm's current ratio, signifying a reduction in liquidity. The ratio is comprised of current assets divided by current liabilities. A decrease in the ratio could be attributed to (1) current assets staying constant and current liabilities increasing; (2) current assets declining and current liabilities staying constant; (3) current assets declining more than current liabilities decline; (4) current assets declining and current liabilities increasing; and (5) both current assets and current liabilities increasing, but current liabilities more so.

Beyond these possible combinations, the changes in assets, liabilities, or both could be attributed to a price change, a quantity change, or both price and quantity changes. If assets changed, which ones and why? Could the change be due to losses, random fluctuations, a change in marketing and inventory policies, a change in size of firm, or a change in enterprise mix? If current liabilities changed, which ones and why? Could the change be due to changes in interest rates, carryover financing due to losses, growth and capital investment, new inventory financing, larger household demands, other reasons?

Finally, consider the possible reasons for a firm experiencing a decline in its debt-to-equity (leverage) ratio from .50 to .40 during the past year. On the surface, one might conclude that the firm has made substantial progress in reducing financial risk. However, a careful examination of the balance sheet might indicate that this business sold much of its assets at a substantial loss in order to meet its financial obligations. By selling these assets, the firm paid off a large volume of debt, thereby decreasing its leverage ratio. In the process, however, the firm's net worth was reduced considerably.

One must determine for each firm what the target leverage should be. Many farmers and lenders prefer low leverage ratios and interpret most movements toward lower ratios as indicating financial progress. However, we will see in Chapter 6 that higher leverage ratios, under proper circumstances, generate more rapid rates of firm growth. Moreover, as leverage increases, the average cost of capital usually decreases to some point, then moves up sharply. Thus, increasing the leverage ratio could be a managerial goal and indicator of financial progress.

Additional analysis is *always* needed beyond the computation of ratios in order to determine what, if any, action should be taken. A ratio serves the financial manager in about the same way that a patient's high temperature serves a diagnostic physician. It indicates that conditions may not be as expected, and that additional investigation is needed.

Comparative Financial Analysis

We can demonstrate the types of comparisons that arise in financial analysis using several years of historic and projected data for Farmer A. Organizing the impórtant summary figures from the balance sheets and income statements into the "Spread Sheet" formats in Tables 4.1 and 4.2 simplifies the comparisons of measures over time and with the norms and tolerance ranges that apply to the particular farming situation. In this case, the budgeted results for the

Table 4.1. Spread Sheet, Farmer A

Item	Year 1	Year 2	Year 3	Budget Year
Assets (year end)				
1. Cash	2,000	12,000	1,000	15,955
2. Inventory	3,500	3,500	3,500	3,500
3. Total current assets	5,500	15,500	4,500	19,455
4. Machinery	44,800	53,600	48,000	60,000
5. Livestock and facilities	0	0	0	32,440
6. Total intermediate assets	44,800	53,600	48,000	92,440
7. Buildings and improvement	23,000	22,000	21,000	20,000
8. Land (original cost)	200,000	200,000	250,000	310,000
9. Reappraisal increment	50,000	50,000	50,000	50,000
10. Total fixed assets	273,000	272,000	321,000	380,000
11. Total assets (3 + 6 + 10)	323,300	342,100	373,500	491,895
Liabilities and Net Worth (year end)				
12. Accounts and notes payable	8,258	0	0	0
13. Current portion, int. debt	6,600	8,927	10,000	23,750
14. Current portion, fixed debt	3,068	2,871	2,686	4,000
15. Total current liabilities	17,926	11,798	12,686	27,750
16. Intermediate liabilities	19,400	21,073	10,000	27,500
17. Fixed liabilities	211,062	213,069	227,874	268,537
18. Total liabilities (15 + 16 + 17)	248,388	245,940	250,560	323,787
19. Net Worth (11 − 18)	74,912	96,160	122,940	168,108
20. Total liabilities and net worth	323,300	342,100	373,500	491,895
Income Statement				
21. Operating receipts	126,440	138,508	162,950	231,080
22. Operating expenses: noninterest	79,602	78,174	89,615	121,660
23. Operating expenses: interest	14,048	16,011	21,195	33,892
24. Inventory change	(4,000)	0	0	0
25. Capital change	(5,100)	(4,500)	(5,600)	(11,560)
26. Profit (Loss)	23,690	39,823	46,540	63,968
27. Off-farm income	0	0	0	0
28. Proprietor withdrawal	12,600	18,575	19,760	18,800
29. Addition to retained earnings	11,090	21,248	26,780	45,168

Table 4.2. Financial Ratios, Farmer A

Ratio	Year 1	Year 2	Year 3	Budgeted Year	Norm for Farmer A	Range
Profitability Measures						
1. Return on assets (average)	NA	11.2%	13.4%	18.3%	15%	12% to 18%
2. Return on equity (average)	NA	19.4%	24.4%	31.0%	20%	15% to 25%
3. Gross ratio	.74	.68	.68	.67	.65	.60 to .70
4. Turnover ratio	.39	.40	.43	.47	.45	.40 to .50
Liquidity, Solvency, and Coverage						
5. Current ratio	.31	1.31	.35	.70	1.50	1.25 to 1.75
6. Intermediate ratio	2.31	2.54	4.80	3.36	1.75	1.50 to 2.00
7. Current plus intermediate ratio	1.35	2.10	2.31	2.03	1.75	1.50 to 2.00
8. Fixed ratio	1.10	1.28	1.41	1.42	1.75	1.50 to 2.00
9. Leverage ratio: Total liab./net worth	3.32	2.56	2.04	1.93	1.50	1.00 to 2.00
10. Leverage ratio: Total liab./total assets	.77	.72	.67	.66	.60	.50 to .67
11. Interest coverage	1.79	2.33	2.26	2.33	2.00	1.75 to 2.25
12. Cash flow coverage	1.05	1.12	1.13	1.26	1.30	1.20 to 1.40
13. Interest to total operating expense	.15	.17	.19	.22	.20	.15 to .25

coming year (see Chapter 5) are also included to further generalize the analysis.

The norms and ranges for the financial ratios are those which Farmer A and his lender have agreed upon, based on their judgment, experience, and observations of comparable measures from similar farms. If the measures fall within the stipulated range, the performance is considered acceptable. If the measures fall outside the range, especially toward the weaker values, then careful study of the causal factors and possible corrective actions is needed. Ideally, unacceptable measures will trend toward the acceptable range over time.

Farmer A's performance likely typifies a recently established business operated by a young manager who has experienced high leverage, low liquidity, and strengthening profitability as the business becomes established and grows in size. Rates of return on assets and equity show positive trends, with recent and projected values exceeding the upper bounds on the anticipated range. Moreover, the downward trend in the gross ratio shows a widening margin between operating costs and receipts, perhaps resulting from managerial experience or size economies in an expanding operation. A clear upward trend is evident in the levels of intermediate and fixed assets, as well as in the various liabilities. The faster growth in net worth indicates strong financial progress.

Measures of liquidity, solvency, and coverage also show favorable trends, although further progress and some restructuring of liabilities appear warranted to bring these measures into line with the desired performance levels. The current ratio has been quite low, although projections for the budgeted year indicate a more acceptable level. The intermediate ratio has been consistently high, and the current plus intermediate ratio has remained above the range as well. The fixed ratio shows a favorable trend, but remains below the acceptable level. Thus, this farm situation is characterized by a strong reliance on financing the acquisition of fixed assets and the resulting liquidity demands for meeting repayment commitments on longer term debt. However, the growing profitability and reinvestment of earnings through debt repayments and capital acquisition should provide for a more balanced financial structure in the future that is consistent with the established norms.

The measures of leverage and coverage also show this farm's heavy reliance on debt capital, although the projection indicates that the favorable trend will continue, bringing the leverage measures within the acceptable range. The trend is less clear in the coverage measures for interest and cash flow, perhaps reflecting the effects of an upward trend of interest rates during the period of analysis.

Formulating spread sheets like those in Tables 4.1 and 4.2 is an essential part of financial management. It aids financial analysis and control and contributes to improved credit management for both borrower and lender. The particular entries in the spread sheet, as well as the norms and ranges on the performance measures, must be tailored to each farm business. Experience over time and with different types and sizes of farm businesses will aid in specifying this vital information.

Topics for Discussion

1. Identify the steps of the financial control process. How are they related to time and uncertainty? Identify some possible data sources for developing norms and tolerance ranges for the various measures of business performance.

2. Contrast the use of absolute measures versus ratio measures in analyzing a firm's financial performance. How are they useful in various types of comparisons?

3. How is ROA distinguished from ROE? Which is the more valid measure? Why?

4. Suppose a farm business indicates an average cost of debt of 12 percent, an ROA of 15 percent, and a ratio of debt-to-equity of 1.0. What is the firm's ROE? What would its ROE be if the debt-to-equity ratio increased to 2.0?

5. Suppose a firm experiences a decline in its current ratio from 1.8 to 1.2. Is this a favorable or unfavorable change? Why? What factors might explain the decline in the ratio?

6. Explain how the intermediate and fixed ratios are useful in analyzing liquidity. If you observe a firm with a current ratio of 0.50 and an intermediate ratio of 5.0, what is the firm's liquidity position, and what corrective actions can be taken?

7. Explain the concepts of solvency and financial risk. How are they related to the firm's leverage position? What are typical ranges of leverage for farm businesses?

8. Distinguish between solvency and coverage ratios. How are they related, and which financial statements are involved?

9. Following is a summary of Phil Farmer's balance sheets for the last two years:

		Year 1	Year 2
Assets			
	Current	$ 80,000	$ 20,000
	Intermediate	40,000	160,000
	Fixed	220,000	520,000
	Total	$340,000	$700,000
Liabilities			
	Current	60,000	200,000
	Intermediate	40,000	0
	Fixed	40,000	260,000
	Total	$140,000	$460,000
Net Worth		$200,000	$240,000

Please use this information to evaluate changes in Phil's operation according to the following criteria.

a. Profitability
b. Liquidity
c. Solvency and financial risk

References

1. Frey, T. L., and R. Behrens, *Lending to Agricultural Enterprises*, American Banking Institute, New York, 1982.
2. Helfert, E. A., *Techniques of Financial Analysis*, 4th ed., Richard D. Irwin, Inc., Homewood, Illinois, 1977.
3. Lee, W. F., et al., *Agricultural Finance*, 7th ed., Iowa State University Press, Ames, 1980.
4. Van Horne, J. C., *Financial Management and Policy*, 5th ed., Prentice-Hall, Inc., Englewood Cliffs, New Jersey, 1980.

Chapter 5

FINANCIAL PLANNING AND
FEASIBILITY ANALYSIS

In this chapter we establish the fundamental concepts and tools for projecting and evaluating the overall financial position and progress of a farm business. The characteristics of various agricultural assets and their financing needs are considered first. Emphasis is placed on the design of financing programs to support the firm's production, marketing, and capital acquisition, as well as meeting the cash needs of the farm family. The techniques of cash flow budgeting and pro forma projections are established and then applied to analyzing financial feasibility.

An Overview of Financial Planning

The development of business plans for farm firms occurs within the three organizational areas of finance, production, and marketing. The focus here is on the financial organization, although it is important to recognize that the financial decisions interact with production and marketing decisions.

In designing an acceptable financing program for a farm business, a major consideration is the relationship between cash flows and loan repayment obligations and the firm's financial performance. The expenditures and cash flows associated with the acquisition and use of resources need careful coordination. Each lending program sets in motion a particular pattern of future cash flows. Each of these flows must be considered together with other cash flows arising from production and marketing activities. Cash flow requirements of the family must also be considered. All too frequently, the formulation of a sound financing program is jeopardized by the addition of short- or intermediate-term loans that were not anticipated or that require repayment faster than cash is being generated.

In developing an optimal loan program, a borrower would prefer (1) a maturity structure of debt that matches the length of the payoff periods for the assets being financed and (2) a repayment pattern over time that matches the asset's earnings pattern. The result is a set of *self-liquidating* loans with the various assets pledged as collateral to secure the loan. A self-liquidating loan is made for a purpose that generates sufficient income to repay the loan within the maturity period. Loans for current assets such as fertilizer or feeder livestock are generally self-liquidating, since a single repayment is scheduled to occur upon sale of the crop or livestock being produced. A self-liquidating loan for intermediate assets such as machinery and breeding livestock should be long enough (5 to 10 years) to allow periodic payments from earnings generated by the asset over its economic life to fully repay the loan. Moreover, the repayment pattern should match the time pattern of the asset's earnings. The same principles hold for financing fixed assets, although longer loan maturities and more flexible repayment schemes are needed.

If the loan maturities are too short of if they are not well coordinated with the time pattern of earnings, then liquidity problems and cash flow pressures arise. Moreover, when business and financial risks occur, there is need for flexible financing arrangements in order to adjust loan maturities and repayment obligations in response to unanticipated variability in cash flows. Hence, credit reserves with the lender must be large enough to provide additional loans to meet the borrower's financial obligations in periods of adversity and flexible enough to restructure excessive indebtedness for more orderly payoffs. Then, the financing program should be designed to restore a more acceptable debt structure when adverse conditions have passed.

The coordination of cash flows is simplified if all the financing (short-, intermediate-, and long-term loans) is provided by one lender. But most agricultural lenders are not able to meet all of a farmer's financing needs. Farmers generally utilize different lenders for financing non-real estate and real estate assets. Examples of these lenders are commercial banks and production credit associations for non-real estate loans, and federal land banks and life insurance companies for real estate loans. Exceptions occur when banks offer complete loan services by serving as loan agents for life insurance companies or other long-term lenders. Nonetheless, there is merit for the single "package" lender to still have separate loans for financing assets with distinctly different time dimensions. The different loan maturities permit more precise analysis of repayability for each financing need, thus providing borrowers with a wider range of choices.

Financing Current Assets

Financing current assets in farm businesses mostly involves the acquisition of annual operating inputs. However, considerable financing of grain inventories and other stored commodities occurs as well. In this section, we consider the characteristics of operating inputs, the analysis of operating loans, and the types of operating loans.

Characteristics of Operating Inputs

Examples of annual operating inputs include fertilizer, chemicals, seed, irrigation water, livestock feed, feeder livestock, veterinary services, labor services, machine fuel and repairs, and utilities. These inputs have several unique characteristics which distinguish them from other productive assets. First, as the name implies, they are generally "used up" or converted into other forms during production. Hence, as a rule, they are not carried from one year to another. Feed, for example, is consumed by livestock and coverted into animal products, while fertilizer is converted into crop products. In both cases, the use of the asset in production means that it cannot be recovered in its original form. Similar results apply to water in irrigated crop production and to fuel and labor services in machine operations.

These conversion features rule out the possibility of rental or leasing for most operating inputs. One cannot rent the use of fertilizer for a production period as with land, tractors, or even breeding livestock. Moreover, these assets make less effective loan collateral because they do not generate easily reclaimable assets. Generally, the lender must rely on a security interest in other fixed assets as well as in the growing crops and livestock to provide the necessary collateral. Feeder livestock is an important and interesting exception to this generalization, as is a warehoused inventory such as grain.

Operating inputs also tend to have a high marginal-value product (MVP) associated with the first few units of use. The payoff from the use of sufficient chemicals to control a serious disease, for example, is very great. Similarly, the marginal returns from hiring labor for harvesting crops are substantial if no other harvest labor is available. Up to some point, each operating input has a sufficiently high MVP that, in its absence, a farmer might justifiably pay a very high price for a limited supply. However, the MVP of annual operating inputs tends to fall considerably as their use increases. Thus, capital tied up in excess quantities of operating inputs may generate low or even negative returns.

The high payoff associated with annual operating inputs creates a high-priority claim on a farmer's financial resources. The lack of financing for operating inputs may terminate production and jeopardize the business. In contrast, borrowing to finance firm growth or to replace old equipment can likely be postponed without seriously jeopardizing business productivity or profitability, at least for a time.

These conditions indicate the farmer's urgent need to (1) secure sufficient financing to acquire the inputs needed for profitable production, (2) obtain appropriate financing terms, and (3) hold adequate reserves of credit or other financial assets to cope with unexpected events. The more critical financing terms for operating inputs are loan maturities and repayment schedules, although collateral requirements and interest rates are also important.

In order for the operating loan to be self-liquidating, loan repayments should be scheduled to come from income generated by sales of products being financed. Thus, loans to finance the purchase of fertilizer in the spring of the year should be scheduled for repayment with income arising from the sale of the products grown with that fertilizer. Such sales generally occur at harvest in the fall, although many producers may utilize storage or contract arrangements that modify the timing of crop sales and cash receipts. In these cases, the financing terms should be modified to reflect the producer's commodity-marketing policies, assuming, of course, that these policies are acceptable to the lender.

Another characteristic of operating inputs arises from the seasonality of farm production which influences the timing of flows of funds and short-term financing needs. Different patterns of seasonality mean that the timing of acquiring operating inputs may differ. Crop production is influenced greatly by climatological factors. Livestock production can also exhibit seasonality, although it is often reduced by farmers' efforts to achieve more continuous marketing. Moreover, both crop and livestock have rather lengthy production periods.

The high degree of divisibility provided by operating inputs is an advantage in acquiring, managing, and financing these assets. In contrast to the bulkiness or indivisibility of investments in land and most depreciable assets, operating inputs can be purchased and used in very small-sized units. However, quantity discounts and prepayments need to be considered.

Analyzing Operating Loans

The acquisition of operating inputs influences the firm's profits, risk, and liquidity in much the same fashion as investment in durable assets. However, these influences all generally occur within one production period. Hence, the need for evaluation procedures that directly account for the time value of money is reduced. This does not mean that the time value of money is no longer relevant. Time is definitely important, as evidenced by crop or livestock producers who must acquire their operating inputs several months prior to the sale of products. These producers must still consider the opportunity costs of funds committed to the acquisition of operating inputs. However, because the product sales occur within a year of the cash outflows for input acquisition, the opportunity costs are smaller and easier to account for. Moreover, if operating inputs are financed by borrowing, the money costs of borrowing are directly reflected in interest charges.

Effects on risk and liquidity are also important. If inputs are purchased with cash, the transactions reflect a restructuring of the firm's current assets, which, on balance, reduces liquidity due to the use of these inputs in production. If inputs are purchased with credit, the transactions reduce the firm's credit reserve, thereby depleting a valuable source of liquidity, and they build the firm's leverage, thereby adding to its financial risk. Further effects on risk and liquidity are associated with meeting the loan-repayment obligations.

The terms of most operating loans are generally set so that the loan is self-liquidating. Under these conditions, the borrower is setting aside the funds to repay the loan when operating expenses are charged against farm sales. Even if cash is paid for the operating inputs, the borrower is essentially committing a future set-aside of cash from product sales to replenish the cash balances.

To illustrate, consider the case described in Table 5.1. During the year, Farmer B produced and sold $120,000 worth of fed cattle, his only product sold. To finance his annual operations, he borrowed a total of $90,000. Of this amount, $82,000 was used to finance the purchase of feeder steers, feed, and other operating expenses. The remaining $8,000 was used to provide funds for family living expenses. Interest costs were $4,000, making the total bank payment $94,000. When the cattle were later sold, the $120,000 sales value was used as follows:

1. Bank payment for

    a. Enterprise financing $82,000
    b. Family financing   8,000
    c. Interest   4,000

           Total $ 94,000

2. Income taxes   3,000

3. Cash balances

    a. Depreciation reserve $10,000
    b. Retained earnings   13,000

           Total   23,000

           Total $120,000

Thus, the process of charging $86,000 operating expenses and $8,000 for family living, as illustrated in Table 5.1, sets aside $94,000 from cash receipts to repay the operating loan. This result is comparable to the effect of charging depreciation to set aside funds from

Table 5.1. Farmer B's Income Statement

Receipts—Cattle Sales		$120,000
Operating Expenses		
Feeder cattle purchases	$60,000	
Feed purchases	10,000	
Fertilizer and chemicals	6,000	
Other	10,000	
Total		$ 86,000
Net Cash Income		$ 34,000
Depreciation		10,000
Proprietor Withdrawals		
Income taxes	$ 3,000	
Family living	8,000	
Total		$ 11,000
Retained Earnings		$ 13,000

sales to service an intermediate-term loan to purchase the depreciable asset.

Types of Operating Loans

Three types of loans are used to finance the purchase of operating inputs: the regular or standard operating loan, a nonrevolving "line of credit," and a revolving "line of credit." The *standard operating loan* consists of separate borrowing transactions and notes each time financing is needed. In each transaction the borrower and lender agree on the loan purpose, loan size, interest rate, and repayment date. The borrower signs a note specifying these terms, and the lender provides the loan funds. This process is cumbersome and inefficient when the borrower needs several loans over a short period of time. The crop producer, for example, who must borrow money in four consecutive months in the spring would have at least four different notes to repay under the standard operating loan. This approach essentially implies that no cash flow budgeting was used to forecast borrowing needs and loan repayments.

Under a *nonrevolving line of credit*, the lender agrees at the beginning of the planning period to supply the loan funds at the times and in the amounts indicated in a cash flow budget. Generally, the budget is formulated on a monthly basis, although any number or any length of time periods can be used. The size of the line of credit is the total amount of borrowing projected for the coming year. However, the funds are advanced only as specified in the budget, and repayments occur when cash inflows exceed cash outflows. This approach minimizes the borrower's cost of using the borrowed funds and better assures their availability throughout the year.

The outstanding-loan balance at any one time may not necessarily reach the total line of credit due to repayments that occur before all borrowing is complete. The loan agreement or master note usually specifies the size of the credit line and the maximum-loan balance at any one time. It also specifies that funds are available as budgeted in the cash flow projection, although some flexibility is provided to account for reasonable deviations in timing and size of individual transactions. Other loan terms and performance conditions may also be stipulated in the loan agreement.

The nonrevolving line of credit provides several advantages in liquidity management and financial control for both borrower and lender: (1) it indicates the uses of the borrowed funds and their sources of repayment, (2) it indicates the expected timing of borrowing and repayments based on the projected cash flows, and (3) the cash flow budget provides an instrument of financial analysis and control for both borrower and lender. The size and timing of actual transactions can be checked against the budget. Deviations can be calculated and explanations provided for those that appear extraordinary. The borrower can assess the quality of financial planning, while the lender can assess repayment performance. In this fashion the cash flow budget jointly serves the purposes of financial planning, analysis, and control.

A *revolving line of credit* provides additional freedom to the borrower in using the loan funds. The lender and borrower agree on a maximum line of credit for the next planning period (e.g., three months, six months, one year) as determined from the results of a cash flow budget and from analysis of the firm's profitability, risk, and liquidity. The borrower can then borrow freely up to this limit, but not above it, whenever funds are needed. Repayments occur whenever surplus funds are available. This arrangement is especially useful when the borrower has recurring needs for and repayments of large amounts of financing in a short period of time. Cattle feedlots and broiler operations with large inventories of feed and animals that turn over rapidly are examples of businesses needing this kind of financing. The lender must be assured that the budgeted funds will be used frequently, effectively, and for the purposes requested. Generally this type of financing is limited to borrowers who provide accurate, detailed, and reliable cash flow budgets and who exhibit superior financial performance.

Interest on these three types of operating loans is generally charged at the contractual rate on the outstanding-loan balance. Hence, interest obligations only occur for the time in which the funds are borrowed. Moreover, the concept of simple interest rather than compound interest is generally used in calculating the interest obligation on operating loans. Simple interest means that accrued interest is not added to the loan balance after each day, month, or other conversion period. Hence, interest is not charged on interest during the operating loan.

To illustrate the interest charge, suppose that a crop farmer borrows $100,000 on April 1 at a 12 percent annual rate with interest charged daily on the outstanding- or remaining-loan balance. The cash flow budget projects $75,000 from crop sales available for loan payment on October 1 and $50,000 from added crop sales available for repayment on November 1. Using equation (5.1), the total interest obligation is found as follows:

$$I = (P)(i)(T) \qquad \text{(5.1)}$$

where I is the interest paid, i is the interest rate, and T is the fraction of the year the loan is outstanding.

October 1 $\qquad I = (100,000)(.12)(\dfrac{183}{365}) = 6{,}016$

November 1 $\qquad I = (25,000)(.12)(\dfrac{31}{365}) = \underline{255}$

$$\phantom{November 1 \qquad I = (25,000)(.12)(\dfrac{31}{365}) = } 6{,}271$$

The $100,000 outstanding for 183 days from April 1 to October 1 incurs $6,016 interest, which is payable along with the $75,000 principal payment on October 1. The $25,000 outstanding for 31 days in October incurs $255 interest, which is paid on November 1 along with the final $25,000 loan payment, making total interest and principal payments during the year of $106,271.

Some lenders require that interest always be paid whenever principal payments are made. Others let interest on the outstanding balance accumulate throughout the year, with payment required when the operating loan is fully repaid. In the latter case, it is to the borrower's advantage to repay loan principal first, then interest, rather than pay interest along with each principal payment.

Financing Intermediate and Fixed Assets

Financing of intermediate and fixed assets in farm businesses mostly involves the acquisition of machinery, equipment, breeding livestock, and farm real estate. Included in farm real estate are farm land, buildings, residences, storage facilities, fences, water handling facilities, and other types of real estate improvements. Various types of financial assets are considered intermediate or fixed as well.

Several characteristics of intermediate and fixed assets distinguish them from current assets. Especially important is their use in a farm business over several years. Thus, they are considered durable assets. However, except for farm land and the financial assets, these intermediate and fixed assets eventually wear out and must be replaced. That is, they experience depreciation as they yield their productive services to the business over the years of their economic life.

Intermediate and fixed assets make up the capital base of a farm business. They contribute significantly to the size of the farming operation, and their acquisition is of major importance to growth in a firm's size and income-generating capacity. New technology and related economies of size are often involved in the growth process. Compared to operating inputs, intermediate and fixed assets generally come in larger size units and involve larger acquisition costs. Most can be either purchased or leased. Moreover, unless replacement of worn out assets is urgent, intermediate and fixed assets offer more flexibility than operating inputs in the timing of acquisition. The acquisition can generally be postponed if business income is low or financing costs are high. Even though intermediate and fixed assets depreciate over time as their productive capacity and years of life decline, they often experience capital gains in response to inflation and other factors. Finally, many intermediate and fixed assets are effective loan collateral because they generate reclaimable assets for lenders. Thus, they contribute importantly to a firm's credit worthiness.

Following the principles of self-liquidating loans, a proper financing program for intermediate and fixed assets should synchronize the asset's length and time pattern of earnings, as reflected by the depreciation schedule, with the length and time pattern of repayment obligations on a loan made to acquire the asset. Thus, loans (or leases) made to finance the asset can be repaid at the same pace the assets are paying for themselves in the business. The cash flows for earnings and debt servicing would then be coordinated.

Intermediate assets with economic lives of 5 to 10 years should be financed with intermediate-term loans having maturities of 5 to 10 years. Longer loan maturities are needed on fixed assets to reflect the longer payoff periods. In this fashion, the loan repayments compel a "setting aside" of cash to cover the asset's rate of depreciation. Loan maturities shorter than an asset's payoff period would require a diversion of funds from the business's net income to meet the payment obligation.

Consider, for example, a farmer who acquires a $40,000 machine for use in the business over an eight-year period, after which the machine has no remaining value. Assuming uniform use over the eight years, which implies straight-line depreciation, the machine should pay for itself at an annual rate of $5,000 = $40,000/8 years. Suppose the lender requires a 25 percent downpayment to provide an adequate safety margin of the farmer's equity capital in the investment. A $30,000 loan payable in eight equal annual payments of $3,750 (plus interest) would be required to make the loan self-liquidating, while still satisfying the lender's desired safety margin. If, however, the lender provides only a five-year loan, the required principal payments would be $6,000 each year. The added $1,000 over the $5,000 attributed to depreciation would have to come from net income, thereby reducing the funds available for family living or other investments.

In practice, it is difficult to exactly match the loan repayment obligations with the asset's earnings pattern. The patterns of earnings for many capital assets (machinery, buildings, equipment) are difficult to precisely identify and are subject to high uncertainty. Moreover, the institutional characteristics and the preferences of the firm's lenders for repayment and loan security may strongly influence the financing terms. Thus, a general guideline is to synchronize as closely as possible the cash flows from the asset's earnings and the repayment obligations.

The use of intermediate-term loans in farm lending has increased in recent years, although the loan maturities for most intermediate and fixed assets are still less than the asset's anticipated payoff periods. Thus, these loans are not completely self-liquidating. Moreover, some non-real estate lenders prefer to finance farmers' capital acquisition solely through short-term operating loans and carry unpaid debts over to following years until they are fully repaid. For the lender, this practice provides effective financial control, especially for high-risk borrowers. However, this lending practice leaves the borrower fully dependent on the lender for continued financing and provides little capacity for the borrower to adjust the financial organization to changing business conditions.

Financing programs for farm land are subject to the characteristic that farm land is not used up in the production process. In principle, then, land could be financed with permanent debt, requiring no loan repayment until the property is sold. In practice, of course, farm real estate lenders do require loan repayments, although the loan maturities are sufficiently long (30 to 40 years) to make the loans highly self-liquidating. Moreover, many borrowers periodically refinance real estate loans to restructure or stretch out repayment obligations. Thus, the self-liquidating feature is often achieved by the use of informal or ad hoc financing practices.

Financing programs for intermediate and fixed assets are generally based on installment loans in which the loans are "amortized" with regularly scheduled payments. Two alternative payment schedules are used to amortize farm loans: (1) *constant payment*, in which the total payment in each period remains constant over the term of the loan, with varying proportions allocated to interest and principal as each payment occurs; and (2) *constant payment on principal*, in which an equal payment on principal plus interest occurs each period. In both cases, interest is calculated on the remaining balance. Figure 5.1 compares the pattern of annual payments on a $20,000 loan amortized over 20 years for these two methods. The total payments (interest plus principal) are lower for the *constant payment* method during the early years of the loan. Eventually, however, the payments become lower for the *constant payment on principal* method. We have indicated curvilinear and linear relationships in Figure 5.1. If payments occur at discrete intervals (annually, monthly), the relationships would have discrete steps.[1]

Although the length of time required to repay the loan is the same under both methods, the outstanding loan balance for any year is greater for the constant payment method. Thus, the total interest paid during the loan is greater for the constant payment method. This method may seem less attractive to some borrowers. However, the higher payment obligations during the early years of the constant payment on principal method reduces the amount of cash flow available for other uses. In particular, it reduces the cash available for servicing non-real estate loans.

A similar situation arises for shorter versus longer maturities on long-term loans. The total interest costs will be less for the shorter-term loans. However, the cash flow required each year to repay principal and interest will be higher, thus adversely affecting non-real estate credit. Hence, an incentive exists for longer-term real estate loans.

A potential disadvantage of a farm mortgage loan is the fixed commitment represented by the amortization payment. If possible, this payment should be scheduled within each year to coincide with the seasonal patterns of the borrowers' cash flows. Scheduling the payments when cash is available from crop or livestock sales is an example. On occasion, however, payments on intermediate- and long-term debt are met from the firm's operating line of credit.

---

[1]The methods of calculating amortization payments are developed in Chapter 9, and the effects of these repayment schedules on the costs of debt capital are considered in Chapter 14.

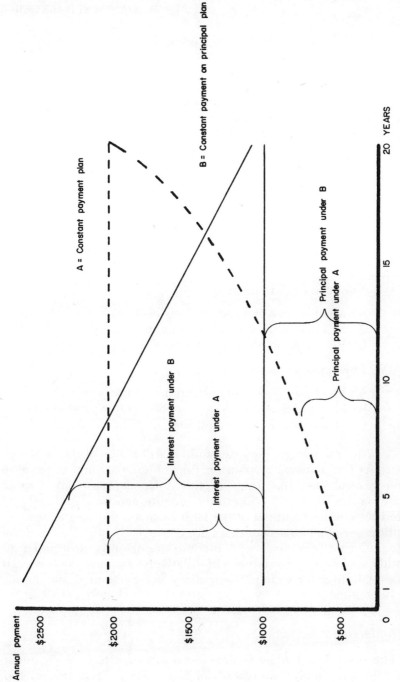

Figure 5.1. Comparing interest and principal payments for a $20,000 real estate loan under alternative repayment plans.

Cash Flow Budgeting

The cash flow budget is the mechanism used for projecting the firm's performance under specified financing programs and provides the data needed to evaluate the financial feasibility of the business plan. The cash flow budget brings together in one framework the projected level and timing of cash flow generated by:

I. Production and Marketing

    A. Operating receipts
    B. Operating expenses

II. Investment and Disinvestment

    A. Capital expenditures
    B. Capital sales

III. Nonbusiness Transactions

    A. Meeting family needs and tax obligations
    B. Making nonbusiness investments
    C. Receiving nonbusiness income

IV. Financing Transactions

    A. Meeting repayment obligations on previous debts
    B. Meeting financing requirements for new investments
    C. Designing the operating line of credit

A cash flow budget indicates future cash needs of the business. It permits the manager to plan for financing needs and to exercise closer control over the firm's liquidity. Conceptually, it is quite simple—a recorded projection of the amount and timing of cash expected to flow into and out of the farm business during the next accounting period. The accounting period is usually one year, and the projected cash expenses and income are usually grouped into monthly summaries. For farms with relatively constant monthly cash flows—dairying, for example—quarterly or semiannual summaries may be sufficient.

The Budgeting Process

The cash flow budget is developed after most of the business plans are tentatively formulated for the coming year. Hence, the budget reflects decisions on productive enterprises, marketing strategies, and investment programs that appear to contribute best to the manager's objectives. These decisions give rise to transactions for acquiring resources and selling products over the budget period. In planning the crop program, the manager will determine the number of crop acres and the amount of fertilizer, seed, and chemicals to be applied to each crop as well as the amount of labor to produce and harvest that crop. This physical information is converted to costs which are expected to occur at particular months during the year. Crop yields are projected along with plans for either feeding or selling crop products. If they are to be sold, the amount and timing of sales can be projected.

Similarly, when developing the livestock program, the amount and timing of livestock purchases and sales are projected. The manager estimates the total feed requirements (including grown and purchased feed), breeding expenses, and other anticipated livestock expenses. The machinery plans for the year provide information on machinery and equipment purchases and sales and unusual repairs. Other operating and overhead expenses can likely be estimated from the previous year's records and modified by plans anticipated for the budgeted year. Capital expenditures are budgeted, and scheduled payments on previously incurred debts also are identified. In practice, the information reported by the financial statements introduced in Chapter 3 provides much of the biophysical and financial data needed for forward planning.

The manager can now summarize these data into an annual cash flow budget. Convenient budgeting forms for crop, livestock, and machinery programs as well as forms for projecting cash flows can be obtained from the agricultural extension service in most states. Many lending institutions also have convenient summary forms available for their agricultural clients. Table 5.2 illustrates one such form for cash flow budgeting.

The Budgeting Worksheet

The first section in Table 5.2 summarizes projected farm operating receipts by months, followed by a summary of operating expenses. All capital transactions are projected in Section II, including capital sales and capital expenditures. Section III covers nonbusiness transactions. Included here are off-farm wages, dividends from nonfarm investments and other off-farm income (line 26), and all

Table 5.2. Monthly Cash Flow Budget

	Jan.	Feb.	Mar.	Apr.	May	June	July	Aug.	Sept.	Oct.	Nov.	Dec.	Total
I Operating Transactions													
Receipts													
1. Crops							77,400			121,680			199,080
2. Livestock							16,000					16,000	32,000
3. Other													
4.													
5. Total							93,400			121,680		16,000	231,080
Expenses													
6. Livestock	2,610	1,810	1,810	1,810	1,810	1,810	3,090	1,810	1,810	1,810	1,810	3,090	25,080
7. Crop	8,400	11,600	2,770	5,880	1,780	3,820			15,390				49,640
8. Machine	4,130	1,600	1,260	1,600	1,070	700	1,560	1,080	1,710				14,710
9. Labor	670	670	670	670	670	670	670	670	670	670	670	670	8,040
10. Property taxes	1,600						1,600						3,200
11. Insurance	200						200						400
12. Rent							8,100		9,900				18,000
13. Utilities	100	100	100	110	120	130	130	150	130	120	100	100	1,390
14. Other	100	100	100	100	100	100	100	100	100	100	100	100	1,200
15. Total	17,810	15,880	6,710	10,170	5,550	7,230	15,450	3,810	29,710	2,700	2,680	3,960	121,660
II Capital Transactions													
Sales													
16. Livestock													
17. Machinery													
18. Real estate													
19. Other													
20. Total													
Expenditures													
21. Livestock	35,000												35,000
22. Machinery	20,000												20,000
23. Real estate	60,000												60,000
24. Other													
25. Total	115,000												115,000

III Nonbusiness Transactions

Line item													
26. Receipts (wages, invest.)													
27. Outlays (family, taxes, invest.)	2,900	900	2,900	900	2,900	900	2,900	900	2,900	900			18,800

IV Payments on Previous Debt

Line item													
28. Intermediate —principal												10,000	10,000
29. —interest												2,000	2,000
30. Long-term —principal											1,424	1,262	2,686
31. —interest											13,175	6,733	19,908
32. Total											14,599	19,995	34,594

V Cash Flow Sub-totals

Line item													
33. Total cash inflow (line 5+26)							93,400			121,680		16,000	231,080
34. Total cash outflow (line 15+25+27+32)	135,710	16,780	7,610	13,070	6,450	8,130	18,350	4,710	30,610	5,600	18,179	24,855	290,054

VI Flow-of-Funds Summary

Line item													
35. Cash balance—beginning	1,000	0	0	0	0	0	0	0	0	0	65,626	47,447	1,000
36. Cash inflow (line 33)							93,400			121,680		16,000	231,080
37. Cash outflow (line 34)	135,710	16,780	7,610	13,070	6,450	8,130	18,350	4,710	30,610	5,600	18,179	24,855	290,054
38. Cash difference (line 35+36−37)	(134,710)	(16,780)	(7,610)	(13,070)	(6,450)	(8,130)	75,050	(4,710)	(30,610)	116,080	47,447	38,592	NA
39. Borrowing —long	45,000												45,000
40. —intermed.	55,000												55,000
41. —operating	34,710	16,780	7,610	13,070	6,450	8,130		4,710	30,610				122,070
42. Repay long—principal												337	337
43. —interest												3,600	3,600
44. intermediate—principal												13,750	13,750
45. —interest												4,950	4,950
46. operating—principal							75,050			47,020			122,070
47. —interest										3,434			3,434
48. Cash balance—ending	0	0	0	0	0	0	0	0	0	65,626	47,447	15,955	15,955

VII Debt Outstanding

Line item													
49. Long-term 230,560	275,560	275,560	275,560	275,560	275,560	275,560	275,560	275,560	275,560	275,560	274,136	272,537	NA
50. Intermediate 20,000	75,000	75,000	75,000	75,000	75,000	75,000	75,000	75,000	75,000	75,000	75,000	51,250	NA
51. Operating	34,710	51,490	59,100	72,170	78,620	86,750	11,700	16,410	47,020	0	0	0	NA
52. Interest balance—operating	260	646	1,089	1,630	2,220	2,870	2,958	3,081	3,434	0	0	0	NA

withdrawals of cash for family living, income taxes, and off-farm investments (line 27). All payments on existing debts scheduled during the year are recorded by months in Section IV (lines 28 through 32). Section V (lines 33 and 34) is used to summarize projected cash inflows and outflows. Section VI presents the flow-of-funds summary, while Section VII indicates the various loan balances and interest accrued in each month.

To illustrate how these sections are used, let's suppose that Sections I through V have been completed for the year and that the manager is ready to begin the flow-of-funds summary (Section VI) for January. The first task is to record the beginning-cash and loan balances. The beginning-cash balance of $1,000 is recorded in the January column of line 35. Any beginning balances on loans are recorded prior to the January columns in lines 49, 50, and 51.

The next step is to transfer the total-cash inflows from line 33 to line 36 and the total-cash outflows from line 34 to line 37. Then add the beginning-cash balance (line 35) for January to the cash inflow (line 36) and subtract the cash outflow (line 37) to obtain the cash difference (line 38). If the cash difference is *positive* or exceeds any minimum-required cash balance, either transfer this figure to the beginning-cash balance (line 35) of the following month or make payments on this year's operating debt (line 46) and accrued interest (line 47). Reduce the operating-loan balance (line 51) and accrued interest (line 52) by the amounts of these payments (lines 46 and 47). If the loan balances are zero, then excess cash may be invested in highly liquid financial assets to earn interest.

If the cash difference (line 38) is *negative*, or less than a minimum-required cash balance, then project the level of borrowing (lines 39, 40, 41) needed to maintain a minimum-cash balance. For Farmer A, a cash balance of zero is assumed. Project long-term borrowing in line 39 and any repayments on this year's loan principal in line 42 and interest in line 43. Adjust the long-term loan balance (line 49) for borrowing and principal payments. Project intermediate-term borrowing in line 40 and any repayments this year on principal and interest in lines 44 and 45, respectively. Adjust the intermediate-term loan balance (line 50) for the borrowings and principal payments. Project operating loans in line 41 that are needed to balance the monthly budget. Add each month's operating loan to the operating loan balance (line 51) and accrue the monthly interest (line 52). Carry the ending-cash balance to the beginning of the next month and repeat these procedures for all months of the year.

The total column for Section VI summarizes the annual sources and uses of funds. Thus it provides a cross-check on arithmetic. The cash on hand at the beginning of the year goes in the total column for line 35. Ignore line 38 in the total column. The cash balance projected for the end of December should correspond to the cash balance obtained from adding the cash inflows and subtracting the cash outflows in the total column. The annual summary for Farmer A is shown in Table 5.3; it indicates that gross cash flows are projected to total $454,150 along with the amounts associated with the various sources and uses.

Table 5.3. Projected Sources and Uses of Funds, Farmer A

Sources	
Cash on hand—beginning	$ 1,000
From sale of crops	199,080
From sale of livestock	32,000
Borrowed during the year	222,070
Total funds available	$454,150
Uses	
Farm operating expenses	$121,660
Capital expenditures	115,000
Payment on debt	148,843
Interest expenses	33,892
Proprietor withdrawal	18,800
Cash on hand—end	15,955
Total funds used	$454,150

With a reliable cash flow budget the manager can project the timing and magnitude of the operating line of credit (line 41) and the schedule of loan repayments (lines 46 and 47). Basing the financing program on the cash flow budget provides information vital for liquidity management to the lender as well as to the borrower. Moreover, the operating loans can be designed according to the loan types described earlier: the standard operating loan, a nonrevolving line of credit, or a revolving line of credit. All borrowings that occur in the operating line are generally expected to be repaid within the coming year. Most lenders are reluctant to enter into financing programs which show a planned carryover in the operating line, unless expenditures for breeding livestock, machinery, and other fixed assets are financed with operating loans. Then carryover of unpaid debt to the following year is inevitable.

The Family Living Budget

It is important to separate family budgets and accounts from those of the farm business. Proper accounting, as well as cash control, is greatly enhanced when the family has a separate checking account. Funds could be transferred from the farm-business account to the family account each month, as specified in line 27 of Table 5.2. Family living expenses are then paid from the family account instead of from the farm-business account. If expected family expenditures are constant from month to month, a total annual allowance for family living is divided by 12 to get monthly totals. However, many family expenditures are seasonal, such as income and social security taxes, insurance, children's educational expenses, and vacation expenses. Others occur infrequently, but in large amounts, such as the purchase of household furnishings. Consequently, carefully anticipating family expenditures is a part of the cash flow budgeting process.

The specific form that is used to summarize a family budget should be consistent with historic records of family living expenses. One form is suggested in Table 5.4. Line 16 of Table 5.4 provides the information used in line 27 of the cash flow budget of table 5.2.

Pro Forma Financial Statements

The term *pro forma* refers to setting up accounting information in advance. Thus a pro forma balance sheet projects the asset and liability position of the firm at a specific time in the future. Similarly, a pro forma income statement projects a firm's net income over a future accounting period.

Table 5.5 shows the beginning-of-year balance sheet for Farmer A and the pro forma year-end balance sheet for the budgeted year. The ending cash balance comes from line 48 of the cash flow budget in Table 5.2 as $15,955. Capital sales and capital expenditures come from lines 20 and 25, respectively. Projected liabilities come directly from lines 49, 50, and 51. Closing inventory values must be projected for saleable livestock, crops, feed, etc., and for breeding livestock. Annual depreciation charges are estimated from established depreciation schedules and from new assets acquired during the year. These estimates are included in Table 5.5. A comparison of the beginning and year-end figures indicates that Farmer A's net worth is expected to increase by $45,168 during the year (from $122,940 to $168,108). However, the data also indicate that he is continuing to increase fixed assets and current liabilities.

Table 5.4. Family Living Budget, Farmer A

	Total	Jan.	Feb.	Mar.	Apr.	May	June	July	Aug.	Sept.	Oct.	Nov.	Dec.
1. Food and	2,280	190	190	190	190	190	190	190	190	190	190	190	190
household operating	2,100	175	175	175	175	175	175	175	175	175	175	175	175
2. Household equipment and furniture	500		100		100	100			100		100		
3. House repairs and rent	300			150			150						
4. Clothing and personal	1,310	30	105	55	105	105	55	30	105	205	105	205	205
5. Entertainment, recreation, and education	780	65	65	65	65	65	65	65	65	65	65	65	65
6. Medical care and drugs	960	80	80	80	80	80	80	80	80	80	80	80	80
7. Contributions	480	40	40	40	40	40	40	40	40	40	40	40	40
8. Auto (personal share)	1,320	110	110	110	110	110	110	110	110	110	110	110	110
9. Other	420	35	35	35	35	35	35	35	35	35	35	35	35
10. Total family expenditures	10,450	725	900	900	900	900	900	725	900	900	900	900	900
11. Life insurance	350	175						175					
12. Additions to savings and investments													
13. Income tax and social security	8,000	2,000			2,000			2,000			2,000		
14. Nonfarm business expenses													
15. Total investments and nonfarm business expenses	8,350	2,175	-0-	-0-	2,000	-0-	-0-	2,175	-0-	-0-	2,000	-0-	-0-
16. Total family and nonfarm business expenses	18,800	2,900	900	900	2,900	900	900	2,900	900	900	2,400	900	900

Table 5.5. Beginning- and End-of-Year Balance Sheets

	Beginning		Ending	
Assets				
Current				
Cash	$ 1,000		$ 15,955	
Inventory	3,500		3,500	
Other				
Total		$ 4,500		$ 19,455
Intermediate				
Machinery	$ 48,000		$ 60,000	
Livestock			32,440	
Other				
Total		$ 48,000		$ 92,440
Fixed				
Real Estate	$300,000		$360,000	
Other	21,000		20,000	
Total		$321,000		$380,000
Total		$373,500		$491,895
Liabilities				
Current		$ 12,686		$ 27,750
Intermediate		10,000		27,500
Fixed		227,874		268,537
Total		$250,560		$323,787
Net Worth		$122,940		$168,108
Change in Net Worth				$ 45,168

    The pro forma income statement is estimated with data provided by the cash flow budget and the pro forma balance sheet. Projected operating receipts are taken directly from line 5 of the cash flow budget. Operating expenses are obtained by combining the total of line 15 (business operating expenses) with the interest charges reported on lines 29, 31, 43, 45, and 47 of Table 5.2. Information on changes in inventory is obtained from the beginning and projected closing inventory. Information on adjustments for changes in capital items comes from several sources. Capital gains (losses) are the differences between the sale prices of capital items sold and their book values. Changes in the number and value of livestock raised should be listed separately. Depreciation will come from depreciation records.

    Table 5.6 illustrates the pro forma income statement for Farmer A. Livestock sales are expected to begin in the budgeted year and will be aided by higher crop sales resulting from increased acreage. Projected profits exceed last year's, due to higher sales. Depreciation charges will increase because of heavy investments in machinery.

Table 5.6. Pro Forma Income Statement, Farmer A

Operating Receipts

Wheat	$ 77,400	
Cotton	121,680	
Hogs	32,000	
Total Operating Receipts		$231,080

Operating Expenses

Livestock	$ 25,080	
Machine Maintenance and Repair	14,710	
Crop	49,640	
Labor	8,040	
Property Taxes	3,200	
Insurance	400	
Rent	18,000	
Utilities	1,390	
Miscellaneous	1,200	
Interest	33,892	
Total Operating Expenses		$155,552
Net Income from Operations		$ 75,528

Adjustments for Changes in Inventory

	Notes & Accts. Rec.	Crops	Market Livestock	Supplies	
Beginning	-0-	2,000	-0-	1,500	
Closing	-0-	2,000	-0-	1,500	
Net Change ±	-0-	-0-	-0-	-0-	-0-

Adjustment for Changes in Capital Items

Gain or Loss from Sale of Capital Items	-0-	
+Increment from Capitalization of Raised Animals	-0-	
−Depreciation	−11,560	
Total Adjustment for Changes in Capital Items		−11,560
Profit		63,968
Off-farm Income		-0-
Proprietor Withdrawal		−18,800
Addition to Retained Earnings		$ 45,168

Several important differences between the cash flow projection and the pro forma income statement should be clearly understood. Inventory changes, depreciation, and unpaid operating expenses are included in the income statement but do not enter the cash flow projection.

On the other hand, projected principal payments on debt do not enter the pro forma income statement, and anticipated capital expenditures enter only indirectly. However, both items do enter the cash flow projection. The pro forma income statement includes all expenses projected to be *incurred* (whether paid for or not) and all receipts projected to be *earned* (whether converted into cash or not);

in contrast, the cash flow projection identifies the amount and timing of all projected inflows and outflows of cash. Neither summary is sufficient by itself for financial planning and management. The pro forma income statement projects profitability but does not indicate liquidity or loan repayability. The cash flow budget shows liquidity and loan repayability but not profitability.

Analyzing Financial Feasibility

A plan is considered financially feasible if it satisfies the financing terms and performance criteria that are agreed upon by the borrower and the lender. The major performance criteria are profitability, risk, and liquidity; however, these criteria may be viewed differently by the borrower and the lender. Borrowers are concerned with the profitability of the farm business primarily for the sake of their financial progress. Lenders are more concerned with loan repayment capacity (a liquidity characteristic) and loan security (a risk characteristic) for their own sakes.

Repayment capacity refers to the firm's ability to generate sufficient cash from product sales to repay the loan plus interest according to the contracted financing terms. Loan security refers to the availability of assets that can be pledged as collateral to the lender. Both of these factors are important determinants of the firm's credit worthiness, although agricultural lenders vary in the weights they attach to each. Moreover, effective financial and risk management by borrowers may further influence credit worthiness by improving prospects of loan repayability, by lowering the need for loan security, or both.

The cash flow budget not only projects the level and timing of borrowing and repayments in each month, but also shows how the borrowing accumulates through time. The accumulated borrowings measure the firm's total indebtedness, or outstanding loan balance, at any one time. When total indebtedness reaches a peak—generally in the summer months for crop operations—the firm experiences its greatest financial risk. This maximum indebtedness is the amount which must eventually be repaid; moreover, it must be secured by assets available for loan collateral.

Achieving Financial Feasibility

If the results of the financial-feasibility analysis indicate that the firm's credit worthiness is sufficient to finance the proposed operation and still assure adequate coverage of risk and liquidity, then the plan is deemed feasible. Besides the monthly cash flow analysis, an annual sources-and-uses-of-funds analysis should be conducted for the next three to five years to assure that intermediate- and long-term debts can be adequately serviced.

If, on the other hand, credit is not judged sufficient to finance projected demands for cash, then the plan is deemed financially infeasible. Various alternatives to achieve feasibility can then be considered. These alternatives include one or more of the following, all of which influence profitability, liquidity, and/or risk in varying degrees.

1. Changing the production plans: changing enterprise combinations, substituting labor for capital, using less fertilizer, etc.

2. Changing the marketing plans: holding less inventory, using forward contracting, and gaining price premiums on high-quality products or large-volume transactions.

3. Improving cost control: conserving fuel, utilizing labor to a greater extent, utilizing machinery and used equipment more fully, and gaining price discounts on volume purchases.

4. Improving consumption control: producing more home-grown food, postponing household expenditures, and conserving the family living budget.

5. Refinancing: refinancing existing term debt or carryover operating debt for more orderly payoff.

6. Instituting other financing sources and methods: lower downpayments, longer loan maturities, lower interest rates, government loan and guarantee programs.

7. Considering leasing instead of purchasing new capital items.

8. Postponing expenditures: postponing new investments—including asset replacements—to future years when liquidity and risk are improved.

9. Introducing new equity: bringing new equity into the business to finance expansion or retire existing debt.

10. Liquidating assets for partial or total debt repayment.
    a. Financial assets: stocks, bonds, life insurance-cash value, annuities.

    b. Intermediate assets: selling breeding livestock or machin-
       ery inventory.

    c. Fixed assets: selling land and buildings.

Case Example

    The following case example illustrates the procedures of finan-
cial feasibility analysis for Farmer A, whose historic financial data
were introduced in Chapters 3 and 4, and whose cash flow budget
was formulated earlier in this chapter. Now the focus is on analyzing
the feasibility of Farmer A's financial plans. Recall that the farm consists of crops grown on 700 acres of owned land, with all production
sold at harvest or shortly thereafter. Similar production and marketing plans are anticipated for the coming year. In addition, the producer is planning on three new investments to expand the size and
diversity of the operation.

    One of these investments is the purchase of additional land for
$60,000 to expand the crop enterprise. Another is the purchase of
$20,000 of additional equipment. The third investment achieves di-
versification into livestock production by establishing a hog enterprise. Investment required for the hog enterprise is $35,000. Hence,
capital expenditures budgeted for the coming year total $115,000.

    Financing plans include an intermediate-term loan for the
$55,000 investment in machinery and hogs, payable in four annual
installments of $13,750 each, plus interest on the remaining balance.
The land purchase is financed from a long-term lender requiring a 25
percent downpayment with the balance of $45,000 payable in
equally amortized annual installments of $3,937 each over a 30-year
period. The first payments on both term loans are scheduled in December. Both of these loans are in addition to existing-term loans that
were incurred in prior years. All other financing is to be provided by
the operator and by operating loans.

    The data in Table 5.2 indicate the monthly cash flow budget for
the coming year, including the above capital expenditures. Operating
receipts (Section I) for the total business are budgeted at $231,080
with sales occurring in only three months, all in the second half of
the year. Operating expenses total $121,660 and are projected to
occur in every month. All capital expenditures (Section II) are
budgeted for the beginning of the year. Nonbusiness outlays (Section
III) occur each month for family living and quarterly payments on
estimated income taxes. Payments on previous intermediate- and

long-term debts (Section IV) occur in November and December. The sub-total summary of cash flows in Section V indicates much variation in level and timing of monthly net cash flows and implies the need for considerable use of operating loans.

The flow-of-funds summary in Section VI combines the firm's beginning cash balances with all other sources and uses of cash in each month to determine the level and timing of operating loans and their repayment, including interest. Operating loans (line 41) occur in eight months, totaling $122,070 for the year and reach a maximum balance of $86,750 in July. Repayments also total $122,070, indicating that the line is fully repaid. Interest paid on the operating loans totals $3,434. End-of-year loan balances for term debts are reported in the December column of Section VII.

At first glance, the business plans appear financially feasible. There is no carryover of operating debt, all scheduled payments are met, and the firm projects a sizeable ending-cash balance that exceeds its beginning-cash balance. However, first impressions do not assure financial feasibility. More detailed analyses of profitability, risk, and liquidity are needed. Profitability is evaluated by checking the validity of data and by estimating pro forma income. Data on prices, yields, costs, feeding rates, etc., used in formulating the production and marketing plans must be realistic and appropriate. Otherwise, performance measures reflected by the budget will not be valid. Generally, however, these data are carefully considered *prior* to formulating the cash flow budget.

Table 5.6 reports the pro forma income statement. Additions to retained earnings of $45,168 are projected for the coming year, providing a $45,168/122,940 = 36.7 percent rate of return on beginning-of-year equity capital. Clearly, profitability appears high. However, financial leverage also appears high, and it is important to evaluate risk and liquidity.

Estimating a pro forma balance sheet and comparing it to past-balance sheets is one approach to evaluating risk and liquidity. Table 5.5 contains beginning- and end-of-year balance sheets which indicate that the firm has generally experienced good financial progress during the year. Net worth has increased by $45,168, which is the amount of the firm's addition to retained earnings. All operating loans have been retired. Term debts have increased, although in support of intermediate and fixed assets purchased to expand the size of operation. The intermediate ratio has declined and the fixed ratio remains the same. The firm's leverage has also declined. Moreover, the larger cash balance has increased the firm's asset liquidity. Further financial strength is likely reflected by appreciation in value of previously owned land, although it is not shown on the balance sheet. In sum, the prospects for financial feasiblity appear quite good so far.

Despite these evidences of strength, the analysis has not treated the effects of seasonality, length of the production process, and marketing policies on the firm's financial exposure to risk. These factors are very important. The cash flow budget clearly indicates that substantial borrowing occurs on the operating line of credit before any cash is generated by product sales. Additional operating loans are also needed after the first crop sale in July. The pattern of loan balances in Section VII of Table 5.2 indicates that the debt outstanding for the operating loan and for all debt reaches a maximum in June. Hence, an important element of the test of financial feasibility is accounting for the period when the firm is experiencing its greatest financial risk. At this point, loan repayability and loan security are most crucial and must be assured.

Formulating a series of monthly balance sheets, based on results of the cash flow budget, together with other information on inventory and capital accounts, is an effective way to evaluate the seasonality of financial risk. Table 5.7 reports these monthly balance sheets for the case farm, while Table 5.8 indicates the effects of seasonality on selected financial ratios.

Outstanding loan balances on the monthly balance sheets are taken directly from Section VII of the cash flow budget. Also included as current liabilities are the current portions of intermediate- and long-term debt, and interest accrued on all indebtedness. Real estate is valued at acquisition cost, and intermediate assets are valued at original cost less depreciation prorated on a monthly basis throughout the year. Cash balances are taken directly from line 48 of the cash flow budget. A $3,500 inventory of supplies is also maintained each month.

Accounting for the values of operating inputs used in production is especially difficult in asset valuation. As examples, the values of fertilizer, fuel, chemicals, seed, and labor that are used in production must be reflected in the value of the growing crop. Similarly, livestock feed, veterinary services, and labor are reflected in the value of livestock being fed for market sale.

The values for crop and livestock production in the current-asset section of Table 5.7 reflect their accumulated costs of production in

Table 5.7. Monthly Pro Forma Balance Sheets for Case Farm[1]

	Begin	Jan.	Feb.	Mar.	Apr.	May	June	July	Aug.	Sept.	Oct.	Nov.	Dec.	Begin
Assets														
Current														
Cash	1,000	0	0	0	0	0	0	0	0	0	65,626	47,447	15,955	15,955
Inventory	3,500	3,500	3,500	3,500	3,500	3,500	3,500	3,500	3,500	3,500	3,500	3,500	3,500	3,500
Crop production (cost basis)	0	13,080	26,830	31,410	39,440	42,840	47,910	30,012	31,642	59,192	0	0	0	0
Livestock production (cost basis)	0	2,730	4,660	6,590	8,520	10,450	15,110	4,660	6,590	8,520	10,450	12,380	0	0
Other														
Total	4,500	19,310	34,990	41,500	51,460	56,790	66,520	38,172	41,732	71,212	79,076	62,827	19,455	19,455
Intermediate														
Machinery	48,000	67,336	66,670	66,002	65,336	64,669	64,002	63,334	62,667	62,000	61,334	60,667	60,000	60,000
Livestock	0	34,783	34,570	34,357	34,144	33,931	33,718	33,505	33,292	33,079	32,866	32,653	32,440	32,440
Other														
Total	48,000	102,119	101,240	100,357	99,480	98,600	97,720	96,839	95,959	95,079	94,200	93,320	92,440	92,440
Fixed														
Real estate	300,000	360,000	360,000	360,000	360,000	360,000	360,000	360,000	360,000	360,000	360,000	360,000	360,000	360,000
Other	21,000	20,917	20,834	20,751	20,668	20,585	20,502	20,419	20,336	20,253	20,170	20,083	20,000	20,000
Total assets	373,500	502,346	517,064	522,608	531,608	535,975	544,742	515,430	518,027	546,544	553,446	536,230	491,895	491,895

(Continued)

Table 5.7. (Continued)

	Begin	Jan.	Feb.	Mar.	Apr.	May	June	July	Aug.	Sept.	Oct.	Nov.	Dec.	Begin
Liabilities														
Current														
Operating loan	0	34,710	51,490	59,100	72,170	78,620	86,750	11,700	16,410	47,020	0	0	0	
Intermediate loan —current portion	10,000	23,750	23,750	23,750	23,750	23,750	23,750	23,750	23,750	23,750	23,750	23,750	0	23,750
Fixed debt—current portion	2,686	3,023	3,023	3,023	3,023	3,023	3,023	3,023	3,023	3,023	3,023	1,639	0	4,000
Accrued interest	0	3,878	6,794	9,768	12,840	15,961	19,142	21,761	24,416	27,799	26,397	15,883	0	
Other														
Total	12,686	65,361	85,057	95,641	111,783	121,354	132,665	60,234	67,599	101,592	53,170	41,232	0	27,750
Intermediate (less current portion)	10,000	51,250	51,250	51,250	51,250	51,250	51,250	51,250	51,250	51,250	51,250	51,250	51,250	27,750
Fixed (less current portion)	227,874	272,537	272,537	272,537	272,537	272,537	272,537	272,537	272,537	272,537	272,537	272,537	272,537	268,537
Total liabilities	250,560	389,148	408,844	419,428	435,570	445,141	456,452	384,021	391,386	425,379	376,957	365,019	323,787	323,787
Net worth	122,940	113,198	108,220	103,180	96,038	90,834	88,290	131,409	126,641	121,165	176,489	171,211	168,108	168,108

[a]Balance sheets for January through December indicate end-of-month data. Beginning balance sheets indicate January 1 data.

Table 5.8. Projected Financial Ratios, Farmer A

	Begin	Jan.	Feb.	Mar.	Apr.	May	June	July	Aug.	Sept.	Oct.	Nov.	Dec.	Begin next year
Current ratio	.35	.29	.41	.43	.46	.47	.50	.63	.62	.70	1.49	1.52	0.00	.70
Intermediate ratio	4.80	1.99	1.98	1.96	1.94	1.92	1.91	1.89	1.87	1.86	1.84	1.82	1.80	3.36
Current plus intermediate ratio	2.31	1.04	1.00	.97	.93	.90	.89	1.21	1.16	1.09	1.66	1.69	2.17	2.03
Fixed ratio	1.41	1.40	1.40	1.40	1.40	1.40	1.40	1.40	1.40	1.40	1.40	1.40	1.40	1.42
Total assets/total debt	1.49	1.29	1.26	1.25	1.22	1.20	1.19	1.34	1.32	1.28	1.47	1.47	1.52	1.52
Total debt/net worth	2.04	3.44	3.78	4.06	4.54	4.90	5.17	2.92	3.09	3.51	2.13	2.13	1.93	1.93

the respective months. For livestock, these costs are the accumulated balance of the entries in line 6 of the cash flow budget plus 18 percent of the labor charge in line 9. The value of growing crops is reflected by the accumulation of entries in lines 7 and 8 plus the rest of the hired-labor charge. These accumulated costs of production provide one source of security for coverage of operating loans used to finance these costs and, more importantly, indicate the source of loan repayment when the products are sold.

The monthly ratios for the case farm in Table 5.8 clearly indicate the impact of seasonality on the firm's financial risk. The current ratio declines immediately and rises slowly, only exceeding 1.0 in November and December after most of the sales and much of the debt servicing have occurred. The ratio of intermediate assets to intermediate liabilities also declines immediately, reflecting the three new investments, and then declines further, reflecting the monthly depreciation. The ratio of current plus intermediate assets to current plus intermediate liabilities declines in the early months, falling below 1.0 in March and not rising above 1.0 until July. Hence, a lender who provides both current and intermediate financing to the case farm and who takes a security interest in current and intermediate assets would experience several months in which the indebtedness is not covered by available collateral.

The ratio of fixed assets to fixed liabilities remains constant through the months. The ratio of total assets to total liabilities declines steadily, reaching a low of 1.19 in June, before rising to an end-of-year value of 1.52. The leverage ratio (debt/equity) is directly related to the ratio of assets to liabilities. It rises to a maximum in June and declines to the year's low in December. Indeed, the monthly series of leverage ratios provides a striking contrast to the beginning- and end-of-year values. Leverage exceeds 4.0 in four months and reaches 5.17 in one month. These high values indicate considerable financial risk and require careful consideration by both lender and borrower in evaluating financial feasibility.

In this case, the firm's plans for marketing crops and livestock tend to limit the financial exposure to risk. Products are sold as soon as they are ready for market, with the sale proceeds used to repay the operating loan. However, many farmers do not sell their crops immediately at harvest or experience delays in payment for other reasons. Some store their crops in inventory in hopes of more favorable prices in the future. Others contract their sales through marketing cooperatives, who assume the farmer's storage and sale functions.

Pricing is accomplished through pooling of cooperative returns with a partial payment when the product is delivered. The balance is payable at the end of the cooperative's marketing season.

In either case—storage or cooperative marketing—the delayed receipt of cash-from-product sales means that the farmer must carry the operating loan for a longer period of time. Additional operating loans may even be needed to meet other financial obligations. The general result is to prolong and increase the firm's maximum exposure to risk. The production risk is reduced, since harvest has occurred, but risk of adverse price fluctuations continues.

What is the verdict? Are the business plans for the case farm financially feasible? The final test would be whether or not a lender is willing to provide the financing. Moreover, the projections for Farmer A need to be considered in the context of the firm's historic performance, as evaluated in Chapter 4. Even with Farmer A's favorable trends, the evidence for the budgeted year leans toward infeasibility. The seasonality of the ratios is the key point. Some ratios clearly exceed the norms and tolerance limits that are commonly used in financial analysis of agricultural firms. For most lenders, the firm's borrowing needs likely exceed its borrowing capacity. Even if financing were available, the remaining credit reserve would be extremely small. The major point is that these data and procedures for financial analysis are appropriate to use and should lead to sounder judgments in financial management.

Topics for Discussion

1. Explain the concept of a self-liquidating loan. Indicate how the time pattern of earnings for current, intermediate, and fixed assets is taken into account in formulating self-liquidating loans.

2. Contrast the various types of operating loans: standard, nonrevolving, and revolving. Which is best suited for a cash grain farm? A dairy farm? A large cattle feedlot?

3. Calculate the total interest charge on a $200,000 loan on March 1 at a 10 percent annual interest rate with repayments projected as $100,000 on October 1, $50,000 on November 1, and $50,000 on December 1.

4. Design an appropriate financing program for a farm to purchase an $80,000 tractor and related equipment. The machine will be used for six years, and the lender requires the farmer to make a 25 percent downpayment as an equity margin.

5. Explain the role of the cash flow budget in financial feasibility analysis.

6. Explain how seasonality in cash flows in a farming operation influences financial risk and liquidity.

7. If the results of a cash flow budget indicate excessive financial risk, what changes can be considered to make the plans financially feasible? What priorities are held by these possible changes?
8. Distinguish between the liquidity of a farm business as indicated by (a) its balance sheet, (b) its income statement, and (c) its cash flow budget. Why are these important?

References

1. Baker, C. B., "Credit in the Production Organization of the Firm," *American Journal of Agricultural Economics*, 50(1968):507-521.
2. Frey, T. L., and R. Behrens, *Lending to Agricultural Enterprises*, American Banking Institute, New York, 1982.
3. Frey, T. L., and D. A. Klinefelter, *Coordinated Financial Statements for Agriculture*, Century Communications, Inc., Skokie, Illinois, 1978.
4. Hanson, G. D., and J. L. Thompson, "A Simulation Study of Maximum Feasible Farm Debt Burdens by Farm Types," *American Journal of Agricultural Economics*, 62(1980):727-733.
5. Lee, W. F., et al., *Agricultural Finance*, 7th ed., Iowa State University Press, Ames, 1980.
6. Mauldon, R. G., "Financial Control Within Commercial Family Farms," *Australian Journal of Agricultural Economics*, 17(1973):33-42.
7. Mueller, A. G., "Flow of Funds Analysis in Farm Financial Management," *Journal of Farm Economics*, 48(1966):661-667.
8. Richardson, J. W., and G. D. Condra, "Farm Size Evaluation in the El Paso Valley: A Survival/Success Approach," *American Journal of Agricultural Economics*, 63(1981):430-438.
9. Van Horne, J. C., *Financial Management and Policy*, 5th ed., Prentice-Hall, Inc., Englewood Cliffs, New Jersey, 1980.
10. Weston, J. F., and E. F. Brigham, *Essentials of Managerial Finance*, 6th ed., Dryden Press, Hinsdale, Illinois, 1982.

SECTION III

Capital Structure, Liquidity, and Risk Management

Chapter 6

CAPITAL STRUCTURE, LEVERAGE, AND FINANCIAL RISK

In previous chapters, we assumed that a firm's desired mix of debt and equity capital was already established. In financial management, however, decisions about leverage are of major importance and have profound effects on expected profitability, risk, and liquidity. In this chapter, we treat financial leverage as a decision variable in financial planning and develop concepts and measures for evaluating how leverage influences business performance.

The following section establishes the theoretical relationship between financial leverage and the firm's costs of debt and equity capital. Then conceptual models are developed that relate a firm's profitability and risk to leverage and other business characteristics. Numerical examples demonstrate that under proper conditions higher leverage can accelerate the growth rate of equity capital (a profitability measure), but also increase the risk of loss of equity. This risk-return trade-off means that the optimal level of leverage will differ among farm businesses, depending on the decision maker's risk-return attitudes. The final sections of the chapter consider the relationships between leverage and other performance factors.

Capital Costs and Leverage

The term *costs of capital* refers to the costs a firm must pay or incur for its financial capital. *Financial capital*, in turn, refers to the debt and equity claims comprising the liabilities side of the firm's balance sheet. The combination of debt and equity reflects the firm's financial leverage or capital structure. Together, debt and equity provide the means for financing the firm's total assets.

Both debt and equity command payments—interest for debt and profit shares for equity—which constitute costs to the firm. Thus, one conceptual approach to specifying optimal leverage is to seek the firm's least cost combination of debt and equity capital. Once the minimum cost leverage is found, the firm continues to finance its assets with that combination of debt and equity.

To evaluate the relationships between capital costs and leverage, we begin with the following propositions about the costs of equity and debt. First, the cost of the debt should be less than the cost of equity because of the equity holder's higher financial risk. Second, we accept the traditional view in finance theory that the costs of both debt and equity will eventually increase as leverage increases. Equity costs increase because of greater financial risk associated with higher financial leverage. Debt costs increase because of the greater likelihood of repayment problems, reduced liquidity, and other lending risks associated with higher leverage. With these propositions we can determine how the firm's average cost of capital responds to changing financial leverage.

These relationships between capital costs and leverage are illustrated in Figure 6.1. Suppose, for example, that the cost of equity capital at zero leverage ($D/E = 0$) is 14 percent and that as leverage increases, the cost of equity also increases, as shown by line i_e in Figure 6.1. Let the cost of debt at zero leverage be 12 percent, and let it also increase with leverage as shown by line i_d. Line i_a indicates the weighted average cost of debt and equity as leverage increases.

At zero leverage, where no debt is used, the average cost equals the cost of equity. As leverage increases, the substitution of lower cost debt for higher cost equity lowers the average cost until higher costs of both debt and equity cause the weighted average to increase.

The derivation of a weighted average cost of debt and equity is illustrated in Table 6.1, based on five leverage positions and using the weighted average cost of capital formula (4.6). In Chapter 4, the focus was on partitioning the Returns on Assets into Returns on Equity and Costs of Debt based on measured returns to assets, debt, and equity and on the weights of debt and equity relative to total assets. The equation was expressed as:

$$ROA = (COD)(D/A) + (ROE)(E/A)$$

Here, we relabel the weighted average equation in order to achieve consistency with the cost concepts identified above. The relabeled equation is:

$$i_a = (i_d)(D/A) + (i_e)(E/A) \qquad\qquad (6.1)$$

where i_d is the cost of debt capital, i_e is the cost of equity capital, and i_a is the weighted average cost of debt and equity using D/A and E/A as the weights. This approach assumes that the costs of debt and equity are known values that serve as a basis for establishing leverage policies.

This equation is used to estimate the weighted average costs of capital for the five leverage positions in Table 6.1. For $D/E = 1.0$, for example, the weights are $D/A = .5$ and $E/A = .5$, and the costs of debt and equity are $i_d = .12$ and $i_e = .14$. The average cost of capital is then

$$i_a = (.12)(.5) + (.14)(.5)$$
$$= .130, \text{ or } 13.0\%.$$

Average costs for other levels of leverage are found in a similar fashion. Through a leverage of 1.0, the costs of equity and debt remain constant, thereby lowering the average cost as leverage in-

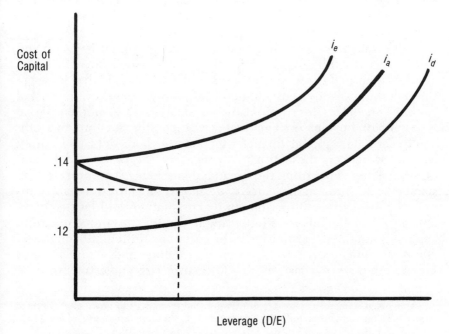

Figure 6.1. Relationship between cost of capital and leverage.

Table 6.1. Weighted Average Cost of Debt and Equity Capital for Alternative Leverage Positions

| Leverage D/E | Debt Capital | | Equity Capital | | Weighted Average |
	Cost i_d	Weight D/A	Cost i_e	Weight E/A	i_a
.00	.12	.00	.14	1.00	.140
.50	.12	.33	.14	.67	.133
1.00	.12	.50	.14	.50	.130
1.50	.14	.60	.16	.40	.148
2.00	.16	.67	.18	.33	.167
2.50	.18	.71	.20	.29	.186
3.00	.20	.75	.25	.25	.213

creases. For leverage of 1.5 and above, the average cost increases due to higher costs of both debt and equity capital. These leverage positions represent five of the points on the average cost of capital line, i_a, in Figure 6.1.

The optimum combination of debt and equity occurs at the minimum average cost of capital—a leverage of about 1.0 in Figure 6.1.[1] In concept the firm should finance its growth in assets by using the least cost combination of debt and equity. Hence, each new dollar of assets should be financed with $0.50 of debt and $0.50 of equity.

The concept of a minimum average cost of capital is sound and instructive. It explicitly identifies the factors associated with leverage decisions and expresses the risks associated with higher leverage through the respective costs of debt and equity. However, the cost of capital concept is less applicable to smaller-scale, non-corporate types of farm businesses. The large, corporate firm generally has efficient access to national financial markets for both debt and equity capital. Moreover, these firms can measure the costs of debt and equity, using data from the financial markets.[2] In contrast, the smaller-scale firms in agriculture are mostly organized as farm proprietorships, partnerships, and family corporations and lack comparable access to markets for equity capital. Their main source of equity capital is retained earnings whose costs are difficult to measure, whose amounts are subject to high uncertainty, and whose rates of growth often are not fast enough to finance large investments. As a

---

[1] Financial economists have vigorously debated the impact of leverage on optimal capital structure for corporate firms. Good references on these topics are [9] and [13].

[2] Procedures for measuring the costs of debt and equity capital are considered in Chapter 14.

result, agriculture has relied heavily on borrowing and leasing, as well as retained earnings to finance its growth. Unrealized capital gains, especially on farm land, have also been a significant source of equity capital.

Those few larger agricultural operations that can attract outside equity capital generally find that conditions in financial markets limit the amounts. Generally, the managers of such operations must decide whether to raise a large block of equity or debt, but not both, to finance a new investment. Consequently, rapidly growing farm firms tend to utilize higher leverage to meet their growth objectives.

Firm Growth in Agriculture

The growth of agricultural firms is a long standing phenomenon, as evidenced by increasing sizes of agricultural operations and declines in farm numbers. Two important features of firm growth are measures of growth and economic incentives for growth.

Measures of Firm Growth

The term *growth*, as used in financial management, refers to increases in business size. Rates of growth refer to how fast changes in size occur over time. Hence, measures of size and growth are closely related.

Several types of growth measures are possible. The measures can be financial or physical and may focus on inputs or outputs. Examples of physical measures of growth for inputs and outputs include acres, litters of hogs, cattle fed, cows milked, and broilers raised. However, these physical measures of size have limited usefulness in comparing different types of businesses. Acreage, for example, may be useful for comparing the size of two wheat farms. But acreage is meaningless for broiler operations or cattle feedlots where the birds and cattle are raised in confinement with purchased feed.

Financial measures of growth are easier to compare. Gross income, for example, may be satisfactory for comparing growth in size for businesses of similar type and capital intensity. However, gross income may not be appropriate for comparing farm types with different ratios of cash expenses to gross receipts (dairy cattle versus feeder cattle, for example).

Financial measures provide for more useful growth comparisons among farms with different operating characteristics. Rate of growth of equity or of net income flows reflects the firm's profitability. As indicated earlier, and developed further below, we will use the rate of return to equity capital as the growth measure. It is synonymous with the expected rate of growth of equity.

Economic Incentives for Growth

In this section, we review the incentives for firm growth in agriculture. These incentives provide a basis for studying the relationships between financial leverage, profitability, and risk in agricultural firms.

Conditions for growth exist when the firm has underutilized resources, less than optimal resource allocation, or savings from disposable income to be invested. Moreover, two types of incentives for economic growth can stimulate the manager. One is a "push" incentive, in which the manager seeks growth as a means to fully exercise management ability. The manager is seeking greater control and stronger challenges from the environment; expanding the business is one means of accomplishing these goals. The second is a "pull" incentive, in which the business grows in order to operate more efficiently, achieve economies of size, and enhance income-generating capacity. These two incentives are not independent; elements of both generally guide growth-oriented decisions. Moreover, their relative importance depends upon the economic environment of farm businesses.

The pull incentive is attributed to the combined effects of several farm characteristics in U.S. agriculture. The farm sector is largely comprised of relatively small firms, despite having relatively large capital investments per person employed. Low price and income elasticities for many farm commodities, subject to weather and other uncontrollable events, have led to wide swings in commodity prices. Moreover, individual farmers in general have had little capacity to influence either resource or commodity prices. These factors have traditionally destabilized farm income and placed downward pressure on profit margins per unit of farm production.

The 1930s through the 1960s witnessed a long, steady period of structural change in the numbers and sizes of farms in the United States and in their financial and market characteristics in response to these income and resource problems. Farm numbers declined and many human resources left agriculture. The remaining farms experienced substantial mechanization, modernization, and growth in size as farmers responded to the cost efficiencies associated with new technologies and the quest for greater income-generating capacity. Farmers also became more dependent on markets for acquiring farm resources. In response to these events, the per capita income for farm families has become comparable in the 1980s to the income of nonfarmers. Moreover, farmers' reliance on nonfarm income grew as well, especially for the many small, part-time farming operations.

These structural changes occurring in an increasingly inflationary environment were financed by farmers' growing use of debt capital and continued reliance on leasing of farm land. Financial leverage in farm businesses has increased over time, especially for larger farming operations, thus obligating a growing proportion of farmers' income to debt servicing. Moreover, the longer term growth in returns to farm assets along with the dominance among assets of real estate and capital investments have brought much of farmers' total returns as unrealized capital gains. When subject to financial analysis, these patterns of returns and farm financing indicate relatively high solvency in most farm businesses due primarily to unrealized capital gains on farm assets that are collateral for the growth in debt; however, farm businesses are also subject to chronic liquidity problems and cash flow pressures resulting from the continued low but volatile current rates of return to production assets.

Prospects for the future suggest continued incentives for firm growth in agriculture, although the pace of change in numbers and sizes of firms will be less than in past decades. Projections to the year 2000 by the U.S. Department of Agriculture suggest an increasing proportion of large farms, continuation of many small farms with nonfarm activities, and a declining proportion of medium-sized farms [12]. The commercial component of these future farms should have strong survival capacities, high quality of management, and well developed skills in managing production, marketing, and finance. They will seek economic growth in a risk environment that is richer and more complex than in the past. Farmers will continue to experience the traditional sources of risk—variations in crop yields, livestock production, commodity prices, etc. Other risks will come from high financial leverage and unanticipated variations in interest rates and debt-servicing requirements. Thus, the development of appropriate leverage policies will be a challenging task.

Financial Leverage and Firm Growth

Financial leverage influences a firm's growth through its effects on the expected returns to equity capital. In general, increasing financial leverage will increase the growth in equity so long as the marginal returns from the use of a loan exceed the costs of borrowing. To illustrate, consider the financial organizations of two farm businesses that are similar in all respects except for their levels of financial leverage. Both Farmer C and Farmer D expect returns to assets of 16 percent and interest rates on debt of 12 percent. They each have an income tax rate of 20 percent and a consumption rate of 50 percent from net after-tax income. They each have $100,000 of equity capital; however, Farmer C's financial structure indicates a debt-to-equity ratio of 0.5, while Farmer D's debt-to-equity ratio is 1.0.

Table 6.2 indicates the balance sheets for Farmers C and D, along with the set of calculations needed to project their rates of growth in equity capital. As the calculation procedures show, the returns to assets (line 5) are reduced by the interest obligation on debt (line 6) to yield taxable income (line 7). Payments for taxes (line 8) and consumption (line 10) according to the specified rates yield the returns to equity (line 11). Dividing returns to equity by the level of equity capital gives the rate of growth of equity—7.2 percent for Farmer C and 8.0 percent for Farmer D. Thus, Farmer D's higher leverage yields a higher expected growth rate for equity capital, with all other variables equal.

Table 6.2. Rate of Growth in Equity for Different Leverage Ratios

Item	Farmer C	Farmer D
Balance Sheet		
1. Assets	$150,000	$200,000
2. Debt	50,000	100,000
3. Equity	100,000	100,000
4. Leverage (D/E)	0.5	1.0
Income Statement		
5. Returns to Assets (16% of line 1)	$ 24,000	$ 32,000
6. Interest on debt (12% of line 2)	6,000	12,000
7. Taxable income	18,000	20,000
8. Taxes (20% of line 7)	3,600	4,000
9. After-tax income	14,400	16,000
10. Consumption (50% of line 9)	7,200	8,000
11. Returns to equity	7,200	8,000
12. Rate of growth of equity (line 11 ÷ line 3)	7.2%	8.0%

The calculation process in Table 6.2 is generalized by developing a growth model that expresses the rate of growth in equity capital as a function of the rate of return on assets, the interest rate on debt, the rates of taxation and consumption, and the level of financial leverage. The model is formulated as:

$$g = (rP_a - iP_d)(1 - t)(1 - c) \qquad \textbf{(6.2)}$$

or, more briefly, as:

$$g = (rP_a - iP_d) k \qquad \textbf{(6.3)}$$

where k = $(1 - t)(1 - c)$ and

g = the rate of growth of equity capital

r = the average net rate of return, except for interest (i) and taxes (t), on total assets owned by the firm

i = the average interest rate paid on debt

t = the average rate of income taxation

c = the average rate of withdrawals for family consumption, dividends, and other nonbusiness flows.

P_a = the ratio (or proportion) of assets to equity, and

P_d = the ratio (or proportion) of debt to equity, which is called the *leverage* ratio.

For greater generality, leverage is modeled in proportional terms as the weights of assets (P_a) and debts (P_d) per dollar of equity capital. To illustrate, Farmer D's balance sheet in Table 6.2 shows $2 of assets and $1 of debt for every $1 of equity capital. Thus the weights (or ratios) of assets and debts relative to equity for Farmer D are P_a = 2.0 and P_d = 1.0, and the value of P_d represents the leverage ratio. Following the balance sheet identity, in which assets minus debt equals equity, these weights must satisfy the relationship $P_a - P_d$ = 1.0.

Using equation (6.2) and the data introduced above, Farmer D's projected rate of growth of equity is:

$$g = [(.16)(2.0) - (.12)(1.0)] (1 - .2)(1 - .5)$$

$$= .080, \text{ or } 8.0\%.$$

Similarly, the projected growth rate for Farmer C is:

$$g = \left[(.16)(1.5) - (.12)(.5)\right](1 - .2)(1 - .5)$$
$$= .072, \text{ or } 7.2\%.$$

Notice that the weights of assets and debt relative to equity for Farmer C are $P_a = 1.5$ and $P_d = 0.5$, reflecting the composition of Farmer C's balance sheet. These weights satisfy the requirement 1.5 − 0.5 = 1.0.

While this model presents a simplified functional form, it includes the major variables affecting a firm's rate of equity growth. The model combines balance sheet (P_a, P_d) and income (r,i) elements as well as specifying external cash withdrawals (c,t). Thus the model can be used to measure the effects on growth of each component.

Growth rates determined by leverage ratios ranging from 0.0 to 5.0 and rates of return ranging from 8 percent to 30 percent are indicated in Table 6.3 when rates of interest, taxes, and consumption are .12, .20, and .50, respectively. These ranges of values for r and P_d include the values found among most farm businesses.

Table 6.3. Growth Rates for Alternate Returns to Assets and Leverage

Leverage (D/E)	Returns to Assets (r)					
	.08	.12	.16	.20	.25	.30
	percent					
0.00	3.20	4.80	6.40	8.00	10.00	12.00
0.50	2.40	4.80	7.20	9.60	12.60	15.60
1.00	1.60	4.80	8.00	11.20	15.20	19.20
2.00	0.00	4.80	9.60	14.40	20.40	26.40
3.00	−1.60	4.80	11.20	17.60	25.60	33.60
4.00	−3.20	4.80	12.80	20.80	30.80	40.80
5.00	−4.80	4.80	14.40	24.00	36.00	48.00

Row 1 shows the growth rates for a debt-free situation at each rate of return in the column headings. These rates are calculated with equation (6.4), which is the reduced version of (6.3) when $P_a = 1.0$ and $P_d = 0.0$.

$$g = rk. \tag{6.4}$$

Thus, for an earnings rate of 12 percent, the rate of growth is

$$g = (.12)(.80)(.50) = .048, \text{ or } 4.8\%.$$

Notice that when $P_d = 0.0$, the growth rates are wholly determined by the returns to assets (r) and the k factor. The growth rate (g) is less than r because of the dampening influence of consumption and tax payments. Notice also, from Table 6.3, that equity growth is unaffected by leverage when the interest rate equals the net rate of return on assets. When both i and r equal 12 percent, all earnings from additional borrowing are used to pay interest. Moreover, if r is less than i, then the growth rate declines with higher leverage and eventually becomes negative.

The remainder of the table illustrates the close relationship between leverage (P_d) and the rate of return on assets (r), and their effects on growth in equity, given the values of i, t, and c. If the rate of return exceeds the interest rate and other variables remain constant, increases in financial leverage will increase the rate of growth, and thus the firm's profitability.

The effects on growth of changes in consumption, taxation, and interest rates are evaluated by holding other factors constant. The reader may explore these effects by varying these variables. The growth rates are increased by higher rates of return, low costs of debt capital, and low rates of consumption and taxation.

This analysis suggests that additional borrowing to finance investments and accelerate the rate of growth is quite profitable. However, it is unusual to find agricultural firms with leverage ratios that exceed the 1 to 2 range. Hence, limits on leverage and on rates of growth tend to occur. We need to consider those factors which reduce the incentive for higher leverage.

Leverage and Risk

One factor affecting the faster growth in equity attributed to higher financial leverage is the increase in the firm's financial risk. The effects of farm business risks are magnified considerably when leverage increases.

Financial risks arise in several forms. As expansion occurs with borrowed capital, the potential loss of equity capital increases, the variation of expected returns to equity increases, and liquidity provided by credit reserves is reduced. These effects are important because, as leverage increases, unfavorable events have greater impact on the firm than do favorable events. These greater variations arise from the fixed contractual obligations associated with interest payments and liabilities.

Moreover, in recent years high-volatile interest rates and greater use of floating rate loans by most farm lenders have created considerable uncertainty about the costs of borrowing. Many interest rates are now variable, thus adding a new source of financial risk to consider along with leverage and business risk.

Leverage and Business Risk

The risk effects of financial leverage are illustrated by showing how a 10 percent reduction in both asset values and returns to assets influences the level of equity and growth rates for Farmers C and D. Table 6.4 indicates the changes in equity and growth rates as asset values (A_0) decline by 10 percent to A_1, and as asset returns (R_0) decline by 10 percent to R_1, with levels of debt, interest, taxes, and consumption remaining the same.

Table 6.4. Effects of Financial Risk for Alternative Levels of Leverage

Item	Farmer C	Farmer D
Balance Sheet		
1. Assets A_0	$150,000	$200,000
2. A_1	135,000	180,000
3. Debt	50,000	100,000
4. Equity E_0	100,000	100,000
5. E_1	85,000	80,000
6. Percentage change in E	15%	20%
Income Statement		
7. Returns to Assets R_0	24,000	32,000
8. R_1	21,600	28,800
9. Interest	6,000	12,000
10. Taxes	3,600	4,000
11. Consumption	7,200	8,000
12. Returns to Equity I_0	7,200	8,000
13. I_1	4,800	4,800
14. Growth rate, g_0	7.2%	8.0%
15. g_1	4.8%	4.8%
16. Percentage change in g	33%	40%

For Farmer C, a 10 percent decline in asset values causes a 15 percent decline in the level of equity and a 33 percent decline in the projected growth rate, given Farmer C's leverage ratio of 0.5. For Farmer D, the same 10 percent decline in asset values causes a 20 percent decline in the level of equity and a 40 percent decline in the projected growth rate. The relative decline is greater for Farmer D, due to his higher leverage ratio, and the fixed obligations associated with debt and interest as asset values and returns to assets fluctuate.

Even with adjustments for the rates of taxation and consumption, the relative decline would still be greater for higher leverage.

As above, the relationship between financial leverage and risk can be generalized by extending the growth model to account for both the expected rate of growth and its variability, as measured by the standard deviation. Suppose that the rate of return on assets (r) is viewed as a normally distributed random variable with an average expectation of $\bar{r} = .16$, or 16 percent, and a standard deviation of $\sigma_r = .06$, or 6 percent. Recall from Chapter 2 that the standard deviation is a measure of the amount of variability of returns, and thus an indicator of risk. This measure of variability means, for example, that asset returns should fall within 6 percentage points of the expected value about 66 percent of the time and within 12 percentage points of the expected value about 98 percent of the time.

Suppose also that the interest cost of borrowing is fixed at $i = .12$, or 12 percent, once borrowing occurs and does not vary over the term of the loan. Hence, for now the standard deviation of the interest rate is zero ($\sigma_i = 0$).

The expected rate of growth under risk is still:

$$\bar{g} = (\bar{r}\,P_a - i\,P_d)\,k. \tag{6.5}$$

The standard deviation of the growth rate is:

$$\sigma_g = \sigma_r\,P_a\,k, \tag{6.6}$$

which is the weighted standard deviation of the risky assets, adjusted by the withdrawals (k) for taxation and consumption.

The relative risk for a given level of leverage is shown by the coefficient of variation (CV), which is the standard deviation of growth divided by the expected rate of growth (see Chapter 2).

$$CV = \sigma_g/\bar{g}. \tag{6.7}$$

For Farmer C, whose financial data are shown in Table 6.2 and whose leverage ratio is 0.5, the expected rate of growth is:

$$\bar{g} = [(.16)(1.5) - (.12)(.5)]\,(.8)(.5)$$

$$= .072, \text{ or } 7.2\%,$$

and the standard deviation is:

$$\sigma_g = \sigma_r\,P_a\,k$$

$$= (.06)(1.5)(.4)$$

$$= .036, \text{ or } 3.6\%$$

The coefficient of variation is thus:

$$CV = \sigma_g/\overline{g} = \frac{.036}{.072} = .50.$$

Farmer D's risk position should be greater than C's, due to D's greater leverage. The expected rate of growth for Farmer D is:

$$\overline{g} = [(.16)(2.0) - (.12)(1.0)](.8)(.5)$$
$$= .080, \text{ or } 8.0\%.$$

The standard deviation for D is:

$$\sigma_g = (.06)(2.0)(.4)$$
$$= .048, \text{ or } 4.80\%,$$

and the coefficient of variation is:

$$CV = \frac{4.80}{8.00} = .60.$$

The higher coefficient of variation for Farmer D indicates the greater financial risk from higher leverage. That is, the amount of variability relative to the expected rate of growth is greater for the higher leverage position. Greater variability, in turn, means a greater risk of loss in equity capital.

Table 6.5 (Section A) indicates expected values, standard deviations, and coefficients of variation of growth rates for several leverage ratios. Higher leverage increases the expected rates of growth, given the values of other growth-related variables. However, higher leverage increases the variability of growth even faster. Thus a business's

Table 6.5. Expected Values and Risk Measures for Growth Rates Under Different Leverage Positions, Excluding and Including Interest Rate Risks

	Leverage (D/E = P_d)						
Measure	0.0	0.5	1.0	2.0	3.0	4.0	5.0
A. No interest rate risk							
Expected growth rate, $\overline{g}$, %	6.40	7.20	8.00	9.60	11.20	12.80	14.40
Standard deviation, σ_g, %	2.40	3.60	4.80	7.20	9.60	12.00	14.40
Coefficient of variation, $\sigma_g/\overline{g}$	.38	.50	.60	.75	.86	.94	1.00
B. With interest rate risk							
Expected growth rate, $\overline{g}$, %	6.40	7.20	8.00	9.60	11.20	12.80	14.40
Standard deviation, σ_g, %	2.40	3.69	5.05	7.88	10.73	13.60	16.47
Coefficient of variation, $\sigma_g/\overline{g}$	.38	.51	.63	.82	.96	1.06	1.14

total risk relative to expected growth increases with greater leverage, as indicated by the increasing coefficients of variation.

Leverage and Interest Rate Risk

Now, suppose that interest rates on debt are also subject to unanticipated variation so that the expected rate is $\bar{i} = .12$, or 12 percent, and the standard deviation of interest rates is $\sigma_i = .04$, or 4 percent. This measure of variability means that interest rates should fall within 4 percentage points of the expected rate (a range of 8 to 16 percent) about two-thirds of the time. In general, we would expect that interest rate risk would add to the business total risk, and thus diminish the incentive for higher leverage. This, indeed, is the case, although the complexity of the growth model increases relative to the situation where interest rates are known with certainty.

The expected rates of growth, $\bar{g}$, for different levels of leverage are the same as before; however, the variability of expected growth increases with higher leverage to reflect the presence of interest rate risks. The standard deviation of growth is now expressed as:[3]

$$\sigma_g = \sqrt{(\sigma_r{}^2 P_a{}^2 + \sigma_i{}^2 P_d{}^2)\, k^2} \qquad \textbf{(6.8a)}$$

or

$$\sigma_g = \left[(\sigma_r{}^2 P_a{}^2 + \sigma_i{}^2 P_d{}^2)\, k^2 \right]^{1/2}. \qquad \textbf{(6.8b)}$$

Continuing the numerical examples, the expected rate of growth for Farmer C, with a leverage ratio of 0.5, is still $\bar{g} = .072$, or 7.2%. Including interest rate risk, the standard deviation of Farmer C's growth rate is now:

$$\sigma_g = \sqrt{\left[(.06)^2 (1.5)^2 + (.04)^2 (.5)^2 \right] (.4)^2}$$

$$= .037, \text{ or } 3.7\%.$$

This result indicates that the standard deviation of growth has increased from 3.6 to 3.7 percent in response to interest rate risk—a minor increase, reflecting Farmer C's relatively low leverage. Farmer C's coefficient of variation increases to CV = .51 = (3.7/7.2), compared to CV = .50 without interest rate risk.

For Farmer D, the presence of interest rate risk increases the standard deviation of growth to:

---

[3]These formulas first find the statistical variance of the growth rate and then take the square root to yield the standard deviation.

$$\sigma_g = \sqrt{[(.06)^2 (2)^2 + (.04)^2 (1)^2] (.4)^2}$$
$$= .051, \text{ or } 5.1\%,$$

compared to a standard deviation of 4.8 percent without interest rate risk. Thus, the magnitude of risk increase is greater for Farmer D than for Farmer C, reflecting Farmer D's higher leverage. Farmer D's coefficient of variation increases to CV = .64 (= 5.1/8.0), compared to CV = .60 without interest rate risk.

The impacts of interest rate risk on total risk (σ_g) and on the coefficients of variation are shown in Section B of Table 6.5 for the other levels of leverage. Again, the coefficients of variation increase as leverage increases and exceed the CV values for the same levels of leverage without interest rate risks, although by rather modest amounts.[4]

The Leverage Choice

Clearly, the choice of a desirable level of leverage is not so clear when risk considerations are introduced. In the absence of risk, higher leverage appears quite attractive. In the presence of risk, however, managers must consider the level of risk *relative* to expected rates of growth.

We have focused primarily on the potential losses arising from higher leverage rather than the potential gains, even when the expectations on each are of equal amount and probability. We do this because risk aversion, of varying degrees, tends to dominate investor behavior. The leverage incentive declines because an assumption of diminishing marginal utility of money reflects greater utility from avoiding losses than acquiring gains. Businessmen have more to fear (bankruptcy) than to hope for (spectacular profits), and different attitudes toward risk are, in effect, different assessments of the utility of expected gains and losses.

A primary consequence of financial risk is the firm's increased need for liquidity in countering uncertain expectations and meeting financial obligations. However, as borrowing increases, the firm's liquidity position is reduced. Thus, the concepts of leverage and

---

[4]This analysis has assumed that the rates of return on assets and interest rates on debt are statistically independent. That is, they exhibit zero correlation. This assumption may be reasonable in practice, since the level of market interest rates and farm income are not strongly related. If, however, these rates are not independent, then the degree of covariation must be included in the risk analysis [4, 8].

liquidity must be jointly considered in explaining managerial behavior and in guiding decision making. If profits could be projected
with certainty, unlimited leverage would be a reasonable objective.
However, the risk of loss of equity, illiquidity, and even bankruptcy
may outweigh the potential gains from leverage, even when the
likelihood of gains exceeds that of losses. We will pursue the discussion of leverage, credit, and liquidity management further in the next
chapter.

Proprietor Withdrawals

Expenditures for family consumption, income tax payments, and
other withdrawals of funds can drain farm income and cash flow
quite rapidly. As such, they influence reinvestment in the business
and can severely constrain growth. If capital accumulation were the
predominant goal, a minimum level of current consumption would
be desirable. But, consumption also has value to the manager. Thus,
growth decisions must consider the time value of money and its implications for savings versus consumption.

Although consumption is likely to increase as income increases,
it is commonly observed that above some minimum level, consumption increases less rapidly than income. Such a consumption pattern
is influenced by several factors: (1) expected increases of income, (2)
capital gains, (3) level of wealth, (4) leverage, (5) type of farm, and (6)
stage of life cycle. The manager should examine the withdrawal rate
(c) for any possible waste. Again, the objective is not simply to
minimize the family consumption rate but to insure that the family
members are getting their money's worth from the level of consumption and the rate of firm growth.

Tax management can also play a significant role in farm planning. When personal and corporate income tax rates require 15 to 50
percent or more of net income as taxes, efficiency in tax management
becomes important. The growth-conscious manager should examine
the farm records and tax situation to see if the tax obligation (t) can
be reduced through better planning, record keeping, and analysis.
We should stress, however, that the objective is not to minimize
taxes but to maximize *after-tax* profits.

An interesting effect on growth rates arises from the interaction
of tax and consumption rates. As income increases, the tax rate (t)
also likely increases. On the other hand, the rate of family consumption expenditure tends to decrease as income increases. Hence, the

rate of savings (k) from higher income is likely more stable than it first appears.

Resource Productivity and Growth

How does firm growth affect the rate (r) of returns to business assets? Is r expected to increase, remain constant, or decrease? The matter is not so simple. Some factors generate economies of size, and other factors generate diseconomies as firm size increases. At the same time, changes in technology can alter the productivity of resources and perhaps increase the earning potential of new investments which are fully utilized. For example, a more efficiently designed milking parlor and feeding system may reduce average costs of milk production if the system is used to capacity. Nonetheless, we generally expect diminishing returns (r) to occur at some firm size. But how do diminishing returns actually appear?

Part of the answer lies in the adjustment of management to new large-scale investments. As financial growth occurs, lags may occur in the adjustment of management to new technology and increased size of business. These lags in managerial productivity arise from the new production decisions needed for crop, livestock, machinery, and labor management; from new marketing skills needed for buying and selling; and from the need for more effective management of investments, financing, and cash flows. The dairy farmer, for example, who rapidly expands herd size and mechanizes operation, has difficulty maintaining a high level of milk production per cow. Eventually, as expansion slows, the manager can exercise more intensive culling, more precise feeding and health care, and master the "mechanics" of mechanization. Thus, management experience is essential in attaining high levels of production efficiency.

These managerial lags often are not properly accounted for in business planning. Generally, a constant level of management productivity is used for planning. This approach overlooks any temporary reductions in production efficiency. The lags in management may severely jeopardize the firm's financial position, especially when a large investment reduces the firm's liquidity. Overcoming these lags is important when financial obligations require a rapid investment payoff.

While diminishing productivity of firm resources may slow the rate of growth, other attributes of resources may also hamper their acquisition. The land market may be inactive. High-quality hired labor, seasonal or full-time, may not be available. Many resources are lumpy or indivisible in size. Examples include land, buildings, feeding systems, large-sized machinery, and irrigation equipment. Even full-time labor represents a lumpy kind of resource. This lumpiness requires large blocks of financial capital to purchase the assets and may sharply change the firm's leverage, risk, and liquidity.

External Finance

Access to external financing, as reflected by the firm's credit, significantly influences its growth rate. Moreover, as we shall see, the terms of external financing can influence both the rate and the direction of firm growth. Our concern in this chapter is with the rate of growth.

We use the term *external capital (or credit) rationing* when a borrower has exhausted all sources of loanable funds but still finds that the marginal value product of resources acquired with borrowed capital exceeds the marginal cost (interest and noninterest) of borrowing. Under these conditions, a firm's economically desirable rate of growth exceeds its financially supportable rate of growth.

External-credit rationing arises from the behavior of lending institutions. In turn, they are influenced by loanable-funds supplies, alternatives in lending and investment, and their evaluation of a borrower's credit. (The properties of credit will be discussed in detail in Chapter 7). The typical farm manager will probably have exhausted all available credit, as evaluated by conventional lenders, at a debt level about equal to the equity of the farm: a leverage ratio of 1.0. Leverage ratios ranging up to 2.0 or beyond usually denote either a superior financial manager or a manager who is in pending financial disaster as evidenced by the depletion of assets or excessive debt.

The operator who can secure a land purchase contract may attain a leverage as high as 3.0, provided non-real estate lenders do not curtail credit for financing other assets. Some nonfarm businesses attain much greater leverage. A number of commercial banks, for example, operate with a leverage exceeding 20.

We also need to consider the response of interest rates (i) as borrowing and leverage increase. In theory, interest rates are expected to differ among borrowers, with variations in loan risk, purpose, length, or size. However, considerable evidence suggests that interest rates on agricultural loans from specific lenders do not vary much among borrowers over a relatively short time period. Instead, interest rates mostly vary over time in response to changes in the lender's costs of acquiring loan funds.

The reliance of agricultural lenders on nonprice responses to differences in lending risks among borrowers is changing, however. Some production credit associations have adopted risk classes in pricing loans so that borrowers with higher lending risks pay a higher interest rate to compensate the lender for the added risk. Commercial banks are also tending to tailor interest rates to the risk and other characteristics of farm borrowers. Results from a 1981 nationwide survey of agricultural banks in the United States indicated that more than half of these banks charge different interest rates to borrowers at any one time. Moreover, about 95 percent of the banks charging farm borrowers different rates do so because of differences in the borrowers' credit risks.[5]

Thus, lending risks are becoming a more important factor in loan pricing. Nonetheless, agricultural lenders still rely heavily on nonprice responses to differences in borrowers' credit worthiness. These nonprice responses may occur as differences among borrowers in loan limits, security requirements, loan maturities, loan supervision and documentation, and other means of credit administration. These price and nonprice responses of lenders combine to limit leverage and raise the total costs of borrowing as leverage and risk increase. In turn, these external credit effects diminish the growth possibilities of higher leverage.

Market Demand

Market demand is beyond the control of most individual producers. Yet, market factors which influence product prices also influence the rates of return to farm business assets. Thus the growth of a farm business is not solely attributed to the firm's capacity to produce; an expanding business is necessary but not sufficient for financial growth. Growth in demand for farm products must also occur.

The generally low price elasticity of demand for farm products, together with the competitive structure of commodity markets, complicates the situation. Thus, the aggregate implications of firm growth and individual investment decisions must be considered. In fact, market-oriented farmers who are considering long-term invest-

---

[5]Other factors associated with differences in interest rates include differences in the borrowers' deposit balances, size of loan, loan maturity, and loan purpose. A review of the survey results is found in reference [6].

ments in highly specialized capital equipment are quite concerned with demand conditions. They are increasingly aware that product prices and farm incomes may be adversely affected when many farmers invest in a fashion that increases total production.

Not all individual farm investments increase output in the aggregate. When a farmer expands farm size by purchasing or leasing a neighboring tract of land, it will not increase aggregate output if the same cropping patterns are maintained. It will simply add to the expanding farm's resource base and income-generating capacity. On the other hand, if a farmer expands by adding to livestock-producing capacity, then aggregate livestock output increases. If numerous farmers follow suit, the impact on aggregate output may be substantial. Given an inelastic demand for that livestock product, the increased livestock output could result in a relatively larger decline in price product and thus gross returns to its producers.

The effects on producers' net income depend on the cost-reducing impact of the new investment. If costs per unit decline by a relatively greater proportion than prices decline, income may actually increase in the short-run. The prospects of higher income may in turn attract further investments by new producers, thus putting renewed pressure on the cost-price margin and bringing additional resource adjustments in the future.

The dynamics of the situation affect different producers in different ways. As an example, the early investors in new technology may benefit substantially from cost reductions and increased volume before price declines from increased output by later investors. The demise of some later (or inefficient early) investors may alleviate the pressure. By then, still newer technologies may come along to continue the process. All these factors influence the rate of earnings (r) over time and, thereby, the growth of the firm.

Topics for Discussion

1. Explain the concept of a weighted average cost of capital. A minimum cost level of leverage. Contrast the ability of large corporate firms and smaller-sized businesses to maintain minimum cost leverage over time.
2. Explain why the costs of debt and equity are expected to increase as leverage increases.
3. What is the average cost of capital when the cost of debt is 12 percent, the cost of equity is 16 percent, and the ratio of equity to assets is .40?
4. Contrast and critique the use of physical and financial measures for evaluating the growth of agricultural firms.

5. Given the following information about a farm business:

Debt-to-equity ratio	2.0
Expected return on assets	18%
Expected interest rate on debt	13%
Consumption rate	60%
Tax rate	20%
Standard deviation of return on assets	5%
Standard deviation of interest rate	3%

   a. What is the expected rate at which this firm could grow?
   b. What might the manager do to increase the rate of growth?
   c. What level of risk is associated with the rate of growth found in a?
   d. Suppose another lender allows a maximum debt-to-equity ratio of 2.5, with an interest rate of 12 percent and a standard deviation of 4 percent. How do expected growth and risk for these conditions compare with the terms cited above?

6. With a tax rate of 20 percent, a consumption rate of 50 percent, a rate of return on assets of 14 percent, and an interest cost of 7 percent:

   a. What leverage ratio must a farmer achieve in order to grow at a 12 percent rate?
   b. What factors should both this farmer and the lender consider when deciding on whether to increase the farmer's leverage to this point?

7. Explain the relationship between business risks as evidenced by variability of prices, yields, asset values, etc., and financial risk associated with borrowing and greater leverage.

8. Discuss how the effects of diminishing returns are modified over time for a firm.

References

1. Baker, C. B., and J. A. Hopkin, "Concepts of Financial Capital for a Capital Using Agriculture," *American Journal of Agricultural Economics*, 51(1969):1055-1065.

2. Barry, P. J., and C. B. Baker, "Financial Responses to Risk," *Risk Management in Agriculture*, Iowa State University Press, Ames, 1983.

3. _____, "Management of Financial Structure: Firm Level," *Agricultural Finance Review*, 37(1977):50-63.

4. Barry, P. J., C. B. Baker, and L. R. Sanint, "Farmers' Credit Risks and Liquidity Management," *American Journal of Agricultural Economics*, 63(1981):216-227.

5. Brigham, E. F., *Financial Management: Theory and Practice*, 3rd ed., Dryden Press, Hinsdale, Illinois, 1982.

6. Calvert, J., and P. J. Barry, *Loan Pricing and Customer Profitability Analysis in Agricultural Banks*, AE-4533, College of Agriculture, University of Illinois at Urbana–Champaign, 1982.

7. *Economic Growth of the Agricultural Firm*, Tech. Bull. 86, College of Agriculture Research Center, Washington State University, Pullman, 1977.

8. Fama, E. F., *Foundations of Finance: Portfolio Decisions and Securities Prices*, Basic Books, Inc., Publishers, New York, 1976.

9. Fama, E. F., and M. H. Miller, *Theory of Finance*, Dryden Press, Hinsdale, Illinois, 1972.

10. Lee, W. F., et al., *Agricultural Finance*, 7th ed., Iowa State University Press, Ames, 1980.

11. Levy, H., and M. Sarnat, *Capital Investment and Financial Decisions*, 2nd ed., Prentice-Hall, Inc., Englewood Cliffs, New Jersey, 1982.

12. Lin, W. G., G. Coffman, and J. B. Penn, *U.S. Farm Numbers, Sizes, and Projected Structural Dimensions: Projections to Year 2000*, TB-1626, ERS, USDA, Washington, D.C., 1980.

13. Modigliani, F., and M. H. Miller, "Cost of Capital, Corporation Finance and the Theory of Investment," *American Economic Review*, 68 (1968):261-297.

14. Van Horne, J. C., *Financial Management and Policy*, 5th ed., Prentice-Hall, Inc., Englewood Cliffs, New Jersey, 1980.

Chapter 7

CREDIT AND LIQUIDITY

The manager who seeks a high rate of firm growth by increasing financial leverage, while simultaneously preferring a high degree of liquidity, will likely be frustrated. A firm that is growing and profitable may not be liquid, for it has probably experienced high leverage to finance its growth. All these practices—reduced borrowing capacity, new repayment obligations, and acquisition of fixed assets—reduce the firm's liquidity.

Liquidity is measured by cash on hand, by cash that can be generated from asset sales, by the potential for additional borrowing, and by "contingent reserves" available through insurance. However, liquidity is acquired and maintained at a cost. One cost is the returns foregone by converting assets from illiquid to liquid forms. Another cost is the reduction in economic value of the firm if productive farm assets are converted into more liquid, yet lower-yielding, financial assets. Still other costs of liquidity include the interest and other costs associated with borrowing and the premiums on insurance.

One of the most commonly used sources of liquidity in farm businesses is unused borrowing capacity, or credit. Yet, borrowing capacity also provides the funds for achieving higher leverage for more rapid growth. Hence, any manager must consider leverage and liquidity *jointly* in making financial decisions.

This chapter investigates more thoroughly the composition of a manager's credit and its influence on leverage, resource allocation, and liquidity. In this fashion, the chapter will help to provide a setting for later discussions of alternatives in managing risks and controlling resources.

Building Leverage with Credit Expansion

The Lender and Credit Evaluation

Credit or borrowing capacity can be considered a resource which the manager can either use in borrowing or hold in reserve. The decision presumably rests on the value of credit in each use. On the one hand, as shown in Chapter 6, total returns and rate of growth can be increased by higher leverage, assuming, of course, that the return on assets exceeds the cost of borrowing. On the other hand, credit held in reserve may provide a valuable source of liquidity. The liquidity value may be difficult to measure; nonetheless, these two values must be jointly considered in credit-allocation decisions. For either leverage or liquidity, however, the growth-conscious manager is interested in expanding total credit. Hence, our first concern is to investigate those factors which determine a firm's credit.

Borrowers are probably the least likely persons to evaluate their own credit. In practice, borrowers do not actually perform the evaluation. Rather, the borrower's credit is evaluated by *lenders* who are relied upon for borrowing. Nevertheless, the borrower may have formed some expectations on the lender's behavior. Moreover, as we shall see, knowledgeable managers can often influence lender response and, thus, credit evaluation through their own managerial decisions.

Lenders are guided by their own objectives regarding profits, risk, liquidity, and planning horizon as well as by forces operating in the financial markets. Hence, the lender's viewpoint in a loan transaction may differ from the borrower's on several counts. For example, loans constitute the earning assets for lenders. They prefer a high rate of return over a short period of time. Conversely, loans generate liabilities and costs for borrowers. Hence, they prefer low-cost loans for a relatively long period of time. The borrower participates directly in any gain or loss that arises from the financed investment. Lenders do not. They are restricted to returns called for by the debt contract. They only indirectly benefit from profits through the borrower's growth in financing needs over time.

Lenders must conform to the regulations of their own institutions. Moreover, they are affected by all elements of their financial markets. For example, to meet their short-term obligations to depositors, commercial banks must maintain a high degree of liquidity in their asset structure, an important part of which is their loan portfolio. Hence, to meet liquidity needs, the lender may prefer a payoff period shorter than the economic life expectancy of the asset being financed. The borrower likely prefers a longer payoff period. Finally, some lenders are limited by law in their loan maturities.

We do not imply that all agricultural lenders are a homogenous group viewing each lending situation in a like manner. Lenders differ substantially with respect to financial markets. Yet, the financial characteristics of lending institutions—rather narrow profit margins, high leverage ratios, and relatively rigid liquidity requirements—generate certain features of credit evaluation which are common to all those engaged in lending activities.

The Credit Profile

We can portray the credit evaluation process in a credit profile or matrix (Table 7.1), wherein the farmer's internal sources of credit are valued by the firm's lenders. Factors which comprise the farmer's credit include four items: (1) assets available for loan security, (2) income and repayment expectations, (3) personal characteristics, and (4) other financial management practices. These financial practices include the borrower's attempts to manage risks, liquidity, taxes, and other factors that may influence the lender's credit evaluation.

The classes of lenders in the column heads of Table 7.1 are highly aggregated and reflect the major institutional sources of lending in financial markets. More detailed classifications could be based on type of lender (i.e., real estate, non-real estate) and type of debt instrument (open account, promissory note, note secured by a real estate mortgage, or a sales contract).

The letter notations in the table represent loan limits by source of loan and source of credit. Hence, to determine total credit (L) generated by land, the manager would sum the loans from each lender across the land row in the table. Alternatively, to determine the total credit (B) available from a bank, the manager would sum the loan limits down the bank column. Summing the totals available from the internal or external sources of credit yields the firm's total credit (T).

Differing degrees of specialization among farm lenders means that all lenders will not consider all of the farm sources of credit. In addition, one lender's response to a loan request might depend on whether the borrower owes a debt to another lender and the loan terms and repayment obligation involved. Federal Land Banks, for example, are primarily interested in land as security for real estate loans. Once they have a lien on the land, then other lender's use of land as security (or credit) is subject to the Federal Land Bank's prior lien. Similar cases exist when other lenders have liens on machinery,

Table 7.1. Credit Profile of the Farm Firm

Farm Sources of Credit	Lender						
	Bank	Trade Firm	Production Credit Association	Federal Land Bank	Other Institutions	Individuals	Total
Assets and Security							
Land	b	a	p	f	o	i	L
Buildings and Other Improvements	b	a	p	f	o	i	B
Crops	b	a	p	f	o	i	C
Livestock	b	a	p	f	o	i	L
Machinery and Equipment	b	a	p	f	o	i	M
Others	b	a	p	f	o	i	O
Income and Repayment Prospects							
Farm	b	a	p	f	o	i	F
Nonfarm	b	a	p	f	o	i	N
Management Practices							
Production	b	a	p	f	o	i	P
Marketing	b	a	p	f	o	i	M
Finance	b	a	p	f	o	i	F
Personal Factors	b	a	p	f	o	i	F
Total	B	A	P	F	O	I	T

growing crops, and livestock. Thus, some coefficients in the table will be zero in given situations. Moreover, uncoordinated borrowing from several lenders may reduce overall credit.

To illustrate the credit-evaluation process, let's apply some typical lender rules of thumb to a case-farm situation with the balance sheet and income expectations expressed in Table 7.2. We will assume that a primary real estate lender requires a one-third equity in purchased land. This requirement implies a maximum debt-to-equity ratio of two. Non-real estate lenders are assumed to allow a maximum debt-to-equity ratio of one $(D/E = 1)$ for non-real estate assets. In addition, operating credit arising from profit projections for a typical farm manager is generated at 70 percent of the expected gross value of crop production and 80 percent of the expected gross value of cattle feeding.

Table 7.2. Evaluating Credit Capacity of a Case Farm

Source of Credit	Asset Value A	Debt Out-standing D	Equity in Assets E=A−D	Maximum D/E	Credit Capacity (E)(D/E)
A. Asset Credit					
Real Estate	$100,000	0	$100,000	2	$200,000
Non-real Estate Assets	60,000	0	60,000	1	60,000
Total	$160,000	0	$160,000		$260,000

	Gross Value per Unit	Credit Rate	Credit per Unit	No. of Units	Credit Capacity
B. Income Credit					
Crops	$300/acre	70%	$210	250 acres	$52,500
Cattle	$300/head	80%	$240	150 head	36,000
Total					$88,500

From Table 7.2, we observe for the case farm that the $100,000 equity in real estate will support $200,000 of real estate credit, while the $60,000 equity in non-real estate assets will support $60,000 of non-real estate credit. Thus, total asset-generated credit is $260,000. Operating credit generated by income expectations is estimated at $52,500 for 250 crop acres and $36,000 for 150 cattle. Hence, total operating credit capacity is $88,500.

Thus, under the rules of thumb just assumed, the case farmer could expect a total credit of $348,500 at this point in time. Changes in asset structure and income expectations would change the credit. So would changes in the lender's rules of thumb. It is important to note that this approach determines the maximum amount that *could* be borrowed from available lenders. This amount may or may not have been borrowed. The *use* of credit in borrowing is considered shortly.

Managing Credit Expansion

Now let's return to the credit profile in Table 7.1 to consider other sources of internal credit. Personal factors, such as honesty, integrity, and reliability, are essential attributes of credit worthiness. The absence of any of these factors could quickly reduce loan limits to zero. They are, therefore, of first priority for the financial manager.

What financial management practices can the borrower utilize to expand or re-structure credit? Obviously, growth in equity, or improved production efficiency and marketing which increase income expectations, would generate increased credit. Yet, such growth often depends upon the availability of greater credit. Thus, we must also focus on other financial strategies.

The farmer can seek lenders who are knowledgeable about current production techniques and farm financing requirements of agriculture. Knowledgeable lenders can more accurately assess loan proposals. They may provide more liberal financing for better managers. More traditional farm lenders generally rely heavily on asset value, relative to income expectations, and have a strong preference for short-term loans. A high payoff may accrue to farmers who can persuade these lenders that loans based on prospective management and repayment capacity are better for both parties. Farmers with lenders who use these criteria are in a favorable position.

Farmers can also demonstrate superior profitability, financial progress, and loan repayability to lenders. This demonstration generally relies on information and documentation furnished by the borrower to support a loan request. Complete records of farm income, balance sheets, and cash flow about past progress and future potential are essential tools in merchandising credit. Accurate and complete financial planning, including capital budgeting, helps to reduce risk, especially for investments involving long payback periods.

The various strategies farm managers use to manage risks in production, marketing, and finance may significantly influence the firm's credit. The producer who fixes the crop price by contracting at planting time for its later sale may increase the credit generation rate—possibly beyond the 70 percent of expected gross value indicated in Table 7.2. Similarly, the cattle feeder who reduces price uncertainty by effective hedging on the futures market may raise credit to 90 percent or more of the expected gross value of the cattle. The use of insurance may also expand credit.

Credit also depends upon the terms of obligation undertaken by the borrower. The amount of borrowing on an open account may be small. It can usually be increased, however, if the borrower is willing to sign a promissory note. It may increase even more if security is pledged as a surety of loan repayment.

In Figure 7.1, the credit profile is extended by outlining a hypothetical supply function relating credit to the rate of interest. Available evidence suggests that a given lender is not likely to respond to a higher interest rate with more loan funds for a given borrower. Thus, lines L_1, L_2, L_3, and L_4 represent different lenders willing, at successively higher interest rates, to loan larger amounts. Farmers who exhaust one loan source must move to higher-cost sources. However, each lender may be willing to lend more to bor-

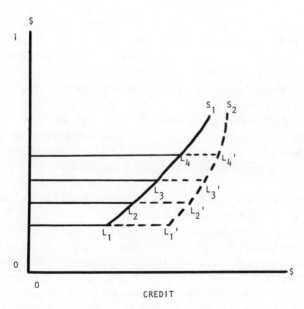

Figure 7.1. Credit supply for the individual farmer.

rowers who exhibit effective financial management and a willingness to undertake more binding debt commitments. This is illustrated by the dotted lines L_1L_1', L_2L_2', L_3L_3', and L_4L_4'. The result is a positively sloped supply curve, relating credit to interest, which shifts to the right as lenders respond to more preferred borrowers.

The lender's working environment cannot be assumed constant in the credit-evaluation process. Changes in loan regulations and legal requirements, as well as the development of new lending institutions, new debt instruments, and new loan policies, may influence credit evaluation. The alert financial manager will take such changes into account in estimating the "credit profile."

Lender Preferences and Resource Allocation

The rate at which the manager's credit is used up by borrowing depends on the compatibility between the loan characteristics and the preferences of the lender. Less preferred, high-risk loans will use up one's credit at a rapid rate. The result is relatively low limits for these loans. Consequently, the farmer's credit decisions are influenced by the loan purpose.

In general, lenders tend to prefer well-secured loans with a high degree of reclaimable assets. The result is an *asset-generating loan.* In addition, loans that finance activities with rapid rates of turnover are preferred—preferably, *self-liquidating loans.* Finally, lenders prefer borrowers with high-management ability. High-management ability may even substitute for other loan preferences. However, we will hold the borrower's management constant as we consider the lender's loan preferences.

On the basis of reclaimability of assets, a loan to purchase feeder cattle is an asset-generating loan. In fact, cattle become more valuable as they grow to market weight. Their high marketability enhances their reclaimability. Financed machinery also generates an asset. But this asset depreciates over time. A loan to purchase fertilizer is not strictly asset-generating since fertilizer is not reclaimable once it is applied. Loans for buildings, permanent fixtures, and drainage do not generate easily reclaimable assets. However, land is a readily reclaimable asset and is one of the most sought-after securities for loans.

Lenders also prefer to lend for self-liquidating purposes: purposes that generate sufficient income to repay the loan within the maturity period of the loan. Such loans reduce the lender's risk. Most loans for feeder cattle and fertilizer have maturities that allow for repayment upon sale of the fed cattle or crop. Machinery, equipment, and buildings rank lower on grounds of self-liquidation since their economic life generally exceeds the loan maturity.

Funds to repay nonself-liquidating loans must come from the net income of the business rather than from the gross income. The result is either a reduction in the firm's liquidity or a reduction in family withdrawals. Loans for land are not self-liquidating since net income must be used to pay for the land.

These two loan criteria (asset-generating and self-liquidating) combine to determine the relative merits of alternative loan purposes for lenders and, in turn, for borrowers. This situation is illustrated in Table 7.3. Loan purposes ranking high in both self-liquidation and asset reclaimability are most preferred by the lender. Loan purposes ranking high on one criterion but low on another have an intermediate preference from the lender's standpoint. The reader can classify other loan purposes in Table 7.3. Where, for example, is a loan to purchase breeding livestock or dairy cows located? What maturities do such loans require, to be self-liquidating?

Table 7.3. Lender Preferences for Combinations of Loan Characteristics

Loan Characteristics	Self-liquidating	Nonself-liquidating
Asset-Generating	High	Intermediate
Nonasset-Generating	Intermediate	Low

In summary, an important element of credit management is recognition that lender behavior influences, and is influenced by, the farm manager's resource allocation and product choices. More loanable funds may be available for some purposes than for others. The effects of these lender responses may cause expansion in what appears as a less-profitable enterprise simply because financing is more readily available for this purpose. Under these conditions, the traditional economic theory of the firm, with resource allocation and product choices based on marginal value productivity, must be modified to account for the effects of financing.[1] In fact, resource allocation can be influenced whether or not borrowing actually occurs,

---

[1]The appendix of this chapter contains a more detailed theoretical discussion and illustration of the effect of financing on resource allocation and product choice.

because credit liquidity is valuable to the farmer and because any transformation of assets affects the credit of the firm. And, following the leverage propositions in Chapter 6, the borrower's access to borrowing will also influence the rate of growth.[2]

These factors suggest that numerous borrowing and debt-management strategies arise from alternatives in production and marketing, in choice of lender, in the sequence and source of borrowing and repayment, in choice of financing instrument (e.g., note, mortgage, contract, lease) and financing terms, and in interactions between credit evaluations by different types of lenders. These factors are important to both borrowers and lenders because each choice modifies those attributes of loan purposes which are desirable from the lenders' point of view: asset generation and self-liquidation of loans.

Liquidity Management

Evaluating Needs for Liquidity

Liquidity must not be confused with solvency. A firm is solvent when the current market value of its assets exceeds its debt obligations and when it can meet these obligations over a sufficiently long period of time. Liquidity is a shorter-run concept. A firm may be solvent and either liquid or illiquid. Conversely, it may be insolvent and either liquid or illiquid. Clearly, however, the two concepts are related, with important implications for financial management.

Liquidity is needed to provide for market transactions and cash obligations as they come due. In addition, liquidity is needed to respond to either unfavorable or favorable events that occur unexpectedly.

First, let's consider the transactions' need for liquidity. In U.S. commercial agriculture, most of the items needed for production or

---

[2]The influence of financing on rate of growth and allocation of resources is not unique to farm management. It permeates all types of production and consumption decisions. Consider, for example, the purchase of a house. The amount of available financing may influence the size of the house which can be purchased. Similarly, the financing terms which reflect the preferences of the lender may influence the type or age of a house one buys. It is often easier to purchase a new house than an older house when, except for financing, the price of the old house might be more attractive. The financing terms on the new house generally include a lower downpayment, lower interest rate, longer maturity, and lower monthly payments than do the financing terms for the older house. This discrepancy reflects the higher-lending risk for the older house.

family consumption are acquired with cash outlays. Generally, the seasonal pattern of cash outflow on most farms differs from the pattern of cash inflow from product sales. This difference gives rise to seasonal cash deficits and/or cash surpluses—the deficits must be met, and the surpluses must be managed.

As an example, a dairy farm typically generates a more uniform flow of cash through the year than does a grain farm. Thus, a dairy farmer's problems in managing cash flows are less demanding. The grain farmer must manage cash and credit to cope with relatively large seasonal deficits.

Liquid reserves are also needed to meet unpredictable fluctuations in seasonal cash flow caused by variable prices, yields, expenses, etc., or to cope with severe hazards, such as fire, hail, tornado, sickness, or death. The increased reliance on markets and cash transactions can also generate uncertainties. In farm production, prices for most farm products are more variable than are farm input prices. Moreover, expenditures for family consumption tend to increase over time and become fixed at the higher levels, despite variability of farm income.

The firm's liquidity needs are also affected by investment and financing decisions. While a new machine may improve the firm's productivity, its purchase likely reduces liquidity and diverts cash for a downpayment and to meet future debt payments. This reduction in liquidity occurs at a time when greater borrowing and associated financial risks have increased the firm's need for liquidity.

Sources of Liquidity

Assets

The most obvious source of liquidity is a firm's cash balance. It is tempting to say that cash is the most accessible source as well. In many respects it is. Yet, in many firms, borrowing occurs while cash remains on hand. Clearly, the manager must perceive an advantage in leaving some cash on hand, even when borrowing. Nearly everyone has a "reservation price" or required return that must be met to use additional cash for either production or consumption. The same concept applies to holdings of other financial assets.

Other assets also contribute to the firm's liquidity position. The contribution varies over a wide continuum from cash, already discussed, through near-cash substitutes (demand and time deposits, government securities, etc.), through assets held primarily for sale (grain inventories, market-finished livestock, etc.), through intermediate assets (machinery, breeding animals, etc.), and through real property (land, land improvements, buildings, etc.). As indicated in Chapter 3, accountants generally classify these assets into three broad categories (current, intermediate, and fixed), which generally reflect their liquidity.

The degree of liquidity in farm assets depends upon an asset's sale value relative to its economic value to the firm. An asset is considered perfectly liquid if its sale generates cash equal to or greater than the reduction in the value of the firm resulting from the sale. Assets become less liquid as their potential sale reduces the value of the firm by more than their expected sale value.

There are several reasons why an asset's sale value might be less than its contribution to the firm's economic value. One reason is the transaction cost needed to complete the sale. These costs include commission charges, transportation costs, opportunity costs, and losses in transit. For most financial assets, the costs for transportation and handling are insignificant. However, these costs are much more important for most intermediate and fixed farm assets and for inventories of grain and livestock as well.

Another liquidity cost involves the degree of market perfection. A market is perfect only if the asset can be either bought or sold for the same price at any one time. Hence, a perfect market for an asset implies perfect liquidity. Clearly, transaction costs are a kind of market imperfection. The quality of market information, volume of trading, number of participants, and other factors that cause differences between an asset's purchase and sale price at a given time are also important. Forced sales of assets with relatively inactive, informal markets (e.g., land, forage, growing crops, many kinds of equipment) may experience significant price discounts to accomplish the sale.

Liquidity is also influenced by the urgency to generate cash and by liquidity risk, defined as the potential variation in the asset's market price. Generally, the less urgent is the liquidity need, the higher is the asset liquidity. Moreover, the less variable the asset's market price, the higher is the asset liquidity.

All these characteristics will differ among farm assets. Few nonfinancial assets are perfectly liquid, although some are nearly so. Examples are finished feedlot cattle, market-weight hogs, and an inventory of grain. Markets for these products are well established, and, with some adjustment for marketing costs, sales can be quickly accomplished at prices known in advance.

Other assets are less liquid. Growing crops are not easily liquidated. To sell a breeding or dairy animal prior to time of optimal replacement would lower the firm's total value. The same would be true for selling machinery and equipment. Other assets such as buildings, land, or land improvements are highly illiquid. Marketing costs for these assets are generally high. An adequate collection of willing buyers for land or purebred livestock may not be quickly available. Finally, to liquidate many fixed assets is an act toward dissolution of the firm itself.

Credit Reserves

A firm's credit reserve is its unused borrowing capacity. The size of the credit reserve depends upon the outcome of the credit-evaluation process, as outlined earlier, and on the amount of credit already used up by borrowing. Loan purposes, credit sources, financing terms, and debt instruments all affect this rate of use. In fact, all the manager's efforts to build credit influence the size and structure of the credit reserve. If no borrowing has occurred, then the entire credit capacity serves as a liquid reserve.[3]

As an example, consider the data in Table 7.4. This table presents the credit capacities for the case farm (Table 7.2) as limits on long-, intermediate-, and short-term borrowing. When long-, intermediate-, and short-term borrowing actually occur at $150,000, $40,000, and $45,000, respectively, the remaining credit reserves are $50,000, $20,000, and $43,500, respectively. These credit reserves could be drawn upon to finance further investment or to borrow in an

Table 7.4. Evaluating the Credit Reserve of the Case Farm

Source of Credit	Credit Capacity	Credit Used in Borrowing	Credit Reserve
Long-term Assets	$200,000	$150,000	$50,000
Intermediate-term Assets	60,000	40,000	20,000
Short-term Operating Credit	88,500	45,000	43,500

[3]For some individuals, self-imposed limitations on borrowing represent moral judgments against debt. In these cases, unused credit provides no liquidity.

emergency. We emphasize that this is a simplified version of borrowing capacity. Often, for example, unused long- and intermediate-term borrowing capacity can be used to support short-term borrowing above its apparent limit. Still, the example portrays the credit-reserve idea.

Holding credit reserves may be a more efficient way to provide liquidity than holding various types of assets. Using credit does not greatly disturb a farm's asset structure or production organization, its transactions costs are relatively low, and institutional sources of loan funds generally are available in rural financial markets.

However, costs of maintaining and borrowing from credit reserves must be considered. Holding reserves reduces returns from investment opportunities that are foregone from further financial leverage; interest is paid when loans occur; and noninterest charges, such as deposit balances and loan fees, sometimes occur to compensate lenders for establishing lines of credit. Moreover, there is uncertainty about future costs and availability of credit.

Conceptualizing credit allocation according to the value of credit to the manager in its respective uses may help explain borrowing behavior. In an optimal allocation of credit between loans and reserve, the manager must consider the liquidity value of the credit reserve and the value of the borrowed funds.

The allocation process for one source of credit is illustrated in Figure 7.2. The horizontal axis measures the percentage of credit used for loans. Movement to the right, along the axis, indicates more of credit used for loans. The remainder constitutes the credit reserve. The vertical axis measures the value of credit used in borrowing or in reserve. The familiar law of diminishing marginal returns indicates that the returns (marginal-value product) from additional units of resources and resource services acquired with borrowed funds (i.e., used credit) will decline at an accelerating rate as indicated by curve V_L. Thus, curve V_L measures the opportunity cost of credit held in reserve.

How can we conceive of the liquidity value of unused credit? As the credit reserve is reduced by borrowing, it is logical to expect the remaining units of unused credit to become increasingly valuable. Just as a thirst-craved wanderer on a desert would value highly his last drops of liquid, so a debt-ridden borrower would value highly his last "drops" of liquidity. We illustrate this relationship by the upward sloping liquidity value curve (V_R) in Figure 7.2, where r represents the liquidity value of the marginal units of unused credit.

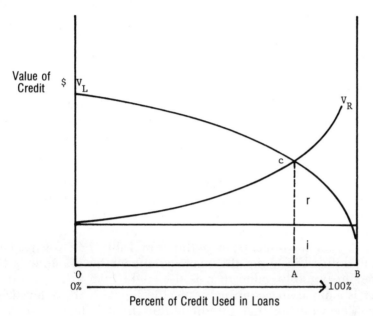

Figure 7.2. Equilibrium in credit allocation.

The addition of the liquidity value (r) to the interest rate (i) yields a total cost of borrowing. A liquidity value of 10 cents, for example, indicates that the manager requires a 10 percent net return above the interest rate on the next unit of credit used. Thus, the next dollar of unused credit has a net value of 10 cents to the manager.

The liquidity-value measure is determined by the manager's level of risk aversion. The more averse the manager is to risk, the higher is the position of V_R. It seems plausible to assume that an individual's liquidity-value curve could shift and change shape over time as a result of experience, age, preference changes, or other changes that alter the importance of risk.

Given V_L as the marginal value product of additional assets required with loans and V_R as the marginal value of liquidity from credit held in reserve, the optimum level of borrowing is OA, with AB the amount of reserve credit. At this point, the marginal-value product of assets (V_L) equals the marginal cost of borrowing, including both the interest (i) and the liquidity value (r). The marginal returns to the manager of using additional credit in borrowing are less than the marginal cost of borrowing (i + r). If r were ignored or considered to be zero, the optimum borrowing is found by equating V_L

with i. Since farmers seldom borrow to this point, they do reserve credit as a part of their liquidity management.

The reader will note the interesting implication that the demand for credit is a broader concept than the demand for loans. We should also note that very conservative lenders may restrict the size of total credit so that the MVP curve (V_L) encounters the right-hand margin of the diagram in Figure 7.2 before it crosses cost curve (V_R). In this situation, the borrower is confronted with external credit rationing. In addition, the interest line (i) may show an upward curvature, if farmers face higher-cost loans as borrowing increases. Finally, the amount of credit (c) may change frequently and be subject to considerable uncertainty. Changes in credit in turn influence the total cost of borrowing and introduce an additional source of financial risk.

Credit reserves can also be differentiated by the classes of lenders and debt instruments, as outlined in Table 7.1. Nonspecialized credit, defined in terms of a commercial bank for example, is likely higher in liquidity value than is the credit from a trade firm. The latter is unique in acquiring a specific input, such as fertilizer or feed. The value of trade credit is thus limited to transactions in which inputs are acquired. On the other hand, the general-purpose liquidity, based on credit at primary lenders, is relatively high in value. This proposition helps to explain why some managers may borrow from merchants and dealers at a higher interest rate, while they still have unused credit at their bank. The total cost of borrowing from the bank, including interest *and* liquidity, could exceed the comparative cost of trade credit.

The liquidity-value concept is rather abstract because it is difficult to measure the behavioral characteristics of decision makers. Yet, appeal to common sense suggests that it does help to explain borrowing behavior. Hence, the liquidity-value concept will help guide the manager's financing decisions. As an exercise, we challenge readers to measure their own liquidity values—assuming, of course, they permit borrowing to be a relevant alternative in consumption or business activities.

Topics for Discussion

1. Describe the notion of "credit." Who evaluates credit? How is the evaluation accomplished? What leads to increased credit? What can credit be used for?
2. In what ways can credit evaluation and borrowing influence a manager's resource allocation decisions?

3. Why is liquidity important to a farm manager? What determines an asset's liquidity?
4. Explain the paradox that is created when borrowing builds leverage and accelerates growth, yet simultaneously uses up a valuable source of liquidity.
5. What are the major factors that influence a farmer's credit worthiness? Explain how changes in these factors may influence the level of available credit.
6. Contrast the effects on credit for loans to finance (a) feeder cattle, (b) storage facilities, and (c) dairy cows.
7. Identify the factors affecting the liquidity of various assets. How would you rank the liquidity of (a) grain inventories, (b) farm land, (c) farm machinery, and (d) U.S. Treasury bills. Why do they differ in liquidity?
8. Explain the concept of a credit reserve. How is the credit reserve related to actual amounts of borrowing? Why is the credit reserve considered a source of liquidity? How can the value of the credit reserve be expressed? How does the liquidity associated with a credit reserve differ among farm lenders?

References

1. Baker, C. B., "Credit in the Production Organization of the Firm," *American Journal of Agricultural Economics*, 50(1968):507-520.
2. Baker, C. B., and J. A. Hopkin, "Concepts of Financial Capital for a Capital Using Agriculture," *American Journal of Agricultural Economics*, 51 (1969):1055-1065.
3. Barry, P. J., and C. B. Baker, "Management of Financial Structure: Firm Level," *Agricultural Finance Review*, 37(February 1977):50-63.
4. _____, "Reservation Prices on Credit Use: A Measure of Response to Uncertainty," *American Journal of Agricultural Economics*, 53 (1971):222-227.
5. Barry, P. J., and D. R. Fraser, "Risk Management in Primary Agricultural Production: Methods, Distribution, Rewards and Structural Implications," *American Journal of Agricultural Economics*, 58 (1976):286-295.
6. Barry, P. J., and David R. Willmann, "A Risk-Programming Analysis of Forward Contracting with Credit Constraints," *American Journal of Agricultural Economics*, 58(1976):61-70.
7. Barry, P. J., C. B. Baker, and L. R. Sanint, "Farmers' Credit Risk and Liquidity Management," *American Journal of Agricultural Economics*, 63(1981):216-227.
8. Boehlje, M. D., and L. D. Trede, "Risk Management in Agriculture," *Journal of the American Society of Farm Managers and Rural Appraisers*, 41(1977):20-29.
9. *Economic Growth of the Agricultural Firm*, Tech. Bull. 86, College of Agriculture Research Center, Washington State University, Pullman, 1977.

10. Robison, L. J., and J. R. Brake, "Applications of Portfolio Theory to Farmer and Lender Behavior," *American Journal of Agricultural Economics*, 61(1979):158-164.

Appendix to Chapter 7

Financing and Economic Efficiency of the Firm

In terms of the economic theory of the firm, an optimal combination of resources is achieved when the marginal rate of resource substitution equals the inverse price ratio:

$$-\frac{dX_1}{dX_2} = \frac{PX_2}{PX_1}$$

where P_i is the price of the input (X_i). When borrowing is considered as a means of financing inputs, this portrayal of economic equilibrium is modified to incorporate the cost of financing:

$$-\frac{dX_1}{dX_2} = \frac{PX_2 + f_2}{PX_1 + f_1}$$

where f_i is the marginal cost of financing a unit of X_i, including interest and the value of the credit liquidity involved in the transaction. Given the discrepancy between the preferences of the lender and of the borrower, as reflected by varying loan limits and erroneous farmer expectations of lender behavior, there is little reason to expect that $f_2/f_1 = PX_2/PX_1$. Hence, optimal resource allocation can be influenced, whether or not borrowing occurs.

In Figure 7.3, the cost of producing output (Y) is minimized with X_1^1 and X_2^1 when it is assumed that the ratio of financing costs equals the ratio of input prices (i.e., $f_2/f_1 = PX_2/PX_1$). However, when lenders favor X_2 over X_1, either through a lower interest rate or through a higher loan limit, such that $f_2/f_1 < PX_2/PX_1$, then the optimum allocation of inputs shifts to X_1^2 and X_2^2.

Similarly, when lenders favor one product or enterprise over another, the optimal product combination is altered. An optimum allocation of given resources among competing production alternatives is achieved when the marginal rate of product substitution equals the inverse of the product price ratios:

$$-\frac{dY_2}{dY_1} = \frac{PY_1}{PY_2}$$

where P_i is the price of enterprise Y_i. When the firm is dependent upon loan funds to finance the expansion of Y_1 and/or Y_2, then the economic equilibrium must be modified to incorporate the impact of financing:

$$\frac{dY_2}{dY_1} = \frac{PY_1 + L_1}{PY_2 + L_2}$$

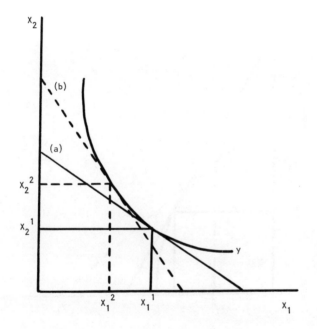

(a) $\dfrac{PX_2 + f_2}{PX_1 + f_1}$ where $f_2/f_1 = \dfrac{PX_2}{PX_1}$

(b) $\dfrac{\dot{P}X_2 + f_2}{PX_1 + f_1}$ where $f_2/f_1 < \dfrac{PX_2}{PX_1}$

Figure 7.3. Effects of financial costs on cost minimizing combinations of X_1 and X_2.

where L_i is a composite term reflecting any difference in interest rates between products as well as values of credit generated for the firm by the production of Y_i and the values of the credit lost in borrowing to finance the production of Y_j. Again, there is little reason to expect that $L_1/L_2 = PY_1/PY_2$. If this equality does not hold, then product combinations based only on expected prices may result in a production organization that is suboptimal.

In Figure 7.4, the returns from resource level (X) are maximized by producing Y_1^1 and Y_2^1 when it is assumed that lender preferences do not deviate from price expectations (i.e., $L_1/L_2 = PY_1/PY_2$). However, when lenders, through their credit evaluation and loan limits,

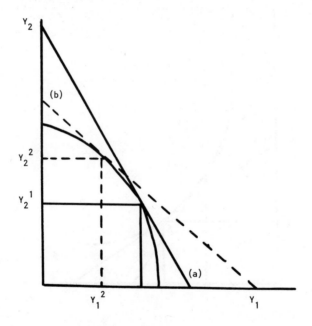

(a) $\dfrac{PY_1 + L_1}{PY_2 + L_2}$ where $L_1/L_2 = PY_1/PY_2$

(b) $\dfrac{PY_1 + L_1}{PY_2 + L_2}$ where $L_1/L_2 < PY_1/PY_2$

Figure 7.4. Effects of finance costs on profit maximizing allocations of resources between Y_1 and Y_2.

favor Y_2 over Y_1, such that $L_1/L_2 < PY_1/PY_2$, then the optimum allocation of products shifts to $Y_1{}^2$ and $Y_2{}^2$.

In essence, economic planning of a farm firm must jointly consider production relations, market prices, and the behavioral properties of the lender and the response thereto of the farmer.

Chapter 8

RISK MANAGEMENT

Risks are pervasive in agriculture. Business risks for farmers include: (1) production and yield risks; (2) market and price risks; (3) losses from severe casualties and disasters; (4) social and legal risks from changes in tax laws, government programs, trade agreements, and so on; (5) human risks on performance of labor and management; and (6) risks of technological change and obsolescence. Financial risks arise from the financial claims on the firm. The greater the financial leverage, the greater are the risks in meeting financial obligations to lenders and lessors. Financial risks are further increased by unanticipated variations in interest rates, credit availability, and other changes in loan terms, as well as in leasing terms.

Business and financial risks combine to magnify potential losses in farmers' equity capital and create inefficiencies in resource use by hampering business planning. Risk management involves the selection of methods for countering business and financial risks in order to meet a decision maker's risk-averting goal. However, lower risk is generally associated with a reduction in expected returns. Thus, it is important to account for the risk-return trade-off in designing risk management strategies.

In this chapter we identify the major choices in risk management for farmers, emphasizing financial responses to risk and their relationships to production and marketing responses. The risk management process is established and the fundamentals of diversification are presented. Then the major methods of responding to risks are presented and analyzed.

A Risk Management Perspective

The process of managing risks is based on the steps of financial control outlined in Chapter 4—setting goals, measures, norms, and tolerance limits; designing an information system; and initiating corrective actions when needed. Control occurs over time and under uncertainty. Within the control process, risk management focuses on the strategies and corrective actions needed to cope with possible adversities in business performance.

The first phase in risk management is designing strategies to cope with risks. These generally are long-range plans that should hold over a period of years and over a range of uncertain events. The second phase in risk management is the implementation of risk responses when adversity occurs. The third phase restores the firm's capacity to implement the risk strategies when distress conditions have passed. Our emphasis here is on phase one of the risk management process—the design of appropriate strategies.

Some risk responses may focus on reducing risks within the business. Effective diversification over several types of assets and business enterprises is an example. Other responses may focus on transferring the risks outside the business. Hedging through forward or futures contracts for commodities or farm inputs is an example. Still other risk responses may not reduce the likelihood of occurrence, but may better enable the firm to bear risks when they occur. Holding liquid reserves of cash or credit, or using insurance, illustrates the building of risk-bearing capacity within the firm. Finally, some risk responses may exhibit several of these effects, as with purchasing insurance which builds liquidity and transfers risk acceptance outside the business.

Some methods of managing risks are feasible for all types of farms. Others are only feasible for certain sizes and types of farms, qualities of management, financial structures, and other characteristics. The methods can be categorized in terms of the production, marketing, and financial organizations of farm businesses. In production these risk responses include enterprise diversification, informal insurance (pesticides, reserve equipment, supplemental irrigation), organizational flexibility, and avoidance of high-risk enterprises. In marketing, they include inventory management and forward and futures contracts. Participation in government programs may be a response to production or marketing risks, or both, depending on the program. Vertical integration may also present opportunities for reducing some production and marketing risks. Financial responses to risk reflect the firm's capacity to bear risks in production and marketing, and mostly involve the management of leverage and liquidity.

The payoffs associated with these methods of managing risks are often difficult to measure because they involve the protection of the firm's equity from possible losses. Furthermore, the financial responses to risk may involve other risk responses too. Trade-offs generally exist between the risk responses in production, marketing, and finance. Thus, emphasis on one means of countering uncertainty (e.g., liquidity) may allow an investor to carry greater risks in production or marketing. The reverse may also be true.

Fundamentals of Diversification

The fundamentals of diversification are important in risk analysis. It may be possible to reduce the total variability of returns by combining several assets, enterprises, or income-generating activities without unduly sacrificing expected returns. As a rule, higher (lower) risk investments carry higher (lower) expected returns. Thus reducing risk usually involves lower expected returns, as well. Frequently, however, gains in business planning and risk efficiency can occur by following the principles of diversification.

To illustrate, let's consider an investor who is evaluating two farm units, one located in the Corn Belt and the other in the Great Plains area of the United States. A financial analyst reports to the investor that the two farm units have about the same expected profitability and risk. More specifically, each farm unit is expected to earn a 20 percent return to assets, with a standard deviation of 10 percent. These data mean that returns from either investment should average 20 percent over time, and should fall between 10 and 30 percent about two-thirds of the time, or between 0 and 40 percent about 95 percent of the time. Moreover, the chance of returns falling below zero is about 2.5 percent.

Based on these figures, the investor should be indifferent between the two farm units. But suppose the investor could divide available funds and invest equally in the Corn Belt and Great Plains units. What gains would arise from this investment strategy? The expected returns would still be 20 percent, but the standard deviation of returns from the combined investments would decline to 7.07 percent. The diversified investment reduces the anticipated variability of returns, and thus the investment's risk, without reducing the expected levels of returns. Hence, the diversified investment would be preferred over investing in only one unit.

Why does risk decline from combining two seemingly comparable investments? The answer is based on the statistical relationship between the two investments. We develop this relationship using a portfolio model.

Portfolio Model

The word "portfolio" refers to a mix, or combination, of assets, enterprises, or investments. It is most commonly used to describe holdings of financial assets such as stocks and bonds. However, it can also be applied to holdings of tangible assets like grain inventories, growing crops, livestock, machines, land, apartment buildings, and cars. Hence, the portfolio of a grain-livestock producer is considered to hold two investments—grain and livestock—although different crops and livestock could further broaden the portfolio. Or, the investor described above could hold two different farm units in the portfolio.

The portfolio model indicates how different combinations of investments may reduce an investor's risk more than having only a single investment. Holding combinations of investments is called diversification, with the potential for risk reduction determined by: (1) the number of investments held and (2) the covariation (or correlation) among the expected returns of the individual investments. In particular, we will demonstrate how the gains in risk reduction from diversification increase as the correlation among investments declines and as the number of investments in a portfolio increases.

Positive covariation means that high profits in one investment are associated with high profits in another investment. Negative covariation means that high profits in one investment are associated with low profits in another investment. Zero covariation means that there is no statistical association between the variations of returns of these investments. The investments are statistically independent.

Diversification as a risk-reducing strategy becomes more effective, as the covariation among investments is lower. These effects are demonstrated with statistical measures of standard deviation, variance, covariance, and correlation. To illustrate, let X_1 and X_2 be two investment alternatives having expected rates of return $\bar{r}_1$ and $\bar{r}_2$, respectively. Let P_1 and P_2 be the proportions of total resources invested in X_1 and X_2, respectively, with $P_1 + P_2 = 1$ to assure that all resources are accounted for.

The portfolio's expected return $(\bar{r}_t)$ is now:

$$\bar{r}_t = \bar{r}_1 p_1 + \bar{r}_2 P_2 \qquad (8.1)$$

Let σ_1 and σ_2 be the standard deviations of X_1 and X_2, and σ_{12} be their covariance. An alternative expression of covariance is $\sigma_{12} = c\sigma_1 \sigma_2$, where c is the correlation coefficient between returns r_1 and r_2. The correlation coefficient varies between plus and minus 1 ($-1 \leq c \leq 1$) with a positive value indicating positive covariation, a negative value indicating negative covariation, and a zero value indicating no covariation.

The total variance of the portfolio is:

$$\sigma_T^2 = \sigma_1^2 P_1^2 + \sigma_2^2 P_2^2 + 2P_1P_2 \, c\sigma_1\sigma_2 \tag{8.2}$$

and the total standard deviation is[1]

$$\sigma_T = \sqrt{\sigma_T^2}. \tag{8.3}$$

Total variance, or portfolio risk, now depends on the relative proportions (P_1,P_2) of X_1 and X_2 in the portfolio, their variances, and the correlation of their returns. Formula (8.2) clearly shows that the higher the value of c, the higher the portfolio risk for any combination of investments X_1 and X_2. Similarly, the lower the value of c, the lower the portfolio risk for any combination of investments X_1 and X_2. Hence the lower the correlation, the greater the reduction in risk associated with diversification.

The risk estimates for portfolios of X_1 and X_2 in formula (8.2) can be combined with the portfolio's estimates of expected returns in order to evaluate risk-return trade-offs for different combinations of X_1 and X_2. These formulas can also be expanded to include other investments by adding terms representing their expected returns, standard deviations, correlations with other investments, and weights in the overall portfolio.

Portfolio Analysis

To illustrate the gains in risk reduction from diversification, con-

---

[1]Some special cases of the portfolio model are expressed as follows:
If all resources are in X_1, so that $P_1 = 1.0$ and $P_2 = 0.0$, then:

$$\sigma_T^2 = \sigma_1^2.$$

For the following correlation value, total variance is:

$$c = -1, \sigma_T^2 = \sigma_1^2 P_1^2 + \sigma_2^2 P_2^2 - 2P_1P_2\sigma_1\sigma_2$$
$$c = 0, \sigma_T^2 = c_1^2 P_1^2 + \sigma_2^2 P_2^2$$
$$c = 1, \sigma_T^2 = \sigma_1^2 P_1^2 + \sigma_2^2 P_2^2 + 2P_1P_2\sigma_1\sigma_2.$$

sider again the investor's choice between farm units in the Corn Belt (X_1) and the Great Plains (X_2). Recall that their expected returns and standard deviations are 20 percent and 10 percent, respectively, and assume a zero correlation between their returns. These data are expressed as:

$$\bar{r}_1 = .20, \bar{r}_2 = .20, \sigma_1 = .10, \sigma_2 = .10, \text{ and } c = .00$$

Investing in either the Corn Belt unit or the Great Plains unit would yield an expected return $(\bar{r}_t)$ of 20 percent and a standard deviation (σ_t) of 10 percent. Moreover, a portfolio comprised of equal proportions $(P_1 = P_2 = .50)$ of the Corn Belt and Great Plains units would yield expected returns

$$\bar{r}_t = (.20)(.50) + (.20)(.50) = .20, \text{ or 20 percent.} \qquad \textbf{(8.4)}$$

However, using formula (8.2), the total variance of the diversified portfolio is:

$$\sigma_T^2 = (.10)^2(.50)^2 + (.10)^2(.50)^2 + 2(.50)(.50)(.00)(.10)(.10) \qquad \textbf{(8.5)}$$

$$= .0025 + .0025 + .0000$$

$$= .0050$$

and the standard deviation is:

$$\sigma_T = \sqrt{.0050} \qquad \textbf{(8.6)}$$

$$= .0707, \text{ or 7.07 percent.}$$

Thus the diversified portfolio yields the same expected return but with less risk, based on an assumption of zero correlation between the returns of these investments. If the correlation were less than zero, the risk reduction from diversification would be still greater.

In this example, an assumption of zero correlation for the returns of these investments may be realistic, since the farm units are far apart geographically and perhaps subject to different economic forces. Suppose, however, that the investor was considering two farm units (X_{1A}, X_{1B}) in the Corn Belt located immediately adjacent to one another. Both farm units have an expected return of 20 percent and a standard deviation of 10 percent. However, because the units grow the same crops and are subject to the same risks, their returns are perfectly positively correlated; that is, $c = 1$.

Are there any gains from diversification now? The total variance of a portfolio with equal proportions of the two investments is:

$$\sigma_T{}^2 = (.10)^2(.50)^2 + (.10)^2(.50)^2 + 2(.50)(.50)(1)(.10)(.10) \qquad \textbf{(8.7)}$$

$$= .0025 + .0025 + .0050$$

$$= .0100$$

and the standard deviation is:

$$\sigma_T = \sqrt{.0100} \qquad \textbf{(8.8)}$$

$$= .10, \text{ or } 10 \text{ percent.}$$

Thus, no gains in risk reduction occur from diversification between investments with returns that are perfectly positively correlated. This case is an exception, however. Diversifying does reduce risk for less than perfect correlation, with the reduction in risk increasing, the lower the level of correlation.

Next consider how portfolio risk declines as the number of assets held in the portfolio increases. To illustrate, suppose a third farm unit (X_3), located in the Pacific region, is added to the portfolio, along with the units in the Corn Belt and Great Plains regions. Let the expected return and standard deviation of X_3 also be 20 percent and 10 percent, respectively, and assume independence (0 correlation) among the returns of the three investments. Using an expanded version of formula (8.1), the expected returns from a portfolio comprised of equal proportions ($P_1 = P_2 = P_3 = .333$) of the three investments will be:

$$\bar{r}_t = (.20)(.333) + (.20)(.333) + (.20)(.333) \qquad \textbf{(8.9)}$$

$$= .20, \text{ or } 20 \text{ percent.}$$

Similarly, the total variance of the portfolio is:[2]

$$\sigma_T{}^2 = \sigma_1{}^2 P_1{}^2 + \sigma_2{}^2 P_2{}^2 + \sigma_3{}^2 P_3{}^2 \qquad \textbf{(8.10)}$$

$$= (.10)^2(.333)^2 + (.10)^2(.333)^2 + (.10)^2(.333)^2$$

$$= .003327$$

and the standard deviation is

$$\sigma_T = \sqrt{.003327}$$

$$= .0577, \text{ or } 5.77 \text{ percent.}$$

Comparing the standard deviation of 5.77 percent for the three-

---

[2]The covariance terms are zero, and thus deleted from the formula.

investment portfolio to the standard deviation of 7.07 for the two-investment portfolio and to 10 percent for the single-investment portfolio indicates the gains in risk reduction from diversification as the number of investments increases. Recall that this example assumed zero correlation among the investments. In reality, the correlation coefficients among assets that make up large portfolios usually average greater than zero, but much less than 1. As a result, diversification over more investments does indeed reduce portfolio risk, although the gains in risk reduction diminish as the number of investments increases. Evidence from portfolios of financial assets, for example, indicates that holding 15 to 20 common stocks largely exhausts the possible gains in risk reduction.

Enterprise Diversification in Agriculture

Diversifying among several types of farm enterprises, and even between farm and nonfarm activities, is a traditional approach to risk management in agriculture. It is premised on the condition that low or negative correlation of returns among some enterprises will stabilize total returns over time. When the income of one enterprise is low, the income from another is high.

Enterprise diversification in farm businesses should be carefully considered, although most farms experience a limited range of available enterprises without sacrificing too much expected returns. Moreover, both prices and yields of most crops grown in a given area tend to be positively correlated, often highly so. This correlation occurs because, in roughly the same location, most crops experience similar weather patterns, use similar resources, and experience similar market factors. Combining livestock and crops is likely the most promising approach.

Examples of correlations among enterprise returns are provided by two studies of farmers' risk management. In a study of Iowa farms [4] over the 1965-74 period, the only negative correlations in enterprise returns occurred between soybeans and various livestock enterprises (hogs, feeder cattle, dairy). Small positive correlations were reported between hogs and dairy (.179), beef cows and dairy (.248), and fed cattle and dairy (.254). Other correlations were higher, as in the case of hogs and fed cattle (.658), beef cows and corn (.648), and corn and soybeans (.481).

A similar study in Georgia [13] focused on a wider range of crops and found negative correlation between net returns of such dissimilar crops as wheat and tobacco (−.63), cotton and tobacco (−.50), and cotton and peanuts (−.16). Correlations were positive between corn and wheat (.24), corn and grain sorghum (.95), corn and soybeans (.68), and between other feed grains.

A major problem with enterprise diversification is the loss in efficiencies and returns from specialized production. These losses could outweigh any risk reduction from diversification. Consequently, specialization often increases rather than decreases as farms become more commercialized, to gain the higher expected returns. The result is greater emphasis on other methods of risk management.

As illustrated in the earlier examples, geographic diversification may hold more promise for large-scale firms than enterprise diversification. This involves spreading production out over a wide space. By diversifying location and seasonality of production, lettuce growers in the Western United States have greatly stabilized annual income, expanded credit, and increased their rate of firm growth. Similar patterns of geographic diversification are developing for other perishable products and could occur for grain production and integrated beef operations, as far as yield risks are concerned. Even farming several tracts of land within a small geographic area (a township or county) may help in coping with yield uncertainty, where the uncertainty comes from such events as hail and flood. The gains from reduced risk must be compared, however, with possible reductions in expected returns from the geographically disbursed operations.

Marketing Choices

Marketing choices provide other methods of risk management for farmers. The grain producer who stores the crop at harvest meets a considerable price risk during the storage period. Without effective inventory management to protect against unfavorable price movements, the producer must maintain a large reserve of liquidity.

Inventory management refers to production and storage policies that influence the timing and magnitude of market transactions. Inventory policies can reduce risk through greater flexibility and frequency in marketing. Spreading sales over time results in price averaging over the marketing period and reduces the total variability of returns. In effect, spreading sales amounts to diversifying transactions over time rather than over different enterprises. Following the principles of diversification in the preceding section, the more frequent the sales, the lower the variability of returns; and, the lower the correlation of prices and returns over time, the lower the variability of returns.

While much investment in on-farm grain storage has occurred, farmers have only just begun to consider sequential marketing as a variable strategy. A recent survey of farmers in Indiana [14] showed, for example, that 70 percent of the surveyed farmers spread their sales of corn, with 31 percent of these farmers selling corn six times or more in any one year. About 58 percent of the farmers spread their sales of soybeans, but less so than corn.

Spreading sales is likely more common with livestock, where production is less seasonal. Linkages with financial risk are also important, since a farmer who invests in storage facilities may have to borrow money to finance the investment and carry the inventory.

Another response to price risk involves hedging. At harvest time, the producer could sell a futures contract timed to be consistent with the firm's storage policy. If, during the storage period, the price increases, the producer gains in terms of stored grain but loses in terms of the futures contract. The reverse could hold should the price movement be reversed. The net result is to cancel most of the price risk associated with storage. The principles of diversification are involved in hedging too. A perfect hedge occurs only if the cash price and futures price for the commodity are perfectly correlated. In practice, these prices are not perfectly correlated, so that new risks associated with hedging—called basis risk—must be considered.

A major problem with hedging is the scarcity of opportunities to hedge. For many farm products no futures contracts exist, or the specifications on product quality, sizes of contract, or delivery dates do not coincide well with the characteristics of the producer's crop. Past history also suggests the need for educational activity to improve producers' understanding of hedging. On the other hand, hedging may not be warranted if the producer expects the product price to increase and has sufficient liquidity to assume the risk. A hedge would lock in the low price and lose the expected gain. Finally, margin requirements by commodity brokers in response to price changes during the hedging period require a flexible credit arrangement. Hedging may be better suited for buyers of farm products (grain elevators, cooperatives, livestock dealers), who by hedging themselves can extend its benefits to farmers through forward contracts.

Forward contracting directly with a buyer is another market response to risk. Forward contracts provide the manager with more certain price expectations and more precise planning. Contracting the sale of output may even increase the farm's credit, since lenders prefer the greater price certainty.

Forward contracting has limitations as well. Procurement contracts will probably specify production performance, harvest conditions, and terms of sale. These specifications reduce the manager's flexibility and freedom of decision making. Forward contracts that stipulate delivery amounts also produce an interaction between yield and price risk. Shortfalls in yields can force the producer to purchase from the cash market at harvest to cover the contracted volume of production. Contracts may also reduce price expectations because of the need to reward the buyer for accepting the price risk.

Choosing products with markets influenced by government programs may offset some price and production uncertainty. Through production and price specifications, these programs may add stability to the respective markets. Cotton, wheat, rice, feed grains, soybeans, peanuts, tobacco, and dairy products are some of the major farm products that benefit from political action to reduce uncertainties. Yet, new uncertainties arise about future changes in government programs and underlying economic conditions. Over-reliance on foreign markets, for example, to sell farm products may be risky in the long run.

For some commodities, pooling arrangements perhaps available through marketing cooperatives enable farmers to transfer the storage, sale, and pricing function to a larger organization. Frequent marketing of pooled commodities helps stabilize farmers' returns. The market firm's knowledge of market conditions, large size, and specialized management may add to expected profits as well.

Flexibility

Greater flexibility in the business organization enables the manager to respond more quickly as new information flows to the firm. Flexibility does not directly reduce risk; it provides a means of coping with risk. We can consider cost, time, resource, and behavioral flexiblity.

One way to increase flexibility is to reduce fixed costs relative to variable costs. Short-lived assets can be changed more often than long-lived assets. Organizing grain and livestock enterprises to use more labor relative to capital investments increases enterprise flexibility. Consider, for example, a hog producer who can choose between a capital-intensive, specialized confinement system of production, or a pasture system using more labor. This means of flexibility is declining, however, as labor resources become more scarce and more costly. More flexible organizations often add to total cost and forego possible size economies. Hence, the manager usually chooses an organization that is less flexible and more efficient on the basis of present information.

Another common way to achieve flexibility is to choose nonspecific resources in place of specific resources. In this strategy, general-purpose buildings and machines are preferred to specialized buildings and machinery. Dual-purpose animals replace beef or dairy animals. General-purpose inputs can respond to changes in market opportunities. However, these general-purpose inputs usually have high costs per unit of output.

Behavioral attributes of flexibility are important too. A manager must recognize when changes are needed and be willing to make the changes as conditions warrant. Searching for new information about market conditions and production techniques is an example. The quality of expectations is improved, the degree of uncertainty is reduced, and the firm can better respond to changing conditions.

The general shortcoming of some types of flexibility is similar to that of diversification. With a flexible organization, the manager loses the benefits of specialization. The higher total costs of flexibility may make its choice infeasible. While flexibility is effective in some cases, it is generally limited as a risk response for modern commercial farms. It is usually cheaper to choose a more specific input and then elect other means to counter risk.

Financial Responses to Risk

Financial responses to risk refer to a firm's capacity to bear risks in production, marketing, and financing, and to spread these risks among the financial claimants on the firm. In larger corporate firms, the wide dispersion of ownership spreads business risks over a large number of stockholders who may themselves be well diversified. The smaller-scale, non-corporate structure of the farm sector reduces the feasibility of this risk response. An exception occurs in leasing of farm land where extensive use of share rents allocates expected business risks between the farm operator and the landlord.

Most of farmers' financial responses to risk involve the management of leverage, liquidity, and formal insurance. These actions affect both the firm's assets and its liabilities and are related to the risk responses cited above. Some sources of liquidity were presented in Chapter 7; they are briefly reviewed here along with other financial responses to risk.

The Pace of Investment

Maintaining flexibility in the pace of farm investment is an important financial response to risk. Postponing capital expenditures, including asset replacement, is a favorite financial control mechanism under adversity. It has the multiple effects of postponing large financial outlays, reducing cash outflows, and restraining indebtedness. Generally, alternative rates of capital investments offer more flexibility in timing than do production and marketing activities, which must be carried on each year to sustain the firm's operations. Ultimately, of course, capital assets must be replaced to sustain the firm's productivity.

The Pace of Disinvestment and Withdrawals

As discussed in Chapter 7, many assets have important liquidity attributes and provide relatively low cost access to cash. Willingness to liquidate assets to meet financial obligations is a crucial financial response, especially under crisis conditions. Drawing down financial reserves is the first step. However, for younger operators with expanding operations, liquid financial assets are relatively scarce, and the opportunity costs of asset liquidation are relatively high. Growing-crops and livestock in feedlots are also considered illiquid assets. In contrast, harvested crops held in storage are highly liquid assets and contribute importantly to risk management.

Other farm assets are dominated by land, machinery, breeding livestock, and other fixed assets whose liquidation is costly and disruptive. Selling these capital assets is usually a last resort effort, although depleting livestock herds is a common cyclical behavior. Selling a tract of land is perhaps the most anxiety-producing response, especially in traditional family farms. But if land acquisition is part of the growth strategy, then land disposal can be part of the risk control strategy as well. In general, when businesses experience heavy stress, asset sales can generate cash in larger amounts and more quickly than most other types of risk response.

Control of withdrawals by family members and other business owners for consumption, taxes, and other purposes is also an important risk response. However, farmers today are more dependent on cash purchases and have less capacity than in the past to adjust family living to swings in farm income. Options in meeting tax obligations provide further opportunities for stabilizing income, especially in shifting taxable gains and losses among years.

Credit Reserves

Much reliance in farming is placed on establishing sound, lasting credit relationships with commercial lenders. These relationships may enable the borrower to carry over loans, defer payments, refinance high debt loads, or otherwise utilize credit liquidity during times of financial distress. Using credit avoids disturbing the firm's assets, but it shifts financial control to lenders and brings new risks about repayment prospects, changes in interest rates, and future availability of funds. As shown in Chapter 7, the firm's credit position, as evaluated by lenders, is strongly sensitive to factors affecting the farm's credit worthiness, including risk responses in production and marketing. Moreover, borrowers must consider differences among farm lenders as they plan, coordinate, and communicate in establishing the borrower-lender relationships. Nonetheless, working with commercial lenders is a prominent risk response for many farmers.

Part of the credit relationship involves establishing acceptable targets on a farm's financial leverage. Basing leverage on risk-return considerations, adequate safety margins in collateral, and projected repayment capacity under normal conditions sets the stage for effective financial control when adversity occurs. Cash flow budgets, capital budgets, and pro forma analyses with careful documentation and sensitivity analysis are important tools in managing leverage and liquidity.

Credit reserves provided by public programs are important to farmers as well, although subject to their own uncertainties. Price and income support programs administered through the Commodity Credit Corporation of the U.S. Department of Agriculture provide a sophisticated financial control program for crop farmers who participate in the program. These programs provide inventory financing for farmers, mechanisms for stabilizing commodity prices, added flexibility in marketing crops, and maintenance of farm incomes. Longer-term storage and commodity reserve programs extend the inventory financing and shift part of marketing control to the public sector.

Other public credit programs in the United States administered mainly through the Farmers Home Administration provide direct credit liquidity for high-risk borrowers, including those who experience natural or economic disasters. Farmers Home lending to farmers occurs through direct loan programs, guarantees of farm loans made and serviced by commercial lenders, and various emergency loan programs that often have concessionary terms. In the later 1970s, the concept of emergency financing was broadened to cover various kinds of economic emergencies, including shortages of credit from commercial lenders. These public credit programs introduce added uncertainties about their continuation over time.

Insurance

Insurance provides a specialized source of liquidity. Instead of reserving cash, savings, or credit to counter the effects of hail damage, a crop farmer might buy an insurance contract which provides a reserve of funds contingent upon the occurrence of the insured event. Commercial insurance indemnifies an asset or flow of income against the occurrence of specified events. Examples include life, crop, loan, and household against debt or accident, yield loss, default, and fire, respectively. If certain statistical properties are met relative to the event and the indemnifiable property, the insurance company can maintain the reserve more cheaply than the individual farmer. In general, events with a very low and highly predictable probability of occurrence, but with a large potential loss, are well suited to insurance coverage.

An event's probability of occurrence to a farmer is the same whether insurance or other liquid reserves are provided. The major concern is the best means of providing liquidity for responding to an unfavorable event. Elements of an insurance decision for a farmer include: (1) the insurance premium, (2) the liquid reserve needed without insurance, (3) the earnings rate of the liquid reserve, and (4) the earnings rate for investing the reserved funds in the business. These elements can be specified in the following model.

$$I = S (b - e) - P \qquad (8.11)$$

where I = the gain from insurance,

S = the size of needed reserve,

P = the annual insurance premium,

b = the opportunity cost of the reserve (i.e., its earning rate if funds were invested in the business), and

e = the earnings rate of the liquid reserve.

Decision rules are specified as:

If I > 0, insure,

If I = 0, indifference,

If I < 0, do not insure.

Consider a manager who is evaluating insurance for a $40,000 (S) building with a $600 annual premium (P). The manager can earn a 10 percent return (e) on a liquid reserve in a savings account. However, the funds will earn a 14 percent return (b) if invested in the business. Substituting in equation (8.11) yields:

I = 40,000 (.14 − .10) − 600

I =   1,600 − 600 = 1,000.

Thus the manager earns an additional $1,000 by insuring and investing the $40,000 directly in the business. In fact, the manager should insure if the difference in earnings rates (b − e) of the reserves exceeds P ÷ R—in this case .015.

Most farmers do not have liquid reserves available for each event which may be insurable, nor do they have such reserves available for new investments. An insurance company can generally provide the reserve more cheaply. While the premium for insurance is an obvious cash outflow, the protective returns from insurance are intangible and more difficult to measure. Yet, the consequences of many insurable events may jeopardize the firm's ability to survive. Even if the dollar cost of insurance may exceed the dollar return in the long run, the utility or security generated by equity protection can make insurance quite favorable.

Unfortunately, insurance does not exist for many farm situations. Examples are prices of farm products and farm outputs, some weather events, failures in contractual relationships, and human performance. For events such as these, the manager must depend on other liquid reserves to meet the consequences.

Concluding Comments

The consequences of business and financial risks in agriculture heighten the need for farmers to develop skills in managing risk. Especially important is the formulation of comprehensive strategies dealing with the multiple sources of risk. Understanding concepts and measures of variability and correlation is important too. Risk management jointly considers the asset and liability structure of farm businesses, and accounts for the sources of risk and methods of managing risks in production, marketing, investment, and financing. High-performance managers will compare the costs and returns for all risk management alternatives in developing their strategies.

Still, however, the most common and often the only available methods of risk response in agriculture are financial in nature. Most grain farmers and livestock producers have limited opportunities for enterprise diversification. Even then, the relatively high correlations among yields and among prices on those diversifiable enterprises diminish its payoff. Farmers have also made limited use of marketing policies (contracts, hedging, sequential selling) in responding to risk. If these observations are correct, then risk responses are mostly financial ones—managing leverage, credit, and insurance—and will likely continue so in the future.

Topics for Discussion

1. Explain the relationship between risk management and the financial control process.
2. Explain the concept of a risk management *strategy*. How is a strategy related to a specific method of risk management?
3. Explain how trade-offs may arise among various methods of managing risks. Why, for example, may hedging reduce the need for holding liquid reserves? Suggest and evaluate some other examples.
4. What conditions must exist for diversification to be an effective risk response? Explain how the correlation effect is involved? The number-of-investments effect?
5. What factors limit farmers' use of enterprise diversification and flexibility in responding to risks?
6. What factors affect the use of hedging and forward contracting as methods of risk management?
7. Contrast asset sales and credit reserves as sources of liquidity. What are their advantages and disadvantages? Which, if either, is preferred?
8. A farmer is evaluating insurance for a $50,000 facility with a $400 annual

premium. He can earn a 12 percent return on a liquid reserve and 16 percent if funds are invested in the business. Is insurance a profitable choice?

9. Given the following information:

	Investment A	Investment B
Expected rate of return	.15	.20
Standard deviation	.12	.15
Correlation coefficient	.5	

a. Find the expected value and standard deviation of a portfolio with equal proportions of Investments A and B. How do these results compare with holding only A or B?

b. Suppose the correlation coefficient declines to −.5. What are the impacts on portfolio risk? How do these results compare to A?

c. Suppose Investment C is considered with expected return .25, standard deviation .20, and correlation of .5 with A and B. Using the data in a, evaluate a portfolio with equal proportions of the three investments. Contrast the results with those in a and b.

References

1. Barry, P. J., *Risk Management in Agriculture*, Iowa State University Press, Ames, 1983.

2. Barry, P. J., and D. Fraser, "Risk Management in Agricultural Production: Methods, Distribution, Rewards and Structural Implications," *American Journal of Agricultural Economics*, 58(1976):286-295.

3. Barry, P. J., C. B. Baker, and L. R. Sanint, "Farmers' Credit Risk and Liquidity Management," *American Journal of Agricultural Economics*, 63(1981):216-227.

4. Boehlje, M. D., and L. D. Trede, "Risk Management in Agriculture," *Journal of the American Society of Farm Managers and Rural Appraisers*, 41(1977):20-27.

5. Fama, E. F., *Foundations of Finance: Portfolio Decisions and Securities Prices*, Basic Books, Inc., Publishers, New York, 1976.

6. Francis, J. C., and S. H. Archer, *Portfolio Analysis*, Prentice-Hall, Inc., Englewood Cliffs, New Jersey, 1979.

7. Gabriel, S., and C. B. Baker, "Concepts of Business and Financial Risk," *American Journal of Agricultural Economics*, 62(1980):560-564.

8. Haley, C. W., and L. D. Schall, *The Theory of Financial Decisions*, 2nd ed., McGraw-Hill Book Company, New York, 1979.

9. Heady, E. O., *Agricultural Production Economics and Resource Use*, Prentice-Hall, Inc., Englewood Cliffs, New Jersey, 1952.

10. Leuthold, R. M., and P. E. Peterson, "Using the Hog Futures Market Effectively While Hedging," *Journal of the American Society of Farm Managers and Rural Appraisers*, 44(1980):6-12.

11. Mapp, H. P., et al., "An Analysis of Risk Management Strategies for Agricultural Producers," *American Journal of Agricultural Economics*, 61(1979):1071-1077.

12. Markowitz, H. M., *Portfolio Selection*, John Wiley & Sons, Inc., New York, 1959.

13. Musser, W. N., and K. G. Stamoulis, "Evaluating the Food and Agriculture Act of 1977 with Firm Quadratic Risk Programming," *American Journal of Agricultural Economics*, 63(1981):447-456.

14. Patrick, G. F., *Risk and Variability in Indiana Agriculture*, Bull. 234, Agricultural Experiment Station, Purdue University, July 1979.

15. Paul, A. B., R. G. Heifner, and J. W. Helmuth, *Farmers' Use of Forward Contracts and Futures Markets*, Agricultural Economics Report 320, ERS, USDA, Washington, D.C., 1976.

SECTION IV

Capital Budgeting and Long-Term Decision Making

Chapter 9

THE TIME VALUE OF MONEY

The introductory discussion of profits and risk in Chapter 2 indicated that economic values of assets are largely determined by (1) the level, timing, and risk of their projected annual profits and (2) the time and risk preferences of investors. We briefly showed how these factors provide a basis for long-term financial decision making.

This chapter develops the basic ideas underlying the time value of money and presents the necessary tools for determining the effects of time on financial decisions. Emphasis is given to time preferences and compound interest and to the use of discounting and compounding techniques in valuing flows of payments at a common point in time. Various applications of these concepts and tools appear in following chapters.

Concepts of Time Value

Interest rates serve as the pricing mechanism for the time value of money. They reflect the collective effects of all investors' time preferences for money. The rate (i) is considered an exchange price between present and future dollars. Thus $1 today exchanges for 1 + i dollars one period in the future. Or alternatively, a $1 payment made one period in the future exchanges for 1/1 + i dollars now.

In financial markets, interest rates play the vital role of equating present and future claims for financial assets of different maturities. Interest rates may also account for risk and inflation, but for now we focus solely on the time differences. These rates respond to changes in supply and demand for alternative financial assets, including money, just as other commodity prices respond to changes in their supply and demand.

Nearly all individuals display positive time preferences for money, wealth, and other desired objects. Hence, interest rates are always positive. The positive time preference means that the sooner the money is available, the greater its value. A dollar received today is preferred to a dollar received tomorrow or, alternatively, a dollar cost is better postponed from today to tomorrow.

These time preferences occur because there are always other valuable opportunities for using the money. Interest rates reflect the opportunity costs of not immediately putting the money into the best of these other uses. For example, if we lend money, the rate (i) is paid to us for our foregone consumption or foregone earnings on other investments. If we borrow, the rate (i) is paid by us to the lender to compensate for his or her foregone consumption or earnings. The level of interest rates reflects the value of these opportunities and the strength of time preferences.

Compound Interest

The time value concept uses compound interest as a basis for determining present and future values. Compound interest differs from simple interest. Simple interest means that only the original principal, or amount of money, earns interest over the life of the transaction. Consider the purchase of a bond for $1,000 that pays 5 percent interest each year. The interest payment is $50 at the end of the first year. Since only the principal earns interest, the interest payments at the end of the second and third years are also $50. Hence, the total interest paid over the three years is $150.

Compound interest means that each time interest is paid, it is added to or compounded into the principal and thereafter also earns interest. As the principal increases through time from compounding, so do the interest payments which provide the source of the compounding. At the end of the transaction period, the total principal available is called the compound amount; the difference between the original principal and the compound amount is called compound interest. The rate of interest is called the compound interest rate. The magnitude of the compound amount is determined by the original principal, the number of compound or conversion periods, and the rate of interest per conversion period.

Suppose you have $1,000 to invest in a bank paying interest annually at a 5 percent annual compound rate (i = .05). After one year you will have:

$$1,000 + (1,000)(i) = 1,050$$

or

$$1,000(1 + i) = 1,000(1.05) = 1,050.$$

After two years, you will have:

$$1,000(1 + i)(1 + i) = 1,000(1.05)(1.05) = 1,102.50$$

or

$$1,000(1 + i)^2 = 1,000(1.05)^2 = 1,102.50.$$

The $1,102.50 is the compound amount, or *future value*, of the $1,000 principal, or present value, invested at a 5 percent compound interest rate for two years. The compound interest earned is $102.50.

If the investment is left for a third year, its future value will be $1,158 yielding compound interest of $158 over the three-year period. The compound interest of $158 exceeds the simple interest of $150 earned when the compounding process was not used.

Future Value of a Present Sum

A general formula that uses compounding to determine the future value of a present value is:[1]

$$V_N = V_o (1 + i)^N \qquad\qquad (9.1)$$

or

$$\frac{\text{Future}}{\text{Value}} = \frac{\text{Present}}{\text{Value}} \times \left(1 + \begin{array}{c}\text{interest rate} \\ \text{per conversion} \\ \text{period}\end{array}\right)^{\text{number of conversion periods}}$$

In the above example the future value of $1,000 compounded at 5 percent for 10 years is:

$$V_{10} = 1,000(1.05)^{10} = 1,629.$$

The term $(1 + i)^N$ can always be computed. However, the procedure becomes tedious for high values of N. Fortunately, numerical results of such equations are tabulated for many values of i and N. Appendix Table I at the end of the book shows the conversion factors for $V_o = \$1$ for selected values of i and N.

---

[1]Notation N is used to designate the number of compound periods, while n refers to the series of payments n = 0, 1, 2, . . . N. In addition, the conversion factors taken from the appendix tables are rounded to the third decimal point in this chapter.

These values are substituted into equation (9.1) and multiplied by V_o for convenient solutions. Turn to Appendix Table I, and locate the appropriate conversion factors used above for i = .05 and N = 2 and 10. These values should correspond to the values used in the examples. Using the table, confirm that V_{20} in the above problem is $2,653.

The same procedures can also be quickly performed on an inexpensive pocket calculator. Moreover, a number of pocket calculators have built-in business programs that perform many types of compounding and discounting procedures at the touch of a few buttons.

Present Value of a Future Payment

Suppose that we already know the future value, the interest rate, and the number of conversion periods. The present value is found by solving equation (9.1) for V_o. The result is a general formula for determining the present value of a future sum:

$$V_o = \frac{V_N}{(1 + i)^N} \tag{9.2}$$

or

$$\frac{\text{Present}}{\text{Value}} = \frac{\text{Future Value}}{\left(1 + \begin{array}{c}\text{interest rate}\\ \text{per conversion}\\ \text{period}\end{array}\right)^{\text{number of conversion periods}}}$$

Note that:

$$V_o = \frac{V_N}{(1 + i)^N} = V_N(1 + i)^{-N}. \tag{9.2}$$

Formula (9.2) shows that present value equals the future value divided by the conversion factor for interest rate (i) and conversion period (N). The process of finding present values is called *discounting* because the future value is discounted to a lower present value to account for the difference in the time value of money. The discount reflects the earnings lost by the investor's not being able to immediately invest the future sum in the alternative investment opportunity yielding interest rate (i).

What is the present value of a $1,102.50 payment available two years from now, if the annual interest rate is 5 percent?

$$V_o = \frac{1,102.50}{(1.05)^2} = 1,000$$

The present value is \$1,000 and the discount for time is \$102.50. Note that this level of discount equals the compound interest earned by investing \$1,000 for two years at an interest rate of 5 percent. Discounting to compute present values is precisely the inverse of compounding, as was demonstrated by deriving equation (9.2) from equation (9.1). Hence, the present value (V_o) of a sum available in N years (V_N) is the amount which, if invested now and compounded for N years, yields V_N—provided, of course, that the interest rates used in compounding and discounting are the same.

The appropriate discount factor could be taken from Appendix Table I and substituted directly into equation (9.2). However, multiplication is usually simpler to visualize and perform than division. So Appendix Table II lists conversion factors for present values of V_N = \$1 at selected values of i and N, for:

$$V_o = \frac{1}{(1+i)^N} = (1 + i)^{-N}.$$

These values are substituted into equation (9.2) and multiplied by V_N to give the solution. To illustrate, consider the present value of \$1,629 available 10 years from now, using an annual interest rate of 5 percent. Appendix Table II lists the conversion factor for i = .05 and N = 10 as 0.614. Therefore:

$$V_o = 1,629(.614) = 1,000.$$

Confirm that the present value of \$2,653 available 20 years from now is \$1,000—again, assuming an interest rate of 5 percent.

Applications of Single-Payment Formulas

Situation

You can purchase a note that will pay \$10,000 five years from now. What is the note's present value with an annual interest rate of 10 percent?

Answer: Use Appendix Table II

$$V_o = 10,000(1.10)^{-5}$$

$$= 10,000(.621)$$

$$= 6,210.$$

Situation

Suppose you borrow $6,210 now and agree to repay the loan in five years plus interest charged at a 10 percent annual rate. Find the future value of the note at the end of year 5.

Answer: Use Appendix Table I

$$V_5 = 6,210(1.10)^5$$

$$= 6,210(1.611)$$

$$= 10,000.$$

Situation

Farm land in Champaign County, Illinois, has been selling for $3,500 per acre. If it is expected to increase in value at a compound rate of 6 percent per year, what will its value be in 25 years? (Note: In this situation, the interest rate is interpreted as a growth rate.)

Answer: Use Appendix Table I

$$V_{25} = 3,500(1.06)^{25}$$

$$= 3,500(4.292)$$

$$= 15,022 \text{ per acre.}$$

Situation

If this same land has been increasing at an annual rate of 10 percent, what was its price six years ago?

Answer: Discount the $3,500 value to a present value for six years ago.

$$V_o = 3,500(1.10)^{-6}$$

$$= 3,500(.564)$$

$$= 1,974 \text{ per acre.}$$

Situation

Mr. Young Lender just joined the Agricultural National Bank at a salary of $16,000. What will his salary be at retirement after a 40-year career and an average annual raise of 7 percent?

Answer:

$$V_{40} = 16,000(1.07)^{40}$$
$$= 16,000(14.974)$$
$$= 239,584.$$

Situation

Mr. Retiring Lender observes that his starting salary 40 years ago was $1,000. How would this compare with today's $16,000 salary, assuming a 7 percent annual increase?

Answer: Discount the $16,000 salary to a present value for 40 years ago.

$$V_o = 16,000(1.07)^{-40}$$
$$= 16,000(.067)$$
$$= 1,072.00.$$

Annual Interest and Compounding

It is always important to determine the interest rate per conversion period when compounding or discounting for time. Sometimes the interest rate is expressed as an annual rate, while compounding occurs more frequently, perhaps on a semiannual, quarterly, or daily basis. Under these circumstances, the interest rate must be changed from an annual rate to a rate per conversion period. The result is:

$$V_N = V_o(1 + \frac{i}{m})^{mN} \qquad \textbf{(9.3)}$$

where m is the number of conversion periods per year and N is the number of years. Suppose, for example, that a bank offers a savings account paying a 6 percent annual rate of interest with interest compounded quarterly (every three months). The number of conversion periods each year is four and the interest rate per period is 1.5 percent. By investing $1,000 for one year, you will have:

$$V_i = 1,000(1 + \frac{.06}{4})^{(4)(1)} = 1,061.40$$

or an annual yield of 6.14 percent rather than the annual quoted rate of 6 percent. As will be seen later, this procedure is especially important in determining interest rates on many kinds of loans.

Present Value of a Series of Payments

One of the most general problems of financial management is to determine the present value of an investment that generates a series of payments over several years in the future. The procedure for determining the present value of a series of payments is an extension of the procedure for determining the present value of a single future sum. That is, discount each future payment in its respective year to a present value and add them all up.

$$V_o = \frac{P_1}{1 + i} + \frac{P_2}{(1 + i)^2} + \dots + \frac{P_N}{(1 + i)^N} \qquad \textbf{(9.4)}$$

or

$$V_o = \sum_{n = 0}^{N} \frac{P_n}{(1 + i)^n} \qquad \textbf{(9.4)}$$

where

$V_o =$ the present value of payment series

$P_n =$ the payment for each conversion period (n) and (n = 0, 1, 2, ... N)

$i =$ the interest rate

$\Sigma =$ the summation for n = 0 to N.

To illustrate, find the present value of an oil royalty expected to pay \$3,000 at the end of year one, \$4,000 in year two, \$5,000 in year three, \$6,000 in year four, and \$7,000 in year five. Use an interest rate of 8 percent. The present-value model is set up as follows:

$$V_o = \frac{3,000}{1.08} + \frac{4,000}{(1.08)^2} + \frac{5,000}{(1.08)^3} + \frac{6,000}{(1.08)^4} + \frac{7,000}{(1.08)^5}.$$

Calculations involve multiplying the respective payments by the conversion factors in Appendix Table II for i = .08 and values of n ranging from 1 to 5:

$$V_o = 3{,}000(.926) + 4{,}000(.857) + 5{,}000(.794) + 6{,}000(.735)$$
$$+ 7{,}000(.681)$$
$$= 19{,}353.$$

The present value of the oil-royalty payments is \$19,353, using an interest rate of 8 percent. The present value of the series using a zero interest rate (i.e., undiscounted) is \$25,000. Hence, the difference of \$5,647 represents the size of discount for delayed receipt of the payments. It reflects the earnings lost by not investing the payments in an alternative investment yielding the 8 percent return. Anyone paying \$19,353 for the right to receive this five-year series of payments would realize an annual compound rate of return (or yield) of 8 percent. Using a higher discount rate (10 percent) yields a lower present value, while using a lower discount rate (6 percent) raises the present value.

Present Value of a Uniform Series

The discounting procedure is simplified if the payments are equal in each conversion period. Then we are determining the present value of a *uniform* series of payments (an annuity), and equation (9.4) reduces to:

$$V_o = A \left[\frac{1 - (1 + i)^{-N}}{i} \right] = A \left[USPV_{i,N} \right] \tag{9.5}$$

where A equals the annuity payment in each period. $USPV_{i,N}$ is used as a simplified notation for a *uniform series present value* over N periods at interest rate (i).

Assume now that the oil-royalty payments in the preceding section are a uniform series of \$5,000 paid at the end of each of the next five years. The present value is expressed as:

$$V_o = 5{,}000 \left[\frac{1 - (1.08)^{-5}}{.08} \right] = 19{,}965.$$

We can use Appendix Table II for values of $(1 + i)^{-N}$. For i = .08 and N = 5, the conversion factor is .681. This value can be inserted into equation (9.5) to solve for V_o. The answer is \$19,965. As a shortcut, however, Appendix Table IV lists directly the present values of an annuity of \$1 for selected value of i and N. For i = .08 and

N = 5 the conversion factor is 3.993. Multiplying this factor by the annuity (A) of $5,000 also gives the present value of $19,965.

Thus, the present value of a series of $5,000 payments received at the end of five successive years is $19,965, assuming an 8 percent interest rate. Alternatively, one can say that $19,965 invested currently at 8 percent interest will provide an annuity of $5,000 per year for five years.

Using Appendix Table IV and equation (9.5) confirms that the present value of a $5,000 annuity payable over 20 years is $49,090; a similar annuity for 50 years has a present value of $61,167.

Present Value of an Infinite Uniform Series

As N increases for a given annuity, the present value of the annuity increases at a decreasing rate. Each additional conversion period adds another payment to the income stream. However, that payment is discounted over an additional time period. At some point in time the present value of the last annuity payment approaches zero. In equation (9.5), this condition is signified when the term $(1 + i)^{-N} = 0$. When this condition occurs (i.e., as N approaches infinity), the present value of the annuity approaches its absolute limit, and equation (9.5) reduces to:

$$V_o = \frac{A}{i}. \hspace{2cm} \textbf{(9.6)}$$

This is the standard capitalization equation used by real estate appraisers. It is applicable whenever a uniform series can be projected to occur perpetually into the future.

Actually, most situations involving the time value of money have measurable time periods. The projected economic life of a machine may be only 5 years, or the planning horizon for a farm family considering a real estate investment may be 10 to 20 years or less. Consequently, the capitalization equation (9.6) has limited application in financial analysis.

Future Value of a Series of Payments

Not all valuation occurs as present values. It is often appropriate to value in the future and to define procedures for determining the future value of payments. Earlier we observed that present values (V_o) and future values (V_n) are related to each other through the interest rate i and the number of compounding periods. This same procedure applies to estimating the future value of a series of payments. The future value of each payment is determined using equation (9.1) and then summed as:

$$V_N = P_0(1 + i)^N + P_1(1 + i)^{N-1} + P_2(1 + i)^{N-2} + \ldots + P_N$$

$$= \sum_{n=0}^{N} P_n(1 + i)^{N-n} \tag{9.7}$$

where

V_N = the future value of the series of payments

P_n = the payment for each conversion period (n) and (n = 0, 1, 2, ... N)

i = the interest rate.

To illustrate, find the future value of the oil royalty expected to pay $3,000, $4,000, $5,000, $6,000, and $7,000 in each of the next five years, respectively, using an 8 percent interest rate. The future-value model is set up as follows:

$$V_5 = 3,000(1.08)^4 + 4,000(1.08)^3 + 5,000(1.08)^2 + 6,000(1.08) + 7,000.$$

Note that there is no payment in period zero; the first payment is made at the end of year 1 and is compounded over the four remaining years. The fifth payment is received at the date of future valuation and is not compounded.

Calculations involve multiplying the respective payments by the conversion factors in Appendix Table I for i = .08 and values of n ranging from 1 to 4:

$$V_5 = 3,000(1.360) + 4,000(1.260) + 5,000(1.166) + 6,000(1.08)$$

$$+ 7,000$$

$$= 28,430.$$

The future value of the series of oil-royalty payments is $28,430, using an interest rate of 8 percent. The future value of the series using a zero interest rate (i.e., uncompounded) is $25,000. The difference of $3,430 represents the compound interest earned by reinvesting the payments in the investment opportunity yielding 8 percent.

Note the linkage between the derivation of present and future values for this series of payments. The present value of this non-uniform series of oil-royalty payments is $19,353. The future value of the $19,353 figure compounded for five years at 8 percent interest is:

$$V_5 = 19,353(1.08)^5 = 19,353(1.469) = 28,430$$

which is also the future value of the series as calculated with equation (9.7).

The valuation of the payment series can occur at any point in time, with the choice largely resting on ease of calculation and on the intended use of the derived values. Clearly, however, to compare the values of two series of payments, they must be valued at the same point of time—either at the present, which is generally the case, or at the same future date.

Future Value of a Uniform Series

Again, the procedure for finding the future value of a uniform series is simplified if the payments are equal. Then we are determining the future value of a uniform series of payments, and equation (9.7) reduces to:

$$V_N = A \left[\frac{(1 + i)^N - 1}{i} \right] = A \left[USFV_{i, N} \right] \tag{9.8}$$

where A is the annuity payment in each period and $USFV_{i,N}$ stands for *uniform series future value* over N periods at interest rate (i).

Now the future value of the five-year uniform series of $5,000 oil-royalty payments is:

$$V_5 = 5,000 \left[\frac{(1.08)^5 - 1}{.08} \right] = 5,000 \left[USFV_{.08,5} \right] = 29,335.$$

Appendix Table III lists conversion factors for the future value of an annuity of $1 for selected values of i and N. For i = .08 and N = 5, the conversion factor is 5.867. Multiplying 5.867 by the annual payments of $5,000 yields the future value of $29,335. Using Appendix Table III, confirm that V_{10} for this annuity is $72,433.

Applications of Series Formulas

The formulas for present and future values of a series of payments are used in numerous kinds of capital budgeting models that will be introduced in Chapter 10 and applied in subsequent chapters. However, it is useful to illustrate some applications now, in order to gain experience with their use. The formulas themselves have only mathematical content. They acquire financial relevance when they are applied to problems in investment and financing.

Situation

Mr. Young Lender, who accepted the $16,000 salary from the Agricultural National Bank, had passed up another banking alternative with a $13,000 starting salary. Assuming the salary differential persists over his 40-year employment, what is the annual difference of $3,000 worth now, using a 7 percent interest rate?

Answer: Find the present value of a uniform series of $3,000 payments for $i = .07$ and $N = 40$.

$$V_o = 3,000 \left[USPV_{.07,40} \right]$$
$$= 3,000 \left[13.331 \right] = 39,995.$$

Situation

Cletus Hoopster is a professional basketball player who has just signed what the newspapers describe as a $5 million contract. The terms are 10 annual payments of $500,000 each. Determine the present value of the contract to Cletus, assuming his interest rate is 10 percent.

Answer: Find the present value of a uniform series of $500,000 payments for $i = 10$ percent and $N = 10$.

$$V_o = 500,000 \left[USPV_{.10,10} \right]$$
$$= 5,000,000 \left[6.145 \right] = 3,072,500.$$

Financial managers may need to determine the rate of savings needed to accumulate a given sum, or the annual payments needed to repay an installment loan. Equations (9.5) and (9.8), which measure the present and future values of annuities, are used to answer these questions. In these cases, the manager knows the present or future values (V_o or V_N), the interest rates (i), and the number of periods (N). Given this information, the manager must determine the level of annuity (A) per period.

Situation

The manager projects a need for $15,000 ($V_N$) in five years and can invest savings at a 6 percent annual interest rate, compounded semiannually. How much must be saved each period to reach the objective?

Answer: Find the annuity which, when invested for 10 periods at i = .03 per period, yields a future value of $15,000. (Note that the semiannual compounding defines 10 conversion periods in the five years, with an interest rate of 3 percent per period.) This information is substituted into equation (9.8).

$$15,000 = A \left[USFV_{.03,10} \right].$$

Solve for A and find the conversion factor for i = .03 and N = 10 from Appendix Table III:

$$A = \frac{15,000}{\left[USFV_{.03,10} \right]} = \frac{15,000}{11.464} = 1,308.44.$$

The manager must invest $1,308.44 each six months at a 6 percent annual rate, compounded semiannually, in order to accumulate $15,000 in five years. This type of fund is generally called a sinking fund.

Situation

The manager is borrowing $6,000 ($V_o$) to purchase a car and will repay the loan in 30 equal monthly payments at an interest rate of 1 percent per month. What is the level of monthly payment?

Answer: Find the level of annuity (monthly payment), whose present value is $6,000 when discounted over 30 conversion periods at an interest rate of 1 percent per period. This information can be substituted into equation (9.5) and solved for A:

$$6,000 = A \left[USPV_{.01,30} \right]$$

$$A = \frac{6,000}{\left[USPV_{.01,30} \right]} \quad \text{(See Appendix Table IV)}$$

$$A = \frac{6,000}{25.808} = 232.49.$$

Thus, monthly payments of $232.49 for 30 months will completely repay the original loan plus the interest. This is called a capital recovery problem in the finance literature. It represents the process of amortization, in which equal payments are made each conversion period to repay a debt within a specified time.

Present Value of a Constant Growth Series

Previously it was assumed that the payment series was uniform over time. Now suppose that the payments experience a constant rate of growth, g. Let P_0 be the current payment, and assume that it was just paid so that it does not enter into the present value computations. The series of growing payments thus starts with the payment at the end of the first period, $P_1 = P_0(1 + g)$. The payment at the end of the second period is $P_2 = P_0(1 + g)^2$, and so on.

The present value is:

$$V_0 = \frac{P_1}{1 + i} + \frac{P_2}{(1 + i)^2} + \ldots + \frac{P_n}{(1 + i)^n}$$

which is equivalent to:

$$V_0 = \frac{P_0(1 + g)}{1 + i} + \frac{P_0(1 + g)^2}{(1 + i)^2} + \ldots + \frac{P_0(1 + g)^n}{(1 + i)^n}.$$

If the series of constant growth payments is for a specified number of periods, then the present value model reduces to:

$$V_0 = \frac{P_1 \left[1 - \left(\dfrac{1 + g}{1 + i} \right)^n \right]}{i - g}. \qquad (9.9)$$

If the series is perpetual and the rate of growth is less than the discount rate i, then the term with the exponent in the brackets approaches zero as N grows very large. Under this condition, equation (9.7) reduces to:

$$V_0 = \frac{P_1}{i - g}. \qquad (9.10)$$

To illustrate, suppose the series of oil-royalty payments is growing at a 3 percent annual rate. For a five-year period and an 8 percent discount rate, the present value is:

$$V_o = \frac{5{,}000 \left[1 - \left(\dfrac{1.03}{1.08} \right)^5 \right]}{.08 - .03} = 21{,}107.75$$

If the payments occur in perpetuity, the present value is

$$V_o = \frac{5{,}000}{.08 - .03} = 100{,}000$$

The Effects of Time and Interest on Present and Future Values

The important variables determining present and future values of single payments or a series of payments are (1) the number of conversion periods and (2) interest rate per compounding period. Both factors interact to determine the total effects of discounting or compounding on present or future values. The impacts are clearly evident in the levels of conversion factors in Appendix Tables I through IV. At low rates of interest, the number of time periods has only a modest effect on either present or future values. For example, the future value of $1,000 invested now at 1 percent interest, compounded annually, is $1,105 in 10 years and only $1,220 in 20 years. Similarly, the present value of $1,000 available 10 years from now, using a 1 percent interest rate, is $905, compared to $820 for a similar sum available in 20 years.

At higher interest rates, however, time has a more significant effect on present and future values. Confirm, for example, from Appendix Tables I and II that with an interest rate of 20 percent:

1. The future value of $1,000 is:
   (a) $6,192 at the end of 10 years and
   (b) $38,338 at the end of 20 years
2. The present value of $1,000 is:
   (a) $162 if it is to be received in 10 years
   (b) $26 if it is to be received in 20 years

Figures 9.1 and 9.2 provide an alternative approach to visualizing the relationship between time and interest in determining future and present values. Figure 9.1 plots $V_N = (1 + i)^N$ for interest rates of 1, 10, and 20 percent, respectively, over a range of N values. Notice the acceleration in the slope of the curvilinear relation as i increases. Similarly, Figure 9.2 plots $V_o = V_N(1 + i)^{-N}$ for interest rates of 1, 10, and 20 percent over a range of N values. Notice again the acceleration in the negative slope of the curvilinear relation as i increases.

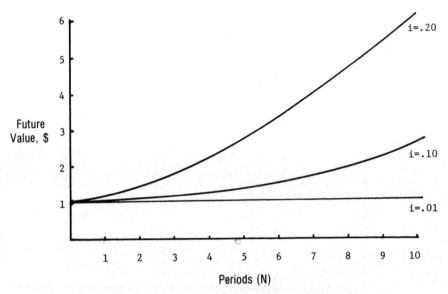

Figure 9.1. Effects of time and interest rate on future value.

The same results occur in the calculation of present or future values of an annuity. In fact, the impact is magnified, since a new payment is received each conversion period. Again, the influence of time on the future value of an annuity increases as the interest rate increases. At 1 percent compounded annually, an annuity of $1,000 has a value of $5,101 after 5 years and $16,097 after 15 years. At a 20 percent rate, however, this annuity is worth $7,442 after 5 years and $72,035 after 15 years. The reverse is true, however, for present values, as indicated in Table 9.1, for varying rates and years.

Notice again, that at high interest rates, the capitalization equation gives reasonably accurate estimates of present value for the series of payments when the number of time periods exceeds about 20. For low interest rates, however, the accuracy of the capitalization equation is unacceptable.

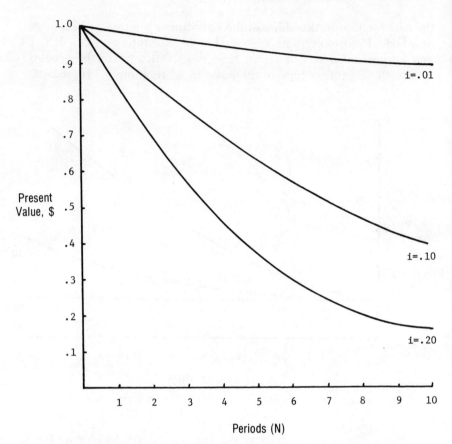

Figure 9.2. Effects of time and interest rate on present value.

Table 9.1. Present Values of an Annuity of $1,000 for Selected Times, Conversion Periods, and Discount Rates

Selected Number of Conversion Periods	Selected Discount Rates (i) (percent)			
	1	10	20	25
5	$ 4,853	$ 3,791	$2,991	$2,689
15	13,865	7,606	4,675	3,859
30	25,808	9,427	4,979	3,995
50	39,197	9,915	4,999	4,000
Capitalization Equation				
$\dfrac{\$1,000}{i}$	$100,000	$10,000	$5,000	$4,000

Review of Formulas

The formulas used in compounding and discounting are presented in summary form to facilitate their use in following chapters.

Notation Summary

V_0 = present value of a future payment(s)

P_0 = payment at time period 0

P_n = payments in other conversion periods

V_N = future value of a present payment or series of payments

n = a conversion period (n = 0, 1, 2, ... N)

i = interest rate per conversion period

A = uniform annuity payment made each conversion period

g = rate of payment growth per conversion period.

1. The present value of a future value is:

$$V_0 = \frac{V_N}{(1 + i)^N} = V_N(1 + i)^{-N}.$$

2. The present value of a series of payments is:

$$V_0 = \frac{P_1}{1 + i} + \frac{P_2}{(1 + i)^2} + \ldots + \frac{P_N}{(1 + i)^N} = \sum_{n = 0}^{N} \frac{P_n}{(1 + i)^n}.$$

3. The present value of a uniform series of payments is:

$$V_0 = A \left[\frac{1 - (1 + i)^{-N}}{i}\right] = A\left[USPV_{i,N}\right].$$

4. The present value of a perpetual uniform series of payments is:

$$V_0 = \frac{A}{i}.$$

5. The future value of a present value is:

$$V_N = V_0(1 + i)^N.$$

6. The future value of a series of payments is:

$$V_N = \sum_{n=0}^{N} P_n (1 + i)^{N-n}.$$

7. The future value of a uniform series of payments is:

$$V_N = A \left[\frac{(1 + i)^N - 1}{i} \right] = A \left[USFV_{i,N} \right].$$

8. The present value of a constant-growth series is:

$$V_o = \frac{P_1 \left[1 - \left(\dfrac{1 + g}{1 + i} \right)^n \right]}{i - g}.$$

9. The present value of a perpetual constant-growth series is:

$$V_o = \frac{A}{i - g}.$$

Topics for Discussion

1. Explain how interest rates serve as the pricing mechanism for the time value of money.
2. Distinguish between compound interest and simple interest.
3. Distinguish between compounding and discounting.
4. You have two opportunities to invest $5,000 for 10 years. The first provides a yield of 8 percent annually, compounded quarterly. The second provides a yield of 8.5 percent annually, compounded annually. Which of these investments provides the higher returns? By how much?
5. Which would you prefer? $10,000 now, $20,000 10 years from now, or $30,000 20 years from now, assuming
   a. a 6 percent annual interest rate
   b. an 8 percent annual interest rate
   c. a 10 percent annual interest rate
6. You have the opportunity to purchase a note that still has four years to run. It pays $750 per year, with the first payment due a year from now. It can be purchased for $2,700. Should you buy the note, assuming you can earn 6 percent on an alternative investment?
7. A farm can finance a tractor purchase with a $25,000 loan at the local bank. The financing terms include a four-year loan, a 12 percent annual interest rate, and equal quarterly repayments of principal and interest. Given this information, calculate the level of the quarterly payments.
8. Henry Bleacher is a professional baseball player who has just signed a $2 million contract. The terms are five annual payments of $400,000 each.

Determine the present value of the contract to Henry, assuming his interest rate is 10 percent.

9. Suppose that Henry is able to reinvest his annual payments of $400,000 in an investment yielding 10 percent per year. How much will Henry have after five years?

References

1. Ayres, Frank, Jr., *Mathematics of Finance*, (Schaum's Outline Series) McGraw-Hill Book Co., New York, 1963.

2. Bierman, H., Jr., and S. Smidt, *The Capital Budgeting Decision: Economic Analysis of Investment Projects*, 5th ed., Macmillan Publishing Co., Inc., 1980.

3. Boudreaux, K. J., and H. W. Long, *The Basic Theory of Corporate Finance*, Prentice-Hall, Inc., Englewood Cliffs, New Jersey, 1977.

4. Van Horne, J. C., *Financial Management and Policy*, 5th ed., Prentice-Hall, Inc., Englewood Cliffs, New Jersey, 1980.

5. Weston, J. F., and E. F. Brigham, *Essentials of Managerial Finance*, 6th ed., Dryden Press, Hinsdale, Illinois, 1982.

Chapter 10

CAPITAL BUDGETING METHODS

This chapter develops a procedure for evaluating the effects of a farm manager's investment choices on a business's profitability, risk, and liquidity. The procedure is called *capital budgeting, or investment analysis.* "Investment" refers to the addition of durable assets to a business. Alternatively, "disinvestment" refers to the withdrawal of durable assets from the business. "Financing" refers to the means of acquiring control of assets: ownership by cash purchase or borrowing, or leasing. An investment can be financed in several ways, and each may affect its profitability and risk. Hence, the capital budgeting procedures must be designed to jointly consider investment and financing decisions.

Capital budgeting is an orderly sequence of steps that produces information relevant to an investment choice. These steps are: (1) the identification of investment alternatives, (2) the selection of an appropriate method, (3) the collection of relevant data, (4) the analysis of data, and (5) the interpretation of results. These steps are developed in the following sections.

Identification of Alternatives

Searching for profitable investments is an important managerial function that needs systematic and thorough attention. While profitable investments may contribute to firm growth, capital obsolesence and price declines can lock a manager into a poor investment for many years. Similarly, using high financial leverage to acquire fixed assets can significantly modify the firm's risk and liquidity. Nonetheless, the manager must generate enough investment opportunities to efficiently utilize all retained income. Hence, the identification of investment opportunities is a crucial function of management.

Investment opportunities in agriculture fall into several categories:

1. Maintenance and replacement of depreciable capital items.
2. Adoption of cost-reducing investments to produce a given volume of output.
3. Adoption of income-increasing investments that expand the volume of output.
4. A combination of the above.

As an example, consider the case of a cattle feeder with a labor-intensive operation, who is planning some changes. Some worn-out facilities need to be replaced. Due to high labor costs, the adoption of a mechanized-feeding system should be considered. However, to fully utilize the mechanized system, the size of the operation must be increased. At the same time, relatively low returns from cattle feeding are encouraging the cattle feeder to consider a hog enterprise in which some of the assets could be purchased or leased. Many investment alternatives need to be analyzed with appropriate capital budgeting methods.

Capital Budgeting Methods

The next step is to choose a method of capital budgeting for ranking, accepting, or rejecting various investment alternatives. We will discuss four methods often used by, or suggested for, business planners: (1) simple-rate-of-return, (2) payback period, (3) net present value, and (4) internal-rate-of-return. As will be clear shortly, only the net present-value and internal-rate-of-return methods directly account for the time value of money. Hence, they are generally considered superior methods. However, the other methods are developed as well, since they are commonly used and are applicable in selected situations.

There are several reasons why different investments have unique time patterns of cash flow. First, the inherent characteristics of the agricultural enterprises cause differences in timing of returns. Investments to establish orchards, improve pastures, and expand beef-cow herds generally have long-payoff periods. On the other hand, investments in livestock-feeding facilities generally pay off more quickly. Second, new investments by inexperienced producers may exhibit a buildup in cash flow due to growing productivity of management. Third, the terms of financing—downpayment, length of loan, and method of repayment—influence the timing of cash flows. Fourth, inflation and risk may influence the time pattern of returns. Finally, alternatives in tax management also influence the timing of cash flows. All these factors indicate the need for capital budgeting methods which account for both the level and the timing of expected cash flows.

To illustrate these capital budgeting methods, we consider the case of Mr. Farmer, who needs to evaluate three agricultural investment alternatives. Each alternative requires an initial outlay of $20,000 and will be evaluated over a five-year period. We assume equity financing, no income tax obligations, no risk, and complete depreciation over the five-year period. Projected cash flows for the three investments are reported in Table 10.1. Time period 0 reflects the current date, and the negative $20,000 is the initial investment.

Table 10.1. Cash Flows for Three Investments

Year	Investment A	Investment B	Investment C
0-present	$-20,000	$-20,000	$-20,000
1	2,000	5,800	10,000
2	4,000	5,800	8,000
3	6,000	5,800	6,000
4	8,000	5,800	3,000
5	10,000	5,800	1,000

Notice that investment A exhibits increasing returns over the planning period. It might reflect an investment in beef-cow production requiring pasture establishment, range improvements, and a buildup of expected returns over time. Investment B exhibits fairly uniform returns and might reflect an investment in grain production, where the returns are about the same each year. Investment C might reflect irrigated crop production from an exhaustible water supply and thereby exhibits declining returns over time. Each of these investments will be evaluated with the four methods of capital budgeting.

Simple-Rate-of-Return

The simple-rate-of-return is a commonly used method. It expresses the average net profits generated each year by an investment as a percent of either the original investment or the average investment over the investment's expected life. There are several ways to compute simple-rates-of-return, and one is expressed as:

$$SRR = \frac{Y}{I} \qquad\qquad (10.1)$$

where Y = the average annual profits (depreciation has been subtracted) projected for the new investment

I = the initial investment

SRR = the simple-rate-of-return.

Individual investments are ranked according to their SRR's and judged as to profitability by comparison with the investor's required-rate-of-return (RRR). The investment choice is then based on the following decision rules: if SRR exceeds RRR, accept the investment; if SRR equals RRR, be indifferent; if SRR is less than RRR, reject the investment. Of course, information on risk, liquidity, and other factors must also be considered before making the final decisions.

The projected returns and average annual-rates-of-return for investments A, B, and C are summarized in Table 10.2. Based on the simple-rate-of-return method, investment A is selected first, followed by investment B, with investment C ranked last. All are profitable so long as the required-rate-of-return is less than 8 percent. Note also that if the average investment ($10,000) is used rather than the initial investment, the simple-rates-of-return are much higher.

Table 10.2. Simple-Rates-of-Return for Three Hypothetical Investments

Project	Total Gross Returns	Total Depreciation	Average Annual Profits	SRR Original Investment	SRR Average Investment
A	$30,000	$20,000	$2,000	10%	20%
B	29,000	20,000	1,800	9%	18%
C	28,000	20,000	1,600	8%	16%

The simple-rate-of-return method does not consider the timing of cash flows. This limitation is crucial when the differences in time patterns of cash flow are large. The simple-rate-of-return can lead to erroneous conclusions, as illustrated later.

The Payback Period

The payback period is also a widely used method of investment analysis. It estimates the length of time required for an investment to pay itself out.

The payback period (P) is determined as:

$$P = \frac{I}{E} \qquad\qquad\qquad \textbf{(10.2)}$$

if the projected cash flows (E) are uniform, or as the value of n giving:

$$P = \frac{I}{\sum\limits_{n=0}^{N} E_n} = 1 \qquad\qquad\qquad \textbf{(10.3)}$$

when the projected cash flows are non-uniform

where I = the initial investment; E = the projected cash flow per period (n) from the investment; and P = the payback period, expressed in number of periods.

Individual investments are ranked according to their payback periods, with the shortest being the most favored; acceptability is determined by comparison with the investor's required payback period (RPP). The investment choice is then based on the following decision rules: if P is less than RPP, accept the investment; if P equals RPP, be indifferent; if P exceeds RPP, reject the investment.

For the cash flows projected in Table 10.1, the payback period for investment A is 4 years, for investment B about 3.4 years, and for investment C about 2.3 years. Hence, with the payback period, C is preferred to B, which is preferred to A—the reverse of the rankings based on the simple-rate-of-return.

The appeal of the payback criterion rests on its simplicity, on its relevance for firms with low liquidity who must concentrate on quick cash recovery, and on the contention that future returns beyond some required payback period are too uncertain to rely on. However, the payback method has been severely questioned for several reasons. First, it does not consider earnings after the payback date. This penalizes investments with returns which increase over time, as is the case with investment A. These large future returns are often quite important. Second, the payback method does not systematically account for differences in timing of cash flows prior to the end of the payback period. Third, the payback period does not really measure an investment's total profitability; rather, it measures the speed of recovery of the initial investment, which may not be a true indicator of profitability.

Net Present Value

The net present-value (NPV) method uses the discounting formulas for a non-uniform (9.4) or uniform (9.5) series of payments to value the projected cash flows for each investment alternative at one point in time. In this fashion, the net present-value criterion directly accounts for the timing and magnitude of the projected cash flows. An important step in implementing the net present-value method is the identification and collection of appropriate data. Five types of data are needed:

1. INV = the initial investment.
2. P_n = the annual net cash flows attributed to the investment that can be withdrawn each year.
3. V_N = any salvage or terminal investment value.
4. N = the length of planning horizon.
5. i = the interest rate or required-rate-of-return; also called the cost of capital or discount rate.

The present-value model is then set up as follows:

$$NPV = -INV + \frac{P_1}{1 + i} + \frac{P_2}{(1 + i)^2} + \ldots + \frac{P_N}{(1 + i)^N} \qquad \textbf{(10.4)}$$

$$+ \frac{V_N}{(1 + i)^N}.$$

Alternatively, if the projected net cash flows are a uniform series of payments (A), the NPV model is:

$$NPV = -INV + A\left[USPV_{i,N}\right] + \frac{V_N}{(1 + i)^N}. \qquad \textbf{(10.5)}$$

These models indicate that each projected net cash flow is discounted to its present value and then added together to yield a net present value. Any terminal-investment value is included as a cash flow in the last year of the planning horizon. The projected cash flows (P_n) can be either positive or negative. Hence, a projected operating loss in year (n) enters the cash flow with a negative sign and is discounted to a present value. The initial investment (INV) is negative, since it reflects a cash outlay.

The sign and size of an investment's net present value determine its ranking and acceptability. If the investments under consideration are all income generating, as is the case in Table 10.1, then the investment with the largest NPV is the most favored, with the next NPV being second favored, etc. The acceptability of each investment depends on whether the NPV is positive or negative and is expressed in the following decision rules. If NPV exceeds zero, accept the investment; if NPV equals zero, be indifferent; if NPV is less than zero, reject the investment. Note that acceptance of an investment implies that it is profitable, but only relative to the required-rate-of-return implied by the discount rate. Rejection of an investment based on a negative NPV implies that the alternative investment with rate-of-return (i) is *more* profitable than the investment being evaluated.

If the investments under consideration are all cost reducing, then the projected cash flows would reflect cash outlays (i.e., expenses). When cost-reducing investments are compared, the choice criterion is then based on the minimum net present value of cash outlays.

Suppose that the investor evaluating investments A, B, and C in Table 10.1 requires an 8 percent rate-of-return. The net present value of investment A is:

$$NPV = -20,000 + \frac{2,000}{1.08} + \frac{4,000}{(1.08)^2} + \frac{6,000}{(1.08)^3} + \frac{8,000}{(1.08)^4} + \frac{10,000}{(1.08)^5}.$$

The conversion factors for $(1.08)^{-n}$ are taken directly from Appendix Table II for i = .08 and values of n ranging from 1 to 5. The NPV is:

$$NPV = -20,000 + 2,000(.9259) + 4,000(.8573) + 6,000(.7938)$$
$$+ 8,000(.7350) + 10,000(.6806) = 2,730.$$

Similar calculations yield net present values of $3,158 for investment B and $3,766 for investment C. Hence, all three investments are acceptable in terms of the NPV decision rules, although C is preferred to B, which is preferred to A. Note that the payback criterion gave the same ordering while the simple-rate-of-return gave precisely the reverse ordering. These capital budgeting results are summarized in Table 10.3.

Now suppose that the investor's required-rate-of-return, or interest rate, is not 8 percent. In fact, let's start with an interest rate of zero and explore how the ranking and profitabilities change as the interest rate is increased. The net present values for several such interest rates are indicated in Table 10.3. For a zero interest rate, the NPVs of each investment are simply the sum of their undiscounted cash flows—$10,000 for A, $9,000 for B, and $8,000 for C. Now A is preferred to B, which is preferred to C. As the interest rate increases, the profitability declines, as reflected by lower NPVs, although the rankings remain the same through an interest rate of 4 percent. However, for a 5 percent rate, the ranking changes in that C is preferred to A, which is preferred to B. Moreover, at a 6 percent rate, the ranking changes again in that C is preferred to B, which is preferred to A. For still higher rates, the rankings remain the same, although eventually, all the investments become unprofitable.

Why did the changes in rankings occur? Clearly, it is tied to the increasing interest rate, but how? The answer lies in the time patterns of the cash flows and in the implied-rates-of-return (i) earned by reinvesting the cash flows as they are received. The net present-value method assumes that the payments are reinvested in the alternative investment opportunity, whose rate of return is the interest rate (i). Raising the interest rate raises the rate of earnings on reinvesting the payments and increasingly favors those investments with larger payments coming in faster. Clearly, investment B earns larger returns faster than investment A. Moreover, investment C earns larger returns faster than B. Raising the interest or reinvestment rate

Table 10.3. Capital Budgeting Results for Three Investments

Criterion	Investment A	Investment B	Investment C
Simple-Rate-of-Return	10%	9%	8%
Payback	4 years	3.4 years	2.3 years
Net Present Value			
i = .00	$10,000	$9,000	$8,000
i = .02	7,907	7,338	6,824
i = .04	6,013	5,820	5,732
i = .05	5,132	5,111	5,215
i = .06	4,294	4,432	4,715
i = .08	2,730	3,158	3,766
Internal-Rate-of-Return	12.01%	13.82%	17.57%

makes these large early payments more valuable and accounts for the eventual change in rankings.

Internal-Rate-of-Return

In determining the net present value of an investment, we used equation (10.4) or equation (10.5) to determine NPV, given the projected cash flows and the rate of interest. These equations are also used to determine the internal-rate-of-return (IRR) of the investment. This rate is called by various names—the "discounted-rate-of-return," the "marginal efficiency of capital," or the "yield of an investment." It is that rate of interest which equates the net present value of the projected series of cash flow payments to zero.

To find the IRR for an investment, simply set up the NPV model, equation (10.4), with the appropriate projected cash flows (INV, P_n, P_N, V_N), set NPV equal to zero, and solve for i:

$$0 = -INV + \frac{P_1}{1 + i} + \frac{P_2}{(1 + i)^2} + \ldots + \frac{P_N}{(1 + i)^N} + \frac{V_N}{(1 + i)^N}. \quad \textbf{(10.6)}$$

The interest rate that satisfies the equation is called the internal-rate-of-return(IRR). In effect, the IRR equates the present value of the cash flow series to the initial investment (INV), since equation (10.6) can be modified to:

$$INV = \frac{P_1}{1 + i} + \frac{P_2}{(1 + i)^2} + \ldots + \frac{P_N}{(1 + i)^N} + \frac{V_N}{(1 + i)^N}. \quad \textbf{(10.7)}$$

To illustrate, find the IRR for an investment requiring an initial outlay of \$1,000 and yielding a \$1,300 payment one year in the future. The IRR model is set up as:

$$0 = -1,000 + \frac{1,300}{1 + i}.$$

Modifying the equation yields:

$$1 + i = \frac{1,300}{1,000} = 1.3$$

and

$$i = .3.$$

Hence, IRR = 30 percent.

Suppose the $1,300 payment is received at the end of year 2 instead of year 1. The model is respecified as:

$$0 = -1,000 + \frac{1,300}{(1 + i)^2}.$$

Modifying the equation yields:

$$(1 + i)^{-2} = \frac{1,000}{1,300} = .7692$$

and i = .14.

In this case, i is found by using Appendix Table II to find the value of i, which, for N = 2, gives a conversion factor of .7692. To use the table, first locate the appropriate N—year 2, in this case. Then let your eye proceed to the right along row 2 until you reach the conversion factor nearest to .7692. In this case, the conversion factor for N = 2 and i = .14 is .7695. Therefore, the IRR of this investment is approximately 14 percent. When the value of the conversion factor falls between two of the interest rates in the table, then linear interpolation is used to estimate the IRR.

To illustrate the derivation of IRR for a series of payments, let's return to the investment choices in Table 10.1. Consider the IRR for investment B. Since its payments are uniform, we can use equation (10.5) and solve for i as follows:

$$0 = -20,000 + 5,800 \left[USPV_{i,5} \right]$$

or

$$\left[USPV_{i,5} \right] = 3.4483.$$

In this case, Appendix Table IV is used to find the value of i, which, for N = 5, gives a conversion factor of 3.4483. For N = 5, the value listed for i = .14 is 3.4331, while for i = .13 it is 3.5172. Therefore, the IRR for investment B lies between 13 and 14 percent. We can estimate more precisely by linear interpolation:

IRR	Conversion Factor		
13 percent	3.5172		
		689	
?	3.4483		841
14 percent	3.4331		

The linear estimate is $13^{689}/_{841}$, or 13.82 percent.

Finding the IRR for investment A is more difficult because its payments are a non-uniform series requiring the use of equation (10.6):

$$0 = -20,000 + \frac{2,000}{1 + i} + \frac{4,000}{(1 + i)^2} + \frac{6,000}{(1 + i)^3} + \frac{8,000}{(1 + i)^4} + \frac{10,000}{(1 + i)^5}.$$

The procedure is essentially a trial-and-error approach in search of the interest rate (i) yielding a zero net present value. A good way to start is to select a rate of return that you would like to have and discount the cash flows to a net present value at this interest rate. If NPV is positive, your rate is too low. Discount again at a higher rate. If NPV is negative, your rate is too high. In this fashion, you search for the interest rate that yields a zero NPV. For investment (A), an interest rate of 8 percent yields a net present value of $2,730. Try again with a higher rate. For i = .12, the net present value is $3.58, and for i = .13, the net present value is −$605.05. Linear interpolation yields an IRR of 12.01 percent.

As with the other capital budgeting criteria, investments can be ranked and accepted or rejected on the basis of their internal-rates-of-return. Ranking is based on the relative sizes of IRRs, with the largest being the most favored. The acceptability of each investment depends upon the comparison of its IRR with the investor's required-rate-of-return (RRR). Acceptability is based on the following decision rules: if IRR exceeds RRR, accept the investment; if IRR = RRR, be indifferent; if IRR is less than RRR, reject the investment. As with other capital budgeting criteria, these decision rules are still subject to consideration of risk and liquidity. For the investments in Table 10.1, C is preferred to B, which is preferred to A, according to the IRR criterion, and all are acceptable for a required-rate-of-return of 8 percent.

Comparing NPV and IRR

The net present-value and internal-rate-of-return methods are closely linked because each uses the same discounting procedure. However, the NPV requires a specified interest rate, while IRR solves for the interest rate that yields a zero NPV. This linkage is portrayed in Figure 10.1 which graphs the net present values of investments B and C at alternative interest rates. At a zero interest rate, the NPV is highly positive. Increasing the interest rate lowers the NPV until it eventually becomes negative (i.e., below the horizontal

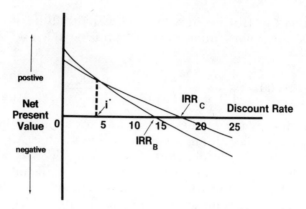

Figure 10.1. Net present value and internal-rate-of-return.

axis). The IRR is found at the point where the NPV line crosses the horizontal axis. It is the interest rate yielding a zero NPV.

The IRR method gives the same ranking of investments as the net present-value method under most circumstances. Both account for differences in the time pattern of cash flows. However, occasional differences in ranking can arise due to different assumptions about the rate of return on reinvestment of the net cash flows. The IRR method implicitly assumes that net cash inflows from an investment are reinvested to earn the same rate as the IRR of the investment under consideration. The net present-value method, on the other hand, assumes that these funds can be reinvested at the firm's interest rate.

The possible differences in rankings are illustrated in Figure 10.1. Both the NPV and IRR methods rank investment C over B as long as the discount rate exceeds i*. At i*, the present value lines intersect, indicating equal net present values. Below i*, investment B has the higher NPV, but lower IRR.

Which reinvestment rate is more realistic? The net present-value rate has the advantage of being consistently applied to all investment proposals. In addition, the net present-value rate may be more realistic if the interest rate is determined by the opportunity cost of capital. On the other hand, IRRs from each investment alternative can be compared against a common RRR, and represent profitability in percentage terms which is often preferred by business managers.

To solve equation (10.6) for the IRR, at least one sign reversal (e.g., one negative sign) must occur among the cash flows. Generally,

INV is negative due to the cash outlay for the initial investment. Multiple IRRs result if more than one sign reversal occurs. In fact, an additional IRR exists for every sign reversal; hence, caution is needed when finding an IRR under these circumstances.

The IRR approach is also tedious to calculate when the payments are a non-uniform series. Fortunately, many pocket calculators and computers are programmed for discounted cash flow analysis according to the preceding procedures. These technological developments greatly simplify the calculations and enhance the usefulness of these capital budgeting methods.

Data Needs

This section discusses the kinds of data needed for using the net present-value and internal-rate-of-return methods of capital budgeting. These data include the initial investment requirements, net cash flows, terminal value, the discount rate, and the planning horizon. First, however, a distinction must be established between returns to assets and returns to equity as the measurement objectives of capital budgeting. This distinction influences the types of financing data needed for the investment analysis.

Returns to Assets or Equity?

As indicated in Chapter 4, returns to assets and returns to equity are two important measures of profitability. Returns to assets measures profitability before interest is paid to a firm's lenders and before any withdrawals or retained earnings are claimed by the firm's owners. Returns to equity measures profitability after the costs of borrowed funds are accounted for. These same concepts apply when the NPV or IRR method is used to measure the profitability of individual investments.

First, consider that the capital budgeting objective is to measure the profitability of the assets committed to an investment project. The return to assets is measured by projecting the expected payment flow for the investment without deducting any charges for interest or loan repayments, and then discounting the payments to a present value, using a weighted average cost of the firm's debt and equity capital as the discount rate. This approach accounts for the effects of the firm's overall financial structure (leverage) in the discount rate. It is based on the assumptions that the firm's leverage determines the

financing costs of an individual investment and that the financing for
an individual investment does not influence the firm's overall cost of
capital.

The returns to assets approach is used for large corporate firms
who can establish and maintain rigorous leverage policies and who
have efficient access to the national markets for debt and equity capital. These firms' leverage and weighted average costs of capital are
relatively stable and predictable over time. Their capital budgeting
procedures need not account for a specific investment's financing
terms.

Now, consider that the capital budgeting objective is to measure
the profitability of the equity capital committed to an investment
project. The return to equity is measured by projecting the payment
flow, net of the cash outflows for principal and interest on debt, and
then discounting the payments to a present value, using the firm's
cost of equity capital as the discount rate. This approach explicitly
accounts for each investment's method of financing. It is based on
the assumption that an investment's financing costs may strongly influence the firm's leverage and cost of capital. This approach is applicable for smaller, non-corporate firms whose leverage fluctuates
over time and who lack access to the national markets for debt and
equity. In smaller firms, including most farm businesses, the large
size and financing terms of new investments often may significantly
change the make-up of assets and liabilities, with the effects lasting
several years.

The choice of measuring returns to assets or returns to equity in
capital budgeting requires careful judgment, based on the characteristics of the business and the investments being analyzed. Either
approach can be used. Here, and in the following chapters, we use
the returns to equity approach because it is consistent with the
smaller-scale, non-corporate structure of most farm businesses.
Moreover, it enables the analyst to develop capital budgets which
include all factors affecting cash flows, thus making the long-term
discounted cash flow analysis more compatible with the cash flow
budgeting outlined in Chapter 5.

Initial Investment Requirements

By initial investment, we refer to the initial equity the investor
commits to the investment. The initial equity depends upon the
value of assets needed to implement the investment and upon the

method of financing. It is important to determine the acquisition cost of the durable assets, since it represents the cost basis for annual depreciation charges. Charging depreciation influences annual cash flows through its effect on income tax obligations. It is also important to account for the type of financing. Use of leverage may spread the cash outflow to pay for the investment over several years, due to the terms of financing. In present-value analyses, these cash outflows for the initial-asset acquisition are combined with other cash flows arising from its productive use. This combination is illustrated in the following section.

One must be sure that all costs necessary to make the investment operational are included in the initial-investment requirement. These costs include freight installations, sales taxes, new components, modifications in buildings, roads, fences, etc., as well as the cost of the asset. They may not all occur in the initial period. Later outlays must be reflected in the periods when they occur.

The trade-in or salvage value of a replaced asset should be subtracted from the purchase price of the new asset in determining net-investment cost. Only the net cash outflow associated with the new investment is relevant—the total purchase price plus installation charges less any trade-in—and, when applicable, the income taxes saved through capital losses on the old asset. For example, consider the replacement of an old machine by a new one that costs $15,000 at the factory. The old machine has a trade-in value of $5,000. Freight costs are $800 on the new machine. The net replacement cost is $15,000 + $800 − $5,000 = $10,800. If the machine is financed with a 25 percent downpayment of equity capital and 75 percent debt, then the initial equity outlay is $2,700.

Net Cash Flows

All capital budgeting methods require some measure of expected future returns for each investment alternative. In the NPV and IRR methods, net cash flow from the business rather than accounting profits is used as the measure of returns. Net cash flows include all cash inflows relating to an enterprise and all cash outflows for operating expenses, capital expenditures, income taxes, and financing. Thus, a net cash inflow is the stream of cash that the owner can withdraw for consumption or reinvestment elsewhere.

Cash flows are not identical with profits or income as derived from an income statement. In fact, changes in income can occur without any corresponding changes in cash flows. This occurs because the accrual accounting system (Chapter 3) differs from a cash basis of accounting. Receipts and expenses are assigned to the fiscal year in which they are earned or incurred rather than when they are received or paid for in cash. Annual depreciation and inventory changes are examples of income statement items which do not directly represent cash flows. However, it is still important to determine the depreciation and other changes in accounting income, since they determine the income tax obligation—a cash flow item.

Under the returns to equity approach, cash flows also account for borrowing and debt repayments associated with the investment. These financing terms can influence investment profitability and modify, often substantially, the pattern of net cash flows. If the machine described in the preceding section were purchased for cash, the initial investment would be $10,800. Thus, $10,800 would enter as a cash outflow at time zero (n = 0). Suppose, however, that the machine were purchased with a 25 percent downpayment or equity commitment, with the debt repaid in three equal annual installments. Only −$2,700 would enter the cash flow for n = 0. Additional entries of −$2,700 for each of the next three years (n = 1, n = 2, n = 3) would cover annual repayments on principal. Interest on the loan would also be added as a cash outflow.

In addition to cash outlays to pay for the assets, most capital investments also affect annual operating costs and receipts. However, some farm investments are cost-reducing rather than output-increasing. A new milk-handling system might permit the reduction of one employee in a large dairy operation, thus saving $6,000 in wages. If the cash-operating expenses for the machine are $1,000, the annual net reduction in cash outflow is $5,000. When several cost-reducing investments are compared, the choice criterion is then the *minimum* net present value of cash outlays. Similarly, a farm manager may be considering investments in buildings or machinery where each investment has about the same effect on revenue but involves different investment requirements and operating costs. In these cases, the analysis can ignore the returns, since they are assumed to be equal. The object is again to select the investment with the lowest present value of projected cash outflows.

We stress that only future cash flows are relevant. Past records are relevant only insofar as they can guide projections of the future. However, the historical data must be supplemented by new information regarding expected prices, costs of production, changes in technology, etc. Accounting for the effects of inflation on revenues and expenses is also important. Most capital budgets involve payment series projected using "nominal" values. Thus they include the effects of inflation.

It is also important to include income taxes in projections of future cash flows. At high levels of income, before-tax income may differ substantially from after-tax income. After-tax income is the important measure. Not all cash outflows are tax deductible. New asset purchases and principal payments on debt fall into this category. Similarly, not all cash inflows generate taxable income. The sale of an asset at its depreciated value or a payment received on a debt owed the business is a nontaxable inflow. Finally, some tax-deductible items are not part of the cash flow. The most notable example is depreciation.

To summarize, the payment series involves the projection of nominal net cash flows that are specified after payment of taxes, interest, and loan principal.

Terminal Value

At the end of the manager's planning horizon, the assets involved in the investment may have a terminal or residual value. For depreciable assets such as machinery, this is often considered a salvage value. Some appreciation in value may also occur, resulting in capital gains at the end of the planning period. This has been true historically for farm land..

If the manager foresees that part or all of the investment could be liquidated to recover a salvage value, then the terminal value should be included as an expected cash inflow in the final year of the payment series. Only the equity portion should be included. Any debt outstanding against the assets should be repaid when they are sold. Moreover, the tax effects of capital gains or losses must also be included.

The Discount Rate

One of the dominant variables affecting present values is the discount, or interest, rate. For these capital budgeting procedures, this rate is a firm's required rate-of-return on its equity capital. It is best understood as an opportunity cost. Thus, the relevant cost of capital for a particular investment is the rate such equity capital could earn in its most favorable alternative use.

The interest rate (i) used in capital budgeting is generally considered to contain three components: a risk-free rate (i_t) for time preference, a risk premium (i_r) reflecting the riskiness of the expected net cash flows, and an inflation premium (i_f) reflecting an anticipated rate of inflation. Hence, the interest rate (i) is expressed in general terms as:

$$i = f(i_t, i_r, i_f).$$

The next chapter will further develop the premiums for risk and inflation and show how these effects are included in capital budgets.

The Planning Horizon

Analyzing an investment in durable assets requires a multiyear planning horizon, since these assets influence cash flows for several years. One factor influencing the relevant length of planning horizon is the productive life of the assets. Good estimates of productive life for most durable assets are available from engineering data. Of course, land that is properly maintained has an infinite lifetime, unless a significant change in land use occurs (e.g., urbanization).

The discounting process also influences the relevant length of planning horizon. The mathematics of discounting implies the declining present value of economic events far in the future. Moreover, the higher the discount rate, the lower the present value. Thus, an economically relevant planning horizon can be thought of as the time span needed to make a decision for the first period. A future event is irrelevant at present if it can assume any expected value, but yet be of no importance for determining actions during the first period. Suppose, for example, that an investor expects the value of a tract of land to be $100,000 in a future year, although the potential variation of the land's value is from $90,000 to $110,000—a $20,000 range. If the discount rate is 14 percent and the planning period is 10 years in length, the present value of this range is $5,395. For a 15-year period, the present value of the variation is $2,802, and for a 20-year period the present value of the variation is $1,455. As the planning period lengthens, the present value of the expected variation of land value becomes smaller and of decreasing importance.

An economically relevant planning horizon may also be influenced by the investor's risk preferences. Adding a risk premium to the interest rate tends to shorten the planning horizon. The greater the risk, the shorter the economically relevant horizon. Accurate and comprehensive forward planning should help to dispel the tendency of uncertainty to shorten planning horizons.

Capital Budgeting Application

The logic and method of capital budgeting under alternative financing methods are illustrated in the following investment situation. Consider a cash-grain farmer who is investing in a hog farrow-finish enterprise to expand the size of the operation. Numerous systems of hog production are available and should be evaluated; however, we will consider a confinement hog operation. It is a capital-intensive system that utilizes the latest technology in feed distribution, waste disposal, and animal care. The system has a capacity of 240 litters per year with 40 sows farrowing every two months.

The investment is evaluated, using the net present-value and internal-rate-of-return methods, for two types of financing. One is a cash purchase of the initial investment, using only the investor's equity capital. The other method assumes that the investor uses that equity capital to finance one-fourth of the initial investment and borrows the remaining three-fourths with an intermediate-term loan. The analysis requires the following data:

1. *Initial Investment*

   The initial investment totals $140,000, with $90,000 required for buildings, $38,000 for equipment, and $12,000 for livestock. We will assume that the appropriate rates of the Accelerated Cost Recovery System are used to depreciate the equipment and buildings (5 years) and breeding livestock (3 years) for tax purposes, and that an investment tax credit of $13,520 is available immediately. Thus the net outlay is $126,480, leaving a depreciable basis of $11,640 in livestock and $121,600 in equipment and buildings.[1]

---

[1] Income tax laws in the United States currently allow a 6 percent tax credit (ITC) on property in the three-year life class and a 10 percent (ITC) on property in the five-year class. The depreciable basis of the property is then reduced by 50 percent of the ITC claimed.

2. Planning Horizon

The investor uses a 10-year planning horizon.

3. Terminal Value

The terminal value in year 10 is projected to be $21,000 and is fully taxable at ordinary income tax rates.

4. Required-Rate-of-Return

The investor stipulates 15 percent as a required-rate-of-return without the use of debt financing and 20 percent as the required return with the use of debt financing (the higher rate reflects the greater financial risk from leveraging).

5. Net Cash Flows

Net cash flows to the investor are determined by deducting projected operating expenses, income tax obligations, and, where appropriate, principal and interest payments from projected operating receipts in each year of the planning period. The initial investment, net of investment tax credit, is a negative cash outflow at present. The terminal value is considered part of the cash flow in the final period. Table 10.4 indicates projected operating receipts, expenses, taxes, and net cash flow to the investor over the 10-year period. In response to inflation, both the operating receipts and expenses are expected to increase at a 5 percent annual rate. For simplicity, an income tax rate of 20 percent is assumed.

Table 10.4 shows a worksheet approach to estimating the net cash flow for the cash purchase (line 10). This is the series of payments to be discounted to a net present value. Annual net cash flow without debt financing is the sum of operating receipts and capital sales less operating expenses and income taxes paid. Income tax obligations are derived from taxable income, which is found by deducting operating expenses and depreciation from operating receipts.

Net present values are calculated with equation (10.4):

$$\text{NPV} = -\text{INV} + \sum_{n=1}^{n} \frac{P_n}{(1+i)^n} + \frac{V_N}{(1+i)^N}$$

Table 10.4 Projections of Net Cash Flows for Hog Enterprise Without External Financing

Item	0	1	2	3	4	5	6	7	8	9	10
						Years					
1. Operating Receipts		158,000	165,900	174,195	182,905	192,050	201,652	211,735	222,322	233,438	245,110
2. Terminal Value											21,000
3. Total Cash Inflow (line 1 + 2)		158,000	165,900	174,195	182,905	192,050	201,652	211,735	222,322	233,438	266,110
4. Initial Equity	126,480										
5. Operating Expenses		130,000	136,500	143,325	150,491	158,016	165,917	174,212	182,923	192,069	201,673
6. Depreciation		21,150	31,175	29,837	25,536	25,536					
7. Taxable Income (line 3 − 5 − 6)		6,850	−1,775	1,033	6,878	8,498	35,735	37,523	39,399	41,369	64,437
8. Income Taxes (line 7 × t)		1,370	−355	207	1,376	1,700	7,147	7,505	7,880	8,274	12,887
9. Total Cash Outflow (line 4 + 5 + 8)	126,480	131,370	136,145	143,532	151,867	159,716	173,064	181,715	190,803	200,343	214,560
10. Net Cash Flow (line 3 − 9)	−126,480	26,630	29,755	30,663	31,038	32,334	28,588	30,020	31,519	33,095	51,550

which, when applying a discount rate of i = .15 to the net cash flows in Table 10.5, yields:

$$NPV = -126,480 + \frac{26,630}{1.15} + \frac{29,755}{(1.15)^2} + \ldots + \frac{51,550}{(1.15)^{10}}$$

$$= 29,257.$$

Similarly, the internal-rate-of-return is found with equation (10.6) and turns out to be 20.47 percent. Hence the hog enterprise is an acceptable investment based on the positive net present value for a 15 percent discount rate and based on the IRR, which exceeds the required-rate-of-return.

Table 10.5 projects cash flows for the situation with external debt financing. The basic difference from Table 10.4 is that net cash flows are calculated after the payments for interest and principal on the loan are accounted for. The following financing terms are specified. The investor's initial equity requirement is one-fourth of the initial investment, or $31,620. The investor obtains an intermediate-term loan for $94,860, payable in 10 equal annual amortized installments of $19,993, based on an interest rate of 16.5 percent. The loan's amortization schedule (annual interest and principal) is shown in lines 7 and 8 of Table 10.5.

Annual net cash flow, as projected in line 12, is now the sum of operating receipts and terminal value less operating expenses, income taxes, principal, and interest paid in each year of the planning horizon. Interest (line 7) is calculated as 16.5 percent of the remaining loan balance, as adjusted by principal payments (line 8) made in previous years. Income tax obligations are derived from taxable income (line 9), which is found by deducting operating expenses, depreciation, and interest from operating receipts.

Applying a discount rate of i = .20 and equation (10.4) to the net cash flows in Table 10.5 yields:

$$NPV = -31,620 + \frac{9,767}{1.20} + \frac{12,749}{(1.20)^2} + \ldots + \frac{32,123}{(1.20)^{10}}$$

$$= 23,552.$$

Similarly, the internal-rate-of-return is 37.82 percent. Hence, the hog enterprise is again judged profitable under this financing arrangement for both methods of capital budgeting.

Notice, however, that the use of external financing, or borrowing, raises the internal-rate-of-return from 20.47 percent to 37.82 per-

Table 10.5. Projections of Net Cash Flows for Hog Enterprise with External Financing

Item	Years										
	0	1	2	3	4	5	6	7	8	9	10
1. Operating Receipts		158,000	165,900	174,195	182,905	192,050	201,652	211,735	222,322	233,438	245,110
2. Terminal Value											21,000
3. Total Cash Inflow (1 + 2)		158,000	165,900	174,195	182,905	192,050	201,652	211,735	222,322	233,438	266,110
4. Initial Equity	31,620										
5. Operating Expenses		130,000	136,500	143,325	150,491	158,016	165,917	174,212	182,923	192,069	201,673
6. Depreciation		21,150	31,175	29,837	25,536	25,536					
7. Loan Interest		15,652	14,936	14,101	13,129	11,996	10,677	9,140	7,349	5,263	2,832
8. Loan Principal		4,341	5,057	5,892	6,864	7,997	9,316	10,853	12,644	14,730	17,161
9. Taxable Income (line 3 − 5 − 6 − 7)		−8,802	−16,711	−13,068	−6,251	−3,498	25,058	28,383	32,050	36,106	61,605
10. Income taxes (line 9 × t)		−1,760	−3,342	−2,614	−1,250	−700	5,012	5,677	6,410	7,221	12,321
11. Total Cash Outflow (line 4 + 5 + 7 + 8 + 10)	31,620	148,233	153,151	160,704	169,234	177,309	190,922	199,882	209,326	219,283	233,987
12. Net Cash Flow (line 3 − 11)	31,620	9,767	12,749	13,491	13,671	14,741	10,730	11,853	12,996	14,155	32,123

cent. Moreover, if we use the same discount rate to evaluate both types of financing, the net present value increases for debt financing. For example, using a 20 percent rate, the net present value is $2,104 without external financing and $23,552 with external financing.

Why does the change in type of financing alter the profitability? The answer involves the principles of leveraging and the cost relationships between debt and equity capital. For the 20 percent required return on equity, leveraging increased the investment's profitability, because lower cost (16.5 percent) debt capital was, in effect, being substituted for higher-cost equity. Moreover, the tax savings on payments of loan interest make debt a still lower-cost source of financing on an after-tax basis. In this case, a before-tax interest rate on debt of 16.5 percent is equivalent to an after-tax rate of 13.20 percent, reflecting the 20 percent tax rate.

Of course, the principles of leverage involve more than the profitability effects. Financial risks increase, and the firm's liquidity tends to decrease as more debt is used relative to equity capital. Thus, the increase in profitability from leveraging is accompanied by greater risk. For the hog example, business risks are already high due to possible unanticipated variations in prices, production, disease, and so on. Leveraging magnifies these business risks because the fixed repayment obligations increase the variation of returns to the equity investor and raise the potential loss of equity. Moreover, borrowing depletes the firm's credit reserve and can hamper repayment capacity on later investment projects.

Thus, these capital budgeting methods indeed generate useful information for decision making. However, the numbers themselves do not make decisions—people do! Clearly, factors such as risk and liquidity need consideration along with the profitibility measures.

Topics for Discussion

1. Contrast and critique the net present value and internal rate of return methods of capital budgeting. What are their similarities and differences? Advantages and disadvantages? Which is generally preferred in capital budgeting?
2. Under what conditions is the payback period a useful capital budgeting method?
3. Explain why changes in discount rates may influence the ranking and profitability of several investment alternatives.
4. Explain the alternative ways of accounting for financing transactions in capital budgets.

5. Discuss some of the problems in obtaining high-quality data for capital budgeting analysis. What kinds of information do managers need to make better investment and financing decisions in their businesses?

6. A farmer is considering replacing a labor-intensive machine system with a more capital-intensive one. He estimates that adopting the new system will increase machinery operating expenses by about $1,000 per year but will replace one hired laborer, whose annual salary is $6,000. The new machinery costs $30,000; however, the trade-in value of the old system is $10,000. Adopting the new machinery will increase annual depreciation by $4,000.

   Further data indicate an eight-year planning horizon, zero salvage value, a 20 percent tax rate, and a 10 percent after-tax cost of equity capital. Please use the net present-value method to evaluate the new machinery system's profitability.

7. A new hog investment requires an initial outlay of $50,000 and is expected to yield annual net cash flows of $8,850 over the investor's 10-year planning horizon. Assuming no salvage value, no taxes, and a 10 percent discount rate, evaluate the investment's profitability using the net present value and internal-rate-of-return methods.

8. In problem 7, determine how the net present value and internal-rate-of-return are influenced by the following financing terms: 20 percent equity downpayment with repayment of the loan balance in eight equal annual principal payments plus interest charged at 8 percent annually on the outstanding loan balance.

9. Suppose the hog investor is in the 30 percent tax bracket. How will this tax obligation influence the capital budgeting results?

10. A large investment company is analyzing the profitability of a farming investment for one of its corporate clients. The investment requires a $10 million outlay to acquire the necessary assets and is projected to yield an annual payment flow of $2 million (before interest payments) over a 20-year horizon.

    The analysts figure a 16 percent cost of equity capital, a 14 percent cost of debt capital, a 20 percent salvage value (of the initial outlay), financing by a bond sale at the 14 percent rate with principal due at the end of the twentieth year, and constant financial leverage as indicated by the corporation's equity-to-asset ratio of .5.

    a. What capital budgeting method would you use to evaluate this investment, and why?

    b. Show clearly how you would set up the capital budgeting model, and show its solution.

    c. Explain your procedures for handling the investment's financing plan.

11. Cletus Farmer is offered the opportunity to invest $5,000 with a promise of receiving $5,700 one year later. His response is: "I reject this investment. I have only $1,000 of my own money, and for a $4,000 loan the bank wants 10 percent interest so that my net return would be only $5,300. Would you be satisfied with a 6 percent return these days?" Did Cletus make the right decision? Critique his analytical approach.

12. Two mutually exclusive investments have projected cash flows as follows:

| | Period | | | | |
Investment	0	1	2	3	4
A. Cropland	–$10,000	5,000	5,000	5,000	5,000
B. Forest land	–$10,000	0	0	0	30,000

    a. Assuming a required-rate-of-return of 10 percent, determine the net present value for each investment.

    b. Determine the internal-rate-of-return for each investment.

    c. Which investment would you select? Why? What assumptions influenced your decision?.

References

1. Aplin, R. D., G. L. Casler, and C. P. Francis, *Capital Investment Analysis*, 2nd ed., Grid, Inc., Columbus, Ohio, 1979.
2. Bierman, H., Jr., and S. Smidt, *The Capital Budgeting Decision: Economic Analysis of Investment Projects*, 5th ed., Macmillan Publishing Co., Inc., 1980.
3. Boudreaux, K. J., and H. W. Long, *The Basic Theory of Corporate Finance*, Prentice-Hall, Inc., Englewood Cliffs, New Jersey, 1977.
4. Brealey, R., and S. Myers, *Principles of Corporate Finance*, McGraw-Hill Book Company, New York, 1981.
5. Brigham, E. F., *Financial Management: Theory and Practice*, 3rd ed., Dryden Press, Hinsdale, Illinois, 1982.
6. Copeland, T. E., and J. F. Weston, *Financial Theory and Corporate Policy*, Addison-Wesley Publishing Co., Inc., Reading, Massachusetts, 1979.
7. Haley, C. W., and L. D. Schall, *Theory of Financial Decisions*, 2nd ed., McGraw-Hill Book Company, New York, 1979.
8. Hirshleifer, J., *Investment, Interest and Capital*, Prentice-Hall, Inc., Englewood Cliffs, New Jersey, 1970.
9. Levy, H., and M. Sarnat, *Capital Investment and Financial Decisions*, Prentice-Hall, Inc., Englewood Cliffs, New Jersey, 1982.
10. Van Horne, J. C., *Financial Management and Policy*, 5th ed., Prentice-Hall, Inc., Englewood Cliffs, New Jersey, 1980.
11. Weston, J. F., and E. F. Brigham, *Essentials of Managerial Finance*, 6th ed., Dryden Press, Hinsdale, Illinois, 1982.

Chapter 11

CAPITAL BUDGETING:
INFLATION, RISK,
AND FINANCIAL PLANNING

In this chapter we extend the capital budgeting concepts to account for the effects of inflation and risk, and to evaluate an investment's financial feasibility. Procedures are also established to evaluate recurring investments with different economic lives. All these extensions make the capital budgeting procedures more complex. However, the effects of inflation, risk, leverage, and financing arrangements have become very important for financial management in agriculture. They must be carefully considered in long-term financial planning.

Inflation and Capital Budgeting

A basic principle of capital budgeting is to consistently account for the effects of inflation both on the flow of payments and on the discount rates used to determine present values. Both of these components of capital budgeting are influenced by inflation. As the following discussion will show, the effects of expected inflation on capital budgeting can occur in one of two ways. One way is to project cash flows in real terms and discount the projected cash flows to present values using a real interest rate that is free of any effects of inflation. A second way is to project cash flows in nominal terms and discount the projected cash flows to present values with an interest rate that includes a premium for inflation. We develop these approaches as follows.

Inflation Concepts

Inflation refers to an increase in the general level of prices for all goods and services in an economy. In contrast, deflation is a decline in the general price level. A rate of inflation refers to the percentage rate of increase (e.g., 6 percent, 7 percent) in the general price level. Most countries develop one or more indexes for measuring inflation. In the United States the consumer-price index and the gross national product (GNP) deflator are commonly used measures.

A positive rate of inflation means (1) the purchasing power of a projected constant payment declines annually by the designated rate of inflation or (2) the nominal or money value of the projected constant payment increases annually by the designated rate of inflation. "Nominal" or "money" values are the actual amount of dollars or other currency comprising the cash flows. In contrast, "real" values reflect the purchasing power today of future cash flows. Real values are found by adjusting nominal values for the rate of inflation.

The process of converting from nominal to real values, or vice versa, uses the same discounting and compounding techniques developed earlier. The main difference is that the inflation rate is used instead of the compound rate of interest for time. We will illustrate these effects in two ways. The first example shows how inflation affects nominal values of future cash flows. The second example shows how *real present values* are found by discounting for *both* inflation and time.

Suppose that the expected annual rate of inflation is 7 percent. For an investment with annual cash flows that respond to inflation, the nominal values of the cash flows increase annually by the factor $(1 + i_f)$. Hence a projected payment of $100 is increased to $100 (1.07) = $107.00 in one year, $100(1.07)^2 = 114.49$ in two years, and so on, to account for inflation. This process uses the future-value formula, although the compound rate (i_f) is the expected rate of inflation rather than the interest rate for time.

Now, suppose an investment has cash flows already projected in nominal terms. Let the investment occur in an annuity, loan, or other fixed-payment financial asset. Under these conditions, an annual inflation rate of 7 percent implies that the purchasing power of the fixed payment declines annually by 7 percent. Thus, the real value, or purchasing power, of a $100 payment received in one year is $P_1/(1 + i_f) = \$100/1.07 = \$93.46$.

Note that real values are not the same as present values. To determine present values, real values must be discounted again at the time preference rate, or at the time preference rate plus a premium for risk. If the time preference rate is 5 percent, then the real present value of the $100 payment is $93.46/1.05 = $89.01.

Modeling Inflation Effects

Finding real present values involves a double-discounting procedure that accounts for both inflation and time. It is expressed as follows for payment P_1 due one year in the future:

$$V_o = \frac{\dfrac{P_1}{(1 + i_f)}}{(1 + i_t)} = \frac{P_1}{(1 + i_t)(1 + i_f)} = \frac{P_1}{1 + i_t + i_f + i_t i_f} \qquad \textbf{(11.1)}$$

The multiplicative term $(i_t i_f)$ in the denominator increases the complexity of this present-value model. Assuming that $i_t = .05$ and $i_f = .07$, the discount factor is:

$$\frac{100}{1 + .05 + .07 + (.05)(.07)} = \frac{100}{1.1235} = 89.01$$

To illustrate further, investment B in Table 10.1 indicated a uniform series of $5,800 payments over a five-year period and an initial investment of $20,000. Suppose that the projected payments are nominal values, the rate for time and risk $(i_t + i_r)$ is 8 percent, and a 4 percent annual rate of inflation is expected. The procedures for finding the real net present value (NPV_r) are outlined in Table 11.1 and are indicated in model form as:

$$NPV_r = -20,000 + \frac{5,800}{(1.04)(1.08)} + \frac{5,800}{(1.04)^2(1.08)^2} \qquad \textbf{(11.2)}$$

$$+ \frac{5,800}{(104)^3(1.08)^3} + \frac{5,800}{(1.04)^4(1.08)^4} + \frac{5,800}{(1.04)^5(1.08)^5}$$

$$= 742.$$

The real net present value is $742. Hence, it is still a profitable investment.

Often the discount factor for finding real net present values is approximated by simply adding together the rates for time and inflation. As is evident in equation (11.1), adding i_t and i_f to yield a discount factor $(1 + i_t + i_f)$ ignores the multiplicative term $(i_t i_f)$. As a result, this approximation procedure slightly underestimates the actual discount rate and therefore overestimates real present values.

To illustrate, suppose the projected nominal net cash flows in Table 11.1 are discounted by the factor $1/(1.12)^n$ rather than $1/(1.04)^n(1.08)^n$. The resulting real net present value is \$907.70, which exceeds the \$742 real net present value found in equation (11.2).

The overestimation of real net present values increases as the rates of inflation and time preference increase. The overestimates could be significant for investments with very lengthy and large net cash flows. Nonetheless, for most investments, simply adding the rates for inflation and time for discounting purposes is satisfactory.

Table 11.1 Real Net Present Value

Year	Nominal Net Cash Flow	Real Net Cash Flow	Real Net Present Flow
0	\$-20,000	\$-20,000	\$-20,000
1	5,800	$5,800/ 1.04 = 5,577$	$5,577/ 1.08 = 5,164$
2	5,800	$5,800/(1.04)^2 = 5,362$	$5,362/(1.08)^2 = 4,597$
3	5,800	$5,800/(1.04)^3 = 5,156$	$5,156/(1.08)^3 = 4,093$
4	5,800	$5,800/(1.04)^4 = 4,958$	$4,958/(1.08)^4 = 3,644$
5	5,800	$5,800/(1.04)^5 = 4,767$	$4,767/(1.08)^5 = 3,244$

Real net present value = \$742

Capital Budgeting Procedures

We can now restate the general principle for capital budgeting under inflation conditions: both the payment series and the discount rate must be specified either in nominal values or in real values, but not in both values concurrently. If the payments are projected in real terms, they must be discounted with a real rate. If the payments are projected in nominal terms, they must be discounted with a nominal rate, that includes an inflation premium. It is inappropriate to discount a payment series specified in real (nominal) terms at an interest rate specified in nominal (real) terms.

In practice, is it better to use real or nominal values? Using nominal values is likely more common. Market interest rates already contain a premium for anticipated inflation that protects the lender's debt claim from loss in its purchasing power. The payment series may also have several cost and return items that respond differently to inflation, and debt servicing requirements are specified in nominal terms. Finally, income tax obligations are based on nominal values rather than real values. Thus, it is important to reflect anticipated inflation in the payment series, if the discount rate is based on market interest rates.

Inflation and Present Values

To show how projections in real or nominal values lead to the same present value, we specify an investment situation in which the payment series and the discount rate respond equally to a constant inflation rate i_f. Let P_o be the current payment and assume that it was just paid; thus it does not enter the present value computations. The series of payments starts with the first year-end payment $P_1 = P_o (1 + i_f)$, followed by the second payment $P_2 = P_o(1 + i_f)^2$, and so on. The discount factor is based on a nominal rate, i, which contains a real rate for time, i_t, and the inflation premium. Following the double discounting concept, the discount factor is expressed as:

$$1 + i = 1 + i_t + i_f + i_t i_f = (1 + i_t)(1 + i_f). \tag{11.3}$$

For a perpetual series of payments, the present value model is formulated in nominal terms as:

$$V_o = \frac{P_o (1 + i_f)}{(1 + i_t)(1 + i_f)} + \frac{P_o(1 + i_f)^2}{(1 + i_t)^2(1 + i_f)^2} \tag{11.4}$$

$$+ \frac{P_o(1 + i_f)^3}{(1 + i_t)^3(1 + i_f)^3} + \ldots$$

Cancelling the expressions for the inflation adjustment in the numerator and denominator reduces the model to real terms:

$$V_o = \frac{P_o}{1 + i_t} + \frac{P_o}{(1 + i_t)^2} + \frac{P_o}{(1 + i_t)^3} + \ldots \tag{11.5}$$

Since this expression involves the present value of an infinite uniform series, it further reduces to:

$$V_o = \frac{P_o}{i_t}. \tag{11.6}$$

Hence, anticipated inflation has no effect on the present value, V_o, at the current time. This present value is simultaneously valued in both real and nominal terms. This makes intuitive sense, because at any time the present value is the amount for which assets can be "cashed in" and represents their purchasing power at current prices.

Inflation does, however, cause the anticipated present value to increase from period to period at the inflation rate i_f, assuming of course that the asset markets are highly efficient and that all other factors stay constant. This change in value is shown by valuing the payment series one period later:

$$V_1 = \frac{P_o(1 + i_f)^2}{(1 + i_t)(1 + i_f)} + \frac{P_o(1 + i_f)^3}{(1 + i_t)^2(1 + i_f)^2} + \ldots \quad (11.7)$$

Cancelling terms and reducing yields

$$V_1 = \frac{P_o(1 + i_f)}{i_t}. \quad (11.8)$$

Recall from (11.6) that $V_o = P_o/i_t$. Thus $V_1 = V_o(1 + i_f)$, which means that the present value in period 1 equals the present value in period o, adjusted for the rate of inflation.

These modeling concepts provide the basis for capital budgeting under inflation and for practical tests about the effects of inflation and other factors on investment and asset values. These concepts underlie the detailed examples of capital budgeting in other chapters.

Risk and Capital Budgeting

To this point, we have assumed complete certainty in the projections of investment performance and cash flows. The net cash flows for each future period have been single-valued projections arising from our best estimate of future outcomes. However, in earlier chapters we identified sources of business and financial risk in agriculture, evaluated their impacts on managerial goals, and considered management responses to risks. The effects of risks are even more pronounced in long-term investment decisions. Hence, accounting for risks in capital budgeting is an important part of investment analysis.

Adjusting the Discount Rate

So far, the discount rate has solely reflected an investor's time preference and an inflation premium. It has been considered a risk-free rate. However, when investments are known to be risky and the investor is risk averse, a simple method of accounting for risk in capital budgeting is to add a risk premium to the risk-free rate. Now the discount rate i has three components—the risk-free rate for time preference i_t, an inflation premium i_f, and the risk premium i_r. The risk premium is the investor's reward for risk bearing; it reflects the difference in rates-of-return required on a risky versus a safe investment.

Adding the risk premium increases the discount rate, thus reducing an investment's net present value. Consider an investment proposal requiring $8,000 initially and returning $2,500 per year for four years. At a risk-free rate of 8 percent, the net present value of the cash flow stream is:

$$NPV = -8,000 + 2,500 \left[USPV_{.08,4} \right]$$
$$= -8,000 + 2,500 \left[3.3121 \right] = 280.25.$$

The positive net present value makes this investment favorable. If, however, a 4 percent risk premium is added to the 8 percent risk-free rate in response to the manager's perception of the investment risk, the net present value for a 12 percent discount rate declines to negative $406.75—an unacceptable level.

In small businesses, the choice of an appropriate risk premium is a subjective process. It must reflect both the investment risk and the investor's risk aversion. Investments may be subject to both business risk and financial risk. Business risk refers to the unanticipated variability of the investment's returns and how these returns are correlated with other business enterprises. Higher variability means greater risk, and thus a greater risk premium. The variability could be offset, however, by low or even negative correlation of an investment's returns with the returns of other assets. In this case, the investment is a good source of diversification and may warrant a lower risk premium.

Financial risk arises from using debt capital to finance an investment. It is expressed by greater variability of returns to equity capital and reductions in liquid reserves of credit and financial assets. Investments financed with debt capital may warrant a higher risk premium to reflect the greater financial risk.

In practice, managers may let their experience help to formulate risk premiums that reflect their risk attitudes and the level of investment risk. Historic data may be helpful since risky enterprises on average yield higher rates-of-return. Some managers define several risk classes for investments, each with a designated risk premium or required rate-of-return. New investments are assigned to the "most suitable" risk class for capital budgeting analysis using the appropriate risk-adjusted discount rate.

Certainty-Equivalent Approach

Some analysts opt for a risk-free discount rate in capital budgeting, adjusting for risk in the numerator or cash flows of the present-value model. This adjustment occurs by multiplying the cash flows (P_n) by a coefficient (α_n), having a value that varies inversely between zero and 1.0 with the degree of risk:

$$V_0 = \sum_{n = 0}^{N} \frac{\alpha_n P_n}{(1 + i)^n} \tag{11.9}$$

where $0 \le \alpha \le 1.0$.

The adjustment coefficient (α_n) makes an investment's projected cash flows equivalent to a completely certain cash flow. Hence, this method is called the *certainty-equivalent* approach.

For example, consider an expected net cash flow of $5,000 for a specific investment. The manager must designate a completely certain cash flow which is equivalent to this expected return. If $5,000 is designated, then $\alpha_n = 1.0$, and the investment is riskless. If $3,000 is designated, then α_n equals $3,000/5,000 = .6$. The smaller value of α_n indicates the larger risk associated with the projected returns. The same procedure determines the level of α_n in all future periods for each investment alternative. Consider an $8,000 investment yielding $2,500 per year for four years. Let's assume that risk increases with time so that $\alpha_0 = 1.0$; $\alpha_1 = .95$; $\alpha_2 = 90$; $\alpha_3 = .85$; $\alpha_4 = .80$. The risk-free rate is 8 percent. The investment's net present value is:

$$NPV = -8,000 + \frac{(.95)(2,500)}{1.08} + \frac{(.90)(2,500)}{(1.08)^2} + \frac{(.85)(2,500)}{(1.08)^3}$$

$$+ \frac{(.80)(2,500)}{(1.08)^4}$$

$$= -715.$$

On a certainty-equivalent basis the project is rejected, as it was using the risk-adjusted discount rate method.

The certainty-equivalent approach is conceptually similar to the risk-premium approach. In fact, we can determine the risk-adjusted discount rate that is comparable to the values of α_n. This rate is the discount rate that equates the net present value of the payment series to $-\$715.00$. This discount rate is 14 percent. Hence, the risk premium is 6 percent—the difference between the 8 percent risk-free rate and the 14 percent risk-adjusted rate.

Both the certainty-equivalent and the risk-premium approaches consider the adjustment in returns needed to make an investor feel indifferent between a risky and a safe investment. Hence, the designation of a certainty-equivalent income is subjective, as is the choice of risk-premium. In both methods, the investor must express the risk aversion by a quantitative measure based on limited judgment. One important difference in the two methods occurs because the risk-adjusted discount rate implies that risks increase exponentially over time, even when the discount rate is constant. Despite their subjective bases, for most purposes, these two methods are the most practical ways of including risk in capital budgeting.

Probability Analysis

A more comprehensive approach to risk analysis in capital budgeting uses probability distributions to measure risks. Recall from the risk section of Chapter 2 that risk measures should reflect how an investor perceives risk. We assumed that risks are perceived as *probability distributions* and that investors express their expectations in probabilistic terms. These distributions are used to estimate three statistical measures—expected value, standard deviation, and coefficient of variation—which help describe an investment's risk. Formulas (2.2), (2.3), and (2.4) and the related text describe these risk measures.

To illustrate probability analysis in capital budgeting, assume the manager uses a risk-free rate to derive net present values for two investments under three kinds of forecasts: optimistic, most likely, and pessimistic. Moreover, the manager has assigned probabilities to each forecast. The basis for the probabilities could be historic performance or personal judgments based on outlook information, advice from peers or other experts, or even a "hunch." The result is the

Table 11.2. Probability Distribution of Net Present Values (NPV) for Two Investments

Forecast	Investment 1		Investment 2	
	V_i	P_i	V_i	P_i
Optimistic	$19,000	.30	$27,000	.10
Most Likely	15,000	.40	20,000	.60
Pessimistic	12,000	.30	11,000	.30

discrete probability distribution of net present values shown in Table 11.2.

Using equation (2.2.), the expected net present values are:

$$E\overline{V}_1 = (.30)(19,000) + (.40)(15,000) + (.30)(12,000) = 15,300$$

$$E\overline{V}_2 = (.10)(27,000) + (.60)(20,000) + (.30)(11,000) = 18,000.$$

Note that the expected value of investment 2 is greater than that of investment 1; however, the standard deviation of investment 2 is also larger:

$$\sigma_1 = \left[(.30)(19,000 - 15,300)^2 + (.40)(15,000 - 15,300)^2 + (.30)(12,000 - 15,300)^2\right]^{1/2} = 2,722$$

$$\sigma_2 = \left[(.10)(27,000 - 18,000)^2 + (.60)(20,000 - 18,000)^2 + (.30)(11,000 - 18,000)^2\right]^{1/2} = 5,020.$$

The relative risks of the two investments are indicated by their coefficients of variation.

$$CV_1 = \frac{\sigma_1}{E(\overline{V})_1} = \frac{2,722}{15,300} = .178$$

$$CV_2 = \frac{\sigma_2}{E(\overline{V})_2} = \frac{5,020}{18,000} = .279.$$

Since the CV for investment 2 is larger, it is the riskier venture. The higher CV indicates greater relative dispersion of outcomes around the expected value. Thus, the likelihood of loss may be greater. The choice between these two investments depends on the manager's risk-return preference. A highly risk-averse manager might prefer investment 1; a less risk-averse manager might prefer investment 2.

This method of analyzing risks could be extended by estimating probability distributions for returns in each year and for each relevant factor determining cash flows (i.e., variations in prices and production). Both expected values and standard deviations could then be discounted to present values. These methods are complex. However, managers who consider this risk framework—expected returns, probabilities, risk aversion—should have a sound basis for decision making.

Financial Feasibility of Single Investments

Financial feasibility analysis for single investments uses present-value methods to test the effects of variations in loan length, interest rate, loan size, and level of payment on the investment's ability to meet these financing terms. If the terms are met, then the investment is judged financially feasible. If, however, the terms cannot be met, then the plans are financially infeasible, and actions to achieve feasibility must be undertaken.

Present-value methods are used because the cash flows associated with the investment occur over a number of years. Hence, the magnitude and timing of these cash flows are important factors influencing financial feasibility. To illustrate, recall the formula for the present value of a uniform series of annual payments:

$$V_o = A[USPV_{i,N}]$$

where V_o = present value

   A = the annual cash flow per period

   i = the interest rate per period

   N = the number of conversion periods.

In financial feasibility analysis the four data in this formula reflect the financing terms associated with the investment. Variable V_o represents the size of loan, A is the level of debt payment, i is the loan interest rate, and N is the length of loan. Variations in values of each variable will influence financial feasibility.

One approach to evaluating financial feasibility is to assume that three of the four data requirements are known. The value of the fourth variable can then be derived. Hence, total-loan size can be determined and evaluated if annual-loan payments, interest rate, and loan length are known. Similarly, the annual-loan payment can be evaluated if the loan size, length, and interest are known. Or, the necessary loan length is found if loan size, interest rate, and annual payments are known. The feasibility of the interest rate can be similarly evaluated.

To illustrate, consider an agricultural producer who is improving pasture land and expanding a beef cow herd by 100 cows. The budget indicates that $20,000 of net-cash income is available each year for debt servicing, consumption, or other uses. This is part of the information needed to evaluate the financial feasibility of the investment. Additional information includes loan size, interest rate, and loan length. Suppose that the investor formulates estimates for two of these variables. The evaluation is as follows:

Case A

The beef investor projects the application of $20,000 annually to debt servicing. For an annual interest rate of 14 percent and a seven-year loan, what is the maximum size loan that can be serviced?

Model

$$V_o = \$20,000[\,USPV_{.14,7}\,]$$
$$= 20,000[\,4.2883\,]$$
$$= 85,766$$

Answer: $85,766.

Evaluation

If a loan greater than $85,766 is needed, then the investment is financially infeasible.

Case B

What is the annual debt (principal and interest) payment on a loan of $85,766 per acre with an interest rate of 14 percent and a seven-year maturity?

Model

$$85,766 = A[\,USPV_{.14,7}\,]$$
$$A = 20,000$$

Answer: $20,000 per year.

Evaluation

If less than $20,000 is available for debt servicing, then the investment is financially infeasible.

Case C

What is the maximum interest rate for a loan of $85,766 for seven years when $20,000 is available annually for debt servicing?

Model

$$85,766 = 20,000[USPV_{i,7}]$$

$$i = .14$$

Answer: 14 percent per year.

Evaluation

If the interest rate exceeds 14 percent, then the investment is financially infeasible.

Case D

What is the minimum length of loan needed for a loan of $85,766 when $20,000 is available annually for debt servicing and the interest rate is 14 percent?

Model

$$85,766 = 20,000[USPV_{.14,N}]$$

$$N = 7$$

Answer: 7 years.

Evaluation

If the available loan is less than seven years in length, then the investment is financially infeasible.

The financial feasibility analysis can be extended to evaluate how changes in values of one or more variables influence financial feasibility. Interactions or trade-offs among these variables can also be evaluated. Examples of possible trade-offs include reduction in interest rates as loan maturity is reduced, reduction in maturity as loan payments are larger, and reduction in interest rate as loan size is increased. Thus, one can jointly analyze these effects on financial feasibility.

Table 11.3 demonstrates analysis for selected values of i, N, A, and V_o. Suppose, for example, that the beef cow investor actually needs a loan in the amount of $100,000. The results of the feasibility analysis for i = 14 percent, N = seven years, and A = $20,000 indicated a maximum-loan size of $85,766. What are the options for achieving financial feasibility? One option, of course, is to reduce the total borrowing to $85,766. However, lower borrowing may not be possible. Other options include (1) lengthening the loan maturity beyond seven years, (2) increasing annual-debt servicing above $20,000, (3) lowering the interest rate below 14 percent, or (4) a combination of (1), (2), and (3).

As Table 11.3 demonstrates, increasing the loan maturity to eight years for i = 14 percent and A = $20,000 increases the loan size to $92,777. Or, increasing debt-servicing capacity to $22,000 with i = 14 percent and N = 7 increases loan size to $94,343. Or, lowering the interest rate to 12 percent for A = $20,000 and N = 7 increases loan size to $91,275. None of these changes yield financial feasibility. However, feasibility is attained by increasing A to $22,000 and lengthening N to 8 with i = 14 percent. Alternatively, feasibility is attained by lowering i to 12 percent and lengthening N to 9 with A = $20,000. Moreover, if payments increase to $22,000 and borrowing occurs at i = 12 percent, a loan of $109,288 could be serviced with an eight-year maturity. Other combinations of variables that provide feasibility can be found in Table 11.3. Moreover, many other values of i, N, A, and V_o can be evaluated.

These results clearly indicate that managers need to carefully

Table 11.3. Maximum Loan Size for Different Interest Rates, Loan Maturities, and Payment Levels

Loan Maturity	Interest Rates					
	12 Percent Payment Level		14 Percent Payment Level		16 Percent Payment Level	
Years	$ 20,000	$ 22,000	$ 20,000	$ 22,000	$ 20,000	$ 22,000
6	82,228	90,450	77,773	85,550	73,694	81,064
7	91,275	100,403	85,766	94,343	80,771	88,848
8	99,352	109,288	92,777	102,055	86,872	95,559
9	106,565	117,222	98,927	108,820	92,131	101,344
10	113,004	124,309	104,322	114,754	96,664	106,331

evaluate the financing terms available from their lenders and their debt-servicing capacity. More favorable financing terms increase the prospects for financial feasibility. In addition, managerial actions which increase yields, upgrade product quality, reduce costs, reduce other debt-servicing obligations, reduce family withdrawals, or increase profits in any other way will increase the serviceable size of loan.

Nonetheless, investments are still undertaken which appear financially infeasible at the outset. Clearly other factors must offset the apparent infeasibility. These factors likely include one or more of the following conditions:

1. The investor uses personal equity capital instead of or in addition to debt capital to finance the investment and is willing to accept a lower rate of return than the interest cost of using debt.
2. The investor has other sources of income which can be used to service debt.
3. The investor obtains more favorable financing terms than those budgeted, perhaps calling for partial amortization with a balloon payment due at loan maturity or a graduated payment plan.
4. The investor's planning horizon exceeds the length of loan maturity.
5. The investor expects increasing annual returns from the investment in the future.
6. The investor expects to realize capital gains from the investment in the future.

Comparing Investments with Different Economic Lives

We conclude this chapter by considering the procedures to use when comparing investments with different economic lives. If these investments are recurring, they must be placed on a common time basis for proper evaluation. As shown below, two methods may be used to achieve this comparison.

To illustrate this situation, consider a manager who must choose between two machines of equal effectiveness. However, they differ as follows:

	Machine X	Machine Y
Original cost	$10,000	$12,000
Projected economic life	4 years	6 years
Projected after-tax annual cash outflows	$3,200	$3,500

Neither machine is expected to have a salvage value.

The differences in economic lives mean that the machines must be replaced at different intervals. The manager's cost of capital is 10 percent. Present values of cash flows are:

$$V_o (X) = -10,000 - 3,200[\text{USPV}_{.10,4}] = -20,144$$
$$V_o (Y) = -12,000 - 3,500[\text{USPV}_{.10,6}] = -27,243.$$

Based on the present value of cash outflows over their respective economic lives, Machine X appears preferable. However, because these values represent different years of service, they are not directly comparable. Even dividing the two present values by their years of service would not produce a satisfactory comparison, since it would not properly reflect the timing of cash flows.

The investments are made comparable either by placing the present-value method on the least-common denominator of time for each investment, or by converting the above present values to annuity equivalents. Both methods lead to the same decision.

The least-common denominator of time for investments with 4- and 6-year lives is 12 years. The present value of cash flows for 12 years with Machine X, including replacement outlays in years four and eight, is:

$$V_o (X) = -10,000 - 10,000(1.10)^{-4} - 10,000(1.10)^{-8}$$
$$-3,200[\text{USPV}_{.10,12}] = -43,304.$$

For Machine Y, the present value for 12 years and one replacement in year six is:

$$V_o (Y) = -12,000 - 12,000(1.10)^{-6} - 3,500[\text{USPV}_{.10,12}]$$
$$= -42,617.$$

On this basis, Machine Y is slightly preferred to Machine X.

The annuity-equivalent method determines the size of annual annuity for the economic life of the investment that could be provided by a sum equal to the present value of its projected cash-flow stream, given the firm's cost of capital. It is given by:

For X: $20{,}144 = A_x[USPV_{.10,4}]$

$$A_x = \frac{20{,}144}{3.1699} = 6{,}355.$$

For Y: $27{,}243 = A_y[USPV_{.10,6}]$

$$A_y = \frac{27{,}243}{4.3553} = 6{,}256.$$

Again, Machine Y is preferred since the annuity equivalent of its cost stream is lower than that of Machine X.

Topics for Discussion

1. Explain the basic principles of capital budgeting under conditions of inflation.
2. Distinguish between real and nominal values of payments. Which is more commonly used in capital budgeting? Why?
3. For a time preference rate of 3 percent and an anticipated inflation rate of 8 percent, find the real value of a $10,000 payment due three years in the future. Find the real present value also.
4. Find the value of an asset yielding a perpetual series of payments of $1,000 per year when the nominal interest rate is 12 percent and anticipated inflation is 9 percent.
5. Find the value of the asset in (4) above when its series of payments starts at $1,000 and increases annually at the general inflation rate of 9 percent (use the 12 percent nominal interest rate).
6. At what annual rate will the values found in (4) and (5) increase over time? Why?
7. Explain the logic and method of using a risk-adjusted discount rate to account for investment risk in capital budgeting. Contrast the risk-adjusted rate approach with the certainty-equivalent approach.
8. Identify some ways to quantify the risk premium used in capital budgeting. How is it influenced by (a) the investment's risk, (b) the investor's risk aversion, (c) the degree of financial leverage, and (d) the investment's correlation with other business enterprises?
9. What sources of information are used in estimating probability distributions on outcomes of risky events?
10. In choosing between two risky investments, does the choice of the investment with the higher coefficient of variation imply a relatively high or low degree of risk aversion?
11. An investor is appraising an investment under the following conditions:

Forecast	NPV	P_i
1	30,000	.10
2	20,000	.15
3	15,000	.50
4	10,000	.25

    a. Find the investment's expected value, standard deviation, and coefficient of variation.

    b. Explain the meaning of each of these measures.

    c. Would the risk averse investor prefer this investment to a risk-free investment with an NPV of $10,000?

    d. Would the risk averse investor prefer this investment to another investment with an expected NPV of $12,000 and a standard deviation of $12,000?

12. A new investment requires an initial outlay of $40,000 and is projected to yield annual net cash inflows of $8,500 over a 10-year period with no terminal value. Evaluate the profitability of the investment, assuming a 3 percent rate for time, a 4 percent risk premium, and a 7 percent expected rate of inflation.

13. The purchase of a new irrigation system is requiring a loan of $61,450 at a 10 percent annual interest rate. The investor figures he can make annual payments of $10,000. Find the length of loan needed to make the investment financially feasible.

    Suppose the loan length is limited to 8 years. What is the effect on feasible loan size? What other actions will affect feasibility?

14. An investor is choosing between the following mutually exclusive investments:

	Investment			
	1	2	3	4
Initial outlay	$48,000	$60,000	$60,000	$36,000
Annual payments	20,000	12,000	16,000	10,000
Lifetime, years	5	15	10	15

The discount rate is 16 percent. Rank the investments according to profitability, assuming they can be repeated in permanent replacement claims.

References

1. Anderson, J. R., J. L. Dillon, and J. B. Hardaker, *Agricultural Decision Analysis*, Iowa State University Press, Ames, 1977.
2. Aplin, R. D., G. L. Casler, and C. P. Francis, *Capital Investment Analysis*, 3rd ed., Grid, Inc., Columbus, Ohio, 1977.

3. Bierman, H., Jr., and S. Smidt, *The Capital Budgeting Decision: Economic Analysis of Investment Projects*, 5th ed., Macmillan Publishing Co., Inc., 1980.
4. Boudreaux, K. J., and H. W. Long, *The Basic Theory of Corporate Finance*, Prentice-Hall, Inc., Englewood Cliffs, New Jersey, 1977.
5. Cooley, P. L., R. L. Roenfeldt, and I. Chew, "Capital Budgeting Procedures Under Inflation," *Financial Management*, 4:4:(Winter 1975):18-27.
6. Copeland, T. E., and J. F. Weston, *Financial Theory and Corporate Policy*, Addison-Wesley Publishing Co., Inc., Reading, Massachusetts, 1979.
7. Hertz, D. B., "Risk Analysis of Capital Investment," *Harvard Business Review*, 42(January-February 1964):95-106.
8. Levy, H., and M. Sarnat, *Capital Investment and Financial Decisions*, 2nd ed., Prentice-Hall, Inc., Englewood Cliffs, New Jersey, 1978.
9. Van Horne, J. C., *Financial Management and Policy*, 5th ed., Prentice-Hall, Inc., Englewood Cliffs, New Jersey, 1980.
10. Weston, J. F., and E. F. Brigham, *Essentials of Managerial Finance*, 4th ed., Dryden Press, Hinsdale, Illinois, 1977.

Chapter 12

CONTROLLING FARM LAND

Farm land is unique among farm resources and thus warrants special attention in long-term decision making. In this chapter we consider its unique characteristics and the forces affecting farm land values. Capital budgeting procedures are applied to evaluate the profitability of farm land investments under various conditions. Characteristics of the leasing market for farm land are also considered.

Characteristics of Farm Land

Land is a durable, immobile resource. Its basic properties either do not change over time or change so slowly that land is considered to have an infinite life. In contrast to other farm resources, land is not used up in the production of farm commodities. Because of its durability and immobility, land has special treatment in such institutional arrangements as taxation, leasing, and government programs. It has a specific legal description with ownership recorded by local governments for taxation and other controls. Specific realty law regulates its use. The availability of land-related resources such as water, minerals, oil, and buildings, as well as conservation practices and recreational uses, may influence land values and the land investment decision. Finally, land has specialized financing instruments and lenders specialized in real estate lending.

Land markets typically exhibit a low rate of market transactions. Only about 2 to 3 percent of the total farm land in the United States is sold each year. Land-leasing markets also have low activity. The terms of farm leases change slowly, and leases change hands infrequently. When tracts of land are sold or leased, they generally occur in large units that involve substantial amounts of capital. Thus borrowed capital is usually employed to finance the sale. Moreover, the lower capital investment involved in leasing explains its importance in a farmer's growth strategy.

Land values are also influenced by special factors that may differ among potential buyers. Some factors are included in the present value analysis. Others are not. To illustrate, a farmer with excess machinery capacity may value a new tract of land higher than will a neighbor who must buy more machinery to operate the added land. Non-monetary factors are illustrated by consumptive phenomena such as pride of ownership, family tradition, hobby farming, and rural living, which may on occasion outweigh the monetary factors.

Alternatives in Land Control

Expansion in farm size and income-generating capacity for most agricultural units requires an increase in the land acreage under the manager's control. The basic choices for controlling additional land are ownership and leasing. Both choices may substantially influence the business's profitability, risk, and liquidity. Thus, analysis of land control decisions must consider these effects.

Numerous options are also available within the purchase or lease alternatives. A cash purchase of land may be the simplest arrangement. However, cash purchases are rare because most land transactions involve large sums of money. Data published by the U.S. Department of Agriculture show, for example, that in 1981, about 90 percent of farm real estate transfers were credit-financed, with buyers borrowing about 78 percent of the funds used to purchase land. Credit purchases are characterized by a downpayment or pledge of equity by the buyer and a note exchanged for the land title—the note being secured by a mortgage or deed of trust on the real estate (see Chapter 15). Alternatively, the buyer could use a land-purchase contract (see Chapter 16), making a small downpayment and paying the remainder to the seller over several years. Title to the land is typically held by the seller or in escrow until the contract terms are fulfilled.

Farm real estate leases may be short-term or long-term and differ substantially in their rental arrangements. Cash rents, share rents, and combinations thereof are common. Moreover, the high inflation, business risk, and interest rates that have characterized the 1970s and 1980s have brought financial innovations and creative financing in both purchase and lease arrangements for farm land. Thus a careful, complete analysis is needed for any land control situation, in which investors consider: (1) the market price of land, (2) the net present value of the land investment *to the investor*, and (3) the financial feasibility of the investment.

Land Values

Determining the market price of land is complicated by the limited availability of timely information about land values and by the effects of many factors that influence these values. In this section, we consider the sources of price information and the approaches to estimating land values.

Sources of Price Information

Most potential buyers and sellers are not able to keep current on precise price levels in the farm land market. The relatively low activity in land transactions limits the availability of pricing information for specific properties. In addition, the size, location, soil quality, water supply, and other factors affecting land values may vary from one tract to another. Local business people, such as lenders, real estate agents, extension personnel, lawyers, and farmers, may have good, timely impressions of the land market, but their information is largely based on opinions, observations, and judgments. Thus, a prospective buyer might want to hire a professional real estate appraiser to make a "market appraisal."

The professional appraiser estimates the price at which land would be exchanged by a willing buyer and a willing seller when each is equally knowledgeable of the situation. Appraisers may use several methods of estimation. First, they might observe recent land values in sales of comparable tracts of land in the same neighborhood. This "comparable sales" method is based on the premise that the values of neighboring tracts of land should be similar, assuming the sale does not occur under extraordinary circumstances.

In addition, appraisers use the capitalization approach, in which the value of property to the "average" or "typical" manager is estimated under average production and price conditions. The perpetual series of returns to land, net of other costs, is capitalized into a land value using equation (9.6): $V_o = A/i$.

Under any appraisal method, the estimated value is adjusted to account for unique features of the land or neighborhood. These include field sizes, dwellings on the property, and nearness to roads, markets, schools, and so on.

The appraised value provides useful information to both buyer and seller in determining price objectives and negotiating strategies. However, the appraisal does not constitute the actual price. It is determined only when the land in question is sold.

Capitalization Models

Much study by economists, appraisers, policy people, and other analysts has occurred to help them better understand the forces that affect farm land values and the efficiency of farm land markets. Indeed, the asset structure of farming is uniquely characterized by the dominance of farm land and the tendency for farm income to be capitalized into land values that appear high relative to current earnings. Profitability in farming has long been characterized by relatively low rates of current (cash) returns to farm assets and a tendency for land values and net worth to increase over time.

This situation has made farm land appear overpriced relative to its current earnings. It also makes highly leveraged investments in land appear financially infeasible when expected cash returns in early years fall short of the debt servicing requirements. These points are illustrated by levels of cash rent for farm land in the U.S. Corn Belt falling in the $100 per acre range compared to land values in the $2,500 to $3,000 per acre range—current rates of return of 3 to 4 percent.

However, new understanding of valuation concepts under inflation and new empirical evidence have developed to suggest that farm land likely is more reasonably priced relative to its recent patterns of earnings growth [1, 7, 10, 11]. These developments indicate that unrealized capital gains or losses in land and other assets should logically be treated as part of farmers' total returns.

The concepts involved here are similar to the "growth·stock" phenomenon in the markets for equity capital. They are complex, but important, and can be illustrated in the following valuation model that uses the formulas and inflation guidelines established in Chapters 10 and 11.

The basic valuation approach is to estimate an asset's current market value by capitalizing its flow of expected future earnings at an appropriate interest (or capitalization) rate. Recall from formula (11.6), and the discussion in the text, that the present value of a perpetual series of payments (P_n), which respond to inflation the same as the nominal discount rate is:

$$V_o = \frac{P_o}{i_t}.$$ (12.1)

This expression means that the asset (land) value is found by dividing the asset's real earnings (P_o) by the real capitalization rate (i_t). Suppose, for example, that an acre of farm land is expected to yield a real rent of \$100 in perpetuity and that the real capitalization rate, net of general inflation, is .04, or 4 percent. Then the land value per acre is \$2,500 (= 100/.04).

Recall that the real interest rate is approximated by subtracting the anticipated inflation rate from the nominal market interest rate, $i_t = i - i_f$. Thus, the land's present value is essentially found by dividing the current rent by the difference between a market interest rate and an inflation premium.

Moreover, the asset (land) is expected to increase in value at the general inflation rate. Thus in a market equilibrium setting, the total annual returns (i) of investors consist of a real rate of return, $i_t = P_o/V$, plus a nominal rate of capital gain, i_f, or:

$$i = i_t + i_f = P_o/V + i_f.$$ (12.2)

The real rate of return consists of a current cash return (adjusted for inflation). Adding the real return to the capital gain from inflation gives the total nominal return.

For the numerical example, suppose that the anticipated inflation rate is 10 percent. The investor's nominal annual return is 14 percent; it consists of the real return of 4 percent (100/2,500) plus the inflation-induced capital gain of 10 percent.

Next, suppose that the asset's earnings experience real growth over time, at rate g, in addition to the growth in response to general inflation. In this case, the expected rental payment to land might grow at an 11 percent nominal rate, while the expected inflation rate is 10 percent. The real rate of growth is approximated as the difference between the nominal rate and the inflation rate, which is 1 percent in this case.

Real growth in the asset's payment series partitions the real rate of return into two parts: (1) a current real return, plus (2) a real capital gain. To see this effect analytically, we combine the time value formula for a growing payment series—formula (10.10)—with the inflation-adjusted valuation model in formula (11.4). The result is:

$$V_0 = \frac{P_0(1 + i_f)(1 + g)}{(1 + i_t)(1 + i_f)} + \frac{P_0(1 + i_f)^2(1 + g)^2}{(1 + i_t)^2(1 + i_f)^2} \tag{12.3}$$

$$+ \frac{P_0(1 + i_f)^3(1 + g)^3}{(1 + i_t)^3(1 + i_f)^3} + \ldots$$

First cancel the terms for $1 + i_f$ in the numerator and denominator of each term. Then, follow the adjustment indicated in Chapter 9 for a constant growth model to yield:

$$V_0 = \frac{P_0(1 + g)}{i_t - g}. \tag{12.4}$$

Now the asset value is found by dividing the asset's real earnings in period 1 by the difference between the real capitalization rate and the real growth rate. To illustrate, suppose as before that the current land rent is \$100 per acre, the real capitalization rate is 4 percent, and the rent is expected to experience real growth at 1 percent per year. Then the land value per acre is:

$$V_0 = \frac{100(1.01)}{.03} = \$3,366.67.$$

The partitioning of the real return into a current real return plus a real capital gain (g) is shown by solving equation (12.4) for i_t.

$$i_t = \frac{P_0(1 + g)}{V_0} + g. \tag{12.5}$$

For the numerical example, the real return of 4 percent contains a current gain of 3 percent ($.03 = 101/3366.67$) plus the 1 percent capital gain.

Higher rates of growth of real payments mean that a higher proportion of real return, i_t, consists of capital gain (g) and a lower proportion as current return. Finally, if the valuation process in (12.3) is repeated a year later, the land value V_1 is found to increase at the compounded rates of inflation and real growth.

$$V_1 = V_0(1 + i_f)(1 + g). \tag{12.6}$$

The combined market effects on investors' returns from inflation and real growth are interpreted as follows. The total annual rate of return i contains a real return i_t plus a capital gain due to inflation:

$$i = i_t + i_f. \tag{12.7}$$

However, when the payments experience real growth, the real return also consists of a current return plus a real capital gain:

$$i_t = \frac{P_o(1 + g)}{V_o} + g. \qquad (12.8)$$

Substituting (12.8) into (12.7) shows that the total return under real growth contains a real current return plus a real capital gain plus a capital gain due to inflation:

$$i = \frac{P_o(1 + g)}{V_o} + g + i_f \qquad (12.9)$$

Total return	=	Real current return	+	Real capital gain	+	Inflationary capital gain

For the numerical example, the total return of 14 percent consists of a current return of 3 percent, plus a real capital gain of 1 percent, plus an inflation-induced capital gain of 10 percent.[1]

Implications for Land Values

The conceptual models described in the preceding section show the way some of the important variables may interact to influence land values, and the mix of current returns and capital gains experienced by investors. These types of models serve as a guide in evaluating the response of land values to changes in these variables.

Recent evidence [1, 7], for example, has indicated that farm earnings, and thus returns to land, experienced real growth during the 1960s and 1970s. Moreover, the real earnings growth appears to have been capitalized into higher land values that have grown at rates roughly comparable to the growth in farm earnings. To the extent that these growth patterns are comparable, then farm land is not necessarily "overpriced" relative to the levels and growth of its expected earnings. Instead, land values adjusted during these times so that investors earn more of their return as capital gains.

Similar, but opposite, effects may occur in response to a decline in the level of expected earnings, or the growth rate of expected earnings. In the early 1980s, for example, levels of farm income

---

[1]These calculations ignore the interaction terms between i_t, g, and i_f. Thus, the calculations are close approximations to the true values.

dropped sharply in the United States, while interest rates reached record highs with much uncertainty about future prospects for farm income and financial market conditions. These factors suggest that the level $(P_1, P_2, \ldots P_n)$ of projected returns to land likely declined, while capital costs (i) were increasing. Expectations on earnings growth (g) may have changed as well. The combined effects of these conditions suggest that land values should have declined rather quickly, as indeed appears to be the case for U.S. farm land nationwide and especially midwestern farm land in the 1981-1982 period.

Further study and evidence are clearly needed about factors affecting land values. The effects of tax policies, government programs, financing arrangements, risk, and expectations are all involved [2.4]. So are nonfarm demands for agricultural land and the efficiency of land markets.

The effects of market efficiency are illustrated as follows. Suppose a sharp change in international trade conditions increases the expected earnings growth for farm land. In an efficient land market, land values would increase immediately to reflect the higher earnings growth and then should continue to grow over time at the new growth rate. However, market imperfections may cause the initial change in land values to be distributed over time, thus blending it with the longer-term growth in land values. Again, similar, but opposite, effects may occur if the land earnings decline and are expected to experience negative real growth $(g < o)$ over time.

Analyzing Land Investments

In this section we consider the analysis of land investment from the individual investor's standpoint, under the assumption that the individual's actions do not influence the aggregate level of land values or other market factors. Individual investors are concerned with the profitability of land investments under their own set of circumstances. This involves each investor's expectations on market prices for resources and products, financing arrangements, inflation rates, tax obligations, length of planning horizon, costs of equity capital, and other relevant factors. Combining information about these variables in a capital budgeting model will show the profitability (NPV) of a land investment or, alternatively, the maximum price an investor can pay for land to earn a stipulated rate of return.

Any analysis of land investments, simple or complex, is still expressed by the basic capital budgeting model shown in equations

(10.4) and (10.5). Using the non-uniform series version and assuming no debt financing, a typical land investment situation is modeled as:

$$NPV = -INV + \sum_{n=1}^{N} \frac{(1-t)P_n}{(1+i)^n} + \frac{V_N - T_N}{(1+i)^N}. \qquad (12.10)$$

The variables are identified as follows:

NPV = the net present value of the land investment

INV = the asking price of the land, perhaps resulting from a land appraisal

i = after-tax cost of the investor's financial capital

N = the length of planning horizon

P_n = the annual net cash flows projected for the land investment. (If subject to growth, then $P_n = P_o(1 + g_p)^n$, where g_p = the nominal growth in the payment series.)

V_N = the terminal land value. (If land values are growing, then $V_N = INV(1 + g_l)^N$, where g_l = the nominal growth in land values.) (Note: depending on the investor's expectations, the expected growth in the payment series, g_p, may differ from the expected growth in land value, g_l.)

t = the ordinary income tax rate.

T_N = a capital gains tax obligation on the change in land values. Current tax laws in the United States require that 40 percent of long-term capital gains are added to ordinary income; thus,

$$T_N = (V_N - INV)(.40)(t).$$

If the investment involves a purchase of land, then V_N represents the land value (net of any outstanding debt for a credit purchase) at the end of the planning period, less any tax obligation on capital gains. If land is controlled under a long-term lease then V_N represents any terminal value of the lease. If land is leased on an annual basis, V_N would likely be zero.

The present value could conceivably be modified to include intangible values in a land investment, such as pride of ownership, prestige in the community, and so on. Although these values may not be quantifiable directly, it is often possible to estimate how large they must be to justify acquiring high-cost land. In the following analysis we will disregard these intangible values and focus on the capital budgeting procedures.

We will begin with a simple investment situation that ignores the effects of taxes, inflation, and external financing; then we will introduce the effects of these variables to show the increasing realism and complexities of the analysis.

Case I Land Purchase: No Taxes, No Inflation,
No External Financing

Consider the case of a farmer who is evaluating the purchase of additional land. The farmer operates 500 acres but can handle another 100 acres with present labor and machinery. A nearby 100-acre farm is being sold from an estate for an asking price of $3,000 per acre. The farmer projects gross income per acre to be $360 per year. The payment of operating costs and property taxes leaves an annual net cash flow of $180 per acre. Other data at this stage of the analysis include a 15-year planning horizon and a 6 percent cost of capital. Taxes, inflation, and financing are not considered.

The net present-value model is specified as:

$$\text{NPV} = -3,000 + 180[\text{USPV}_{.06,15}] + \frac{3,000}{(1.06)^{15}} \tag{12.11}$$

$$= -3,000 + 1,748.20 \qquad + 1,251.80$$

$$= -3,000 + 3,000$$

$$= 0.$$

The present value of the uniform series of A = $180 per year for 15 years is $1,748.20 ($180 × 9.7122). The conversion factor is found in Appendix Table IV for n = 15 and i = .06. The present value of the terminal value of the land ($3,000 in year 15) is $1,251.80, which results from $3,000(1.06)^{-15} = $3,000(.4173). The sum of these two present values is $3,000, which, when added to the initial investment of $3,000, gives a net present value of 0.

The zero net present value means that the land investment has break-even profitability to the investor. If an investor indeed pays $3,000 per acre for the land, the investor will experience a 6 percent yield over the 15-year period, given these data projections. Thus, the

$3,000 present value from the annual earnings and terminal value is the investor's maximum bid price for obtaining the required rate of return. If the bid price equals the asking price, as occurs here, then the net effect is a zero NPV and exact achievement of the targeted return.

If the asking price were lower than $3,000, then the investment would be a profitable one, yielding more than the required rate of return. A higher asking price would yield a lower rate of return. Alternatively, if the investor used a lower cost of capital, the NPV would exceed zero (assuming a $3,000 asking price), indicating a profitable investment. A higher cost of capital would yield an unprofitable investment. Confirm, for example, that an 8 percent cost of capital would yield a maximum bid price of $2,486.44 and a net present value of −$513.56, if $3,000 were bid for the land.

For this situation, changing the length of planning horizon does not change the capital budgeting results. Suppose the planning horizon is lengthened to 20 years. The net present value is:

$$\text{NPV} = -3,000 + 180 \left[\text{USPV}_{.06,20} \right] + \frac{3,000}{(1.06)^{20}} \tag{12.12}$$

$$= -3,000 + 2,064.59 + 935.41$$

$$= 0.$$

The net present value is the same as for the 15-year horizon, although a higher proportion of the maximum bid price of $3,000 is attributed to annual earnings than to the terminal value. In any case, the terminal value plays an important role in the investment's profitability. This phenomenon is typical in land investments.

Case 2 Land Purchase: With Inflation, No Taxes or External Financing

Introducing the effects of inflation and growth will influence the investment's payment series, terminal value, and cost of capital. Investors might expect inflation to affect each of these values differently. Let's assume that the case farmer is evaluating the land investment under an anticipated inflation rate of 7 percent. Adding the 7 percent inflation premium to the 6 percent cost of capital used earlier gives a nominal capital cost of 13 percent. The case farmer also believes that the annual net cash flow will grow at an 8 percent annual rate and that land values will grow at a 9 percent annual rate.

Under these conditions the net present-value model is specified in nominal terms as:

$$NPV = -3,000 + \sum_{n=1}^{15} \frac{180(1.08)^n}{(1.13)^n} + \frac{3,000(1.09)^{15}}{(1.13)^{15}} \tag{12.13}$$

$$= -3,000 \quad + \quad 1,916.00 \quad + 1,747.20$$

$$= 663.20.$$

The calculation procedures using nominal values are more tedious because the payment series is non-uniform. They are calculated each year as P for the preceding year ($P_0 = \$180.000$) multiplied by $(1 + g_p)$. Discounting occurs separately for each year, with the discounted values then summed for all years in the planning period. In this case the present value of the payment series is \$1,916.00. The present value of the land's terminal value is found by compounding the asking price to a future value at the 9 percent growth rate, and then discounting to a present value at the 13 percent cost of capital. This present value is \$1,747.20, which, when added to the discounted earnings value, gives a maximum bid price of \$3,663.20. The net present value is \$663.20, which indicates that the land investment is profitable, relative to the 13 percent required return.

A simpler calculation procedure is to adjust the discount rate for each component of the valuation model by the compound growth rate found in the respective numerators. For the earnings flow, divide the 1.13 discount rate by the 1.08 growth rate in the numerator and subtract 1 from the answer. The result is 4.630. Then find the present value of a uniform series of \$180 payments for N = 15 and i = 4.63. For the terminal value, divide the 1.13 discount rate by the 1.09 growth rate in the numerator and subtract 1. The result is 3.670. Then find the present value of a single payment of \$3,000 for n = 15 and i = 3.67. The net present value is the same as above, and fewer calculations are needed.

$$NPV = -3,000 + 180[USPV_{.0463,15}] \quad + \frac{3,000}{(1.0367)^{15}} \tag{12.14}$$

$$= -3,000 + 1916.00 \quad\quad\quad + 1,747.20$$

$$= 663.20.$$

Table 12.1 reports several maximum bid prices for land, to illustrate the effects of different assumptions about growth in net cash

flows and land values, length of planning horizon, and costs of capital. Subtracting the $3,000 asking price (INV) from each bid price in
the table gives the net present values. Arranging the data in this way
allows an analyst to consider the sensitivity of bid prices and net
present values to changes in individual variables or combinations of
variables. This approach could account in part for some of the investment's risk characteristics.

To illustrate, the results in Table 12.1 show that a higher cost of
capital, with all other variables held constant, will always lower the
net present values. But increasing the planning horizon has different
effects on present values, depending on the values of other variables.
For high costs of capital and lower growth rates for cash flow or land
values, present values may decline as the planning horizon
lengthens. Otherwise, present values increase with longer planning
horizons. Trade-offs between growth rates for cash flow and land
values, given the cost of capital, can also be considered in developing a bid price strategy. But, the analyst should remember that inflation tends to affect growth rates and costs of capital in similar ways.
Thus, sharp differences between changes in the values of these variables need careful justification.

Table 12.1. Maximum Bid Prices of Land Investment for Different Levels of Key Variables, No Taxes or External Financing

| Growth in Net Cash Flow | Horizon | Growth in Land Value | | | | | |
| | | 6 Percent Cost of Capital | | | 8 Percent Cost of Capital | | |
		10%	12%	14%	10%	12%	14%
6 Percent	10 Years	$3,547	$3,076	$2,682	$3,973	$3,431	$2,980
	15 Years	3,754	3,101	2,591	4,311	3,526	2,917
8 Percent	10 Years	3,700	3,211	2,802	4,126	3,567	3,100
	15 Years	4,058	3,356	2,807	4,617	3,781	3,133

Case 3 Land Purchase: With Taxes and Inflation, No External Financing

Introducing income tax obligations means that the appropriate
variables in the capital budget must be expressed on an after-tax
basis. This is shown in equation (12.10). Annual earnings and the
investor's cost of capital are measured after taxes. The terminal value

is also the net of any tax obligations on capital gains or ordinary income, as illustrated by the general model in equation (12.10).

Assuming an ordinary income tax rate of 20 percent (t = .20), the after-tax cost of capital in the example is expressed as: .104 = (1 − .2)(.13). Other data are the same as in Case 2. Table 12.2 summarizes the capital budgeting calculations. The NPV at the bottom of the table is $1,153.44. It is comprised of the sum of the present values for the after-tax cash flows, plus the terminal value, minus the initial investment and the capital gains tax. Comparing the NPV ($1,153.44) for this situation to the NPV ($663.20) in Case 2 without taxes suggests the interesting result that the presence of tax obligations increases the investment's profitability. This is not strictly the case, however.

Table 12.2. Net Present Value for Land Investment with Inflation, Taxation, and No External Financing

Item	Present Value
1. Initial Investment	−3,000
2. Net Cash Flow Series	

$$\sum_{n=1}^{N} \frac{(1 - t)(P_0)(1 + g_p)^n}{(1 + i)^n}$$

Year 1: $(1 - .2)(180)(1.08)(1.104)^{-1} =$	140.87	
Year 2: $(1 - .2)(180)(1.08)^2(1.104)^{-2} =$	137.81	
Year 3: $(1 - .2)(180)(1.08)^3(1.104)^{-3} =$	134.81	
Year 15: $(1 - .2)(180)(1.08)^{15}(1.104)^{-15} =$	103.56	
Total:	1,819.90	1,819.90

3. Terminal Land Value

$$V_N = INV (1 + g_1)^N (1 + i)^{-N}$$

$$= 3,000(1.09)^{15}(1.104)^{-15}$$

$$= 2,477.32 \qquad\qquad 2,477.32$$

4. Capital Gains Taxes

$$T_N = \frac{(V_N - INV)(.4)(t)}{(1 + i)^N}$$

$$= \frac{(10,927.45 - 3,000)(.4)(.2)}{(1.104)^{15}}$$

$$= 143.78 \qquad\qquad -143.78$$

| 5. Net Present Value | 1,153.44 |

The increase in net present value that occurs here is attributed to the sheltering of tax obligations on the investment's terminal value, compared to the implicit assumption that the earnings from an alternative investment, expressed through the discount rate, are fully taxable. Tax obligations on the land's terminal value occur only if the land experiences long-term capital gains; even then, 60 percent of the long-term capital gain is sheltered from taxation. Thus, careful judgment is needed in specifying the cost of capital on an after-tax basis. If, for example, another investment opportunity involves tax shelters from capital gains or other tax provisions, then the after-tax cost of capital should be adjusted accordingly.

Case 4 Land Purchase: With External Financing

Thus far we have assumed that the investor is financing the land purchase only with equity capital. In practice, this seldom occurs. Instead, a downpayment of from 10 to 50 percent of the purchase price usually occurs, with the remaining amount borrowed and re-paid over a series of years. We will now consider how the use of borrowed capital affects the capital budgeting analysis.

The net present value model in equation (12.10) must be mod-ified to include the effects of financing terms on the initial invest-ment, on annual net cash flows, and on the terminal equity in the investment. The model is reformulated as:

$$\text{NPV} = -\text{INV}_{dp} + (1 - t) \, A\big[\text{USPV}_{i,N}\big] \qquad \textbf{(12.15)}$$

$$-\sum_{n=1}^{N} \frac{\big[P_n + (1 - t)I_n\big]}{(1 + i)^n} + \frac{V_N - T_N - D_N}{(1 + i)^N}$$

where INV_{dp} is the downpayment of equity capital, P_n is the repay-ment of loan principal per period, $(1 - t)I_n$ is the after-tax interest payment, and D is the debt outstanding at the end of Year N.

To evaluate debt financing, consider again the land purchase in Cases 2 and 3. The farmer could purchase a tract of land for $3,000 per acre, which would increase the annual net cash flow by $180 per year, with the payment series and land value growing at annual rates of 8 percent and 9 percent, respectively. Assuming a 13 percent cost of capital, a 15-year planning horizon, a zero tax rate, and no external financing, the investment's net present value was $663.20, as in equation (12.14).

Now, let's assume that the financing terms include a cash

downpayment of 20 percent of the asking price, or $600, with the remaining $2,400 to be repaid in equal annual installments over 15 years at 13 percent interest. The size of payment required to amortize $2,400 over 15 years is found by solving for A in:

$$2,400 = A[USPV_{.13,15}] \qquad (12.16)$$

$$A = \frac{2,400}{USPV_{.13,15}} = 371.38,$$

as calculated with the conversion factor for $i = .13$ and $N = 15$ in Appendix Table 4.

Since the tax rate is assumed zero, the total after-tax loan payment (principal plus interest) is $371.38 each year, allowing the debt servicing requirement to be expressed as a uniform series. Including the debt servicing requirement of $371.38 in equation (12.15) and noting that the debt outstanding at the end of the planning horizon is zero results in the following net present value.

$$NPV = -600 + \sum_{n=1}^{15} \frac{180(1.08)^n}{(1.13)^n} - 371.38[USPV_{.13,15}] \qquad (12.17)$$

$$+ \frac{3,000(1.09)^{15}}{(1.13)^{15}}$$

$$= -600 + 1,916.00 - 2,400 + 1,747.20$$

$$= 663.20.$$

Not surprisingly, the net present value is $663.20 which is the same as the NPV when no external financing was used. Thus, in the limiting case, where (1) the interest rate on the land debt is equal to the firm's cost of equity capital, (2) the planning horizon equals the length of loan, and (3) income taxes are disregarded, the terms of financing do not affect the profitability of the land investment.

However, a firm's cost of equity capital should be higher than the interest rate on debt to reflect the higher risk from leveraging. Moreover, the interest paid on debt is tax deductible. And, the investor's planning horizon may be shorter or longer than the loan maturity. Thus, the size and pattern of debt payments do affect cash flows and investment profitability.

To illustrate these effects, consider the following financing terms for the land investment. A 25 percent downpayment is required, with the loan balance of $2,400 per acre to be repaid in equal annual payments of principal and interest over 30 years at a 12 percent interest rate. The investor's expectations on cash flows and growth remain the same, the cost of capital is 13 percent, and the tax rate is zero. Thus, the initial investment of equity capital (INV_{dp}) is $600, the annual debt servicing is $A = \$297.94 = (2{,}400 \div USPV_{.12,30})$, and the loan balance after 15 years is $D_{15} = \$2{,}029.44$.[2]

The net present value model is formulated as:

$$NPV = -600 + \sum_{n=1}^{15} \frac{180(1.08)^n}{(1.13)^n} - 297.94[USPV_{.13,15}] \qquad \textbf{(12.18)}$$

$$+ \frac{3{,}000(1.09)^{15} - 2{,}029.44}{(1.13)^{15}}$$

$$= -600 + 1{,}916.00 - 1{,}925.40 + 1{,}422.71$$

$$= 813.31.$$

The positive NPV indicates that the investment is profitable under these financing terms and that the maximum bid price is $3,813.31. Moreover, the NPV and bid price have increased as a result of debt financing, compared to complete equity financing. The increase in profitability reflects the effects of leveraging, in which lower-cost debt capital (12 percent) is substituted for higher-cost equity capital (13 percent). Moreover, as shown below, the tax deductibility of interest payments further favors the use of debt capital. Of course, leveraging involves greater financial risk too; if a risk premium were added to the cost of equity capital to reflect the greater risk, the payoff from leveraging would be less.

When the tax rate is non-zero, the computations become more tedious, since the amount of the annual loan payment allocated to interest, which is tax deductible, will vary from year to year. As a result, we can no longer use the convenient uniform series factors of Appendix Table 4. Instead, we must compute the present values of the after-tax debt servicing requirements separately for each year, and then sum these values for all years.

To illustrate, consider the introduction of taxes at a 20 percent rate ($t = .20$) in Case 3. Table 12.2 showed the calculation procedures and the resulting net present value of $1,153.44 for the land investment under equity financing. If the investment is financed in

---

[2]The derivation of a loan amortization schedule with annual principal, interest, and loan balances is shown in Chapter 14.

part with debt capital according to the terms used in this section, then the main effects occur on the initial investment, the present value of the loan payments, and the terminal debt. The after-tax present value of the loan payments is represented by the third term of equation (12.15).

$$\sum_{n=1}^{15} \frac{[P_n + (1 - t)I_N]}{(1 + i)^n}.$$

In Table 12.3., we project a 15-year amortization schedule for these financing terms and show the present value of the after-tax payments to be $1,801.61.

Table 12.3. Present Value of Principal and After-Tax Interest Payments

Year	Principal	Interest	After-tax Interest	Discount Factor $1/(1.104)^n$	Present Value $(1 + 3)(4)$
	(1)	(2)	(3)	(4)	(5)
1	$ 9.94	$288.00	$230.40	.906	$217.75
2	11.13	286.01	228.81	.820	196.75
3	12.47	285.47	228.38	.743	178.99
4	13.96	283.98	227.18	.673	162.33
5	15.64	282.30	225.84	.610	147.24
6	17.52	280.42	224.34	.552	133.58
7	19.62	278.32	222.66	.500	121.21
8	21.97	275.97	220.77	.453	110.00
9	24.61	273.33	218.66	.410	99.85
10	27.56	270.38	216.30	.372	90.67
11	30.87	267.07	213.66	.337	82.35
12	34.57	263.37	210.69	.305	74.82
13	38.72	259.22	207.37	.276	68.00
14	43.37	254.57	203.66	.250	61.83
15	48.57	249.37	199.49	.227	56.24
Total					$1,801.61

The summary of the NPV calculations is adapted from Table 12.2, and shown in Table 12.4. The NPV at the bottom of the table is $1,291.74. It is comprised of the sum of present values for the after-tax cash flows plus the land's terminal value minus the initial investment, loan payments, capital gains tax, and terminal loan balance. The positive NPV indicates a profitable investment when borrowed capital is used as a source of financing, and when the effects of inflation and taxation are considered. Moreover, the NPV for debt

Table 12.4. Net Present Value of Land Investment with Inflation, Taxes, and External Financing

Item	Present Value
1. Initial Investment (INV_{dp})	$\$-600.00$
2. Net Cash Flow Series (See Table 12.2)	1,819.90
3. Loan Payment Series (See Table 12.3)	$-1,801.61$
$\sum_{n=1}^{15} \dfrac{[P_n + (1-t)I_N]}{(1+i)^n} = 1{,}801.61$	
4. Terminal Land Value (See Table 12.2)	2,477.32
5. Capital Gains Taxes (See Table 12.2)	-143.78
6. Terminal Loan Balance	-460.09
$\dfrac{D_N}{(1+i)^N} = \dfrac{2{,}029.44}{(1.104)^{15}} = 460.09$	
7. Net Present Value	$\$1,291.74$

financing is higher than the comparable NPV for full equity financing in Table 12.2, indicating the effects of leveraging. The after-tax NPV for the debt financing case also exceeds the pre-tax NPV, indicating the combined effects on profitability of tax shelters associated with the terminal value and interest payments.

Financial Feasibility of Land Investments

Financial feasibility means the ability of an investment to satisfy the financing terms and performance criteria that are agreed upon by the borrower and the lender. A profitable investment may not always be financially feasible, if the financing plan does not accommodate the magnitude and timing of the investment's returns. As we shall see, land investments often present special challenges in financial feasibility and liquidity management, because of the role of capital gains.

Several types of liquidity problems arise for leveraged investors who purchase farm land, subject to expected earnings growth. One liquidity problem is attributed to the nonself-liquidating characteristics of land investments. Because land is not used up in the farm production process, no inherent set-aside of cash occurs to meet debt servicing requirements, as is the case with charging depreciation on durable farm assets and operating expenses on other inputs. Instead, the funds for servicing land debt come from net business income,

thus reducing the funds available for family living or other investments.

A second liquidity problem arises because current earnings from
land investments often are a relatively small portion of the investor's
total return compared to capital gains. The capital gains provide no
cash flows unless the land is sold or used as a basis for refinancing.
The lesser role of cash earnings reduces the investment's liquidity.

Another liquidity problem arises from differences in the kind of
compensation required by lenders and experienced by equity investors in the land. Lenders require all of their scheduled compensation
(principal and interest) in a cash payment, of which part is a real
return and part is an inflation premium, needed to compensate for
the anticipated loss of purchasing power in their debt claim. Borrowers, however, experience only part of their return as a current payment; the rest is capital gain. Thus, if leverage and inflation are high
enough, borrowers will experience a financing gap by having insuffi-
cient cash from the land's early earnings to meet the debt payments.
The borrowers' equity is growing favorably, but not their cash position. Only after several years of earnings growth will the financing
gap disappear.

This situation arises in part because the traditional repayment
schemes based either on constant principal payments or on equal
installment payments make no direct allowances for the pattern of
cash flows arising from the land investment. As shown below, these
repayment practices contribute to financing gaps and trigger various
liquidity responses by borrowers.

The problems in liquidity and achieving financial feasibility are
illustrated with data for the land investment in the preceding sections. The financing terms on the $3,000 per acre purchase included
a $600 downpayment with annual payments of $297.94 fully amortizing the $2,400 loan over 30 years at 12 percent interest. However, the
nominal value of the land earnings in year 1 is $194.40 = $180(1.08).
Thus, ignoring the effects of income taxes, the investor experiences a
cash deficit of −$103.54 = $194.40 − $297.94. The cash deficit con-
tinues at a diminishing amount until year 7, when the nominal value
of the payments series has grown to $308.49 = $180(1.08)^7.

This deficit means that the investment is financially infeasible.
It does not generate sufficient cash from its earnings alone to meet
the debt payment. Recall, however, that the investment is still profitable (positive NPV), although the profitability is largely due to the
growth in earnings and terminal land value.

How can a leveraged investor in farm land, especially a young, first-time farm borrower, make the investment financially feasible when only part of the nominal returns occur as cash flow, and the rest as capital gains? One approach is to postpone the investment until additional equity is accumulated, but this may severely curtail the growth potential.

Another approach is for the farmer to generate cash from other earnings, or perhaps from liquidating other assets, to pay the lender. These sources of cash might come from earnings on rented land, other owned land, livestock enterprises, nonfarm wages, foregone consumption, or sales of capital assets. Short-term borrowing or carryover loans from non-real estate lenders also may occur to meet the long-term debt payments, thus creating additional financial risk. Older, well established operators or nonfarm investors are more likely to use these approaches than are younger farmers. However, for any types of investors, these approaches may substantially alter their leverage and reinvestment policies when measured in real terms.

An alternative approach under inflation is to modify payment policies on debt so that the growth in a borrower's repayment obligations more closely corresponds with the expected growth in debt servicing capacity. These modifications directly involve the lender's participation in the design of the financing plans.

At one extreme, repayments could be waived, with loan principal and interest indexed to the expected growth in the borrower's returns. This would result in permanent indebtedness, with the amount of debt growing at about the same rate as the investor's equity. As a result, the liquidity problems could be resolved and the real financial positions of both lender and borrower remain the same, without the need to divert other earnings or obtain short-term loans to meet long-term payments.

Another alternative to inflation-indexing is to specify full amortization of long-term debt according to an inflation-adjusted repayment scheme. Most such schemes are designed to alleviate cash deficits and financing gaps early in the repayment period. They have been used to finance residential housing and warrant consideration in farm lending, too. Numerous schemes are possible: graduated payments, purchasing power mortgages, partial amortization, interest only, and combinations thereof.

To illustrate, a graduated payment plan might start with the borrower's repayment obligations set at the level of expected land earnings in year 1 ($180 in the example). The payment obligation would then increase at the expected growth rate (8 percent) for several years (5, 7, or 10), after which the remaining loan balance would be refinanced on a conventional fixed payment loan.

These types of plans may be more administratively feasible to lenders, since they involve full amortization of the loan rather than permanent indebtedness. They also can be tailored to selected types of borrowers, and tied to loan insurance or other kinds of risk protection for the parties involved. Even equity participation loans are under consideration by some long-term lenders. Called a "Shared Appreciation Mortgage," this type of loan compensates the lender in part by sharing the appreciated value of the property being financed.

These financing programs involve liquidity responses to inflation that depart sharply from traditional amortization methods based on fixed-payment or declining-payment loans. They also shift the emphasis in credit evaluations more toward evidence of managerial skills and financial progress, and away from repayment history. But these innovative financial programs respond directly to the financial feasibility problems of land investments. They warrant careful consideration, although providing risk protection from swings in farm earnings and possible declines in land values is important too.

Leasing Farm Land

Leasing farm land is a widespread method of financing, especially for farm operators in the growth stage of their life cycle. Nearly 40 percent of the farms in the United States and nearly 65 percent of the farm land have been operated by farmers who lease part or all of the land they operate. Most of the leasing occurs by part owners, with a typical pattern of land control characterized by heavy reliance on leasing by younger operators, followed by combined ownership and leasing for farmers aged 30 through 60, with greater reliance on ownership thereafter.

Leasing also varies with the type of farm. Full owners are dominant for fruit and nut, vegetable, and dairy farms. Ownership is also more important in dairy farms and most types of livestock operations, in which land contributes less to total asset value. Leasing is most common in crop farms where grain, oilseeds, cotton, etc., are the major products.

Lease Contracts

The legal document for renting land is the land lease, a contract conveying control over use rights in real property from one party to another without transferring title. A contract usually stipulates the property's intended use, with extent and conditions of payment for this use. Thus, leasing is a means of financing that enables a manager to control the use of assets belonging to others without making a downpayment or incurring other ownership obligations.

Many land leasing contracts are verbal; however, there are important reasons for using written leases. Specifying the details of the lease in writing improves communication among the parties involved and helps to avoid misunderstandings. On occasions, new participants become involved in leasing transactions. Specifying the terms of the lease in writing insures that these terms will be binding on all parties and reduces the chances of misunderstanding.

Types of Land Leases

Among the more important types of land leases are the cash lease, the crop-share lease, and the livestock-share lease. Cash leases predominate in those states where much of the rented land is publicly owned grazing land. In the Corn Belt, crop-share leasing prevails, along with livestock-share leasing and combinations of cash and share leases.

Under the cash lease, a predetermined cash fee—either per acre or for the total farm unit—becomes a fixed fee to the tenant irrespective of the yields for product prices obtained. This fee may be payable in several payments during the year, some occurring prior to harvest. Thus part of the cash rent may enter a farm's operating line of credit. The cash lease sometimes is modified, however, by indexing the cash rent to an average yield index or to an average product price index. Such a modification shifts some of the production and price risks from the tenant to the landlord.

A fixed fee cash lease may create substantial financial risk for the tenant when business risks from yield and price variations are high. The fixed financial claim associated with the lease is another form of financial leveraging that magnifies the possible loss of the tenant's equity as business risks increase. In poor years, cash renters may have difficulty meeting lease payments, compared to share rent obligations; in contrast, surplus earnings occur in good years under cash rent arrangements.

A logical outgrowth of the high financial risk of cash leases is the product-share lease, which enables the land owner to share with the tenant the risk of variability in yields and prices and to furnish some of the management input. Share leases introduce perfect positive correlation between a farmer's crop returns and the rental obligations, including sharing the financing of annual operations. Thus, share leases are highly risk-efficient financing plans. However, share rents are likely higher on average than cash rents, reflecting the premiums needed to compensate the landlord for accepting greater risk and contributing part of the management.

With a crop-share lease, a specified percentage of the crop is paid to the landlord for use of the land. The share is set so that both parties are properly compensated for the resources which they contribute. Typically, the tenant provides all labor and machinery, the landlord provides the real estate, and both parties share the variable costs of production.

Under a livestock-share lease, the landlord typically furnishes the land and buildings, while livestock are owned by either party or jointly by both parties. Returns from livestock sales, net of any shared cost, are divided between the two parties according to the share arrangements. Generally, the landlord owns half of the livestock and equipment, pays half of the operating expenses (including all feed inputs), shares in management decisions, and receives half the farm receipts.

Share-Leasing Terms

Share leases promote maximum economic efficiency when both parties' shares in farm production are proportionate to their contributions to the business, and when all truly variable expenses are shared in the same proportion as crops are shared. What, then, determines satisfactory rent shares? In the case of land-intensive crops, such as corn, wheat, soybeans, grain sorghum, and rice, why do we find typical rental payments of one-half of the crops in central Illinois, two-fifths of the crops in southwestern Ontario, or one-third or one-fourth of the crops in Texas? Or, why does some land rent for $120 per acre and other land for $60 per acre?

Differences in the quality and value of resources contributed by the tenant and landlord are especially important. Differences in land quality probably have the greatest impact on rent levels. Many of the differences in land quality are attributable to soil productivity. However, lease terms may also reflect differences in water supply, drainage, slope, proportion of tillable land, buildings, and other features which affect the land's earning capacity. For some specialty crops, acreage allotments and market accessibility may be important factors.

The differences in shares arise because the tenant's costs for planting, cultivating, and harvesting an acre of most types of crops should be about the same regardless of location or land quality. To illustrate, suppose we compare the share-lease arrangements on two tracts of land located in geographic regions with significant differences in land productivity. Tract A on average yields $400 of gross returns per acre; tract B averages a $300 gross return per acre. In both cases, the tenant's "costs" average $200 per acre. For tract A, the tenant should receive one-half (200/400) of the crop to cover costs. For tract B, the tenant needs two-thirds (200/300) of the crop to cover the same costs. The landlord receives the residual income as rent. Differences over time in this residual income are capitalized into land values that, in turn, reflect the differences in land productivity.

Failure to share variable expenses in the same proportion as products are shared will reduce the economic efficiency of the lease arrangement. The tenant and landlord may then have different incentives for using the variable inputs. To illustrate, a landlord who does not share the cost of fertilizer would prefer that the tenant apply a yield-maximizing level of fertilizer. However, this would not be a rational level for the tenant, who must bear the full marginal cost of the fertilizer.

Some inputs are difficult to classify. If herbicide applications, for example, only substitute for the tenant's usual cultivation practices, then herbicide costs should not be shared. But if yields increase from the herbicide, then sharing its costs would be consistent with sharing its returns.

Leasing terms and their impact on managerial decisions are largely a result of custom or tradition. Share-rent levels, for example, tend to persist over time, even though changes occur in farm practices and economic conditions. The persistence of 50-50 crop-share leases in the Midwest is a good example. These leasing terms may constitute the only expression of market price for the services of unpaid inputs such as land, operating labor, and management. In share leasing, the economic rent for land is disguised behind a number of associated non-land inputs. Thus, the adoption of new methods of crop harvesting, storage, feeding systems, or herbicides becomes involved in the land-rental problem.

Cash leases are experiencing greater use as improved technology reduces yield variability and as tenants need greater freedom in managing leased land. Cash rents also allow more flexibility in bidding for leased land. Levels of cash rents have likely adjusted to changing conditions more readily than have share rents. This adjustment results in part from increased bargaining between landlord and tenant, a factor which may increase tenure risks if land control shifts frequently to the highest bidder.

Analyzing Land Leases and Financing Arrangements

The framework for analyzing leasing as a means of financing the control of farm land is similar to ownership. The type and length of lease can affect cash inflows and outflows over the manager's planning horizon. The net cash flows can be discounted to a present value for comparison with other land financing methods. Non-economic factors can be considered as well.

With share leases, the major impacts on a farmer's cash flow are the percentage reductions in output and variable costs that are allocated to the landlord. Cash leases have no effect on the farmers' returns, only on the projected costs from the land investment. In either case, estimates of all cash flow items influenced by the lease should be considered in the capital budgeting analysis on an after-tax basis.

The rental arrangements may also impact on the short-term financing of the farm operation. In cash leases, many landlords require more than one payment during the year. If part of the cash rent is due prior to harvest, then the tenant must finance it through the operating line of credit or with cash from other sources. Thus, the timing of the rental payments will influence short-term financial planning.

The timing of rental payments should also influence the level of rent, since earlier payments of rent shift the financing burden from the landlord to the tenant. Suppose, for example, that the typical cash rent in a community is $100 per acre, based on payment at harvest in November. A landlord who requires a full payment six months in advance should be prepared to accept a lower rent to reflect the time value of money. If the interest rate is 12 percent annually, then the discount should be $6.00, based on the six-month time period. The negotiated rent would then be $94.00 per acre.

Share rents also influence short-term financing through the practices followed in sharing variable expenses. In principle, the landlord and tenant should cover, through cash payment or credit, their respective shares of operating expenses as they are incurred. Hence, two lines of credit might be needed—one for the tenant and one for the landlord. In practice, however, the arrangements for sharing the financing of operating inputs vary widely. In many cases a separate billing occurs to the tenant and landlord as expenses are incurred. In other cases, the tenant may act as an agent for the landlord in acquiring and financing operating inputs. A final settlement for expenses (including interest) occurs at harvest time. This latter arrangement is especially useful for farmers having large operations, with land leased from several landlords. In any case, leasing arrangements clearly bring added demands for financial management.

Other indirect costs of leasing are associated with tenure risk and the effects of leasing on credit. When short-run leases are used, with no option for renewal, tenure risk is a special concern to both landlord and tenant. Most farm leases, whether written or unwritten, have been limited to one year. Few investment programs become feasible in a one-year horizon. Consequently, tenants may be reluctant to undertake investments which would be profitable over longer periods. Lenders may be reluctant to finance such investments for similar reasons.

Tenants and landlords can usually gain from increasing the tenure security of the lease contract, especially after a favorable experience with a one-year contract. An example is a three- to five-year contract which is renewable each year. This arrangement extends the contract into the future at least two years. The terms of the lease also should enable either party to terminate the contract if the other party fails to perform satisfactorily. In some states, annual leases are extended automatically if notice of discontinuance is not given prior to the termination date. Arrangements can also be developed for one party to compensate the other for residual values of investments when the lease terminates.

Numerous examples arise of landlord-tenant arrangements which have continued for many years without long-term contracts. The tenant who regularly attains above-average yields and product quality usually has little risk of losing a lease. In fact, such a tenant usually has a waiting list of interested landlords. Similarly, landlords who have a reputation for fairness, integrity, and management skills tend to attract better candidates as tenants.

Leasing adds to the control of resources for a firm with a minimum of financial disturbance. The manager thus avoids the lower liquidity that tends to be associated with ownership through cash purchase or borrowing. No liabilities are created beyond the rent obligation. However, a lender may be reluctant to finance the addition of durable assets on land which may not be available to the tenant in the future. The reclaimability of assets ranks high on lender preferences for loan purposes. However, the degree of reclaimability for the same asset can vary with the tenure of the operator: owner, part-owner, or full tenant. Thus, the credit available for financing durable assets may be less favorable for the tenant than for the owner-operator.

Topics for Discussion

1. Identify the characteristics of farm land that make it unique from other resources. What are the implications for financing land investments?

2. How active is the market for farm land? How does this activity affect land values and their responses to changes in farm income, interest rates, and inflation?

3. Estimate the appraisal value of a tract of land with a current cash rent of $80 per acre, a nominal capitalization rate of 12 percent, and an inflation rate of 8 percent. How would you validate this value? What is the anticipated land value one year in the future? Two years?

4. How would the appraised value in problem 3 change if the current cash rent is expected to experience real growth of 1 percent annually? What would be a land investor's current rate of return and rate of capital gain under this condition?

5. How would the appraised value in problem 3 change if the current cash rent is expected to experience a real decline of 1 percent annually?

6. An individual investor is evaluating the profitability of an anticipated land investment that has an asking price of $2,000 per acre and a current net cash flow of $120 per acre. The investor will pay cash, plans on holding the investment for 10 years, and has a 5 percent cost of capital. No inflation or tax obligations are involved. Evaluate the profitability of the investment.

7. Evaluate the investment in problem 6 under an assumption that the anticipated inflation rate is 8 percent, which equally affects net cash flows, land values, and the cost of capital.

8. Evaluate the investment in problem 7 under the same conditions, except that land values are expected to grow at a 7 percent annual rate.

9. Evaluate the investment in problem 7, assuming that the investor's tax rate on ordinary income is 20 percent.

10. Evaluate the investment in problem 9 with the use of debt financing, assuming a 20 percent downpayment, and a loan at 11 percent interest with equal payments of principal and interest amortized over 30 years. Discuss the possible risks associated with this investment.

11. Evaluate the financial feasibility of the land investment in problem 10. If found to be infeasible, how might feasibility be attained?

12. Explain how an investment can be profitable, yet financially infeasible.

13. Discuss some of the reasons why leasing is an important method of financing the control of farm land.

14. Contrast leases using cash rents with those using share rents. Which is more risk efficient from the tenant's view? Why?

15. Explain some of the financing implications of cash leases and share leases. How do the rental arrangements affect operating lines of credit?

16. Explain why the percentage shares of products between landlord and tenant may differ among geographic regions.

17. Which is the proper observation: "land rents determine land values" or "land values determine land rents"? Why?

18. Explain how land values should respond to (a) an increase or decrease in the level of returns to land, (b) an increase or decrease in the expected earnings growth for land, and (c) an increase or decrease in the cost of financial capital.

References

1. Barry, P. J., *Current Issues in Agricultural Finance: Inflation, Risk, and Financial Instabilities*, W. I. Myers Lecture, Cornell University, October 1981.

2. Castle, E. N., and I. Hock, "Farm Real Estate Price Components 1920-1978," *American Journal of Agricultural Economics*, 64(1982):8-18.

3. Economic Research Service, *Farm Real Estate Market Developments* (annual series), USDA, Washington, D.C.

4. Feldstein, M., "Inflation, Portfolio Choice, and the Prices of Land and Corporate Stock," *American Journal of Agricultural Economics*, 62(1980):910-916.

5. Lee, Warren F., and Norman Rask, "Inflation and Crop Profitability: How Much Can Farmers Pay for Land?," *American Journal of Agricultural Economics*, 58(1976):984-990.

6. Lins, D. A., N. E. Harl, and T. L. Frey, *Farmland*, Century Communications, Inc., Skokie, Illinois, 1982.

7. Melichar, E. O., "Capital Gains vs. Current Income in the Farming Sector," *American Journal of Agricultural Economics*, 61(1979):1082-1092.

8. Reiss, F. J., *Farm Leases for Illinois*, Rev., Agricultural Extension Service Circular 960, University of Illinois at Urbana–Champaign, September 1972.

9. _____ *What Is a Fair Crop-Share Lease?*, Agricultural Extension Service Circular 918, University of Illinois at Urbana–Champaign, October 1965.

10. Robison, L. J., and J. R. Brake, "Inflation, Cash Flows, and Growth: Some Implications for the Farm Firm," *Southern Journal of Agricultural Economics*, 12(1980):131-138.

11. Tweeten, L. G., "Macro-economics in Crisis: Agriculture in an Underachieving Economy," *American Journal of Agricultural Economics*, 62(1980):853-865.

Chapter 13

LEASING NON–REAL ESTATE ASSETS

A lease is a contract by which control over the right to use an asset is transferred from one party (the lessor) to another party (the lessee) for a specified time in return for a rental payment to cover the lessor's costs of ownership. Thus, leasing is a method of financing the control of an asset that separates its use from its ownership. Several types of leasing have developed in agriculture. Especially important is the leasing of farm land, which was addressed in the previous chapter. Also important are operating leases, custom hiring, financial leases, and leveraged leases, which are treated here.

In the following sections we describe the types of non-real estate leases used in agriculture, evaluate their advantages and disadvantages, and apply present value techniques to analyze the economics of leasing for both the lessee and the lessor. Most of the discussion focuses on financial leases for farm machinery and equipment, due to their growing importance. However, the basic principles and tools of lease analysis apply to many other types of agricultural assets.

Types of Leases

Leasing of non-real estate assets has grown in agriculture, but is still less extensive than in other industries such as trucking, manufacturing, computer, and airline industries. Generally, leasing in agriculture involves machinery, equipment, some buildings, and breeding livestock. Most other types of non-real estate assets are less suited for leasing because they are not easily reclaimed when the lease expires. Most manufacturers of farm machinery and equipment offer leasing programs to farmers through dealerships, although these programs receive relatively moderate use. In addition, leasing services may be provided by financial institutions, such as commercial banks and Production Credit Associations, and by independent leasing companies and individual firms or persons offering specialized services. In large agribusinesses, more complex lease arrangements, called "leveraged leasing," may develop to formally involve lenders with the lessor and lessee. In the following sections, we consider the characteristics of these various types of leases.

The Operating Lease

The operating lease is usually a short-term rental arrangement (hourly, daily, weekly, monthly) in which the rental charge is calculated on a time basis. Rental cars, trailers, and retail rental stores are common nonfarm examples. The lessor owns the asset and performs nearly all the functions of ownership, including maintenance. The lessee pays direct costs, such as fuel and labor. These terms vary with the type of machine and length of rental period. When a trench digger is leased for a day or two, the lessor likely pays for all maintenance. In contrast, the lessee might carry most of the maintenance costs on a tractor leased for an entire cropping season. These terms are often negotiated between the two parties.

Companies offering operating leases are usually those who perform maintenance tasks, such as manufacturers or their subsidiaries, dealers, or other specialized businesses. The greatest success for operating leases is with general-purpose items, which have user demands spread over various time periods, or with specific-purpose items, whose demand varies by region or by type of service. Innovation in operating leases may help increase the dealer's merchandising activities and provide a supply of relatively new items for the popular "used" market, especially for machinery.

The operating lease may also be combined with a purchase program. Lease-purchase arrangements in a contract essentially give the lessee the option to apply part or all of the lease payment to an asset's purchase price. Thus, the operating lease may change to a cash or credit purchase.

Custom Hiring

Custom hiring is a form of leasing that combines the hiring of labor services with the use of the tangible asset. Common examples include custom combining for many crops, custom applications of chemicals and fertilizer, and custom feeding of livestock in commercial feedlots. These specific functions are performed by individuals or firms who control the needed machines or facilities and who will supply the services of both the asset and their own labor.

For some locations and farming types, machinery and equipment dealers may offer custom crop services by utilizing their labor and equipment. With good quality of service and established maintenance departments, they can offer custom services on favorable terms. Chemical suppliers may also provide custom applications, thus assuring expert quality of work.

In many areas, land owners can hire the custom operation of their entire farm: soil tilling, planting, cultivating, harvesting, etc. Where cash-crop farming is prevalent, "custom farming" thus offers an alternative to leasing arrangements on farm real estate, although the latter is much more prominent. In livestock areas, especially in the Plains States, many cattle and some hogs are custom fed in commercial feedlots which own neither the animals nor the feed. The cattle owner pays a fee to the feedlot for the production and marketing services.

Custom hiring resembles other types of leasing in that it avoids the financial drain of capital investments and the obsolescence risk of owned capital. It may also improve the accuracy of cost estimates for the various services, thus facilitating projections of cash flows and short-term financing needs. Custom operations may also relieve limitations on the availability of family labor or skilled hired labor for many agricultural enterprises. Custom labor that is specialized to its tasks may perform more efficiently than other types of labor. The timeliness of operations may also improve, although uncertainties may occur about the availability of the custom operator. Finally, custom hiring may be cheaper than either owning or leasing an asset for a specialized task.

Custom services have a long history in agriculture. In the U.S. Corn Belt, for example, the services evolved from the practice of neighborhood work sharing for machines that were too large for single farms to own. Threshing and corn shelling are historical examples. Much custom work is still done by farmers with excess machine capacity. However, in the cotton and wheat areas custom services tend to come from specialized operators.

The Financial Lease

The financial lease is a long-term contractual arrangement in which the lessee acquires control of an asset in return for rental payments to the lessor. The contract usually runs for several years and is noncancellable. Except for price variations of the asset, the lessee acquires all of the benefits, risks, and costs of ownership without having to make the usual investment of equity capital. In many ways, the financial lease is comparable to a credit purchase financed by an intermediate-term loan that provides 100 percent financing, although prepayments of rent have the same cash flow effects as downpayments in credit purchases. The rental charge is established to cover the lessor's expected costs of ownership plus profit.

Financial leases have become more important in agriculture and should have more use in the future. Thus, the rest of this chapter focuses on their characteristics and methods of analysis.

Leveraged Leases

Leveraged leasing is an extension of financial leasing that has developed in large agribusinesses and other corporate firms to finance projects with large capital expenditures and long economic lives. The main feature of leveraged leasing is the formal involvement of a lender in providing debt capital to finance the lessor's purchase of the leased asset. As with a regular financial lease, the lessee selects the asset to be leased and negotiates the leasing terms with the lessor. The difference in a leveraged lease, however, is that the lessor purchases and becomes owner of the asset by providing only part (20 to 40 percent) of the capital needed. The rest of the purchase price is borrowed from one or more institutional lenders, with the loan secured by a first lien on the assets, by an assignment of the lease contract, and by an assignment of the rental payments. Arrangements are carefully developed to assure that the various transactions among the lessee, lessor, lender, equipment manufacturer, and any other parties are soundly conceived and effectively carried out.

In agriculture, leveraged leasing is illustrated by the Banks for Cooperatives' participation as lenders in leasing arrangements between large agricultural cooperatives, lessors or their trustee representatives, and manufacturers. Examples of capital projects that have been financed through leveraged leasing by cooperatives include sugar beet refineries, fertilizer plants, rural electric systems, vessels, production equipment, and commodity handling systems. Farmers and other agricultural producers who patronize and own these cooperatives benefit indirectly from the co-ops' use of leveraged leasing to finance their operations.

Issues in Financial Leasing

The popular view of financial leasing highlights several basic advantages: the conservation of working capital, 100 percent financing, the use of modern equipment and facilities, and possible tax benefits for the lessee and lessor. These issues and many others are important in evaluating the payoffs of using financial leases as a method of financing non-real estate assets. Some of these issues are clearly advantages or disadvantages; others simply need careful consideration in the decision-making process.

Profitability of Leasing

Leasing may be a lower-cost method of financing than controlling assets through ownership and borrowing. Profitability depends on the comparison of the present values of after-tax cash flows for the various financing methods. The effects of income tax obligations on these cash flows are very important. The analytical procedures involved are shown later in the chapter.

Leasing and Borrowing Capacity

Leasing may conserve a farmer's existing sources of credit and might not restrict a firm's borrowing capacity. As explained below, leasing activities seldom are included in a farmer's balance sheet and thus do not directly influence many financial ratios. Indeed, leasing may even increase a farmer's credit over time if working capital is conserved and income expectations improve. However, the effects of leasing on financial and credit analyses should be integrated with the effects of other assets and liabilities to properly evaluate a business's overall financial feasibility. Acquiring a leased asset may on occasion be worse than not acquiring the asset at all, if the financial demands on cash flows are too strong. Under these conditions, a farmer's credit would be adversely affected too.

The relationships between leasing and credit also involve a lender's regulatory and liquidity positions. Some farmers who borrow from agricultural banks, for example, have loan requests large enough to exceed the bank's legal lending limit. The bank then needs an overline loan participation from another lender to fully fund the loan. An alternative is for the farmer to lease some of the assets, perhaps from the agricultural bank's leasing subsidiary, and thus reduce the need for overline participations from higher-cost sources. Similarly, if the bank has a tight liquidity position, as indicated by a high loan-to-deposit ratio, it may encourage its farm customers to lease some assets in order to relieve loan demands. The lender can then include the rental obligation in the farmer's operating line of credit, rather than provide a term loan. Of course, lenders who provide a leasing service must still finance their own leasing activities.

Leasing and Total Financing

Financial leases are often considered to provide the lessee with total financing that does not require the commitment of equity capital through cash purchases or downpayments on a loan. This is not always true, however. The terms of leases often result in cash payments at the beginning of the lease contract, which have cash flow consequences similar to downpayments on a credit purchase. Prepayments on rent and security deposits are common examples. They must be met by the lessee's own funds. Nonetheless, these initial cash payments usually are lower than the downpayment requirements on a credit purchase.

Leasing and Financial Statements

The concepts and practices involved in accounting for leasing activities on a firm's financial statements provide an interesting contrast. In concept, a firm's financial statement should report the full range of activities affecting its assets and liabilities. In this approach, assets and liabilities are broadly defined. Assets include all of the farm's income-generating activities, before the payments of rent, interest, taxes, and equity withdrawals. Included are the values of everything the business controls, whether owned outright or leased. Liabilities are all the claims on assets and income, including those of lenders, lessors, and equity capital. The value of leased assets is thus offset by the value of rental claims.

In practice, however, the effects of leasing have only appeared as operating expenses for rental payments on farm income statements and flows of funds' accounts. No accounting of leasing has appeared on the firm's balance sheets, so that leasing has been characterized as "off-balance-sheet" financing. Sometimes minimal disclosure of leasing activities might occur in footnotes to the financial statements.

Under these arrangements, financial analysis of firms that lease assets has yielded ratios and other measures showing stronger liquidity and solvency than is actually the case. The same situation applies to farmers who lease farm land. Most real estate leases are short-term written or oral contracts that resemble an operating lease more than a financial lease. Consequently, real estate leasing is also considered off-balance-sheet financing.

Accounting procedures changed in the 1970s with generally accepted accounting principles now calling for capitalization on the balance sheet of certain types of leases. A leased asset is to be capitalized on the balance sheet if any one of the following conditions is met:

1. The lease transfers ownership of the asset to the lessee by the end of the lease contract.
2. The lease contains an option to purchase the asset at a bargain price.
3. The lease period equals or exceeds 75 percent of the asset's estimated economic life.
4. At the start of the lease, the present value of the rental payments exceeds 90 percent of the value of the leased assets.

In general, if the lessee acquires essentially all of the economic benefits and risks of owning the leased asset, then the value of the leased asset is shown as an asset and the rental obligation is shown as a debt. These values roughly offset each other on the balance sheet and are reflected in the various measures of balance sheet liquidity. Moreover, information about the leasing terms and the methods of capitalization is to be given in footnotes to the financial statements.

The capitalization process involves both the balance sheet and the income statement. The procedures are summarized as follows. First, determine the present value of the lease by discounting its flow of rental payments to a present value, using an appropriate discount rate (the lessee's borrowing rate or the lessor's implicit interest rate in the lease contract). Enter this value as both an asset and a liability on the firm's balance sheet, distinguishing between the current and non-current portions as appropriate. Then, establish procedures for amortizing these lease values over the contract so that the asset and liability values reach zero by the end of the contract period. The lease's asset value is usually amortized according to the firm's depreciation practices (straightline or accelerated). The lease's liability value is amortized like a long-term-debt obligation into interest and principal portions each year. The leasing charge in the firm's income statement for any year is then the sum of the annual asset amortization plus the calculated interest charge.

These accounting procedures are illustrated in Table 13.1 for a farmer who is leasing a $15,000 micro computer on either an operating lease or a financial lease for a three-year period. In either case the lessor figures the annual rental charge at $6,570 based on a 15 percent implicit interest rate. If the farmer acquires the asset on an operating lease, the $6,570 rent is charged as an expense against each year's income, and no entries occur on the balance sheet. For a financial lease, the asset and liability values for the lease are $15,000, which is the present value of a uniform series of $6,570 payments for three years at 15 percent interest. The asset value is amortized on a straightline basis, yielding annual amortization of $5,000 (column d). The liability value is reduced according to the amortization schedule shown in columns f and g for imputed interest and principal. The annual expense (column h) is the sum of annual amortization (column d) and imputed interest (column f).

Table 13.1. Financial Accounting for Operating Leases Versus Financial Leases

End of Year	Operating Lease		Financial Lease					
	Rental Payment	Annual Expense	Asset Value	Annual Amortization	Liability Value	Imputed Interest	Principal	Annual Expense (d + f)
	(a)	(b)	(c)	(d)	(e)	(f)	(g)	(h)
0			15,000		15,000			
1	6,570	6,570	10,000	5,000	10,680	2,250	4,320	7,250
2	6,570	6,570	5,000	5,000	5,713	1,603	4,967	6,603
3	6,570	6,570	0	5,000	0	857	5,713	5,857
Total	19,710	19,710						19,710

As Table 13.1 shows, the total expenses over the lease contract are the same ($19,710) for the operating and financial leases. However, the time pattern of the expenses differs, with larger charges occurring earlier for the financial lease. Clearly, the accounting procedures for financial leases are more complex than for operating leases and make leasing an "on-balance-sheet" method of financing.

But these procedures also account more fully for leasing's effects on the firm's total financial position.

Leasing and Tax Considerations

The lessee's rental payments are a deductible expense for income tax purposes on operating or financial leases, so long as the transaction clearly qualifies as a lease. The conditions that qualify a transaction as a financial lease, in contrast to a credit purchase, have evolved over time in response to changes in federal laws and guidelines and rulings issued by the Internal Revenue Service in the United States. A major focus of these laws and rulings has been that lease transactions not be used solely for the purpose of transferring tax benefits.

The following guidelines have been in effect to qualify a transaction as a lease for tax purposes:

1. The lessor must have a minimum "at risk" investment of at least 20 percent in the property.
2. The lessee may neither provide investment capital for acquiring the property nor lend to or guarantee the loans of the lessor.
3. The lessee may not have an option to purchase the property at the end of the lease except at the existing fair market value. In no case can the lessee be required to purchase the property.
4. The lessor must expect to receive a profit and positive cash flow from the transaction, independent of the tax benefits.
5. The property should not be limited in use to only the lessee.

In addition, 1982 legislation created a new category of tax lease, called a *finance lease*, which applies to limited use property and which allows the lessee a fixed-price purchase option at 10 percent or more of the property's original cost.[1] Thus, a finance lease is considered to occur in lease agreements that contain a 10 percent fixed-

---

[1]The 1982 legislation contains numerous other stipulations and transitional requirements. For example, the full provisions of the *finance lease* are not in effect until September 30, 1985. Prior to then, various limitations apply to the spreading of investment tax credit, reductions in lessor's tax liability, and percent of lessee's qualifying equipment under lease. However, farm property is eligible for full finance lease treatment up to a maximum of $150,000 of leased equipment for any lessee per calendar year. The $150,000 limit on farm property no longer applies after 1985.

price purchase option or that involve limited use property, where otherwise the lessor is treated as the property owner for tax purposes. The major feature of the finance lease is provision for the fixed-price purchase option. In the past, the requirement that purchases at lease-termination occur only at fair market value created much uncertainty for both lessee and lessor. The fixed-price option reduces the uncertainty and allows residual values to be considered explicitly in setting lease payments and other terms.

Only the lessor, as owner of the leased equipment, may claim depreciation on the leased asset. However, the lessor may elect to pass on the investment tax credit (see Chapter 3) to the lessee, if the leased property is new and meets the specifications for claiming investment tax credit. A lessor cannot pass on the credit for used property to the lessee. Arrangements on transferring the tax credit are often subject to negotiation between the parties involved, based on their tax positions, and may influence the size of the rental obligation.

Leasing and Financing Terms

The variability and length of payment obligations, security requirements, and credit worthiness factors also warrant consideration in evaluating lease versus credit-purchase transactions. In most financial leases, the rental obligation is fixed over the term of the lease contract, in contrast to the increasing use of variable (or floating) interest rates on intermediate-term loans. The risks to the lessor associated with a fixed-rate lease tend to be passed on to the lessee in the form of higher rental payments. Since variable rate leasing contracts are possible, they likely will receive greater use, as lessors respond to changes in their own financing costs.

The comparability of maturities for financial leases and term loans likely varies with the source of leasing and the source of credit. In general, these maturities should be similar, as lessors and lenders increasingly establish contract lengths that approach the economic life of the assets involved. Security requirements and other credit factors should also be similar for financial leases and term loans. Most lessors require that collateral be pledged to secure the lease. Lenders have similar requirements, although often requiring additional collateral as well. In most financial leases, the lessee must demonstrate lease worthiness the same as a borrower demonstrates credit worthiness. Showing repayment capacity, pledging collateral, meeting net worth requirements, and other credit factors may be involved.

Other Leasing Issues

Many other factors unique to the specific situation need consideration in leasing transactions. Leasing may reduce the risk of obsolescence by allowing more rapid replacement of equipment at lower transaction costs, although this is less true for financial leases than for operating leases. Leasing may provide financing for noninterest costs of acquiring an asset. Sales taxes, delivery and installation costs, and others may be included in the rental payments on a lease. Leasing may also introduce "tenure risks" involving the inability to renew the lease when the contract expires. Loss of a leased asset could jeopardize other parts of a business operation, although this risk is greater for leasing farm land than for non-real assets.

Economics of Leasing

In this section we demonstrate procedures for evaluating the economics of leasing for both the lessee and the lessor. For the lessee, leasing is contrasted to ownership based on intermediate-term financing. For the lessor, leasing is contrasted to other forms of investment, with evaluation based on capital budgeting procedures. Both analyses use present-value methods in order to account for leasing's effects on the timing and magnitude of cash flows.

Lease Versus Credit Purchase: Lessee's Position

Consider a farmer who has made the decision to acquire the services of a new tractor. The farmer's main concern at this point is choosing the best financing method. The financing alternatives are numerous. The tractor services could be hired on a custom basis, rented each year on an operating lease, rented on a financial lease with subsequent purchase, or purchased now. If the tractor is purchased, numerous loan sources are also available.

We will assume, however, that the farmer has narrowed the financing choices to two alternatives: (1) a financial lease from a local machinery dealer followed by a purchase when the lease expires and (2) a purchase financed by an intermediate-term loan from a local financial institution. The preferred choice is based on the lower-cost method of financing. Thus, the appropriate "costs" must be identified and measured over the planning period. This involves projecting the cash flows associated with the two financing methods.

The computational procedures are simplified by eliminating all the cash flow elements that are similar for the two alternatives. In this case, machinery operating costs, property taxes, maintenance, and labor are the same for the farmer whether the tractor is owned or leased. So, they can be ignored in the comparison. Only the cash flows that differ between the two financing methods are considered.

These cash flows are projected over the life of the transactions and discounted to their present values. The financing method with the lower present value of net cash outflows is the preferred choice. As the following example will show, the income tax consequences of the lease versus purchase decision are very important.

The relevant data associated with the tractor acquisition are as follows: the tractor is valued at $50,000, and the farmer intends to keep it for seven years. The farmer is in the 30 percent tax bracket and has a 10 percent after-tax cost of capital. Variations in the tax rate and discount rate will be considered later.

The terms for purchasing the tractor with credit financing are a 25 percent downpayment with equally amortized annual payments over five years at an interest rate of 14.5 percent on the remaining loan balance. Thus the downpayment is $12,500, leaving a loan balance of $37,500 and annual amortization payments of $11,055. Depreciation is based on the five-year class of the Accelerated Cost Recovery System (ACRS) (see Chapter 3), with the depreciable basis reduced by half of the investment tax credit. Investment tax credit is claimed at 10 percent rate, and the tractor's residual value at the end of year 7 is projected at $3,150.

The terms of the financial lease include a five-year contract, with annual rental payments of $11,225 due at the beginning of each year. The lessor retains the investment tax credit. At the end of year 5, the farmer purchases the machine for an expected value of $5,000. Depreciation may be claimed on the purchase, but no investment tax credit is allowed. The residual value at the end of year 7 is also projected at $3,150.

Net cash outflows associated with the lease and purchase are projected in Table 13.2 on an after-tax basis. Net cash outflows for leasing in Column d consist of the five annual rental payments less the tax credit (or savings) at 30 percent of the rental payment, lagged one year. Following year 5, the cash flows reflect the tractor pur-

Table 13.2. Net Cash Outflows for Lease Versus Purchase of a $50,000 Tractor

	Financial Lease				Purchase					
Year	Rent and Purchase (a)	Depreciation (b)	Tax Credit (c)	Net Cash Outflow (a − c) (d)	Downpayment and Principal (e)	Interest (f)	Depreciation (g)	ITC and Residual Value (h)	Tax Credit (i)	Net Cash Outflow (e + f − h − i) (j)
0	11,225			11,225	12,500			5,000		12,500
1	11,225		3,368	7,857	5,617	5,438	7,125		3,769	2,286
2	11,225		3,368	7,857	6,432	4,623	10,450		4,522	6,533
3	11,225		3,368	7,857	7,365	3,690	9,975		4,100	6,955
4	11,225		3,368	7,857	8,433	2,622	9,975		3,779	7,276
5	5,000	750	3,368	1,632	9,655	1,400	9,975		3,412	7,643
6			225	−225						0
7	−3,150	1,100	330	−3,480				3,150	−945	−2,205

chase in year 5, tractor sale in year 7, and tax credits for depreciation in years 6 and 7.

The tax credit is determined by multiplying the tax deductible expenses for each alternative by the relevant tax rate. The tax deductible expenses reduce taxable income, thereby reducing the cash outflow for taxes. Since the table expresses net cash outflows, entries in Columns d and j with negative signs represent cash inflows. Although depreciation is not a cash cost, it is a tax deductible expense. Hence, charging depreciation reduces taxes and yields a tax credit.

The net cash outflow for the credit purchase is based on entries in Columns e through j in Table 13.2. Entries in Column e indicate the 25 percent downpayment in year zero and the principal portions of the amortized loan payments for years 1 through 5. The interest portion of the amortized payments is shown in Column f. Annual depreciation is in Column g, and the 10 percent investment tax credit and residual sale value are shown in Column h. The series of tax credits in Column i represents the sum of interest (Column f) plus depreciation (Column g) multiplied by the appropriate tax rate (30 percent). The negative tax credit in year 7 represents the ordinary income tax obligation on the residual sale value. The series of net cash outflows in Column j is the sum of entries in Columns e plus f minus h minus i.

The irregular pattern of net cash outflows in Column j reflects the combined effects of the financing terms and the tax implications of interest, depreciation, investment tax credit, and the residual value. Clearly, these non-uniform patterns in the timing and magnitude of cash flows for both the purchase and the lease alternatives require present-value methods for accurate evaluation. Table 13.3 shows the present value of net cash outflows for the lease and purchase alternatives, based on an after-tax discount rate of 10 percent. The present values are $35,230 for the financial lease and $33,786 for the credit purchase. Thus, the credit purchase is preferred, because it provides a lower present value of net cash outflows.

Table 13.4 shows present values of net cash outflows for the two methods under different assumptions on discount rates and tax rates.[2] For the 30 percent tax rate and other specifications of this example, leasing is only preferred at a zero discount rate. As the discount rate increases, the credit purchase is preferred, with its margin of superi-

---

[2]Readers should be aware that in this example and the following one, some rounding of numbers in the calculation process has occurred.

Table 13.3. Present Value of Net Cash Outflows (10 Percent Discount Rate)

	Financial Lease			Purchase		
Year	Net Cash Outflow	Present Value Factor (1/1 + i)	Present Value	Net Cash Outflow	Present Value Factor (1/1 + i)	Present Value
0	11,225	1.0000	11,225	12,500	1.0000	12,500
1	7,857	.9091	7,143	2,286	.9091	2,078
2	7,857	.8264	6,493	6,533	.8264	5,399
3	7,857	.7513	5,903	6,955	.7513	5,225
4	7,857	.6830	5,366	7,276	.6830	4,970
5	1,632	.6209	1,013	7,643	.6209	4,746
6	−225	.5645	−127	0	.5645	0
7	−3,480	.5132	−1,786	−2,205	.5132	−1,132
Total	40,580		35,230	40,988		33,786

ority increasing for higher-discount rates. In addition, the credit purchase tends to have a wider margin of preference for higher tax rates. The margin of superiority for the credit purchase narrows as the lessee's tax rate is lowered, as shown by reading across the table for selected discount rates. Only for low discount rates (e.g., 5 percent) and low tax rates (or no tax obligation) is leasing preferred.

The major factor that favors ownership here is the owner's full use of the investment tax credit to conserve the net cash outflow in period 1. The Accelerated Cost Recovery System (depreciation) and interest deductions also generate higher tax credits earlier in the investment period for purchase rather than leasing. These influences on the pattern of net cash flows have important effects on the present values.

We must stress that the emphasis is on the methods of evaluating lease versus purchase decisions. The numerical results are specific to the terms and assumptions of the tractor example. Other terms and investment situations could yield different results. Moreover, changes in laws affecting the tax status of leasing and ownership may shift the economic balance of leasing versus purchase over time. Through negotiation, the lessor may also adjust the leasing terms to make them more attractive to a lessee while still meeting the lessor's profit target.

Leasing As an Investment: The Lessor's Position

In this section we consider the profitability of financial leases from the lessor's standpoint. Leasing is an income-generating activity for the lessor; thus the analytical approach uses capital budgeting

Table 13.4. Present Values of Lease Versus Credit Purchase for Different Tax and Discount Rates

	Tax Rates									
	30 Percent		20 Percent		10 Percent		5 Percent		0 Percent	
Discount Rate	Lease	Purchase	Lease	Purchase	Lease	Purchase	Lease	Purchase	Lease	Purchase
0 Percent	40,580[1]	40,988	46,380[1]	47,200	52,186[1]	54,413	55,323[1]	56,619	59,975[1]	64,625
5 Percent	37,722	36,939	42,718	42,465	47,718[1]	47,914	50,313[1]	50,638	52,707[1]	58,124
10 Percent	35,230	33,786	39,586	38,605	43,944	43,425	46,191	45,835	48,294[1]	52,790
20 Percent	31,173	28,931	34,587	32,792	38,002	36,653	39,746	35,584	41,413[1]	44,681
30 Percent	28,082	25,544	30,851	28,721	33,618	31,898	35,023	34,441	36,385[1]	38,922

[1]Leasing yields a lower present value.

procedures to estimate a Net Present Value (NPV) or an Internal-Rate-of-Return (IRR) for leasing. The results can be used to accept or reject leasing as an investment activity, or to rank its profitability relative to other investments. The budgeting procedures are also helpful in evaluating terms (rental payments, residual values, investment tax credit) on leases that will enhance the lessor's competitive position while also improving the lessee's cash flow.

We illustrate the analytical methods with the following case taken from an actual banking situation. The Big Farm Lender (BFL) is considering the adoption of a leasing program for farmers in addition to the lending program which it presently offers and wishes to compare the profitability of leasing to lending. The comparison is based on the following terms and assumptions for financial leasing and intermediate-term lending.

- *Lending:* A $1 million term loan payable in equal annual amortized payments over five years at an interest rate of 18 percent.

- *Leasing*: A $1 million lease transaction with equal rental payments due at the end of the next five years. Rental payments are set at $319,778 to fully amortize the asset cost at 18 percent interest. The asset is fully depreciated over five years. The estimated residual value is 15 percent of the initial asset cost, or $150,000.

The Big Farm Lender is incorporated and pays taxes at the corporate tax rate of 46 percent. Investment tax credit of 10 percent is available immediately. The residual value is fully taxable. The depreciation allowances for tax purposes based upon ACRS are:

	Year				
	1	2	3	4	5
Rate	15%	22%	21%	21%	21%

These rates are applied to the assets' original cost less one-half of the investment tax credit.

The net present-value procedures could be illustrated with a work sheet, as in the previous section, that identifies the various sources of cash flow. In this example, however, the capital budgeting procedures are expressed in a present-value model to show an alternative approach to the analysis. The present-value model for the financial lease is:

$$NPV = -INV + ITC + (1 - t)A[USPV_{i,n}] \qquad (13.1)$$

$$+ \sum_{n=1}^{n} \frac{tD}{(1 + i)^n} + \frac{(1 - t)V_N}{(1 + i)^N}$$

The variables are:

    i = The discount rate, measured here as the after-tax yield on lending.

Thus:

    i = $(.18)(1 - .46) = .097$, or 9.7%

    N = The length of the lease contract, or 5 years

    A = The annual rental payments, or $319,778

    V_N = The residual value of the leased assets, or $150,000

    t = The corporate tax rate, or 46 percent

    INV = The asset's initial cost, or $1 million

    ITC = Investment tax credit retained by the lessor at time zero, or $100,000

    D = Annual depreciation, projected as:

Year	
1	$142,500
2	209,000
3	199,500
4	199,500
5	199,500

    Values of these variables are included in equation (13.1) in order to determine the net present value. Table 13.5 summarizes the calculation procedures. The NPV at the bottom of the table is $140,920. It is comprised of the sum of the present values for the after-tax rental payments, the depreciation tax credit, and the residual value minus the initial investment adjusted for investment tax credit.

    The positive net present value indicates that the financial leas-

Table 13.5. Net Present Value of Financial Leasing for the Lessor

	Item	Present Value
1. Initial Investment:	INV =	−1,000,000
2. Investment Tax Credit:	ITC =	100,000
3. Rental Payments:	$(1 - t)A[USPV_{i,n}]$	
	$(1 - .46)(319,778)[USPV_{.097,5}] =$	659,641
4. Depreciation Tax Credit:	$\sum\limits_{n=1}^{n} \dfrac{tD}{(1+i)^n} =$	

Year 1: $(.46)(142,500)(1.097)^{-1} = 59,754$
Year 2: $(.46)(209,000)(1.097)^{-2} = 79,890$
Year 3: $(.46)(199,500)(1.097)^{-3} = 69,515$
Year 4: $(.46)(199,500)(1.097)^{-4} = 63,369$
Year 5: $(.46)(199,500)(1.097)^{-5} = 57,765$

	Item	Present Value
	Total:	330,293
5. Residual value	$\dfrac{(1 - t)(V_n)}{(1 + i)^n}$	
	$\dfrac{(1 - .46)(150,000)}{(1.097)^5} =$	50,986
6. Net Present Value		140,920

ing activity should be profitable relative to the alternative of intermediate-term lending, even though both investments involve the same before-tax interest rates, payments, and maturity. The differences in timing and magnitude of tax obligations for the two investments account for most of their differences in profitability. The internal-rate-of-return is the discount rate, which yields a zero net present value in equation (13.1). The IRR on the financial lease is 15.33 percent. Thus, compared to a 9.70 percent after-tax yield on intermediate-term lending, the financial lease is profitable according to the IRR criterion as well.

The net present-value model can also be used to evaluate how alternative leasing terms affect the lessor's profit position. Suppose, for example, that the Big Farm Lender is willing to set the five rental payments at a level that yields the same after-tax rate of return as intermediate-term lending; that is, 9.70 percent. This is accomplished by finding the level of rental payments (A) in equation (13.1) that yields NPV = 0, assuming that the values of all other variables remain the same. For the data in Table 13.5, the present value of rental payments (entry 3) would have to be $518,721 to yield NPV equals zero. The after-tax value of A is then:

$$A = \frac{518{,}721}{\text{USPV}_{.097,5}} = 135{,}790$$

Dividing A by $1 - t$ yields a before-tax rental payment of \$251,463.

Similar procedures are followed to determine the rental payments needed to yield a 9.70 after-tax return when a 10 percent residual value is projected for the leased assets. In this case, the before-tax rental payments are \$259,702. Next, suppose the lessor elects to pass the investment tax credit to the lessee, projects a 15 percent residual value, and stipulates a 9.70 percent after-tax return on the lease. For these specifications, the before-tax rental payments must be \$291,513. (Note: No adjustment in depreciable basis is needed when ITC is passed to the lessee.)

Finally, assume in the original specification of the problem that the lessor requires the rental payments at the beginning of the year instead of year end. Confirm in Table 13.5 that advance payments would increase the present value of the rental payments to \$723,626, and the lessor's net present value to \$204,905.

Thus, the effects of numerous changes in leasing terms can be evaluated in order to find mutually acceptable arrangements for both lessor and lessee, based on their cash flow and tax positions.

Topics for Discussion

1. Distinguish between operating leases and financial leases. How do they represent methods of financing? How is custom hiring distinguished? Explain the concepts of leveraged leasing.
2. Critically evaluate the proposition that "leasing provides 100 percent financing."
3. Identify the effects of leasing on a farm's borrowing capacity.
4. Critically evaluate the proposition that "leasing is an off-balance-sheet form of financing."
5. A farmer leases a tractor for five years with annual rental payments of \$11,225 due at the end of each year. Using a 15 percent interest rate, show the impacts for year 1 on the farmer's balance sheet and income statement.
6. Identify the guidelines to qualify a transaction as a lease for tax purposes. What additional features characterize a "finance lease"?
7. How do lessors evaluate the lease worthiness of lessees? Contrast this process with a lender's evaluation of a borrower's credit worthiness.
8. Compare a financial lease with a credit purchase for a \$150,000 asset, depreciable over five years, with a zero residual value. Lease payments are \$37,000, due at the beginning of each of the next five years. Credit

terms are 25 percent downpayment and a loan payable in equal payments of principal and interest over five years at 14 percent interest. The investor's tax rate is 30 percent, and the after-tax cost of capital is 10 percent. Investment tax credit and the Accelerated Cost Recovery System apply.

9. A Production Credit Association is developing a financial leasing program for its farm customers, along with its current lending program. The lending terms on farm tractors are a five-year loan at 13 percent interest, with equally amortized payments. Assuming the PCA's tax rate is 46 percent, find the annual rent the PCA would charge on the lease to give the same yield as the loan rate. Assume a 10 percent residual value on tractors, a five-year term, lease payments at year end, and full use of ITC and ACRS (figure on a per dollar of original tractor value).

How does this rent compare with the farmer's cash payments for a credit purchase? What are the implications for financial leasing by PCAs, and other lenders?

References

1. Barnes, G. D., "An Ag Lender Looks at Leasing," *Agri Finance*, 23(1980):40-48.
2. Brigham, E. F., *Financial Management: Theory and Practice*, 3rd ed., Dryden Press, Hinsdale, Illinois, 1982.
3. Crawford, P. J., C. P. Harper, and J. McConnell, "Further Evidence on the Terms of Financial Leases," *Financial Management*, 10:3(1981):7-14.
4. Levy, H., and M. Sarnat, *Capital Investment and Financial Decisions*, Prentice-Hall, Inc., Englewood Cliffs, New Jersey, 1978.
5. Pritchard, R. E., and T. Hindelang, *The Lease-Buy Decision*, AMACOM, American Management Associations, New York, 1980.
6. Sorenson, J. W., and R. E. Johnson, "Equipment Financial Leasing Practices and Costs: An Empirical Study," *Financial Management*, 6:1(1977):33-40.
7. Van Horne, J. C., *Financial Management and Policy*, 5th ed., Prentice-Hall, Inc., Englewood Cliffs, New Jersey, 1980.

Chapter 14

COSTS OF FINANCIAL CAPITAL

This chapter develops procedures for measuring a firm's costs of debt and equity capital. In previous chapters, we have largely taken these costs as given, in order to evaluate their effects on a firm's profitability, leverage, financial growth, capital budgeting, and financial feasibility. In financial planning and investment analysis, however, these costs must be determined from available data and sound judgment about future conditions.

The following sections apply present-value analysis to estimate the costs of debt capital under different financing terms and from different lenders. Costs of equity capital then are distinguished on the basis of retained earnings and new outside equity brought into a farm operation. Effects of taxes, inflation, and nonmoney costs are also considered in evaluating a firm's average cost of capital.

Money Costs of Debt Capital

Costs of debt capital include money costs to meet interest payments and other noninterest obligations and nonmoney costs associated with financial risks. These costs are generally measured on an after-tax basis with appropriate allowance for inflation. We begin with the money cost of borrowing.

The money cost of borrowing is the difference between the total money that the borrower *receives* from the loan (sometimes different from the total loan, as we shall see) and the total money paid to retire the loan. It is comprised, primarily, of interest cost, but often includes noninterest costs as well. Both interest and noninterest costs are included when computing the percentage, or "rate," cost of borrowed capital.

A discussion of procedures for determining interest rates is complicated by the different methods used to compute interest costs and by the differences in terminology used to identify different kinds of interest rates—the *contractual* rate, the *simple* rate, the *compound* rate, the *real* rate, the *nominal* rate, the *annual percentage* rate, the *actuarial* rate, the *effective* rate, and others. Hence, it is generally not sufficient to base a financing decision solely on an interest rate that is stated on a note.

The Actuarial Interest Rate

Our approach is to develop a basic model for determining money costs of debt capital that may be used for any kind of financing transaction—simple or complex. The approach uses the notion of compound interest developed in Chapter 9, together with the present-value models, to determine an interest rate per conversion period on a loan transaction. This interest rate per conversion period is called the *actuarial* interest rate. The actuarial rate is the interest rate, or discount rate, that equates to zero the sum of the present values of all cash flows associated with the loan transaction. Or, expressed in another way, it is the interest or discount rate that equates the present value of all cash inflows associated with the loan transaction to the present value of all cash outflows.

The concept of the actuarial rate should sound familiar. It is similar to the definition of the internal-rate-of-return discussed in Chapter 10. Only the application is different. The IRR is used to evaluate investment profitability. The actuarial interest rate is used to evaluate money costs of debt capital. Each reflects the interest rate yielding a zero net present value for a series of payments. In fact, the borrower's actuarial interest on a loan would be the same as the lender's IRR on that loan.

To demonstrate the procedures for calculating an actuarial interest rate, let's identify the appropriate present-value model, recalling that we seek a net present value of zero. For a loan with a single payment of principal and interest due at the end of N periods, the model is:

$$0 = V_0 - \frac{P_N}{(1 + i)^N} \tag{14.1}$$

where V_0 is the cash proceeds of the loan received by the borrower, P_N is the repayment of principal and interest, and i is the actuarial interest rate. Notice that the signs of the variables are different from those used in Chapter 10 for analyzing investment profitability. Now V_o has a positive sign reflecting the cash inflow of the loan proceeds to the borrower, while the later payment (P_N) of principal and interest has a negative sign signifying the cash outflow.

To illustrate, let's find the actuarial rate of interest on \$1,000 borrowed on January 1 and repaid a year later with a payment of \$1,120. It is:

$$0 = 1,000 \; - \; \frac{1,120}{1 + i} \tag{14.2}$$

$$i \; = \; \frac{1,120}{1,000} \; - \; 1 = .12, \text{ or } 12 \text{ percent.}$$

Had the loan been repaid after two years with a payment of \$1,254.40, the actuarial rate would be:

$$0 = 1,000 \; - \; \frac{1,254.40}{(1 + i)^2} \tag{14.3}$$

$$(1 + i)^2 = 1.2544$$

$$i = .12, \text{ or } 12 \text{ percent.}$$

From Appendix Table I, an interest of 12 percent is found to be associated with $n = 2$ and a conversion factor of 1.2544. Hence, the actuarial interest rate is 12 percent per conversion period.

For an installment loan in which a series of payments of principal, interest, or both are made to fully repay the loan, the appropriate present-value models are the non-uniform series, if the payments differ among the periods:

$$0 = V_o - \sum_{n\,=\,1}^{N} \frac{P_N}{(1 + i)^n} \tag{14.4}$$

or the uniform series if the payments are the same in each period:

$$0 \; = \; V_o - A[USPV_{i,N}]. \tag{14.5}$$

In each case, the object is to find the value of i that equates the sum of the present value of all the cash flows to zero.

To illustrate, let's find the actuarial rate of interest on a \$1,000 loan that is repaid in four annual payments of \$329.23 each. Total payments over the four years are $(\$329.23)(4) = \$1,316.92$. Hence, interest paid over the four years is \$316.92. Since the annual payments are constant and the conversion periods are equal in length, we can use the uniform series model which is specified as:

$$0 = 1{,}000 - 329.23[\text{USPV}_{i,4}].\qquad(14.6)$$

We must now determine the value of i, which, when substituted into equation (14.6), will equate the sum of the cash flows to zero. First solve for the value of the conversion factor for $[\text{USPV}_{i,4}]$:

$$[\text{USPV}_{i,4}] = \frac{1{,}000}{329.23} = 3.0373.$$

Then, look in Appendix Table IV for the rate of interest that is associated with N = 4 and a conversion factor of 3.0373. In this case, the interest rate is found to be .12, or 12 percent. Hence, the actuarial interest rate on the loan is 12 percent.

This kind of loan is called a fully amortized or constant-payment loan because equal payments comprised of principal and interest are used to fully repay the loan and interest during its period to maturity. It is commonly used on farm real estate loans and on consumer installment loans. Another repayment pattern is the constant payment-on-principal method. This method requires equal principal payments in each period, with interest paid on the remaining loan balance. Because the interest payments are smaller in each successive period, the total payments of principal and interest decline over the period of the loan.

Suppose, for example, that the $1,000 loan is to be repaid in four annual principal payments of $250 each, plus interest in each year. Total payments are $330 at the end of year 1, $310 in year 2, $290 in year 3, and $270 in year 4. To find the actuarial interest rate, we use equation (14.4) and formulate the present-value model as:

$$0 = 1{,}000 - \frac{370}{1+i} - \frac{340}{(1+i)^2} - \frac{310}{(1+i)^3} - \frac{280}{(1+i)^4}.\qquad(14.7)$$

We must again determine the value of i, which, when substituted into equation (14.7), will equate the sum of the cash flows to zero. Because the cash flows are non-uniform, we must use Appendix Table II and follow the trial-and-error method.

For i = .11, or 11 percent, the net present value of equation (14.7) is −20.40. Hence, the interest rate must be increased to yield NPV = 0. In this case, an interest rate of 12 percent yields NPV = 0. Hence, the actuarial interest rate for this loan is 12 percent.

The Annual Percentage Rate (APR)

The annual percentage rate (APR), sometimes called the nominal rate, is found by expressing the actuarial interest rate on an *annual* basis. That is, the APR is the interest rate per year. Clearly, the APR and the actuarial rate are identical when the conversion periods are each one year long. This was the case in the previous examples. Hence, for the $1,000 loan to be repaid in four annual installments of $329.23 each, the actuarial rate of 12 percent is also a 12 percent annual percentage rate.

Differences between the actuarial rate and the APR occur when each conversion period is not one year in length. As examples, monthly payments on a loan create 12 conversion periods within a year. Similarly, quarterly payments on a loan create four conversion periods within a year. Under these circumstances, compounding of loan interest occurs more frequently than once a year, and the actuarial interest rate must be converted to an APR.

To illustrate, consider the case of a loan for $1,000 to be repaid in four quarterly payments of $269.03 each. Again, we can use present-value equation (14.4) or (14.5). However, since compounding of loan interest occurs more frequently than once a year, we utilize equation (9.3), $V_N = (1 + i/m)^{mn}$, to reflect i as an annual percentage rate. In this case, the actuarial rate is expressed as i/m where $m = 4$ due to the quarterly payments. Multiplying the actuarial rate by $m = 4$ will yield the APR.

The problem is set up as follows:

$$0 = 1,000 - \frac{269.03}{1 + i/4} - \frac{269.03}{(i + i/4)^2} - \frac{269.03}{(1 + i/4)^3} \qquad \textbf{(14.8)}$$
$$- \frac{269.03}{(1 + i/4)^4}$$

or, since the payments are a uniform series:

$$0 = 1,000 - 269.03[USPV_{i/4,\,4}].$$

Solve for the conversion factor:

$$[USPV_{i/4,\,4}] = \frac{1,000}{269.03} = 3.7171.$$

Then, find the interest rate $(i/4)$ in Appendix Table IV that is associated with a conversion factor of 3.7171 and $N = 4$. The conversion factor for 3 percent is 3.7171.

Hence, the actuarial interest rate (i/4) for this loan is 3 percent per conversion period. Since each conversion period is one-fourth of a year, the actuarial rate is multiplied by four to yield the annual percentage rate. The result is (3)(4) = 12 percent.

Truth in Lending and APR

Procedures for calculating and comparing interest costs and rates on financing transactions have always been perplexing to many consumers and businesspersons. Often, the lender's quote of a contract interest rate differs considerably from the annual percentage rate, due to different methods of charging interest or to noninterest costs. As a result, federal legislation was passed in the United States requiring lenders to inform borrowers precisely and explicitly of the total amount of the finance charge which they must pay and the annual percentage rate of interest to the nearest 0.10 percent. The purpose was to improve knowledge and understanding of market rates and to reduce the likelihood of fraudulent practices. Truth-in-lending compliance is required of creditors who (1) regularly make loans in the ordinary course of business; (2) levy a finance charge for more than four installment payments; or (3) make loans to a natural person, where the recipient uses the proceeds primarily for personal, family, household, or agricultural purposes. Excluded transactions in the early legislation included loans for commercial or business purposes, loans to partnerships, corporations, cooperatives, and organizations, and loans greater than $25,000, except for real estate loans, where compliance is required irrespective of the amount.

The inclusion of interest disclosure on agricultural loans and not on commercial or business loans concerned many lenders, who felt that these loans should receive comparable treatment. As a result, all agricultural loans were exempt from truth-in-lending requirements. Hence, for most agricultural operations using large amounts of short- and intermediate-term debt, disclosure of annual percentage rates and finance charges is no longer required.

Lenders who comply with truth in lending must report an annual percentage rate which is based on the logic and method of the actuarial rate and compound interest as outlined above. The simplifying differences in truth in lending are that the lender need only report the rate to the nearest 0.10 percent and use tables or computerized techniques in its estimation.

The Contractual Rate

At this point you should be familiar with the notion of the actuarial rate and its linkage to the annual percentage rate. Now we introduce a third rate, called the contractual rate, which may or may not be identical to the actuarial rate and the APR. In simplest terms, the contractual rate is the interest rate stated by the lender on the note—10 percent, 12 percent, 14 percent, etc. In the first example given earlier, where a $1,000 loan was repaid in a single payment of $1,120 one year later, both the actuarial rate and the APR were 12 percent. The contractual rate is also 12 percent per year. It would appear on the note, signifying that the borrower promises to repay the loan in one year with interest calculated at a 12 percent annual rate.

The contractual rate can differ from the actuarial rate or APR when noninterest money costs are part of the loan transaction or when different methods of calculating interest are used. Recall that the actuarial rate is defined as the rate of interest equating the sum of the present value of all cash flows associated with the loan transaction to zero. Included are cash flows for the loan principal, for interest, and for noninterest costs included in the loan payments. Hence, the actuarial rate has a broader meaning than the contractual rate.

Noninterest Money Costs

A variety of noninterest costs are often associated with loans. Although there are no fixed rules on which costs to include in deriving the actuarial rate, some guidelines are offered by paragraph 226.4 of the Rules and Regulations of the Federal Reserve System pertaining to the Truth in Lending Act. With few exceptions, all charges should be included that are payable directly or indirectly by the borrower and imposed directly or indirectly by the lender as incident to or as a condition of the extension of the loan. In addition to interest, they include: (1) service, transaction, activity, or carrying charges; (2) loan-fee points or finder's fees; (3) fees for investigations and credit reports (except those related to real property); and (4) premiums for special insurance required as a condition of the loan for either the lender or the borrower.

When itemized and disclosed to the customer, the following types of charges need not be included in the finance charge: (1) fees prescribed by law paid to public officials for perfecting or releasing any security (or insurance in lieu of perfecting any security interest if the premium does not exceed the latter cost); (2) license, certificate of title, and registration fees imposed by law; (3) taxes; and (4) delinquency, default, and reinstatement charges. In addition, the rules specifically exclude the following charges relating to real-property transactions: (1) fees for title examination, title insurance, and similar purposes, and for property surveys; (2) fees for preparation and/or notarization of deeds and other documents; (3) required escrow payments for future payment of taxes, insurance, etc.; (4) appraisal fees; and (5) credit reports.

As a general rule, one should include all costs arising from borrowing. Moreover, as later examples will indicate, there is also need to account for special requirements by different types of lenders. Examples include compensating deposit balances often required by commercial banks as a loan condition and stock requirements associated with borrowing from production credit associations, federal land banks, and banks for cooperatives.

Methods of Computing Interest

Computing interest rates is further complicated because lenders can use three methods of computing interest, and the interest cost can vary considerably according to the method being used. These methods are called the remaining-balance, the add-on, and the discount methods. The remaining-balance method is most commonly used, although the others, especially the add-on method, have considerable use as well. Each method yields a different time pattern of cash flows associated with the loan transaction, which in turn causes differences in the annual percentage rate.

Remaining-Balance Method

With the remaining-balance method, interest is calculated by multiplying the principal outstanding by the contractual rate for the period in question. The procedure is illustrated in the following formula, where P = loan principal, i_c = the contractual rate, and T = the length of period expressed as a fraction of a year. The interest cost (I) is:

$$I = (P)(i_c)(T). \tag{14.9}$$

For example, a $1,000 loan at a 12 percent annual rate for six months would carry an interest cost (I) of ($1,000)(.12)(1/2) = $60.

To illustrate further, let's return to the constant payment on principal method of repayment indicated in equation (14.7). A $1,000 loan is being repaid in four annual principal payments of $250 each, plus interest at a 12 percent annual rate on the remaining balance. The interest payments in each of the four years are found as follows:

$$I_1 = (1,000)(.12)(1) = 120$$

$$I_2 = (750)(.12)(1) = 90$$

$$I_3 = (500)(.12)(1) = 60$$

$$I_4 = (250)(.12)(1) = 30.$$

These interest payments are added to the $250 principal payments in each year to give total payments of $370, $330, $310, and $280 in each respective year.

The remaining-balance method may also be used in the equally amortized, or constant payment, installment loan, although the procedures for calculating the interest paid in each installment are more detailed. To illustrate, consider the earlier example of a $1,000 loan to be repaid in four equal annual payments of principal and interest at a 12 percent annual rate calculated on the remaining-balance method. To find the annual payment, we solve for the level of annuity (A) that will fully amortize a $1,000 loan over four periods at a 12 percent rate per period. The uniform series model is formulated and solved as follows:

$$1,000 = A[USPV_{.12,4}]$$

$$A = 329.23.$$

The next step is to determine an amortization schedule which shows the breakdown of each payment into principal and interest. Perhaps it is easiest to remember that the interest obligation of the payment must be met first, with the rest of the payment used to reduce the loan balance. This procedure is illustrated in Table 14.1. At the end of the first year, interest is calculated on the $1,000 loan balance as:

$$I = (1,000)(.12)(1) = 120$$

and is added to the balance:

$$1,000 + 120 = 1,120.$$

Then the first payment is deducted to obtain the remaining balance:

$1{,}120 - 329.23 = 790.77$.

Principal paid is the difference between the total payment and the interest payment. The same procedure is followed the next period and every period thereafter; that is, interest is calculated first and then added to the balance before the payment is subtracted.

Columns 3 and 7 in Table 14.1 show the interest and principal payments, respectively, while columns 2 and 6 show the beginning and remaining loan balances. Notice the pattern of interest and principal payments. As the remaining balance of the loan is reduced, the interest payment decreases. Consequently, a higher portion of each payment is principal, which reduces the loan balance. When the last payment is reached, very little is charged as interest.

Table 14.1. An Amortization Schedule for a Fully Amortized, Constant-Payment Loan

Period (T) (1)	Balance, Beginning of Period (P) (2)	Interest Accrued (3)	Total Balance Before Payment (2) + (3) (4)	Payment (A) (5)	Remaining Balance (4) − (5) (6)	Principal Paid (5) − (3) (7)
1	$1,000.00	$120.00	$1,120.00	$329.23	$790.77	$209.23
2	790.77	94.89	885.66	329.23	556.43	234.34
3	556.43	66.77	623.20	329.23	293.97	262.46
4	293.97	35.26	329.23	329.23	0	293.97

These procedures for deriving an amortization schedule characterize any constant-payment installment loan with interest paid on the remaining balance. Procedures are the same whether the payments are made for annual, quarterly, monthly, or other periods. Amortization tables for different rates of interest and different time periods are readily available for the convenience of lenders or others who need this detailed information.

Add-on Method

When lenders say that interest is charged at a 10 percent add-on rate, they mean that interest is calculated on the original loan for the entire period of the loan. The formula for calculating the total interest obligation (I_a) is:

$$I_a = (P)(i_c)(N) \qquad \qquad \textbf{(14.10)}$$

where P is loan principal, i_c is the contractual interest rate per period, and N is the number of periods. The sum of total interest and principal is divided by the number of payments to obtain the amount of each installment.

To illustrate, consider a $1,000 loan for four years with four annual payments, add-on interest, a 10 percent contractual rate, and no noninterest costs. The total interest obligation is:

$$I_a = (1,000)(.10)(4) = 400.$$

The total obligation of principal and interest is then $1,400, and each annual payment is $1,400 ÷ 4 = $350.

The actuarial rate for add-on interest is found using the present-value model as follows:

$$0 = \$1,000 - 350[USPV_{i,4}] \tag{14.11}$$

and, using Appendix Table IV, is associated with an actuarial interest rate of 14.96 percent. Since each conversion period is one year long, the APR is also 14.96 percent. Hence, the 10 percent add-on rate with four annual installments is equivalent to a charge of 14.96 percent per year on the remaining loan balance.

The difference in rates occurs because the add-on method fails to account for the principal payments made on the loan prior to its maturity—payments which reduced the outstanding loan balance. The actuarial rate and the APR for add-on interest can always be calculated by following the above procedures.

Discount Method

When money is borrowed as a "personal" loan, the *discount* method is sometimes used in computing interest. Here, the meaning of discount differs from its earlier use in net present-value analysis. For discount loans, interest is calculated on the original amount of the loan for its full period, and this amount, plus any other loan costs, is subtracted from the amount of the loan at the beginning. The borrower receives the difference. The size of each installment is obtained by dividing the amount of the loan by the number of installment payments.

For the same contractual rate and length of time, the actuarial rate will be higher for the discount method than for the add-on method. This increase in the actuarial rate is due to the payment or discount of interest at the very beginning of the loan transaction. To determine the actuarial rate, as we have indicated before, first identify the timing and magnitude of all cash flows associated with the loan, and then determine the interest rate which makes the present value of the sum of all these cash flows equal to zero. In the above example, suppose the $400 interest obligation for the $1,000 loan was deducted immediately, leaving the borrower with $600 as loan proceeds to use. The loan is then repaid in four annual installments of $250 each. Again, the actuarial rate is found, using the present-value model:

$$0 = 600 - 250[\text{USPV}_{i,4}].$$

The conversion factor is:

$$[\text{USPV}_{i,4}] = \frac{600}{250} = 2.400$$

and, using Appendix Table IV, is associated with an actuarial interest rate of 24.10 percent. The APR is also 24.10 percent. Clearly, the APR for the discount loan is greater than the APR for the add-on loan, and the APR's for both of these methods are greater than the remaining-balance rate.

Effects of Balance Requirements

Commercial banks may require or recommend that borrowers hold part of their loan on deposit with the bank. This "compensating balance" is common in corporate financing by regional or money center banks. Some rural banks use the practice too. Moreover, even if deposit balances are not formally required, the balances provided by a borrower during the year are usually considered in loan pricing. A different, yet analogous, practice is the requirement by the Cooperative Farm Credit System that its borrowers purchase stock in the system from the loan proceeds.

From the borrower's standpoint, these balance requirements increase the loan's APR relative to the contract rate. This increase occurs because the borrower foregoes use of part of the loan. To show the rate increase, consider a single period loan for V_o dollars at contract rate i_c, with b percent of the loan held as a compensating balance. To solve for i (the APR), the present-value model is formulated as:

$$0 = (1 - b)V_o - \frac{V_o(1 + i_c)}{1 + i} + \frac{bV_o}{1 + i}. \tag{14.12}$$

The first term is the borrower's receipt of the loan, net of the balance requirement; the second term is the present value of the repayment of principal and interest one period later; and the third term is the later return of the balance to the borrower, discounted to a present value.

Solving equation (14.12) for i yields the following expression for the APR:

$$i = \frac{i_c}{1 - b}. \tag{14.13}$$

Thus, a balance requirement increases the borrower's APR by the factor $1/1 - b$, relative to contract rate i_c. A loan with a contract rate of 14 percent, subject to a 10 percent balance requirement, would have an APR of 15.6 percent.

An Application: Determining the Money Cost of Debt Capital

To illustrate the application of these procedures for determining borrowing costs, consider the case of Mr. Farmer, who is purchasing new harvesting equipment valued at $50,000 and must determine the best source of financing. He has ruled out the manufacturer of the equipment as a financing source because of its high interest rates. The choice remains between a local Production Credit Association (PCA) (Case 1) and a local bank (Case 2). He identifies the following financing terms offered by each lender:

Terms	PCA	Bank
Downpayment (equity)	$10,000	$10,000
Equipment loan	$40,000	$40,000
Loan length	4 years	4 years
Contractual interest	9%	9%
Payment	annual and equally amortized	annual and equally amortized
Other	10% stock $300 loan-fee	15% compensating balance

While many of the terms are comparable, the differences in stock and compensating-balance requirements make it difficult to compare these two lenders solely in terms of their contractual-interest rates.

To account for the effects of noninterest costs of borrowing, we must derive the actuarial rate and the APR. The first step is to project all cash flows associated with the loan transactions and formulate the present-value models.

Case 1

PCA loans are generally formulated to include the stock-ownership requirement and any loan fees as part of the total loan to the farm borrower. In effect, the borrower uses part of the total loan to pay any loan fees and to pay the stock requirements. The requirement for borrowers to purchase PCA stock at some percent of the loan provides the major source of the PCA's equity capital. The stock is owned by the borrower and can be recovered when the loan is repaid. However, the borrower loses the use of these funds during the period of the loan.

In this case, the farmer must borrow enough to cover the $40,000 for the equipment, the $300 for the loan fee, and the stock requirement. The stock requirement is 10 percent of the total loan, which includes the stock purchase. To find the stock requirement we must recognize that the rest of the loan—$40,300—comprises 90 percent of the total loan. Hence, the total loan must be $40,300 ÷ .9 = $44,778, leaving a 10 percent stock requirement of $44,778 − $40,300 = $4,478.

The total loan of $44,778 is to be repaid in four equally amortized annual payments. The annual payments are found by solving for A in the uniform series present-value model:

$$0 = 44,778 - A[USPV_{.09,4}] \tag{14.14}$$

$$A = \frac{44,778}{[USPV_{.09,4}]} = 13,821.57.$$

All the data are now available to formulate the present-value model of the loan cash flows and solve for the actuarial interest rate (i). The model is set up as follows:

$$0 = 40,000 - 13,821.57[USPV_{i,4}] + \frac{4,478}{(1 + i)^4}. \tag{14.15}$$

The $40,000 entry reflects the cash made available to the farmer to purchase the equipment; the −$13,821.57 entry reflects the uniform series of payments needed to fully amortize the total loan of $44,778; and the $4,478 entry reflects the value of the stock made available to the farmer at the end of the four-year period.[1] Because all the cash flows are not a uniform series, we must use both Appendix Tables II and IV in solving for i by trial and error. We anticipate that the rate will be higher than the contractual rate of 9 percent, so let's try 10 percent as the first estimate:

$$NPV = 40,000 - 13,821.77 \left[USPV_{.10,4} \right] + \frac{4,478}{(1.10)^4}$$

$$= 40,000 - 43,813.15 + 3,058.53$$

$$= -754.62.$$

Because the NPV is negative, we know that 10 percent is too low. Using this same procedure, confirm that the NPV of the cash flows is $68.51 when i = .11. Thus, 11 percent is too high. By linear interpolation, the actuarial rate is found to be 10.92 percent, which is also the APR.

Case 2

The compensating balance required by the local bank means that a specified percentage of the total loan must be held on account at the bank as a demand balance through the length of the loan. When the loan is fully repaid, the demand balance is available to the borrower. However, the borrower loses the use of the compensating-balance funds during the loan period.

The farmer must borrow enough to cover the $40,000 for the equipment and to meet the compensating balance. The compensating balance is 15 percent of the total loan, which includes the compensating balance. To find the compensating balance, we must recognize that the $40,000 for the equipment comprises 85 percent of the total loan. Hence, the total loan must be $40,000 ÷ .85 = $47,058.82, leaving the 15 percent compensating balance of $47,058.82 − $40,000 = $7,058.82.

The total loan of $47,058.82 is to be repaid in four equally amor-

---

[1]Technically, the borrower's stock investment could be reduced as the loan balance is reduced. This reduction would alter the annual cash flows. However, we assume that the stock investment remains constant until the loan is fully repaid.

tized annual payments, which are found by solving for A in the uniform series present-value model:

$$0 = 47{,}058.82 - A[USPV_{.09,4}] \qquad (14.16)$$

$$A = \frac{47{,}058.82}{[USPV_{.09,4}]} = 14{,}525.58.$$

The cash flow model can now be formulated as:

$$0 = 40{,}000 - 14{,}525.58[USPV_{i,4}] + \frac{7{,}058.82}{(1+i)^4}. \qquad (14.17)$$

The $40,000 entry reflects the cash made available to the farmer to purchase the equipment; the −$14,525.58 entry is the uniform series of payments needed to fully amortize the $47,058.82 loan; and the $7,058.82 entry reflects the value of the compensating balance returned to the farmer at the end of the four-year period.

As in Case 1, Appendix Tables II and IV must be used to solve for i. Using i = .11 yields the following:

$$NPV = 40{,}000 - 14{,}525.58[USPV_{.11,4}] + \frac{7{,}058.82}{(1.11)^4}$$

$$= 40{,}000 - 45{,}064.82 + 4{,}649.86$$

$$= -414.96.$$

Because the NPV is negative, we know that 11 percent is too low. Using this same procedure for i = .12 yields NPV = 366.75. By linear interpolation, the actuarial rate is found to be 11.53 percent, which is also the APR.

Hence, for these financing terms, the local bank provides the more costly source of financing, with costs reflecting all the cash flows associated with the loan transaction. This result was probably clear from the initial data. That is, one would expect the cost of the 15 percent compensating balance to outweigh the cost of the 10 percent PCA stock requirement and the relatively small service charge.

The actuarial rates confirm this expectation. Suppose, however, that all the financing terms (equity, length, contract rate, balances) differed between the two lenders. Then, the lower-cost source would be less clear, with even greater reliance placed on finding the actuarial rates.

Other Costs

Interest Rates After Taxes

The above discussion treats interest rates on a before-tax basis. However, both interest and noninterest costs of borrowed capital are deducted from taxable income, thereby reducing the after-tax net cash outflow from borrowing. Hence, it is important to express costs of borrowing on an after-tax basis. If the relevant tax rate is t, then the after-tax interest rate (i_t) is:

$$i_t = i(1 - t) \qquad\qquad\qquad\qquad \textbf{(14.18)}$$

where i is the annual percentage rate. Suppose, for example, that the APR is 12 percent and the tax rate is 20 percent. The after-tax interest rate is:

$$i_t = .12(1 - .2) = .096 = 9.6 \text{ percent.}$$

Note that the after-tax cost of borrowing will differ among borrowers, depending on *their* tax position.

The Real Interest Rate

The term *real interest rate* reflects interest rates measured in *real* terms (see Chapter 11). For example, assume that the annual percentage rate increased from 12 percent to 14 percent over a particular period. During the same period, suppose the rate of inflation also increased by 2 percent. One could then say that no change occurred in the real rate of interest.

The concept of the real interest rate is meaningful in financial management. Unanticipated inflation has the effect of reducing the real cost of borrowing because fixed-debt obligations incurred in the past are being repaid with inflated dollars at present. In the above example, if interest rates had remained at 12 percent while the rate of inflation increased by 2 percent, then the real cost of borrowing would decline by 2 percent. As a result, the payoff from debt increases during such periods. Conversely, unanticipated reductions in the rate of inflation increase the cost of debt.

Nonmoney Costs of Debt Capital

Nonmoney costs of debt capital primarily reflect the premium associated with greater financial risk as leverage increases. In Chapter 7, we indicated that credit reserves (unused borrowing capacity) are an important source of liquidity for most firms. However, this source is consumed rapidly as leverage increases, causing borrowers to place an increasing liquidity value on the diminishing amount of credit reserve. It may be helpful to review the discussion associated with Figure 7.2 to insure a clear understanding of the liquidity value of the credit reserve (identified as R in Figure 7.2).

This premium for financial risk is important in determining the total cost of borrowed capital. Clearly, it is a "nonmoney" cost. Nonetheless, the difficulty of quantifying this cost does not diminish either its reality or its importance in financial management.

The liquidity premium can be determined in a couple of ways. One way is to consider it as a required-rate-of-return, over and above the interest costs of borrowing, that is needed to justify further borrowing. Another way is to measure the cost of utilizing a source of liquidity other than credit. Consider, for example, the dairy manager who raises feed grains in an area subject to crop losses from hail damage. The manager has always held liquid reserves to buy feed in case the grain crop is lost due to hail. This year a credit reserve of $20,000 is maintained for that purpose. Alternatively, $20,000 worth of hail insurance could be purchased to set up a contingent reserve in the event of hail damage. If the annual premium on the $20,000 hail insurance is $420, then the credit reserve has at least a *minimum* value of $420 ÷ $20,000 = 2.1 percent. Because the credit reserve is more flexible in its availability and use than are most insurance reserves, we treat the insurance cost as the *minimum* value of the credit reserve.

Total Costs of Debt Capital

An investor's total costs of debt capital are represented by the real, after-tax money costs of borrowing plus the liquidity premium. One component of this total cost is the actuarial interest rate expressed as an annual percentage rate. Other components include the borrower's tax rate, the rate of inflation, and the liquidity premium. Two of these components—the actuarial rate and the inflation rate— are determined in financial markets. The other two components—the tax rate and liquidity premium—are unique to each investor and will cause differences among investors in their total costs of debt capital.

To illustrate the derivation of the total costs of debt capital, consider again Mr. Farmer, who is purchasing the $50,000 worth of harvesting equipment. His least-cost source of financing occurred from the Case 1 lender with an annual percentage rate of 10.92 percent. Suppose further that his tax rate is 20 percent, the inflation rate is 4 percent, and the liquidity premium on the credit reserve is 6 percent. Mr. Farmer's after-tax cost of debt capital is 10.92 (1 − .2) = 8.74 percent. His real after-tax cost of debt is 8.74 percent minus the 4 percent inflation rate, or 4.74 percent. The total cost of debt is then 4.74 percent plus the 6 percent liquidity premium, or 10.74 percent.

Costs of Equity Capital

Our present concern is with the logic and method of estimating the costs of equity capital. New equity must come either from present owners or from new investors. The present owners may provide equity through reinvestment of earnings from the operation or by investing funds earned from other sources. Equity is raised from outside investors by selling common and preferred stock or by adding partners.

The Costs of Retained Earnings

Historically, most of the new equity capital in agriculture came from retained farm earnings and unrealized capital gains, although debt capital has played a more significant role since the mid-1940s. Because retained earnings do not carry an immediate and specific cash outflow, they are often considered to be costless. However, this is not the case. There are important opportunity costs of retained earnings that reflect either earnings on alternative investments or, perhaps more importantly, family consumption that must be foregone to increase retained earnings.

These costs of retained earnings can be thought of as *required rates-of-return* needed to compensate for foregone consumption. As an example, farmers might ask what rate of return they must have on the last increment (e.g., $100 or $1,000) of disposable income to divert it from consumption to savings. If the response is "a 20 percent rate of return," then 20 percent is the cost of retaining that increment of earnings. Retaining additional increments of earnings will likely have increasing opportunity costs. Moreover, the higher are the business and financial risks associated with the farm operation, the higher is the cost of equity capital, reflecting the premium needed to compensate for bearing the added risk.

In the past, many farmers perceived the cost of equity to be relatively low. Consequently, retained earnings have supplied most of the new capital investment in agriculture. At the same time, farm households lagged behind the rest of the nation in health and dental care, education, and modern conveniences of living. More recently, evidence indicates that the costs of retained earnings have increased, as farm families have sought standards of living comparable to those of urban families. Hence, it has become more costly to reinvest earnings into the farm business.

Larger corporate firms experience similar costs of retained earnings. Conceptually, their costs of retained earnings are the owners' returns, if the retained earnings were paid as dividends. In practice, management tends to depend on stockholders to become vocal when they feel too much of the firm's earnings are being retained in the business. Income tax considerations also influence dividend versus retained-earnings decisions. If earnings are retained in the business, the stockholder avoids the immediate tax on dividends. Delaying present taxes on dividends by the stockholders with the likely prospect of converting the earnings to capital gains makes retained earnings a more economical source of equity capital than selling common stock.

Costs of Outside Equity Capital

The costs of bringing outside equity capital into a farm proprietorship are generally high. A farmer might ask, "How high an expected return on capital would I need to make me invest in a farm like my own if it were operated by someone else?" This answer would help to indicate the costs of obtaining outside equity. The traditional farm proprietorship is seldom attractive to outside investors. Other forms of business organization are much better adapted to this purpose.

Larger corporate firms can consider sales of preferred or common stock as means of raising new equity capital. The cost of preferred stock is closely tied to the fixed-dividend commitment which must be paid from the profits of the firm. Because of the fixed dividend, preferred stock can often be sold for a lower-expected yield than can common stock. The cost of capital for preferred stock is given by:

$$K_{el} = \frac{D}{P_1 - C_1} \qquad (14.19)$$

where D is the annual dividend, P_1 is the sale price of preferred stock, and C_1 is the cost of selling. For example, if preferred stock carrying an annual dividend yield of $2.00 is sold for $20.00 per share with sale costs of $2.50 per share, then the seller will realize a net addition to capital of $17.50 per share. Hence:

$$K_{el} = \frac{2.00}{20.00 - 2.50} = 11.43 \text{ percent.} \qquad (14.20)$$

Since dividends are not tax deductible, this figure is already on an after-tax basis.

The cost of equity capital raised by selling common stock to investors is given by:

$$K_{e2} = \frac{E}{P_2 - C_2} \qquad (14.21)$$

where E is the expected earnings per share if the new investment is not undertaken, P_2 is the expected sale price of common stock, and C_2 is the cost of selling common stock. Suppose, for example, that the business continues to earn $3 per share if no new investments are undertaken. This figure is an estimate of the returns foregone by existing owners, who share these earnings with the new investors. If new shares are sold at $25 per share and sale costs are $4 per share, then the cost of funds by sale of common stock will be:

$$K_{e2} = \frac{3.00}{25.00 - 4.00} = 14.28 \text{ percent.} \qquad (14.22)$$

Again, this rate is already on an after-tax basis.

Using Costs of Financial Capital

Although some of our discussion of the costs of capital has used terms and instruments that are especially relevant for large corporate structures, the logic and methods also apply to farm proprietorships and other small businesses. Equity capital *is* more costly than debt capital, even for a farm proprietorship or partnership. Moreover, the cost of retained earnings to a farmer is very real. Hence, the concept of costs of capital is an important determinant of a firm's optimal leverage. Moreover, the costs of equity capital serve as the basis for defining the interest rate or required rate-of-return to be used in capital budgeting.

Deriving the costs of debt capital considers a number of factors—the financing terms and potential changes in rates of inflation, tax obligations, and liquidity values. The derivation procedures are clearly established, although some factors are easier to quantify than others. Nonetheless, estimating the total costs of debt capital together with equity capital will help the farmer to identify the firm's average costs of capital and to understand better the role of financial leverage.

Topics for Discussion

1. Under what circumstances might the following statement be true? "There are no costs to using your own capital." Explain.
2. Explain the difference between actuarial and annual percentage interest rates.
3. Find the actuarial interest rate on a loan of $30,000 to be repaid in equal annual installments of $6,687.47 each over a six-year period.
4. Find the annual percentage interest rate (APR) on a $5,000 loan to be repaid in equal monthly payments of $180.76 each over a three-year period.
5. Discuss the importance of nonmoney costs of debt capital. What gives rise to those costs?
6. In general, what are the effects of the *add-on* and *discount* methods of computing interest on the annual percentage rate?
7. What are the impacts of income taxes and inflation on the costs of debt and equity capital?
8. A farmer is buying a new tractor valued at $25,000. The dealer will allow $5,000 on the trade-in of the old tractor, leaving a balance to be financed by one of the three methods listed below. Compute the annual percentage rate for each method. Which one is cheapest?

   a. The local PCA will make a four-year loan with equal annual payments of principal and interest at a 12 percent contractual interest rate with a $300 loan fee and a 10 percent stock requirement.
   b. The local bank will also make a four-year loan with equal annual payments of principal and interest at a 13 percent contractual interest rate with a 5 percent compensating balance requirement.
   c. The manufacturer will make a four-year loan with equal payments of principal and interest with interest computed at 10 percent add-on.

References

1. Board of Governors, *Annual Percentage Rate Tables, Truth in Lending,*

Regulation Z, Vols. I and II, Federal Reserve System, Washington, D.C., 1969.

2. ——, "Rules and Regulations," Supplement 1, Regulation Z, Truth in Lending, *Federal Register*, 34:29(February 12, 1969), Federal Reserve System, Washington, D.C.

3. Botts, R. R., *Farmers' Handbook of Financial Calculations and Physical Measurements*, Handbook 230; ERS, USDA, Washington, D.C., 1962.

4. Brake, J. R., *Interest Rate Terminology and Calculation*, Agricultural Economics Department Report 13, Michigan State University, East Lansing, 1966.

5. Fisher, Irving, *The Rate of Interest*, Macmillan Publishing Co., Inc., New York, 1907.

6. Gilson, J. C., *The Cost of Credit*, Department of Agricultural Economics Bulletin 3, University of Manitoba, Winnipeg, 1961.

7. Neifield, M. R., *Neifield's Guide to Installment Computations*, Mack Publishing Company, Easton, Pennsylvania, 1951.

8. Osborn, Roger, *The Mathematics of Investment*, Harper & Row, Publishers, New York, 1957.

9. Solomon, Ezra, *The Theory of Financial Management*, Columbia University Press, New York, 1963, pp. 93-98.

10. Stelson, Hugh E., *Mathematics of Finance*, D. Van Nostrand Company, Inc., Princeton, New Jersey, 1963.

11. Van Horne, J. C., *Financial Management and Policy*, 5th ed., Prentice-Hall, Inc., Englewood Cliffs, New Jersey, 1980.

Appendix to Chapter 14

Approximating Formulas for Interest Rates

Thus far, we have concentrated on present-value techniques for determining the actuarial rate of interest. We have also demonstrated ways for computing an annual percentage rate of interest. Although these measures are generally very accurate, they do have limitations.

The actuarial rate on which the APR is based is difficult to measure when several installments are concerned. Instead, it must be determined by trial and error, using present-value tables, or by electronic means. Consequently, several formulas have been developed for estimating interest rates where equal installment payments are made on the loan. Each of the equations has its own simplifying assumptions concerning the ratio of the amount of interest to the amount of principal in each payment. The simplest of the estimating equations—the constant ratio—assumes this ratio is constant, while others assume it is distributed according to various other patterns. The more realistic this assumption for the particular situation, the more accurate is that particular estimate.

The *constant-ratio formula* assumes a constant ratio between the amount of interest and principal in each payment. It is probably the simplest, yet least accurate, of the estimating equations:

$$i = \frac{2CN}{Bf(N + 1)} \tag{14.23}$$

where C is the total cost of the loan, B is the beginning principal of the loan, f is the length of the loan in years, and N is the number of loan installments. To illustrate, let's apply equation (14.23) to the situation used in equation (14.11) where C = \$400, f = 4, B = \$1,000, and N = 4:

$$i = \frac{2(400)4}{1,000(4)\ (4 + 1)} = \frac{3,200}{20,000} = 16.00 \text{ percent.}$$

This estimate is somewhat higher than the APR obtained from equation (14.11).

Stelson [10] has presented a slight modification from the constant-ratio assumption which increases accuracy over the constant-ratio formula for most situations, but which is still relatively simple:

$$i = \frac{2C}{f(B + a)} \tag{14.24}$$

where a is the amount of each periodic payment. Using the same situation as illustrated above in equations (14.11) and (14.23):

$$i = \frac{2(400)}{(4)\ (1,000 + 350.00)} = \frac{800}{5,400.00} = 14.81 \text{ percent.}$$

The Stelson equation generally underestimates the APR slightly. However, it usually provides a closer approximation than does the constant-ratio equation.

Other estimating equations are available in most standard textbooks on the mathematics of finance. In general, the more limiting the assumptions and the simpler the equation, the less flexible is the equation to fit different situations. We have considered two of the more popular equations.

SECTION V

Financial Markets for Agriculture

Chapter 15

FINANCIAL INTERMEDIATION
IN AGRICULTURE

Financial intermediation is a process of channeling funds and securities between savers and investors. It is a two-way flow. The funds flow originates with savers and terminates with investors (borrowers). The securities flow originates with investors and terminates with savers. The funds flow arises because the investors have needs for funds that exceed their own capacity to generate funds. The securities flow arises to assure the savers (i.e., to provide security!) that the funds will eventually be returned along with an additional payment for their use. These flows are activated by transactions in financial markets.

This flow process is indicated in Figure 15.1. Funds flow along the top of the diagram, and securities flow along the bottom. The funds are divided into two classes called "debt" and "equity." Debt funds are distinguished by the investor's (borrower's) promise to repay the funds at a designated time along with a payment of interest to compensate for using the funds. Equity funds do not have the same kind of repayment promise and are thus considered riskier than debt funds. The payment for providing equity funds is generally a share of the investor's profit.

The securities also can be divided into the two classes that distinguish funds flows. While there are many kinds of securities, we will use the term *note* to refer broadly to debt securities and the term *title* to refer broadly to equity securities. These securities are also called financial assets in that they reflect claims by their holder on the assets of those who issue the securities. Financial assets originate in primary transactions between the saver and investor or, as we shall see, between the saver or investor and a financial intermediary. Such participants constitute a primary market. A secondary market

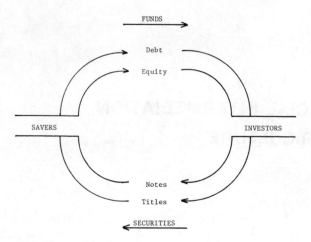

Figure 15.1. Flows of funds and securities in financial intermediation.

makes it possible for a financial asset to be sold through secondary transactions from one holder to another.

In an earlier, more primitive period, financial transactions occurred directly between saver and investor. Such a cumbersome process did not lend itself well to economic development. As a result, specialized financial intermediaries began to develop who could perform the intermediation process more efficiently and safely than could individual savers and investors. Along with the intermediaries came the development of laws and standard financial instruments that facilitated the important role played by financial intermediation in economic development, commerce, and government and consumer finance. Most intermediaries developed in response to a demand for services sufficient to generate a profit for them. Their success thus depends on their efficiency in performing the intermediation process.

Financial intermediaries are distinguished from other firms by two important characteristics: (1) claims on other economic units dominate the assets in their balance sheets, and claims by others dominate their liabilities; and (2) their economic activities center on the purchase, sale, and transformation of such claims. Although commercial banks, savings banks, savings and loan associations, life insurance companies, and finance companies are commonplace in advanced societies, these institutions are of relatively recent origin.

The growth of financial intermediaries in the United States is evident from the 225-fold increase in assets of commercial banks, mutual savings banks, life insurance companies, and savings and loan associations between 1900 and 1981 (see Table 15.1). Nearly half of this increase occurred after 1975. Changes in the ratio of assets held by financial institutions to the value of all tangible national assets are particularly revealing. At the beginning of the nineteenth century, this ratio was below 1 to 10 and had increased to only about 1 to 7 a century later. By 1920, however, it had advanced to nearly 1 to 4. Presently, the value of assets of all financial intermediaries represents well over half of our nation's assets. This doesn't mean that financial intermediaries actually own this much of the nation's assets. The liabilities of these financial intermediaries indicate that other economic units (businesses, individuals, government) in the United States have claim on the assets of financial intermediaries. In the case of banks, these claims occur as demand, savings, or time deposits.

Table 15.1. Total Assets of All Banks, Mutual Savings Banks, Life Insurance Companies, and Savings and Loan Associations for Selected Years

Year	Total	All Commercial Banks	Mutual Savings Banks	Life Insurance Companies	Savings and Loan Associations
		----------- millions of dollars -----------			
1900	14,673	10,011	2,430	1,742	490
1912	31,198	21,822	4,015	4,409	952
1922	65,318	47,267	6,597	8,652	2,802
1929	100,387	65,621	9,873	17,482	7,411
1939	111,469	64,997	11,852	29,243	5,377
1945	230,688	160,262	17,021	44,797	8,608
1950	260,083	157,677	21,439	64,020	16,893
1960	529,762	298,126	40,571	119,576	71,489
1975	1,683,003	934,410	121,056	289,304	338,233
1980	2,985,186	1,703,700	171,564	479,210	630,712
1981	3,142,510	1,781,700	175,612	521,354	663,844

Source: *Federal Reserve Bulletin.*

Financial Characteristics of Savers

Nearly everyone in the United States saves in some form at certain times in life. Not only do most citizens save but businesses also save. So do municipal, county, state, and federal governments. Savings occur for many reasons. Seasonal variations in cash flows lead to a temporary accumulation of funds.[1] Additionally, most individuals, firms, or governments forego spending in the short run to save for one purpose or another. These purposes for saving strongly influence the form of savings.

Incentives to Save

Savings are placed in many investments to assure a reasonable rate of return as well as safety and availability. These three criteria—yield, risk, and liquidity—help the saver select the best form of investment. The relative importance of each depends on the purpose of saving and on the saver's risk-returns preferences. Saving to provide for a large consumption expenditure, such as a vacation or new car, would likely be invested in securities providing high liquidity and minimum risk. The saver would likely be unwilling to sacrifice safety or liquidity for a higher yield.

When the timing and magnitude of the expected need for funds are known, the *interim* liquidity of savings is not critical, provided the funds will be available when needed. An example of this type of saving occurs with insurance companies, where policies carry contingent liabilities which can be forecast actuarially on the expected rate of death or retirement of policy holders. Moreover, many policy obligations occur as annuity payments, which are fixed in size and time. Based on a predictable demand for cash, the insurance company can invest in relatively illiquid assets.

Where savings are needed as reserve against adversity, liquidity considerations tend to dominate the savings decisions. Under these conditions, savers will sacrifice yield for high liquidity. An important phenomenon of the American economy since the 1930s has been the almost universal participation of workers in retirement or pension funds. These funds also assume future payment commitments which can be forecast actuarially. Administrators of these funds are primarily concerned with safety and, to some extent, with yield. They are less concerned with liquidity.

Other savers are primarily concerned with accumulating wealth. Greater wealth provides a base for higher earnings in later years. Such savers vary greatly in their preference for yield relative to

---

[1]It should be clear that we refer here to savings in liquid assets—indeed, principally debt claims held: savings and loan shares, bank accounts, etc., including even currency itself. Savings also occur in other forms of wealth: land, buildings, etc.

safety. Some save voluntarily in investments, varying from passbook savings to "high flying" speculative stocks. Others experience a contractual arrangement of "forced" savings, which automatically allocates a portion of their income to savings. Life insurance policies, annuity investment programs, and various retirement programs illustrate contractual savings. Liquidity tends to be less important than yield or risk for the "forced-savings" group.

Securities for Savers

The numerous financial instruments for saving vary greatly in their liquidity, yield, and risk. Because savers differ substantially in their risk-return-liquidity preferences, evaluating alternatives is largely an individual undertaking.

The problem is made more complex because of different risks associated with holding financial instruments. First, the borrower may default on the repayment obligation, and collection costs may be high. This risk is inherent in loans to individuals, businesses, and farmers.

Second, the financial asset might have to be sold before maturity to generate liquidity. If the value of the asset has declined, the saver experiences a capital loss. This type of risk is inherent in fixed-income securities. There may be little danger of default at maturity. However, the security price fluctuates inversely with the market interest rate, and if the instrument must be liquidated before maturity, the possibility of capital loss or gain is very real.

Third, inflationary declines in purchasing power of money will incur a loss to the holder. This risk is inherent in all financial instruments with value fixed in money terms—including money itself. The risk is directly associated with the security's maturity period and the likelihood of changes in inflation. All savers must evaluate the investment opportunities in terms of their own risk-return-liquidity preference.

The more important savings alternatives in financial markets are listed in Table 15.2. In general, these securities are arranged in order of decreasing liquidity, as reflected by their marketability. There are, however, substantial variations in the market acceptance of various municipal and corporate securities, depending upon the financial strength of the municipality or corporation. Similarly, the liquidity of loans to individuals varies greatly.

Any blanket-risk classification of these securities is arbitrary,

Table 15.2. Savings Alternatives

Security	Institution	Yield	Liquidity	Risk
Currency	Federal Reserve System	Low	High	Low
Demand Deposits	Commercial Bank			
Savings Deposits	Commercial Bank			
Money Market Funds	Investment Company, Broker			
Savings Certificates	Savings and Loan Association			
Certificates of Deposit	Commercial Bank		Moderate	
Certificates of Investment	Savings and Loan Association			
Treasury Bills	U.S. Government			
Government Bonds	U.S. Government			
Agency Bonds	(e.g.) Federal Land Bank	Moderate		
Municipal Bonds	Municipality, County, or State			Moderate
Corporate Securities Bonds	Private Corporation	High,		
Common Stocks	Private Corporation	but		
Mutual Funds	Private Investment Management Company	Highly Variable		
Individual Loan	Directly with Individual			
Futures Contracts and Various Other Contracts	Commodity Exchange, Broker, etc.		Low	High

owing to the different types of risks and their effects on different investors. The risk classification of Table 15.2 pertains only to default and market risks as discussed above. In general, yields vary directly with risk, although notable exceptions occur among and within the various categories.

Some indications of the changes occurring among savers are obtained from Table 15.3. Note the strong upsurge during the last 20 years of depository savings in commercial banks and savings and loan associations. Of particular relevance to financial intermediation for today's agriculture is the substantial increase in the number of savers residing in metropolitan areas, each saving small amounts and preferring high liquidity and low risk. Many of the investments listed in Table 15.2—such as the highest yielding certificates of deposit and government securities—are not available to most "small" investors. Moreover, these savings are not readily available to farm borrowers. Part of the problem is distance. But other difficulties will be more apparent as we examine the changes occurring in farmers' securities. In addition, greater investments in financial assets are occurring through direct investments in securities and money market mutual funds by investors, thus bypassing the traditional financial intermediaries.

Table 15.3. Claims on Selected Financial Intermediaries Held by the Nonfinancial Sector, 1939-1981

End of Year	Commercial Banks	Savings Banks	Savings and Loan Shares	Credit Union Shares	Life Insurance Reserves[1]	Private and Public Pension Reserves[2]	Mutual Fund Net Assets	Money Market Funds
				----billions of dollars----				
1939	58.4	10.5	4.1	0.2	25.8	3.0[3]	0.4[4]	0.0
1945	136.2	15.4	7.4	0.4	38.7	5.4	1.3	0.0
1950	161.3	20.0	14.0	0.8	55.0	11.7	2.5	0.0
1955	200.1	28.1	32.1	2.7	75.4	26.8	7.8	0.0
1960	205.0	36.3	62.1	5.7	98.5	52.7	17.0	0.0
1965	360.2	52.4	110.3	10.6	127.6	92.3	35.2	0.0
1970	440.4	71.6	146.4	17.8	167.6	155.2	47.6	0.0
1975	725.1	109.8	278.7	38.5	235.1	248.6	45.8	3.7
1980	1,187.4	154.8	503.2	71.7	390.3	459.6	134.7	49.1
1981	1,241.2	154.9	518.4	N/A	N/A	N/A	N/A	N/A
Increase								
1939-1950	102.9	9.5	9.1	0.6	29.2	8.7	2.1	
1950-1960	43.7	16.3	48.1	4.9	43.5	41.0	14.5	
1960-1970	235.4	35.3	84.3	11.7	69.1	102.2	30.6	
1970-1980	747.0	83.2	356.8	53.9	222.7	304.4	87.1	

1. Also includes individual and group annuities.
2. Reserves of private noninsured pension funds and state and local pension reserves.
3. Figure is for 1940 rather than 1939.
4. Figure is for 1941 rather than 1939.
Source: Data for commercial banks, mutual savings banks, savings and loan associations, and money market funds are from Board of Governors of the Federal Reserve System, *Federal Reserve Bulletin*, various issues. Those for life insurance companies are from the Institute of Life Insurance, *Life Insurance Fact Book*, 1981. Data for credit unions are from the U.S. Savings and Loan League, *Savings and Loan Fact Book*, 1981. Those for private and public pension reserves are from the U.S. Securities and Exchange Commission, Statistical Bulletin, 1981. Data on mutual fund net assets are from the Investment Company Institute, *Mutual Fund Fact Book*, 1981.

Financial Characteristics of Farm Borrowers

In contrast to the number of savers, the number of farm borrowers has declined by nearly one-half since 1950, while the average total investment per farm has increased to 19 times the 1950 level. Some insights on financial characteristics of farmers are provided by USDA data in *Economic Indicators of the Farm Sector*. These national data are shown on a per farm basis in Table 15.4. Despite the limitations of broad averages, some significant trends can be seen in different types of assets and liabilities of farmers.

Those assets showing the greatest percentage increase between 1950 and 1981 are (1) investment in farm cooperatives, (2) investment in real estate (primarily land), and (3) investment in machinery and equipment. Farm cooperatives and real estate are highly "illiquid" assets. Farm machinery and motor vehicles are becoming increasingly specialized, thus offering less flexibility in use. Consequently, they provide a less liquid asset for securing farm loans. At the same time, farmers' investments in more liquid assets—financial

Table 15.4. Balance Sheet of the Farming Sector: Average per Farm Current Prices, January 1 for Selected Year

	1950	1970	1975	1980	1981	$\frac{1981}{1950}$
Assets						
Physical Assets:						
Real Estate	$13,739	$ 73,085	$134,853	$311,438	$342,577	25.7
Non–Real Estate:						
Livestock and Poultry	2,283	7,949	8,750	25,278	25,168	11.0
Machinery and Motor Vehicles	2,154	10,934	19,851	39,847	42,307	19.6
Crops Stored on and off Farms	1,344	3,697	8,287	13,811	15,044	11.2
Household Equipment and Furnishings	1,524	3,334	5,453	7,996	9,114	6.0
Financial Assets:						
Deposits and Currency	1,607	4,025	5,363	6,534	6,688	4.2
U.S. Savings Bonds	836	1,266	1,542	1,662	1,576	1.9
Investment in Cooperatives	364	2,438	3,744	7,119	8,247	22.7
Total Assets	$23,851	$106,728	$187,845	$413,085	$450,721	19.2
Claims						
Liabilities:						
Real Estate Debt	$ 988	$ 9,879	$ 16,484	$ 34,052	$ 38,040	38.5
Non–Real Estate Debt:						
Excluding CCC Loan	912	7,166	12,545	29,119	32,311	35.4
CCC Loans	305	906	114	1,853	1,805	5.9
Total Liabilities	2,205	17,951	29,143	65,024	72,156	32.7
Proprietors' Equities	21,646	88,777	158,702	348,661	378,565	17.8
Total	$23,851	$106,728	$187,845	$413,685	$450,721	19.2
Debt-to-Asset Ratio	9.2	16.8	15.5	15.7	16.0	1.7

Source: *Economic Indicators of the Farm Sector,* Income and Balance Sheet Statistics, annual series, ERS, USDA, Washington, D.C.

assets and inventories of marketable assets—have increased very modestly.

Farmers increasingly are using debt to finance capital acquisition and growth of their business. Real estate debt outstanding per dollar of real estate value, for example, increased from 7.2 cents in 1950 to a high of 13.5 cents in 1970-71. (See Table 15.5.) Since 1971, however, average farm land values have increased about as fast as farm real estate debt.

Farmers have become important users of borrowed capital to finance growth, investments, asset replacements, and operating expenses. Non-real estate debt outstanding per farm in 1981 was about 35 times its level in 1950, for example (see Table 15.4). The ratio of non-real estate debt outstanding at year-end to production expenses during the year has fluctuated around 50 percent during the last decade, compared to 35 percent in 1950 (Table 15.5).

Table 15.5. The Relationship of Farm Debt to Selected Assets' Values and Income Levels

Year	Real Estate Debt to Value of Farm Real Estate	Total Farm Debt to Total Productive Farm Assets	Non–Real Estate Debt to Production Expenses	Total Debt to Cash Farm Income	Total Debt to Realized Net Farm Income
			percent		
1950	7.2	11.3	35.3	43.8	97.0
1955	8.1	12.5	42.5	59.9	159.2
1960	8.8	13.5	46.4	72.6	223.7
1965	11.1	17.0	53.2	93.5	310.4
1970	13.5	18.8	54.8	104.7	355.5
1975	12.2	17.0	47.1	91.3	393.2
1980	10.9	16.7	57.6	115.7	729.6[1]
1981	11.1	17.0	64.4[1]	132.7[1]	1048.1[1]

[1]Preliminary.
Source: *Economic Indicators of the Farm Sector*, Income and Balance Sheet Statistics, annual series. ERS, USDA, Washington, D.C.

Average total debt per farm increased by nearly 33 fold during this period. More significantly, the ratio of total farm debt outstanding to realized net farm income, which was .970 in 1950, increased to 10.48 in 1981.

On balance, the debt instruments which farmers sell have increased rapidly in total volume, size of loan per farm, and repayment requirement. Moreover, these debts are secured by assets whose liquidity appears generally low. At the same time, an increasing number of people in metropolitan centers are saving small amounts per person, often subject to limiting liquidity requirements. These conditions explain the shift away from direct intermediation between savers and farm borrowers and the need for specialized intermediaries to channel funds to savings-deficit areas.[2]

Functions of Financial Intermediation

These changes indicate the important need for financial intermediation in agricultural finance. First, limited funds available in rural areas must be supplemented by those of metropolitan areas. These savings move, predominantly, into urban and suburban banks and savings and loan associations, into retirement and pension funds gathered into large city banks, and into life insurance companies with accounts in large city banks. The funds are not available to farm borrowers until they are acquired by intermediaries serving farming areas.

Second, for farm lending, funds must be aggregated into larger units than are provided by most savers. In the absence of financial intermediaries, some farmers would borrow directly from 50 to 100 individual savers to acquire the needed funds. Moreover, funds must have unique time dimension to be of value to agriculture. Farmers must finance highly seasonal operating expenses. Their loans can be repaid annually from the sale of farm products. Additionally, farmers need intermediate-term financing for acquisition of depreciable assets and long-term financing for real estate. The need for large blocks of funds with a unified time dimension to fit these special needs gives added emphasis to the need for intermediation.

Third, the liquidity provided in most farm securities must be modified to satisfy most savers. Loans which must be repaid prior to achievement of the loan purpose are of little value to farmers. Yet few individual and corporate savers are willing to commit funds *directly* to such an inflexible schedule of recall. Thus, harmonizing the liquidity needed by savers with the liquidity of farm securities is a demanding task of financial intermediation. This feat is accomplished through the benefits of multilateral trade involving large numbers. In this case, large numbers of savers deposit their funds in a bank, each having a different time requirement for using the funds.

---

[2]An interesting exception to the shift from direct negotiation between savers and borrowers occurs in financing farm-land purchases. Here the saver (the land seller) is an important supplier of finance for land purchases. Reasons for this exception will be explored in the next chapter.

By this means, a commercial bank can make 90- to 180-day loans, for example, based on demand deposits.

Fourth, the risks inherent in most farm loans must be modified if savers are to invest in farm securities. Savers of funds placed in deposit investments prefer deposit insurance by an agency of the federal government. They would require a higher yield to compensate for a small increase in risk. Most of them likely would not loan directly to farmers, because such loans are "too risky."

A financial intermediary modifies risk in several ways. Most importantly, it substitutes its own financial strength for the financial strength of the farmer. Consequently, rural bank depositors do not look to local farmers for deposit security, even though the local bank, in turn, loans funds from those deposits to local farmers. Financial intermediaries also rely on guarantees from the Federal Deposit Insurance Corporation (or another government insuring body) to reduce the saver's risks. Borrowers might also use insurance to guarantee loan repayment, as is done with Federal Housing Administration, Small Business Administration, and Veterans Administration loans. Some intermediaries can spread loan risk over wide geographic areas and over many borrowers. Farm credit banks, for example, jointly sell bonds and notes in the financial market, based on a portfolio of securities offered by thousands of farm borrowers throughout the United States. Similarly, statewide branch-banking systems can spread the weather risks inherent in farm loans over many farming areas of the state.

The Legal Environment

A major feature of the intermediation system for channeling savings into investment is the intangible nature of the services and financial assets that are involved. As a result, considerable confidence, trust, and stability are required among market participants in order for financial markets to develop and function effectively. Accordingly, these markets experience much regulation for purposes of safeguarding savers and investors, modifying competition, responding to imperfections and gaps in financial services, and providing for effective monetary policy. Regulations take many forms: restraints on geographic expansion of financial institutions, as in branching and holding company regulations; mandatory specialization in some services (housing or farm lending, transactions accounts); portfolio diversification through reserve and capital requirements, loan limits, and asset allocations; interest rate controls on deposits and loans; special borrowing privileges; fair trade practices; public programs for credit and insurance; and laws affecting the design, trade, and negotiability of financial instruments.

Regulations yield many positive effects, as intended. However, they also may impose substantial costs on participants in financial markets as changes occur in economic, social, and institutional conditions. Inequities can arise that discourage savings, impede flows of funds, hamper the performance of some intermediaries, and reduce the efficiency of intermediation. Regulations also have induced financial innovations to circumvent government policies, thus further distorting and destabilizing financial markets.

When these costs of regulations become excessive, the stage is set for substantial regulatory change. In Chapters 16 and 17 we will consider the relationships between regulations and specific financial intermediaries in more detail and identify some of the major regulatory issues affecting the current cost and availability of financial services to farmers. Now, however, our focus is on the role played by the legal environment in fostering the development of trade, intermediation, and trading of financial assets in an orderly manner.

In a less developed financial market, in which the lender and borrower negotiate directly, the lender needed evidence of the debt obligation in case legal action was needed to collect the loan. The borrower's written promise to repay—a note—and the pledge of personal or real property—the collateral—as security for repayment greatly strengthened the lender's position. With these two pieces of evidence—the promissory note and the pledge of collateral—the lender found that the note signifying indebtedness could be sold to a third party. Financial intermediation was then underway.

Two sets of legal instruments are essential for extensive financial intermediation and for trading in commodities, either with or without debt financing. The first is the body of financial documents providing evidence of claim on money or other financial assets. The second relates to documents of title to personal and real estate property.

As developed in the United States, laws distinguish between transactions in real estate and personal property (non-real estate). Historically, the development of laws governing contracts and commerce rested with the individual states. As a consequence, a variety of instruments and rules emerged among states which made interstate commerce burdensome and risky. To achieve uniformity of laws, regulations, and instruments among the states, the Uniform

Commercial Code (UCC) was developed, beginning in 1951, pertaining to laws dealing with transactions in personal property. This code has added greatly to the stability and efficiency of financial intermediation.

The reader is referred to the appendix of this chapter for a more detailed discussion of the legal aspects of finance, including: (1) the negotiable instruments used in financial transactions, (2) the application of the UCC relating to transactions involving personal property, (3) regulations and instruments pertaining to real estate transactions, (4) laws pertaining to the co-ownership of property, and (5) other legal instruments important in financing agriculture.

The Financial Market

Many types of financial institutions have emerged in developed societies to provide the necessary linkages between savers and users of funds. In the United States, some are local or regional in their orientation, while others are directed toward the national financial market, which is centered in the Wall Street area of New York City. There one finds offices of the nation's largest banks and insurance companies and many other large financial institutions, the leading underwriters and dealers in debt and equity securities, and many large industrial corporations. Through a far-flung and flexible network of international, national, regional, and local offices and institutions, the market provides continuous linkages between suppliers and users of funds. It uses a variety of financial instruments, some of which were listed in Table 15.2.

The Evolution of Financial Markets
in Agriculture

Prior to World War I, the capital needs of farmers were not especially great. New land was still available through homesteading, and prices on established farm land were low. Machinery use was not widespread, and farmers used few other purchased inputs. Farmers' short-term financing needs were reasonably well met by merchants and dealers and by local banks, except during periods of tight money. However, the local banks and merchants were generally subject to the same kinds of risks as their farm customers. If the farmer prospered and paid off his loans, the banks and merchants survived. If farmers and local merchants did not prosper, the banks risked failure and difficulty in meeting their own financial obligations.

Typical mortgages were of short term (three to five years), high cost, and not amortized. Hence, large, lump-sum repayments were required when the loans matured. Renewals of matured loans were common; however, dependence by farmers on easy renewals was a risky proposition due to the possibility of changing conditions in the money market which, in the absence of a central banking system, tended to be rather unstable.

Concern over the farm-credit situation led to the establishment of several commissions to study farm-credit needs. Particular attention was given to European cooperative farm-credit systems. These studies ultimately led to the establishment of the Cooperative Farm Credit System and Farmers Home Administration as we know them today. They were not born overnight, however. In fact, their initial development covered more than four decades (1910s through 1940s), and they are periodically reviewed and modified.

Because the Farm Credit System was designed to be self-supporting, it was not well suited to high-risk borrowers with inadequate resources or for farmers who experienced drought or other disasters. As a result, various programs of direct government assistance have provided the needed emergency or supervised financing. The current means of providing such financing is through the Farmers Home Administration (FmHA), established in 1946 to provide financing for farmers who could not be served on reasonable terms by other lenders. More recently, the purposes of the FmHA have been broadened to include loans for such items as rural housing, recreation, and other rural development projects.

While these changes were occurring in cooperative and public financial intermediation, the banking system was undergoing important changes also. The Federal Reserve System was established in 1913, providing the tools for closer monetary controls. However, membership in the Federal Reserve System was required of only nationally chartered banks. Many state banks, located primarily in rural areas, chose not to become members—a condition still existing today, although all depository institutions are now subject to reserve requirements administered by the Federal Reserve System. In addition, federal insurance programs were provided for depositors in banks and savings and loan associations. Also, complex interbank relationships were established to help rural banks be more responsive to the financing needs of farmers.

The Local Market for Farm Securities

The growth in farm debt since 1935 and the relative importance of different lenders nationally and by geographic regions are indicated in Tables 15.6 through 15.9. The volume of farm real estate debt outstanding increased 1,729 percent between 1950 and 1982, while the volume of non-real estate loans increased 1,250 percent during the same period. Projections of future capital and credit needs in agriculture indicate continued strong growth in farm credit through the 1980s, although at more moderate rates than in the 1970s.

Farm loans can be divided roughly into three categories, based on the maturity of the note: long-term, intermediate-term, and short-term. Each of these classes of loans is adapted to different loan purposes, loan security, and sources of repayment.

Long-term Loans

With long-term loans, the note is nearly always secured by a pledge of farm real estate through either a real estate mortgage or a deed of trust. An alternative is the land purchase contract. Farm real estate debts normally carry maturities in excess of 10 years and usually range between 15 and 40 years. As shown in Table 15.7, the total farm real estate debt outstanding in the United States declined between 1935 and 1945 to $4.9 billion, then increased to $102 billion in 1982.

Federal land banks have emerged in recent years as the most important supplier of farm real estate financing, showing a growth in outstanding debt of over 4,414 percent in the 1950 to 1982 period. Currently, FLBs hold almost 43 percent of the outstanding farm real estate debt. This percentage varies by regions, however, from a high of over 50 percent in the Delta to about 35 percent in the Pacific states.

A large amount of farm real estate debt, about 27.7 percent of the total, is held by noninstitutional lenders, including individuals who sell their own land either on contract or with a mortgage. Other individuals also become involved in financing and land transfers without the need for a financial intermediary. Following World War II, life insurance companies were the largest institutional lenders of long-term funds to agriculture. In 1955, they held about one-fourth of all outstanding farm real estate loans. However, their relative position has since declined rather steadily to less than 13 percent in 1982.

Table 15.6. Real Estate Farm Debt Outstanding for Selected Lenders in the United States, January 1, Selected Years

Year	Federal Land Banks mil.$	%	Farmers Home Administration mil.$	%	Life Insurance Companies mil.$	%	Commercial Banks mil.$	%	Other Lenders mil.$	%	Total Real Estate Debt mil.$
1935	1,947	25.7	—	—	1,301	17.1	499	6.6	3,836	50.6	7,583
1940	2,815	43.0	32	0.5	948	14.5	534	8.1	2,221	33.9	6,550
1945	1,562	31.6	195	3.9	938	19.0	450	9.1	1,795	36.3	4,940
1950	965	17.3	202	3.6	1,172	21.0	932	16.7	2,308	41.4	5,579
1955	1,280	15.5	379	4.6	2,052	24.9	1,161	14.1	3,374	40.9	8,245
1960	2,335	19.2	676	5.5	2,820	23.1	1,523	12.5	4,828	39.6	12,182
1965	3,687	19.5	1,285	6.8	4,288	22.7	2,417	12.8	7,218	38.2	18,895
1970	6,671	22.9	2,280	7.8	5,734	19.6	3,545	12.1	10,953	37.5	29,183
1975	13,402	29.0	3,215	6.9	6,297	13.6	5,966	12.9	17,408	37.6	46,288
1980	29,642	35.9	7,111	8.6	12,165	14.7	8,623	10.4	25,137	30.4	82,678
1981	35,944	39.1	7,715	8.4	12,928	14.0	8,745	9.5	26,685	29.0	92,017
1982	43,564	42.7	8,744	8.6	13,100	12.8	8,387	8.2	28,250	27.7	102,045
					Percent Change in Volume						
1970-1982	553.0		283.5		128.5		136.6		157.9		249.7
1960-1982	1,765.7		1,193.5		364.5		450.7		485.1		737.7
1950-1982	4,414.4		4,228.7		1,017.7		799.9		1,124.0		1,729.1

Source: Balance Sheet of the Farming Sector, ERS, USDA, September 1977; Agricultural Statistics, USDA, 1981.

Table 15.7. Real Estate Farm Debt by Regions of the United States, January 1, 1982

Region	Total	Commercial and Savings Banks	Life Insurance Companies	Federal Land Banks	Farmers Home Administration	Other Real Estate Debt
	$1 million	-- percent --				
Northeast	4,724	14.1	2.1	38.6	14.1	31.1
Lake States	10,974	8.4	6.2	43.3	7.9	34.2
Corn Belt	23,889	10.3	13.1	41.9	6.3	28.4
Northern Plains	11,158	4.0	12.5	48.7	12.2	22.6
Appalachian	8,454	8.4	13.8	37.9	8.5	31.3
Southeast	7,442	14.2	6.3	46.4	13.1	20.0
Delta States	7,180	9.7	12.0	55.1	8.3	14.9
Southern Plains	5,793	11.5	18.9	44.2	11.2	14.2
Mountain	9,100	1.6	17.5	40.0	10.0	30.9
Pacific	13,330	4.6	19.6	35.4	3.8	36.5
United States	102,045	8.2	12.8	42.7	8.6	27.7

Source: ERS, USDA, 1982.

The volume of farm real estate loans held by commercial banks increased from less than $1.2 billion in 1955 to $8.39 billion in 1982. The proportion of total farm real estate debt held by commercial banks fluctuated between 12 and 14 percent through the 1960s and 1970s, then declined in the 1980s. However, as shown in Table 15.7, this figure also varies greatly by regions. The large amount of mortgage financing in the Northeast and Southeast occurs primarily because banks in these areas tend to use farm real estate as security when financing the farmer's short-term and intermediate-term requirements.

Intermediate-term Loans

Intermediate-term loans have maturities ranging from 1 to 10 years. They are used to finance the purchase of many types of assets, such as breeding livestock, farm machinery, and equipment; the purchase and construction of farm structures; and other improvements, such as orchards, irrigation development, and the modernization of farm facilities. The relative importance of depreciable assets in agriculture is increasing. Many have economic lives of from 5 to 10 years or more. Consequently, the relative importance of intermediate-term farm debt is increasing. The primary markets for intermediate-term loans by farmers are local banks, PCAs, machinery dealers and manufacturers, and FmHA.

Table 15.8. Non-Real Estate Farm Debt Outstanding for Selected Lenders in the United States, January 1, Specified Years

Year	Commercial Banks		Production Credit Associations		Federal Intermediate Credit Banks[1]		Farmers Home Administration		Others[2]		Commodity Credit Corporation[3]		Total
	mil.$	%	mil.$	%	mil.$	%	mil.$	%	mil.$	%	mil.$	%	mil.$
1935	628	52.9	60	5.0	55	4.6	204	17.2	—	—	240	20.2	1,187
1940	900	26.1	153	4.4	32	0.9	418	12.1	1,500	43.5	445	12.9	3,448
1945	949	27.9	188	5.5	30	0.9	452	13.3	1,100	32.3	683	20.1	3,402
1950	2,049	29.8	387	5.6	51	0.7	347	5.1	2,320	33.8	1,720	25.0	6,874
1955	2,934	31.2	577	6.1	58	0.6	417	5.5	3,210	34.1	2,219	23.6	9,415
1960	4,819	38.0	1,361	10.7	90	0.7	398	3.1	4,860	38.3	1,165	9.2	12,693
1965	6,990	39.0	2,277	12.7	125	0.7	644	3.6	6,330	35.3	1,543	8.6	17,090
1970	10,330	43.3	4,495	18.9	218	0.9	785	3.3	5,340	22.4	2,676	11.2	23,844
1975	18,238	51.3	9,519	26.8	374	1.0	1,044	2.9	6,050	17.0	319	0.9	35,545
1980	31,034	41.3	18,299	24.3	666	0.9	8,983	11.9	11,720	15.6	4,500	6.0	75,202
1981	31,567	38.3	20,027	24.3	810	1.0	11,756	14.2	14,000	17.0	4,367	5.3	82,527
1982	32,948	35.5	21,484	23.1	913	1.0	14,452	15.6	15,000	16.2	8,008	8.6	92,805
Percent Change in Volume													
1970-1982	219.0		378.0		318.8		1,741.0		180.9		199.3		289.2
1960-1982	583.7		1,478.5		914.4		3,531.2		208.6		587.4		631.2
1950-1982	1,508.0		5,451.4		1,690.2		4,064.8		546.6		365.6		1,250.1

[1] Loans to and discounts for livestock loan companies and agricultural credit corporations.

[2] Estimates of short- and intermediate-term loans outstanding from merchants, dealers, individuals, and other miscellaneous lenders.

[3] Includes price-support and storage loans made by the Commodity Credit Corporation. Although price-support loans are nonrecourse loans, they are treated as debts. Borrowers must either pay them in cash or deliver the commodities on which they are based.

Source: Balance Sheet of the Farming Sector, ERS, USDA, 1977; Agricultural Statistics, USDA, 1981.

Short-term Loans

Short-term loans are for one year or less. They are mostly used to finance operating inputs. The volume of non-real estate loans to farmers outstanding on January 1 increased from $9.4 billion in 1955 to $92.8 billion in 1982 (Table 15.8). Both short-term and intermediate-term loans are included in these loan figures, however, so they must be considered together.

Noninstitutional lenders ("Others" in Table 15.8) comprise an important but rapidly declining group. Mostly they are merchants, dealers, and other agribusinesses making short- and intermediate-term loans to farmers. Individuals and other miscellaneous lenders are also included in the noninstitutional category. Commercial banks have the largest volume of non-real estate debt, although their market share has declined sharply from its peak in 1975. The proportion held by PCAs has increased steadily since they were established in 1933 and moved up sharply until the mid-1970s. The relative importance of the FmHA in supplying non-real estate loans to farmers declined following the 1940s, and then increased sharply in the 1980s, reflecting various types of emergency loan programs.

Table 15.9 indicates the regional distribution of non-real estate farm debt in 1982. Especially noticeable are the low market shares held by commercial banks in the Appalachian, Southeast, and Delta states, and the high shares held by FmHA in the same regions.

Table 15.9. Regional Distribution of Non–Real Estate Loans to Farms by Principal Lending Institutions, January 1, 1982

Region	Banks	Farmers Home Administration	Production Credit Associations	Federal Intermediate Credit Banks	Total Loans
					thousands of dollars
	---percent --				
Northeast	36.1	25.4	37.7	.8	3,011,448
Lake States	45.7	15.4	37.0	1.9	7,205,110
Corn Belt	58.6	11.3	29.7	.4	14,148,691
Northern Plains	61.8	17.9	19.5	.8	10,466,723
Appalachian	26.4	28.5	44.4	.7	4,973,526
Southeast	18.4	42.8	38.9	0	4,476,391
Delta States	22.8	49.4	26.1	1.7	4,499,628
Southern Plains	52.3	22.9	21.2	3.6	7,156,877
Mountain	45.5	17.5	34.0	3.0	5,829,159
Pacific[1]	52.9	11.0	35.2	.9	8,029,759

[1]Includes Alaska and Hawaii
Source: ERS, USDA, 1982.

Equity Capital

Despite the growing volume of farm debt, *equity* capital dominates the aggregate balance sheet for the agricultural sector. It also is the dominant source of capital for most individual farms, although much of the equity growth is attributed to unrealized capital gains on farm land.

The primary source of new equity capital for agriculture is retained farm earnings. However, "outside" equity capital is becoming increasingly important, particularly in poultry raising, cattle feeding, and fruit and vegetable production and marketing. Such capital might be in the form of equity capital invested in farm operations by local nonfarmers as a joint venture or general partnership, or it might be invested under a more formal legal arrangement, such as a "limited" partnership, or a large industrial corporation that is also engaged in agriculture. In any case, the financial market for outside equity capital for agriculture is not well developed.

Topics for Discussion

1. What is financial intermediation?
2. What important function must be accomplished in financial intermediation for agriculture?
3. How is financial marketing dependent on financial intermediation?
4. Where are time deposits shown in the financial position of a commercial bank?
5. What risks are incurred when a saver buys a U.S. Government Security? A corporate bond? A farm mortgage? How would you expect the yields to vary among these financial instruments? Why?
6. How have changes in the demand for loan funds and preferences of savers accounted for the increasing use of financial intermediation in the flow of funds to farmers?
7. How do you account for the fact that financial intermediation has increased but little in the case of loans to finance land purchases?
8. Why were units of the Farm Credit System established? Have they been effective in reducing the incidence of low-income farmers?
9. What are the roles of legal instruments in the market or exchange system?
10. How is reliability of contract performance related to the evolution of financial markets? To the financial organization of the farm firm?
11. Why might a landlord consent to a "subordination agreement" that makes his claim on farm crops secondary to the claim held by the tenant's lender?

12. What economic factors account for the evolution of such legal instruments as installment notes? Security agreements? Financing statements? Subordination agreements? Convertible debentures?

References

1. American Law Institute, *Uniform Commercial Code*, Chicago, 1963.
2. ———, *Uniform Laws Annotated, Uniform Commercial Code*, Edward Thompson Co., Minneola, New York, 1968.
3. *Economic Indicators of the Farm Sector*, Income and Balance Sheet Statistics, annual series, ERS, USDA, Washington, D.C.
4. Edmister, R. O., *Financial Institutions Management*, McGraw Hill Book Company, New York, 1980.
5. Farm Credit Administration, *Non Real Estate Farm Debt* and *Farm Real Estate Debt*, annual series, Washington, D.C.
6. *Federal Reserve Bulletin*, monthly series, Board of Governors of the Federal Reserve System, Washington, D.C.
7. Goldsmith, R. W., *Financial Institutions*, Random House, Inc., New York, 1968.
8. Henning, C. N., W. Pigott, and R. H. Scott, *Financial Markets and the Economy*, 3rd ed., Prentice-Hall, Inc., Englewood Cliffs, New Jersey, 1981.
9. Hoag, W. L., *The Farm Credit System*, The Interstate Printers & Publishers, Inc., Danville, Illinois, 1976 (out of print).
10. Lee, W. F., et al., *Agricultural Finance*, 7th ed., Iowa State University Press, Ames, 1980.
11. Levi, D. R., *Agricultural Law*, 4th ed., Lucas Brothers Publishers, Columbia, Missouri, 1978.
12. Smith, P. F., *Money and Financial Intermediation: The Theory and Structure of Financial Systems*, Prentice-Hall, Inc., Englewood Cliffs, New Jersey, 1978.
13. Tostlebe, A. S., *Capital in Agriculture: Its Formation and Financing*, Princeton University Press, Princeton, New Jersey, 1957.
14. Van Horne, J. C., *Function and Analysis of Capital Market Rates*, Prentice-Hall, Inc., Englewood Cliffs, New Jersey, 1970.

Appendix to Chapter 15

Legal Aspects of Finance

This appendix summarizes many legal issues important to financial intermediation and to financial transactions for both real estate and personal property. The discussions are grouped into five categories: (1) a summary of the most important negotiable instruments, (2) the Uniform Commercial Code (UCC) as it relates to personal property, (3) regulations pertaining to real estate transactions, (4) laws regulating co-ownership of property, and (5) other legal instruments important to financing agriculture.

Negotiable Instruments

In general, the legal instruments relating to personal property fall into two classes: those which serve as evidence of debt claims and those which serve as evidence of equity claims. Sometimes, however, a particular instrument may have characteristics of each class, or it may be shifted from one to another at the option of one party to the contract—usually the holder.

Article 3 of the UCC deals with commercial paper or negotiable instruments. Four different categories of instruments are listed: (1) promissory notes, (2) drafts or bills of exchange, (3) checks, and (4) certificates of deposit.

The basic document for a loan transaction is the *promissory note*. A *negotiable promissory note* is an unconditional promise in writing made by one person to another to pay a specified sum of money at a fixed or determinable future time to the order of the second party or to the bearer. A simplified promissory note is illustrated in Figure 15.2. There are special types of promissory notes which may or may not be negotiable, depending on their form.

The *simple promissory note* is generally used for unsecured loans. A *collateral note* is a note accompanied by a pledge of personal property to secure the note. If the borrower defaults, the lender may, under specified circumstances, sell the property and apply the proceeds to the debt.

With an *installment note*, the principal and interest are paid in periodic installments until the note is retired. When the note is secured with real estate, a *mortgage note* likely is used. However, transactions relating to real estate are not included in the UCC.

A *draft*, or *bill of exchange*, is an unconditional order in writing requiring the person to whom it is addressed (the *drawee*) to pay on demand, or at some specified future time, a specified sum of money to the person drawing the draft (the *drawer*) or to someone whom the drawer designates. It is, in effect, an order by one person upon a second person to pay a sum of money under a specified set of circumstances to a third person. The drawee is not bound to pay the

Figure 15.2. A promissory note.

NO. 2300-05   Endless Plains, Texas   June 1   19 76 $10,000

FOR VALUE RECEIVED, I, we, or either of us, as principals, promise to pay to the order of

Interest $300.00   Cr. Lfe. —   H & A —

LAST STATE BANK, ENDLESS PLAINS, TEXAS

at said address, the sum of $10,000.00 , payable in 4 monthly installments of $2575.00 ,

the first installment being due and payable on or before the 1st day of July , 19 78 and the remaining installments being due and payable on or before the same day of each succeeding month thereafter until said note is fully paid, with all remaining principal and interest maturing on October 1 , 19 78 .

BORROWER shall pay interest after maturity at the highest legal rate and if this note is collected through judicial proceedings, BORROWER shall pay the amounts actually incurred by HOLDER as court costs and attorney's fees assessed by a court. BORROWER shall have the right at any time during regular business hours to prepay this note in full and shall receive refunds in accordance with the rule of 78's. BORROWER shall pay additional interest for default at $.05 per $1.00 of any installment due and remaining unpaid for 10 days or more. Deferred interest shall be charged as permitted by the Texas Consumer Credit Code. A default in payment of any amount when due will, at holder's option mature the entire unpaid balance of this note, less unearned charges. Borrower and each surety, endorser or guarantor of this note hereby waives presentment, protest, notice of protest, and diligence in collection, and each hereby consents to any extension or extensions of this note which holder may make. Holder is expressly granted the right to offset against this note and all other liabilities of the borrower to holder, all money or other property in its possession held for or owed to the borrower (including without limitation, all deposits and accounts). To secure the payment of the foregoing obligation or any renewal of same and to likewise secure payment of any other indebtedness now or hereafter owed by Borrower, Borrower hereby grants to holder a security interest, subject to the terms and conditions stated on the the reverse side hereof, in the personal property hereinafter described, together with any and all additions and accessions thereto and all proceeds therefrom, all hereinafter collectively called "Collateral".

Model 7000 A TRACTOR

WHEAT CROP   COTTON CROP

BORROWER hereby acknowledges that this combined Note, Truth in Lending Disclosure, and Security Agreement was completed as to all essential provisions and disclosures before it was signed by BORROWER and a copy thereof was delivered to BORROWER at time of signing. NOTICE: See other side for important information.

INS.   x Farmer Q

ADDRESS Star Rt. Box 18   x

PHONE   Address and Signature of BORROWER (S)

NOTE: Truth in Lending Disclosure, Security Agreement, Monthly Installments

---

DISCLOSURES COLUMN

1. Amount of Credit $10,000

$ — Prepaid Finance Charge

$ — Required Deposit Balance

2. $ — Total prepaid Finance Charge and Required Deposit Balance

3. Other charges, Itemized

Credit Life Insurance $ —

Credit A/H $ —

$

4. Amount Financed $10,000.00

5. FINANCE CHARGE $ 300.00

6. Total of Payment $10,300.00

ANNUAL PERCENTAGE RATE 9 %

Credit life or credit life accident and health insurance is voluntary and not required for this loan. This insurance is available for term of loan at cost shown below.

I desire (✓ if applicable) ☐ Credit life at

$

☐ Credit life accident and health at

$

☒ I do not desire insurance coverage.

DATED this the 1st day of June , 19 78

x Farmer Q (Signature of BORROWER)

money unless the terms of the order are accepted. Once the transactions associated with the order have been accepted, the drawer becomes the *acceptor*.

There are several types of drafts. A *sight draft* is payable when the holder presents it to the drawee for payment, or "on sight." The *time draft* is payable at a specified future time, such as "60 days after acceptance." One type of bill of exchange important in agriculture is the *trade acceptance*, where the bill of exchange is sent by a seller of goods to a purchaser with the understanding that if the goods are approved on arrival, the purchaser will accept the instrument immediately and abide by its terms.

A *check* is a bill of exchange drawn on a bank and payable on demand. To be legal, the drawer must have deposits in the bank to cover the check. A *cashier's check* is drawn by a bank on itself directing that it pay the specified sum of money either to the purchaser of the check or to a designated person. A *bank money order* is similar. It is an order by a bank upon itself to pay a specified sum to a third party designated by the purchaser. A *bank draft* is a check drawn by one bank on another bank. These three instruments serve about the same purpose—a means of securing payment to fulfill a contract at a specified time and location. The purchaser of these money instruments must pay to the bank the amount specified on the instrument plus a service charge.

Documents of Title

The development of negotiable instruments has greatly extended both the time and the space dimensions of business transactions. This extension would not have been possible, however, without a similar development in documents evidencing title to goods in storage or in transit. The UCC deals with regulations relating to documents of title in Article 7. Documents of title serve three important functions: (1) as a receipt of bailment, (2) as a contract for storage or shipment, and (3) as a symbol evidencing ownership of the goods.

The two most important documents of title are: (1) *bills of lading*, issued by carriers where the merchandise is accepted for shipment and (2) *warehouse receipts*, issued by firms engaged in storing goods for hire. Other familiar names include air bills, weight bills, air consignment notes, and any other document which, in the regular course of business or financing, is treated as adequate evidence that its holder is entitled to receive, hold, or dispose of the document and of the goods it covers.

Such titles may be either negotiable or nonnegotiable. With negotiable documents, the *bailee* (the individual receiving the property) must deliver the goods only when a negotiable document of title is surrendered. To facilitate transactions, negotiable documents of title, such as order bills of lading, are printed on yellow paper. With nonnegotiable documents of title, the bailee may deliver goods upon a separate written authority and without a surrender of the document of title. Nonnegotiable documents, such as straight bills of lading, are usually recorded on white paper.

Warehouse receipts are important in agricultural financing. Warehouse receipts, certified by a bonded warehouse supervisor, can serve as evidence of ownership of property, with the bonded warehouse certifying the quantity and the quality of goods owned. Such an instrument, therefore, can serve as collateral to secure a loan. The use of *field* warehouse receipts has extended far beyond the traditional "storable" commodities, such as corn, wheat, flour, oil, etc., to include dressed meats in packinghouses, cattle in commercial feed lots, and even cattle on pasture. This service of third party collateral control and certification reduces the lender's uncertainty over the existence and value of collateral and thus augments financing of such items. An extension of the concept of third-party collateral control, which could be of importance to agribusiness, is *accounts receivable certification*, wherein a bonded third party assumes control over and certifies the value of the firm's accounts receivable. With such certification, the lender can advance funds against the accounts received.

A warehouse receipt should contain the location of the "warehouse" (i.e., where the property is stored), the date the receipt is issued, the consecutive numbering of receipts, whether the goods are to be delivered to the bearer or to a person specified on the order, the rate of storage charges, description of the goods being warehoused, a statement of charges subject to lien by the warehouse, and the signature of the warehouse supervisor.

To demonstrate how a warehouse receipt or a bill of lading might be used in a transaction, consider Bill Farmer as the seller who consigns a carload of corn to the Union Pacific Railroad in North Platte, Nebraska, to be shipped to the buyer, Mr. B, in Los Angeles. Mr. Farmer, on delivering the corn to the railroad, gets a bill of lading stating the total amount and grades of corn being shipped. He then draws a draft on Mr. B, the buyer. He attaches the draft to the bill of lading and endorses both of them to his bank in North Platte. At that time, his banker discounts the draft, giving Mr. Farmer the amount of the draft less a fee for servicing and for financing until total collection occurs. The North Platte bank then forwards the draft and bill of lading to its correspondent bank in Los Angeles—for example, United California Bank (UCB). UCB then presents the draft to the buyer, who is the drawee of the draft. On paying the draft, the buyer is given possession of the bill of lading. When the shipment arrives at the depot in Los Angeles, Union Pacific will notify Mr. B, who will then surrender his negotiable bill of lading to the shipper in order to receive the corn. The entire transaction is completed when UCB transfers to the North Platte bank the amount of the draft, less its service charges.

Transactions Secured by Personal Property

As indicated earlier, a promissory note might be secured or supported by a claim against the borrower's personal property. Historically, such claims could take a number of forms. Article 9 of the UCC brings all these devices for securing personal property under one law and presents a comprehensive and unified system for regulation of security interest in personal property.   '

The law classifies personal property collateral as intangible and tangible. Intangible collateral may be of six types: (1) contract rights, (2) accounts receivable, (3) instruments (negotiable), (4) chattel paper (a combination of a note with some other instrument of value), (5) documents, and (6) general intangibles (such as patent rights and other rare or esoteric items having remote value). Tangible property, in turn, is divided into four classes: (1) consumer goods, including items held primarily for personal or household use; (2) equipment; (3) inventory, including all goods not classified as equipment, and goods held for sale or lease or to be furnished under a contract of service; and (4) farm products. The latter category includes crops, livestock, and supplies used or produced in farming operations; products of crops or livestock in their unprocessed state, such as wool, eggs, milk, hides, etc.; and products in possession of the borrower who is engaged in raising, grazing, or fattening cattle or in other farming operations.

Article 9 of the UCC clearly distinguishes farm products from other classes of personal-property collateral by giving farm lenders special consideration with respect to farm products as they are followed beyond the farm. When purchasing farm products, the buyer is responsible for proving that a commodity is free of encumbrances, which is not the case when buying consumer goods or other commodities. This differential might provide farmers with more favorable consideration in financing. But the benefits might be offset by unfavorable considerations in marketing, since the buyer must assure that the title to farm products is free of claims.

The UCC has replaced such security instruments as the chattel mortgage, conditional sales contract, factor's lien, trust receipt, or pledge with a *security interest* created by a *security agreement*. Some of the older instruments continue to be used in a few states. Under the UCC, a *security interest* is a claim, or, lien, which a secured party has on the personal property of the debtor. The *security agreement*, on the other hand, is an agreement which creates a specific security interest. (See Figure 15.3.) It must be in writing, contain a description of the personal property serving as collateral, and be signed by the debtor.

A security interest may arise in two different ways. First, it may originate through the purchase of property. A *purchase money security interest* is created when the seller retains a security interest in the asset in order to secure the purchase loan. Similarly, lenders obtain a purchase money security interest when they loan money to purchase an asset which is used to secure the loan. A purchase money security interest has a high priority against third-party claims, provided the security interest is perfected through proper filing. For example, a dealer sells Bill Farmer a tractor, requiring a 25 percent downpayment and the rest financed through a promissory note secured by a purchase money security interest created by a security agreement. At about the same time (it might be either before or after), the local PCA finances Mr. Farmer and receives a security interest in the farmer's crops and machinery. If Mr. Farmer later goes into bankruptcy, the dealer with a purchase money security interest in the tractor will prevail over the PCA in its claim on the tractor, *provided* the dealer has perfected security interest by proper filing.

The second way a security interest may arise is through a loan or obligation on property already owned. To accomplish this:

1. The secured party must give value (i.e., perform some service, advance some loan, or otherwise incur a legal obligation from the debtor).

SECURITY AGREEMENT

Date June 1, 1978

A. PARTIES

1. Debtor __Farmer A__
   Check one: ☒ individual ☐ partnership ☐ corporation ☐ other
2. Address: __Star Rt. Box 18__　　　__Brook__　　　__Texas__　　　__10000__
   　　　　　　　street or RFD　　　county　　　state　　　zip
   Address shown is ☐ place of business ☐ chief executive office (if more than one place of business) ☐ residence
3. Bank: __Last State Bank__

4. Address: __Endless Plains, Texas　10000__
   (Information concerning this security interest may be obtained at the office of the bank shown above.)

B. AGREEMENT

Subject to the applicable terms of this security agreement, debtor grants to bank a security interest in the collateral to secure the payment of the obligation. A carbon, photographic, or other reproduction of this security agreement may be filed as a financing statement.

C. OBLIGATION

1. The following is the obligation secured by this agreement:
   a. All past, present, and future advances, of whatever type, by bank to debtor, and extensions and renewals thereof.
   b. All existing and future liabilities, of whatever type, of debtor to bank, and including (but not limited to) liability for overdrafts and as indorser and surety.
   c. All costs incurred by bank to obtain, preserve, and enforce this security interest, collect the obligation, and maintain and preserve the collateral, and including (but not limited to) taxes, assessments, insurance premiums, repairs, reasonable attorneys' fees and legal expenses, feed, rent, storage costs, and expenses of sale.
   d. Interest on the above amounts, as agreed between bank and debtor, or if no such agreement, at the maximum rate permitted by law.
2. List notes included in the obligation as of the date of this agreement (show date and amount):
   June 1, 1978　Farm Line of Credit for 1977 in the amount of $80,000,
   　　　　　　　　with draws of various amounts and dates under Bank's
   　　　　　　　　commitment granted December 9, 1977.

D. COLLATERAL

1. The security interest is granted in the following collateral:
   a. Describe the collateral and, as applicable, check boxes and provide information indicated in Item D.1.b. (If debtor's residence is outside the state: give location of consumer goods, farm products, and farm equipment, and if collateral includes accounts arising from the sale of farm products, give location of products sold.)

   MODEL 7000 A TRACTOR
   WHEAT　　COTTON

   b. 1. ☒ The above described crops are growing on or are to be grown on:
   __Farm is located in Brook County, Texas, ten miles west of Endless Plains__
   __on Hwy. 38.__
   　　　　　　　　　　(describe real estate)
   　　2. ☐ The above goods are to become fixtures on:

   　　　　　　　　　　(describe real estate; attach additional sheet, if needed)

   　　3. ☐ The above timber is standing on:_____
   　　　　　　　　　　(describe real estate; attach additional sheet, if needed)
   　　4. ☐ The above minerals or the like (including oil and gas) or accounts will be financed at the well head or mine head of the well or mine located on:_____
   　　　　　　　　　　(describe real estate; attach additional sheet, if needed)
   c. If b.2, b.3, or b.4, above, is checked, this security agreement is to be filed for record in the real estate records. (The description of the real estate must be sufficiently specific as to give constructive notice of a mortgage on the realty.)
   ☐ The debtor does not have an interest of record; the name of a record owner is_____

   d. All substitutes and replacements for, accessions, attachments, and other additions to, and tools, parts, and equipment used in connection with, the above property; and the increase and unborn young of animals and poultry.
   e. All property similar to the above hereafter acquired by debtor.
2. Classify goods under one or more of the following Uniform Commercial Code categories:
   ☐ Consumer goods　　　　　☐ Equipment (farm use)　　　　　☐ Inventory
   ☐ Equipment (business use)　☐ Farm products
3. ☐ If this block is checked, this is a purchase money security interest, and debtor will use funds advanced to purchase the collateral, or bank may disburse funds direct to the seller of the collateral, and to purchase insurance on the collateral.
4. If any of the collateral is accounts, give the location of the office where the records concerning them are kept (if other than debtor's address in Item A.2.)
5. If this security agreement is to be filed as a financing statement, check this block ☐ if products are covered for financing statement purposes. Coverage of products for financing statement purposes is not to be construed as giving debtor any additional rights with respect to the collateral, and debtor is not authorized to sell, lease, otherwise transfer, furnish under contracts of service, manufacture, process, or assemble the collateral except in accordance with the provisions on the back of this security agreement.
   Additional terms on back.

BANK, By: LAST STATE BANK, ENDLESS PLAINS　　　DEBTOR, By: FARMER A
Signature _Jerold Wayne_　　　　　　　　　　　Signature _Farmer A_

Typed
Name and Title JEROLD WAYNE, PRESIDENT　　　　Typed
　　　　　　　　　　　　　　　　　　　　　　Name and Title FARMER A, OWNER

If this Security Agreement is to be filed as a financing statement, Bank must sign.

Figure 15.3. A security agreement.

2. All parties involved must sign a security agreement.

3. The debtor must have rights in the property.

In order for the security interest to prevail against third-party claims, it must be perfected by giving public notice of the secured party's interest in the collateral. This is accomplished by taking possession of the asset (which is often done with intangible assets such as stocks, bonds, or notes) or by filing a *financing statement*, which is a summary or abstract of the security agreement. The distinction between the security agreement and the financing statement can readily be seen by comparing Figures 15.3 and 15.4. A financing statement should contain a description of the collateral by item as well as by type and the signatures and addresses of both parties.

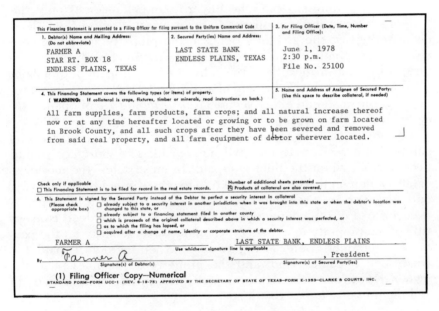

Figure 15.4. A financing statement.

Legal Instruments for Real Property

Ownership interest in land is usually identified as an *estate*. This may be a leasehold estate, which endures for a limited period of time (whether for 1 year or 99), or a freehold estate for an indefinite length of time. A freehold estate may be a life estate, where one holds title only during a lifetime, or it may be a fee-simple estate. This distinction is important because only the latter is inheritable.[3]

The legal instrument used to convey title to real estate is a *deed*. The most important types of deeds in the United States are the general warranty deed, the quitclaim deed, and the trust deed.

Where title to property is transferred by a *general warranty deed*, the grantor or seller is, in essence, promising that there is a clear, fee-simple title to the land except as noted on the deed. If this promise is false, the buyer can sue for damages resulting from reliance on this promise. If a transaction is initiated under the promises of a general warranty deed and the seller cannot provide such a clear title, the buyer usually has grounds for nullifying the contract and recovering costs.

With a *quitclaim deed*, the buyer (grantee) receives only the grantor's interest in the property. In other words, the quitclaim deed claims only that the grantor's rights in the property are being conveyed to the grantee. Thus, a buyer should thoroughly check the nature and extent of the title if the seller insists on using a quitclaim deed to transfer title. To be sure of acquiring a clear title to the property, the buyer should either secure an *abstract of title* or obtain *title insurance* on the property.

A *mortgage* conveys real estate property to the mortgagee as a surety that a real estate loan will be repaid. The mortgage should become void when the debt is repaid. In most states, the mortgage creates a lien on the property, the title to which is held by the owner and borrower. In some states, a *trust deed* or *trust deed mortgage* is used instead of the conventional mortgage. The trust deed conveys title of the property to a trustee, who holds it as security for the payment of the debt. (Refer to Figure 15.5.) When the debt is paid, the trust deed becomes void, and the property is reconveyed to the owner. However, if the debtor defaults, the trustee is authorized to sell the property to pay the debt.

Co-ownership of Property

Co-ownership of agricultural property (both personal and real) is more the rule than the exception. Co-ownership (referred to as con-

---

[3]An estate also can be defined as a legal entity that survives death of the owner and continues until distribution to the heir(s).

NOTICE Prepared by the State Bar of Texas for use by Lawyers only. Revised 1-1-76
*To select the proper form, fill in blank spaces, strike out form provisions or
insert special terms constitutes the practice of law. No "standard form" can
meet all requirements.*

DEED OF TRUST

THE STATE OF TEXAS ⎫
COUNTY OF   ⎬   KNOW ALL MEN BY THESE PRESENTS:
               ⎭

That   Farmer A and wife, Janice A.

of ...... Brook .... County, Texas, hereinafter called Grantors (whether one or more) for the purpose of securing the indebtedness hereinafter described, and in consideration of the sum of TEN DOLLARS ($10.00) to us in hand paid by the Trustee hereinafter named, the receipt of which is hereby acknowledged, and for the further consideration of the uses, purposes and trusts hereinafter set forth, have granted, sold and conveyed, and by these presents do grant, sell and convey unto ...Lyndol Bynum.., Trustee, of ....Brook............................ County, Texas, and his substitutes or successors, all of the following described property situated in ....Brook....................................... County, Texas, to-wit: all that certain tract or parcel of land lying and being situated in Brook County, Texas and being more particularly described on Exhibit "A" attached hereto and made a part hereof.

     TO HAVE AND TO HOLD the above described property, together with the rights, privileges and appurtenances thereto belonging unto the said Trustee, and to his substitutes or successors forever. And Grantors do hereby bind themselves, their heirs, executors, administrators and assigns to warrant and forever defend the said premises unto the said Trustee, his substitutes or successors and assigns forever, against the claim, or claims, of all persons claiming or to claim the same or any part thereof.

     This conveyance, however, is made in TRUST to secure payment of ......one........................ promissory note .... of even date herewith in the principal sum of ....Two hundred thousand and $\frac{no}{100}$ ------------------------------- -- Dollars ($200,000.$\frac{00}{}$..........)

executed by Grantors, payable to the order of ....LAST STATE BANK, ENDLESS PLAINS, TEXAS............

in the City of ....ENDLESS PLAINS........................, ...BROOK............................ County, Texas as follows, to-wit:

Figure 15.5. A deed of trust.

current interest) can exist with any type of land ownership, although it is more prevalent in fee-simple estates. In most states, there are three types of co-ownership: tenancy by entireties, joint tenancy, and tenancy in common. In all three situations, the co-owners have an undivided interest in the property, although the rights as a co-owner are significantly influenced by the type of concurrent interest.

     A *tenancy by entireties* is permitted in some states. It can be held only by a husband and wife. Under this form of co-ownership, when one spouse dies, the surviving spouse automatically becomes the full and sole owner of property held in joint ownership. Consequently, such property need not go through probate. However, during the lifetime of both spouses, the undivided interest of one spouse cannot be conveyed without the consent of the other.

Joint tenancy may be held by any two or more co-owners. Again, the survivors automatically receive the interest of a deceased joint tenant so that the administrative expenses associated with probate of the jointly held property can be avoided. In contrast with a tenancy by entireties, a joint tenancy enables an owner to convey interest in a lifetime deed without the co-owner's consent.

Tenancy in common also may exist between any two or more persons. However, the interest of each co-owner is inheritable rather than passing to the survivor on the death of a co-owner. Furthermore, with tenancy in common, co-owners can convey their respective interest to others without regard to the wishes of the other co-owners.

Some states retain the *community property* system as the basic property ownership law between a husband and wife. With community ownership, each spouse owns in his or her own right an equal, undivided portion of all marital property. Unless otherwise specified, all property belonging to a married couple—except that which one spouse owned before the marriage or acquired during marriage by gift or inheritance—is considered community property. As such, each party's share is inheritable in much the same manner as tenancy in common.

Other Legal Instruments Important to
Financing Agriculture

Several other legal instruments warrant consideration here. In general, a security interest cannot attach to livestock which are not conceived or to crops which are not yet planted. However, an *after-acquired property clause* attached to the security agreement permits the lender to create a valid security interest in livestock offspring which were not conceived at the time the agreement was executed. Similarly, the lender can advance money for crop production before the crop is planted, with the assurance that the security interest will attach to the future crop.

One may *waive* rights under a contract by failing to demand performance by the other party or by failing to object when the other party fails to perform under the terms of the contract. For example, if a contract calls for Bill Farmer to pay the proceeds of all livestock sales from his farm operation to the bank, and the banker is aware that Mr. Farmer has sold livestock from time to time without remitting proceeds, the banker may have waived any rights under the contract to sue Mr. Farmer for violation of contract.

A *subordination agreement* is frequently used in financing agriculture. It is an agreement subordinating one set of claims to another. It might be used in financing a tenant farmer, for example, by requiring that the owner subordinate any claims on cash rent or on a share of the crop to the claims of the lender. Similarly, a lender may require that the commercial cattle feeder subordinate claims under an *agister's lien* for any unpaid feed bills to the claims of the lender who is financing the cattle. With most family farm corporations, the corporation owes an obligation to one or more of the corporate stockholders—usually the father. The lender likely will require that the stockholders subordinate their claims to the assets of the corporation to the security interest of the lender.

A personal *suretyship* is a relationship and procedure by which one person becomes responsible for the debt or undertaking of another person. In the usual father-child farm arrangements, the father may be called on to sign a *guaranty* or *suretyship,* in which he assumes responsibility to repay a loan made to his son, for example, in case the son defaults. In financing partnerships or family corporations the lender might require that one or more of the parties (those with substantial financial strength) sign a guaranty for the indebtedness of the business.

Chapter 16

FINANCIAL INTERMEDIARIES
IN AGRICULTURE

Most countries of the world have several types of financial intermediaries that provide loans and other financial services to farmers. These credit sources include: (1) commercial banks relying
primarily on deposits for funds; (2) specialized farm lending institutions having corporate or cooperative organizations relying on money
market sources of funds; (3) government programs at federal, provin-
cial, or state levels relying on tax sources of funds; (4) credit unions
for members with a common bond; (5) farm-related trade or agribusiness firms; (6) individuals, such as family members, sellers of farm
land, or "money lenders" in developing economies; and (7) other
sources, such as thrift institutions, life insurance companies, and retirement systems.

These credit sources differ among countries in their organizational structures, operating characteristics, sources of funds, and relative importance. But they all perform the basic intermediation functions identified in Chapter 15. Moreover, they also appraise each
borrower's credit worthiness to achieve a desired loan portfolio. In
addition, government programs may be tailored to the credit needs of
particular borrowers, often on concessionary terms.

In this chapter we review the role and characteristics of major
farm lenders in the United States. These lenders have achieved high
performance in financing farmers and timely innovations of new institutions, instruments, and practices for meeting farmers' capital and
credit needs. The farm credit market evolved from strong reliance a
century ago on country or frontier banks, local merchants, land
mortgage companies, and life insurance companies to now include
the Cooperative Farm Credit System, U.S. Government lending
agencies and credit programs, local-regional-national credit programs

of many farm input suppliers, and an extensive and heterogeneous commercial banking system. Considerable financing by individuals, especially sellers of farm land, occurs as well.

Major evolutionary features of the farm credit market are the relatively large size and the regional or national orientation of many intermediaries. The Cooperative Farm Credit System has characteristics of a large national branching organization. Life insurance companies have regional or national orientations in farm lending. So do credit programs of farm input suppliers, through merchants and dealers. Even local offices of the federal government are branches of a national organization. Money center banks, regional banks, many branch banks, and Federal Reserve Banks also are large in size and are part of the national financial markets. In contrast to these size and scope phenomena however, many of these commercial banks most heavily involved in farm lending are smaller community banks located in rural areas.

Commercial Banks

As shown in Chapter 15, commercial banks play a major role in providing credit and related services to U.S. agriculture. Their involvement varies by bank size, location, specialization, and type of branching. The major money center banks (New York, Chicago, San Francisco, Dallas, etc.) generally finance larger operations involved in livestock and poultry production. This type of financing may include the entire United States. Money center banks in states with liberal branching laws may serve both large and small farming operations. These banks are further involved in agriculture by financing agribusinesses and international trade and through loan participations with regional and community banks. Moreover, they are major buyers of securities sold by the Cooperative Farm Credit System.

Regional banks located in medium-sized cities also provide direct loans to large agricultural operations and agribusinesses, and they become involved in loan participations with smaller banks. When banks are ranked by farm loan volume, the top 50 banks are mostly in large cities, even though their loan volume is small relative to other lending activities. Smaller, community-oriented banks located in rural areas are most heavily involved in farm lending.

About half of the total farm loans at commercial banks in the United States are held by about 6,000 banks, with total assets less than $100 million, in which farm loans comprise a relatively high proportion of total loans. The liquidity of these smaller agricultural banks is important because of their heavy involvement in farm lending and their heavy reliance on local markets for sources of funds. Agricultural banks rely on local markets for acquiring deposits as a major source of loanable funds. They have experienced periodic disintermediation problems (a withdrawal of deposits by depositors who reinvest directly into national money markets) in response to interest rate differentials. The problem is serious when legal restrictions limit interest rates that can be paid to depositors. These banks are especially vulnerable to local changes in farm income, which influence loan demands, loan repayments, and deposit activities. These changes cause periodic stresses in bank liquidity and large swings in credit availability for farmers.

Structure of the Banking System

Federal laws about banking structure in the United States reflect an historic concern about undue concentration of economic power, excessive competition, competitive equality between state and national banks, and state sovereignty in setting restrictions on geographic limits in banking. These concerns are expressed in the McFadden Act of 1927, which prohibits interstate branching and reserves intra-state branching policies to each state; and in the Douglas Amendment to the Bank Holding Company Act of 1956, which prevents bank holding companies from buying or establishing out-of-state subsidiaries unless authorized by the states. The result is a diverse set of state limitations on branching and holding companies. Thus, states may be designated as unit banking states, limited branching states, or statewide branching states. Moreover, states differ in their authorizations for banks to be affiliated with single-bank holding companies or multi-bank holding companies.

In a unit banking system, an individual bank maintains only one office or place of business. Rural banks in unit banking states tend to be small. Their size is limited by the amount of business in their communities. Even in traditional unit banking states, however, restrictions have been liberalized to allow drive-in windows and additional offices within specified distances. Moreover, as shown below, these unit banks have correspondent relationships with larger banks to obtain various types of banking services.

Branching refers to multiple offices of a single bank firm. Branching cannot go beyond state boundaries in the United States and within some states is limited to specific areas, such as counties, or groups of counties. This situation contrasts with many other countries that allow national branching. Restrictions on interstate bank branching are easing, however. Banks in the United States are allowed to operate "loan production offices" outside their home state and to open out-of-state offices to finance international trade. Much of the large banks' financing of agriculture occurs through these loan production offices or through other personnel contacts on a wide geographic basis.

A holding company brings one or more banks under the control of a firm which owns a major portion of the banks' stock. Holding companies allow many of the effects of branching to occur, even though the banks involved retain their independent status. Funds can easily flow within a holding company system, specialization and size economies can be achieved, and bank-related activities (leasing, insurance, etc.) may be performed by other units of the holding company.

As of January 1, 1979, only 12 states required unit banking operations, 17 states permitted limited branching, and 21 states permitted statewide branching. Most unit banking states are located in the strong agricultural areas of the Midwest and Plains regions. Hence, these banks experience considerable involvement in farm lending.

Other Regulatory Issues

As shown in Chapter 15, financial institutions in general and commercial banks in particular experience high degrees of regulation to assure desired levels of safety, stability, competitiveness, and responsiveness to monetary policy. Besides the structural issues considered above, other major bank regulations include requirements for legal reserves, capital adequacy, legal lending limits, deposit insurance, and interest rate controls on deposits (Regulation Q) and loans (usury laws). Banks are also subject to periodic audits and examinations to assure regulatory compliance and to appraise portfolio quality and management practices.

Reserve requirements established by federal and state legislation assure minimum levels of bank liquidity. The major emphasis in reserve requirements, however, is shifting to the federal level. The 1980 Depository Institutions Deregulation and Monetary Control Act (DIDMC) established uniform reserve requirements at all depository institutions in the United States: commercial banks, savings and loan associations, mutual savings banks, and credit unions. The act requires depository institutions to hold reserves on all transaction accounts and on all nonpersonal time deposits. Transaction accounts include demand deposits, negotiable orders of withdrawal (NOW), automatic transfers from savings, and other accounts subject to withdrawal for transactions purposes.

Required reserves are specified as 3 percent on a bank's first $25 million of transactions balances, effective in 1981, with this balance figure indexed annually to rise or fall at 80 percent of the rate of increase or decrease in the aggregate of transactions balances in all covered depository institutions. The reserve requirement on larger transactions balances is 12 percent. The reserve requirement on nonpersonal time deposits with maturities of less than four years is 3 percent and for maturities of four years or more is zero percent. The Federal Reserve Board can vary these requirements within specified ranges and can impose supplemental reserves for monetary control purposes. Banks may hold reserves as cash, as balances at a Federal Reserve Bank, or—if not a member of the Federal Reserve System— as pass-through balances in another depository institution that in turn maintains such funds as balances in a Federal Reserve Bank. Thus, the required reserves must be held in a non-earning form.

Legal lending limits to any bank borrower are based on the bank's equity capital. They are designed to limit the concentration of lending risks. For nationally chartered banks, loans to an individual borrower cannot exceed 15 percent of the bank's unimpaired capital and unimpaired surplus fund (a measure of net worth). However, the limit increases to 25 percent for loans to purchase livestock or for loans fully secured by readily marketable collateral (other exceptions are also provided in the law). Loan limits for state chartered banks vary among the states and are in general comparable to those of national banks. Agricultural banks in unit banking states often experience problems in meeting larger farm loan requests that exceed the banks' legal lending limits. These banks must develop loan participations with other lenders for these customers or risk losing their business.

Federal deposit insurance is required of banks that are members of the Federal Reserve System and is used by nearly all nonmember banks as well. Effective 1981, the insurance covers deposits up to $100,000 per account.

Most states have usury limits on loan rates for different types of borrowers. As interest rates increased during the 1960s and 1970s, these limits hampered farm lending in many states. Usury limits have been liberalized in most states, but these modifications have lagged increases in market rates to varying degrees. In addition, the 1980 act preempted existing state usury ceilings on business and agricultural loans for a period of three years, although affected states could override the preemption. State limits were replaced by a floating ceiling of 5 percentage points above the Federal Reserve's discount rate. State usury limits on other types of loans were also preempted. Future federal legislation will likely continue to relax the usury limits.

Commercial banks have also experienced ceiling rates on various types of deposits. These ceilings, called "Regulation Q," have hampered banks' ability to retain deposits and bid for additional deposits during periods of rising interest rates. Minor changes in Regulation Q occurred over time, and banks developed innovative ways to circumvent these rate ceilings. However, Regulation Q became an outdated, ineffective, and inequitable set of controls. Thus, the 1980 act provided for an orderly and complete phase-out by March 31, 1986, of the rate ceilings that banks (and other depository institutions) may pay on deposits and accounts.

Beyond these regulations the adequacy of bank capital is determined by policies of national and state bank examiners. These policies, in the form of guidelines on capital adequacy, liquidity, and asset quality, essentially have the force of law through their long standing use. These policies largely reflect the public's desire, expressed through the regulatory agencies, to protect bank depositors and assure bank soundness.

Banks' Portfolio Management

Banks are commercial businesses, organized as corporations, which operate for profit purposes on behalf of their stockholders, with due consideration given to risk and liquidity. Since farm lending is a major income-generating activity, especially for smaller rural banks, we can consider its contribution to bank profitability, risk, and liquidity.

Figure 16.1 models the various alternatives in managing a bank's assets (uses of funds) and liabilities (sources of funds) in order to achieve the bank's goals. The major uses of funds are categorized as (1) reserves, (2) loans, (3) investments, and (4) services. Funds also are withdrawn from the bank to pay dividends on bank stock and to

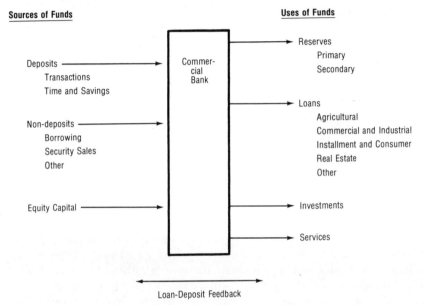

Figure 16.1. Sources and uses of bank funds.

meet income tax obligations. Reserves consist of primary reserves that satisfy legal requirements and secondary reserves held to meet longer-term liquidity needs brought about by seasonal or cyclical factors in the bank's market area. Secondary reserves are interest bearing and generally consist of U.S. Treasury bills or short-term loans (called federal funds) to other banks.

Loans are usually categorized as commercial and industrial, agricultural, installment and consumer, real estate, and other. They make up the major portion of a bank's assets. Lending yields the highest profits but also carries the highest risk and lowest liquidity of all bank investments. Along with some deposits, loans provide the greatest opportunity for differentiating the bank's "products" and competing for a greater market share. The bank's loan portfolio is generally determined by the size, business orientation, and other characteristics of its market area and by bank policy. Larger banks operating in regional or national markets usually have more diverse loan portfolios and more specialized loan officers.

Banks face two policy choices in formulating their loan portfolio. One choice involves the allocation of loanable funds among the various loan categories. This major policy decision is determined by the executive officers and bank directors. The other policy choice involves the allocation of loan funds among the various borrower-applicants that comprise the respective loan categories. Both choices are based on profitability and risk considerations; however, credit decisions at the customer level emphasize the credit-worthiness factors considered in earlier chapters.

Investments involve holdings of various types of securities: U.S. Government bonds, U.S. agency bonds, municipal bonds, and so on. Investment holdings are a residual use of funds after reserve requirements and loan demands are satisfied. Investments have longer maturities than reserves. The expected returns are higher than those of reserves but lower than those of loans, and involve interest returns and capital gains or losses if securities are sold prior to their maturity. Secondary markets for sales or purchases make investments highly liquid assets. Investment risks are relatively low; they primarily involve fluctuations in security prices as market interest rates change. A bank's management of income tax obligations centers on the investment portfolio due to the role of capital gains and losses, the exemption of municipal bonds from federal income taxation, and the exemption of U.S. Government and agency securities from state and local taxation.

Services offered to banking customers include checks, safety deposit boxes, trust and farm management, credit cards, auto licenses, insurance, and many others. These services are generally self-supporting through payment of fees or service charges.

A bank's assets will vary by size and type of bank. The typical agricultural bank located in rural areas will likely have 50 to 60 percent of its total assets in loans, 30 to 40 percent in investments, and 5 to 10 percent in reserves. The bank's building, furnishings, and other fixed assets comprise a small portion of total assets.

Consider next the sources of funds which comprise a bank's liabilities. These sources of funds are mostly deposits, although non-deposit sources have become important, especially for larger banks. Deposits include transactions accounts, like demand deposits and NOW accounts, as well as time and savings deposits. Nearly all deposits are interest-bearing (except for demand deposits), with fixed and variable ceilings that differ by size and length of deposit. However, as noted previously, these rate ceilings on deposits are scheduled to be phased out by 1986. The deregulation of deposit rates and higher reliance on non-deposit funds has increased the rate sensitivity of banks' sources of funds. Greater rate sensitivity increases a bank's portfolio risks and requires careful planning and coordination for the pricing of assets and liabilities.

Non-deposit sources of funds for banks include borrowing from other banks on a daily or longer-term basis, borrowing from Federal Reserve Banks, arranging loan participations with correspondent banks, and, for larger banks, selling commercial paper or bankers' acceptances in the national financial markets. In addition, eligible banks may obtain loan funds for their farm customers from Federal Intermediate Credit Banks by discounting loans, by direct borrowing, or by forming a subsidiary agricultural credit corporation for the same purposes.

Finally, banks must maintain an equity base which combines with deposit and non-deposit funds to form the capital base for asset holdings. A bank's equity capital must grow over time along with the bank's growth in loans and other income-generating activities. For most smaller banks, the main source of equity capital is earnings retained from the profits of lending and investments. Banks must plan carefully to assure that equity grows along with other activities. Banks are highly leveraged firms with equity capital ranging from 5 to 10 percent of total assets, and even lower for very large banks.

Banks manage their assets and liabilities to achieve high profitability subject to risk, liquidity, and competitive conditions. Banking risks arise from several sources: (1) credit risks from potential delinquency or default on repayments by borrowers, (2) investment risks from capital gains or losses on securities sold prior to maturity, (3) liquidity risks from possible loss of deposits and other sources of funds, and (4) risks from costs of funds.

The cost of funds risk (4) has grown more crucial in recent years. In the past, most banks (and other financial institutions) have tended to obtain funds with short maturities at costs that have become increasingly rate sensitive, and then have committed these funds to loans or investments with longer maturities and fixed rates of return. This practice magnified the variability of banks' profits and reduced bank profitability during periods of rising interest rates. Banks responded to this cost of funds risk with improved methods of asset-liability (A/L) management. Included in A/L management are greater use of floating (or variable) interest rates on loans, more precise matching of maturities on assets and liabilities, and, for larger banks, use of financial futures contracts to hedge interest rate risks.

Floating interest rates have gained wide use on farm loans, commercial loans, and, to a lesser degree, on consumer loans. A floating rate loan is periodically repriced prior to loan maturity as changes occur in the banks' costs of funds. This practice enables a bank to achieve a higher correlation between its costs of funds and its returns on loan assets. In the process, interest rate risks are shifted to the borrower.

Farm Lending and Bank Performance

In general, farm lending has contributed favorably to bank goals. Agricultural banks have exhibited strong profitability over time, although subject to the variations in economic performance of farms, agribusinesses, and other farm-related enterprises in their local communities. Most agricultural banks structure their portfolios to accommodate seasonal patterns of loans and deposits in their market area and possible swings in farm and farm-related income. Their ratios of loans to deposits and loans to total assets are generally less than larger banks' ratios.

Recent studies [13, 16] have shown that losses and service costs associated with agricultural loans tend to be lower per dollar of loan than for installment and commercial loans. Much farm lending is highly personalized so that the characteristics of farm customers are well-known by bankers, tending to offset relatively less developed accounting practices by farmers.

Banks are developing improved access to sources of funds for farm loans that should reduce the liquidity problems experienced in the past. Farm loan liquidity is improving too, as evidenced by the growing use of secondary markets for farm and other rural loans guaranteed by the Farmers Home Administration or the Small Business Administration. Through broker services banks can sell the guaranteed portion of these loans while still retaining loan servicing and other contacts with the borrower.

Loan-Deposit Relationships

The loan-deposit relationship is a unique feature of banking that helps to explain banks' policies in formulating their portfolios. This relationship is based on the importance of deposits as a primary source of a bank's capacity to lend and invest and the resulting importance of loan customers who hold deposits. Loans and deposits experience an interactive feedback over time that affects both bank performance and business activity in the local community. This feedback relationship for an individual bank is a micro application of the deposit-creating process that characterizes an entire banking system.

The feedback is expressed by part of the loans to bank customers returning to the bank as deposits. The feedback deposits occur from the combined effects of (1) the borrower's increased business growth arising from the financing, (2) the borrower's increased level of deposits prior to spending the loan proceeds or repaying the loan, and (3) the increased level of business activity in the community. The feedback deposits provide the basis for additional loans whose demand may be strengthened by current loans. In contrast, no such feedback occurs from most investments or from loans to nonlocal borrowers. Instead, these loan funds leave the bank's market area.

The strength of this loan-deposit relationship is difficult to measure. It appears to differ among loans, among borrowers, and with differences in bank structure and competition. It appears especially important in rural financial markets involving relatively few banks. The qualitative aspects of the feedback relationship are evidenced by most banks' practice of lending only to their depositors, by the use of deposit balances in loan pricing, and by the value bankers place on attracting new, nonlocal sources of funds that contribute to the bank's deposit base and to community business activity.

Correspondent Banking

Correspondent banking occurs when a large bank (the correspondent) provides various banking services to a smaller bank in return for compensation provided by the small bank's payment of fees or placement of a demand deposit with the correspondent. Included among correspondent services are check clearing, federal funds transactions, security safekeeping and transactions, international services, leasing services, electronic data processing, investment counseling, loans to bank directors and officers, and loan participations.

Rural banks have long relied on loan participations with correspondent banks to meet farm loan requests that exceed their legal limits and to meet total loan demands that are high relative to available loan funds. Generally, both of the participating banks carry portions of the loan, each receiving interest and security on its respective shares. In addition, the correspondent bank is also compensated by demand balances held on deposit by the rural bank.

These loan participations tend to work well when monetary conditions are relatively stable. However, in the past, problems in the pricing mechanism for participations appeared to increase significantly a rural bank's participation costs during periods of rapidly rising market interest rates. The small bank's farm loan rates tended to remain at lower levels and seriously impaired its ability to fully finance larger farm units. The pricing problem was attributed to the use of balances to pay for correspondent services, a practice which on occasion overcompensates for the services and causes a net outflow of funds from rural areas.

The 1980 DIDMC Act influenced correspondent participations in several ways. The deregulation of banks' costs of funds and the relaxation of usury limits on loans enable a closer match between farm loan rates and national market rates. These conditions along with farmers' willingness to accept higher, more volatile interest rates (perhaps based on floating rate policies) should make them more attractive customers for correspondent banks. The closer relationship between farm loan rates and national market rates will allow farm loans to compete more equitably with correspondents' other investments and will reduce the reliance placed on compensating balances. Thus, interest rates and fees should have greater use in pricing correspondent services.

Other barriers have also hampered correspondent loan participations. Many correspondent banks are not staffed with agriculturally trained and oriented officers. They may lack the ability to evaluate and control agricultural credits, especially if accounting information and loan documentation are limited. Distance between city and rural banks often precludes the correspondent banker from participating directly in the credit evaluation. Finally, some rural banks may hesitate to call on correspondents for fear of losing customers to the larger bank.

Agricultural Credit Corporations

Agricultural credit corporations (ACCs) are commercial corporations organized primarily to provide credit services to farmers. They are profit-oriented businesses that provide farm loans at interest rates which cover costs of funds, operation and administration, and risk bearing. Through a subsidiary arrangement ACCs offer a way for an individual commercial bank or a group of banks to fund farm lending from non-deposit sources. The participating bank or banks must provide initial equity capital for the ACC, which is then levered with other funds, resulting in debt-to-equity ratios that range from 6 to 1 to 10 to 1.

Once equity capital and ACC management are available, the main problem is to develop the source of funds. Two approaches are usually possible: (1) acquiring funds by selling money market instruments and (2) discounting loans with Federal Intermediate Credit Banks (FICBs)—called lending to "other financial institutions" (OFIs) by the FICBs.

The experience of banks with ACCs that sell money market instruments is limited. This procedure is feasible only for banks having close relationships with money center banks or for regional banks having customers (such as cattle feedlots) with large (above $1 million) and continuing credit needs. Smaller banks have difficulty generating enough volume and continuity to maintain money market access through ACCs. They also have high costs in providing the kinds of collateral control or insurance to meet the safety preferences of investors.

Besides serving Production Credit Associations, FICBs are also authorized to loan money and discount loans for eligible ACCs, commercial banks, and OFIs. Although use of FICBs is not extensive, a growing number of rural banks have formed ACCs to use the credit services of FICBs. This arrangement is described more fully below.

Farm Credit System

The Farm Credit System (FCS) is a system of federally chartered but privately owned banks and associations organized as cooperatives with the purpose of providing credit and related services to agricultural producers and their cooperatives in the United States. As of 1982, FCS was comprised of 12 Federal Land Banks (FLBs) and 482 Federal Land Bank Associations (FLBAs), 12 Federal Intermediate Credit Banks (FICBs) and 423 Production Credit Associations (PCAs), 13 Banks for Cooperatives (BCs), a finance office in New York City, and a joint service office, Farm Bank Services, in Denver. These private organizations are completely owned by their borrowers and operate under a federal charter, the Farm Credit Act of 1971, with several amendments. The banks and associations comprising

FCS are supervised and examined by the Farm Credit Administration (FCA), an independent agency in the executive branch of the U.S. Government.

The FCS is characterized by steady, strong growth in loan volume and is now the dominant farm lender in the United States. Its congressional authority requires that it work to improve the income and well-being of American farmers and ranchers by furnishing sound, adequate, and constructive credit and closely related services to credit-worthy borrowers and that it provide these services through favorable and unfavorable economic times.

Compared to other financial intermediaries, the FCS and its various units have a less complex financial structure. The system's assets are dominated by loans made by the various banks and associations to eligible agricultural borrowers. Reserves and physical facilities make up less than 5 percent of the system's total assets. The system obtains its loan funds primarily through the sale of securities in the national financial markets, with the various banks participating in these sales according to their projected financing needs.

In broad terms, asset-liability management by FCS mainly involves the selection of maturity structures, the timing of security sales to minimize the costs of funds acquisition, and the efficient allocation of these loan funds among individual borrowers according to their credit-worthiness. The total volume of FCS lending is largely determined by the borrowers' loan demands. The loan funds are priced to farm borrowers with floating interest rates that are adjusted periodically for changes in the average costs of funds, capital or reserve requirements, and other intermediation costs of the banks or associations making the loans. Interest rates on these loans are also exempt from state usury laws.

The system's personnel include executive officers, loan officers and credit analysts, examining and regulatory personnel, researchers and policy analysts, treasurers and financial managers, and others. By virtue of the cooperative organization, the agricultural borrowers become the system's owners and suppliers of equity capital and are represented by elected boards of directors.

Development of FCS

The FCS dates back to 1916, when the Federal Farm Loan Act, authorizing a cooperative system of 12 Federal Land Banks, was passed. The act also created the National Farm Loan Associations, now called Federal Land Bank Associations, to act as the local lending agents of the FLBs, as well as to service such loans. The 12 FLBs were originally capitalized with $750,000 each, primarily through stock purchases by the U.S. Treasury. As with later FCS units, this original government capital has long since been repaid.

The FLBs were to provide farmers with long-term real estate mortgage loans on terms compatible with the unique characteristics of agriculture and more reasonable than those available from other lending sources. FLBs had a rather conservative posture through the 1920s, but were a primary source of refinancing for many debt-stricken farmers during the depression years of the 1930s. They have since grown to become the major farm real estate lender.

The Federal Intermediate Credit Banks, along with the Production Credit Associations, were the second type of major lending institutions within FCS. Established by the Farm Credit Act of 1923, the 12 FICBs were designed to discount the short- and intermediate-term notes from various institutions, such as commercial banks or finance corporations. Thus, FICBs were mostly intended to provide an additional source of funds for private lenders. During their early years, FICBs experienced relatively slow growth due to conservative lending policies, a narrow spread between the FICB loan rate and the rates banks could charge their customers, and difficulties farmers had in establishing and operating their own finance corporations.

Thus, an enlarged credit program for agriculture was launched in 1933 as Congress authorized the establishment of local Production Credit Associations, which could discount loans with, or borrow directly from, FICBs and make short- and intermediate-term loans to farmers. In addition, the Banks for Cooperatives were also established in 1933 as the third key part of the Farm Credit System. Their mission is to provide seasonal and term loans to farmer-owned marketing, supply, and service cooperatives. All these cooperative organizations—FLBs, FLBAs, FICBs, PCAs, and BCs—became the Farm Credit System as it exists today.

Organization and Control

Figure 16.2 portrays the structural characteristics of FCS and the pattern of ownership and control. The banks and associations comprising FCS are chartered, supervised, and examined by the Farm Credit Administration. FCA is comprised of the Federal Farm Credit

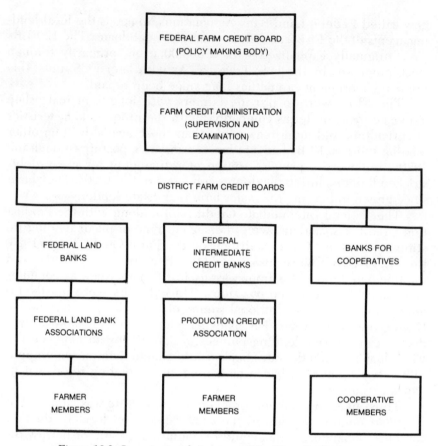

Figure 16.2. Organizational structure of the Farm Credit System.

Board, the governor of FCA, and other personnel employed to carry out the agency's activities. Essentially, the board establishes policies and adopts regulations to implement the Farm Credit Act and its amendments and to assist FCA in its supervision, examination, and coordination of the various banks and associations. The board consists of 13 members, 12 appointed by the president of the United States (one from each Farm Credit district) and one by the Secretary of Agriculture to act as his or her representative.

Following cooperative principles, member borrowers of FCS own the banks and associations through their stock investments and participate in the management and control of these institutions.

Based on the principle of one member–one vote, stockholders directly elect the boards of directors of the FLBAs and PCAs of which they are members. These boards hire management and set loan policies in accordance with the laws, FCS regulations, and bank policies. Similarly, the members of cooperatives holding stock in the district BCs elect the boards of directors of their respective cooperative associations. In turn, the boards of the local associations and cooperatives that use the BCs elect the boards of directors for their respective Farm Credit board. Two representatives are elected from among the FLBAs, PCAs, and BC borrowers, respectively, and a seventh member in each district is appointed by the governor of FCA.

FLBs, FICBs, and PCAs are authorized to make loans to bona fide farmers and ranchers, rural residents, aquatic producers, and persons furnishing on-farm services to farmers. Any person who owns agricultural land or is engaged in producing agricultural or aquatic products is eligible. Partnerships, corporations, trusts, estates, and other business forms may also qualify.

Cooperatives engaged in the processing, handling, or marketing of farm or aquatic products, or in the acquisition of supplies or services for producers of such products, are eligible to borrow from the BCs, provided they meet the minimum specified criteria.

Funding the Farm Credit System

The Farm Credit Banks acquire loanable funds by issuing two types of securities in the national financial markets: Federal Farm Credit Banks Consolidated System-wide Bonds and Federal Farm Credit Banks Consolidated System-wide Notes. These are commonly called Farm Credit bonds and discount notes, respectively. Bonds are issued in book-entry form 16 times a year: on the first of each month and on the twentieth of January, April, July, and October. Bonds with six- and nine-month maturities are issued on the first of each month and sold only in multiples of $5,000. Bonds with maturities of 13 months or longer are available in multiples of $1,000.

Discount notes are designed to provide flexibility in obtaining funds between bond sales. They are comparable to commercial paper issued by corporate firms. These notes are issued daily, with maturities of from 5 to 270 days, and are sold in denominations of $50,000, $100,000, $500,000, $1 million, and $5 million.

Responsibility for selling securities lies with the FCS fiscal agency located in New York City. After each Farm Credit Bank has determined and reported its financing needs, the fiscal agent will consult with bond dealers and with the governor of FCA to determine the amount and terms of the issues to be offered. Bonds and notes are then sold through a nationwide chain of securities dealers. The dealers sell the bonds to private and public investors, mostly comprised of commercial banks, state and local governments, thrift institutions, and corporations. A small but growing amount of Farm Credit bonds are held by foreign investors. The bonds are priced to sell at par in their original issue. They are subsequently traded in an active secondary market at values based on current market yield.

Prior to 1979, the three Farm Credit banks issued their own consolidated securities, and they still have the authority to do so. However, the issuances are now all system-wide. The Farm Credit banks also maintain credit lines with large commercial banks for added liquidity, and they may borrow from other banks within FCS.

Farm Credit bonds and discount notes are treated as "Government Agency Securities" in the financial market even though it is explicitly stated that they are not guaranteed by the federal government against default. Agency status is a significant factor in the ability of FCS to market large volumes of securities at relatively favorable costs. Agency securities generally trade at yields that fall between yields on U.S. Treasury securities and the yields on prime corporate bonds of comparable maturities. While the yield spreads may vary over time, depending on general financial conditions and supply-demand characteristics for these securities, the long-term pattern of spreads holds with a high degree of consistency.

However, other factors are needed along with agency status to achieve the high standing of FCS securities in the financial markets. These other factors include: (1) a strong credit history with no delinquency or default by FCS in meeting obligations on securities and with only minor losses in farm loans; (2) a strong capital structure and financial position for the banks and associations that comprise FCS; (3) strong management within FCS; (4) the large size and nationally federated structure of FCS, which permits effective diversification of loans and pooling of risks among the banks and associations; and (5) an efficient system for issuing and distributing FCS securities as characterized by a stable maturity structure, regular issuances, predictability, large volume, wide dealer involvement, and an active secondary market.

Equity capital of the various banks and associations is obtained through sale of stock to borrowers and by earnings retained from interest, fees, and rental revenue paid by members. In practice, the equity capital from stock sales is created by loaning additional amounts to borrowers to finance their stock purchases. The stock requirement generally poses no cash flow hardship for borrowers, although it slightly increases their annual percentage rate of interest (see Chapter 14).

The banks and associations also differ in their tax obligations, which in turn affects some of the system's financial operations. FLBs, FLBAs, and FICBs are not subject to taxation, except for taxes on the real estate they own. PCAs and BCs are subject to income taxes similar to other corporations operating on a cooperative basis. The exemption from taxation of some units means that credit services can be offered to borrowers at lower costs. In addition, the tax exemption of FICBs creates further opportunities for shifting obligations between FICBs and PCAs to reduce income taxes, and thus borrowing costs.

Federal Land Banks

The 12 FLBs service the long-term loan requirements of farmers and other FCS borrowers. They make direct loans to borrowers with farmer contact, loan servicing, and loan endorsement provided by the FLBAs. Loans can be made for maturities of from 5 to 40 years. Repayments are usually specified as equally amortized annual payments. However, the payments may vary in accordance with the FLB's floating interest rate policy. While the loan proceeds can be used for any purpose, most FLB loans are used for purchasing new real estate, improving land, acquiring buildings, or refinancing previous real estate or non-real estate loans. The principal lending requirement is that all FLB loans be secured by a first lien on real estate.

Loans to individual borrowers are legally limited to 20 percent of the district FLB's equity capital (capital and surplus). Since the equity capital of the 12 FLBs averages over $150 million, the legal lending limit is of no practical significance to most borrowers. Larger loans can be made through participation arrangements with other district FLBs.

The loan amount may also not exceed 85 percent of the appraised value of the real estate pledged as security. This limit increases to 97 percent of appraised value if a government guarantee by the Farmers Home Administration is provided. The actual percentage loaned, however, is commonly less than 85 percent and depends on the borrowers' repayment capacity and other elements of credit worthiness. Published data indicate an average ratio of loan amount to security value of 55 percent for all FLB loans in 1980. FLBs determine appraised values by using "benchmark" farms that represent the major types of farming in the borrowers' local area. The value of benchmark farms is updated periodically (once or twice a year) as changes occur in farming conditions and in actual sales value for farm land in the local community. This procedure results in benchmark values lagging behind changes in market values. Some FLB personnel estimate, for example, that appraised values run about 80 percent of market values when land values are trending upward. This percentage will vary considerably among the FLBAs in the country.

Each borrower must be a member of the local FLBA and must purchase stock in the association of not less than 5 percent nor more than 10 percent of the loan, depending on the bylaws of the FLBA. The current stock requirement is 5 percent. The FLBA in turn buys an equal amount of stock in the district bank. Most FLBs also include a small service fee—1 to 3 percent of the loan. Generally, both the stock requirement and the service fee are included in the loan.

Interest rates are predominantly floating rates, although some FLBs may offer the borrower a choice between floating and fixed rate loans. Advanced payments or total loan repayments may occur prior to maturity without penalty. In fact, few loans actually continue to loan maturity due to the borrowers' early repayment, refinancing, added financing, and renewals.

The timing and pattern of repayment plans can be tailored to the borrowers' repayment capacity and financial situation. The most credit-worthy borrowers, for example, may receive "open-ended" loans in which they may draw upon a future credit commitment over a specified period of time. Normally, however, the loan disbursement and repayments are precisely specified.

Finally, the Farm Credit Act Amendments of 1980 authorized FLBs to participate in real estate loans with non-FCS lenders, similar to PCA's authorization to participate with other lenders. These loans are subject to the same security requirements and terms as direct FLB loans and to the eligibility requirements for FCS borrowers.

FICBs and PCAs

The major activity of the 12 FICBs is to loan to or discount loans from the PCAs located in their respective farm credit districts. In addition, FICBs may loan to or discount loans from other financing institutions, as discussed below. PCAs make short- and intermediate-term loans to farmers and other eligible borrowers for almost any purpose associated with farming, farm-related businesses, on-farm services, and rural life. The maximum loan maturity is 10 years, although most intermediate-term loans for machinery and breeding livestock are in the 5-year range. The terms and repayment patterns of most PCA loans are based on the borrowers' projected cash flows. Funds are advanced to meet projected outlays as needed, and loans are repaid as income becomes available. This procedure keeps interest costs to a minimum. In addition, service fees may be charged to cover the costs of preparing cash flow budgets and loan servicing.

PCAs in general charge floating interest rates set to cover the costs of loan funds borrowed from the district FICB, the costs of operating the PCA, possible loan losses, and retention of earnings to build equity capital. Each PCA monitors its costs of funds on a monthly basis for possible changes in loan rates. Most PCAs charge all borrowers the same interest rate, although an increasing number of associations use multiple rates based on differences in the borrowers' credit risks. At year end, surplus earnings may be allocated to borrowers as patronage refunds that are either paid in cash or retained by the PCA.

Each borrower is required to purchase stock in the association at levels of between 5 percent and 10 percent of the loan, depending on a specific PCA's capitalization policy. Most PCAs have a 10 percent stock requirement. The stock represents the borrowers' ownership claim on the PCA and, since it is normally included in the loan, increases slightly the borrowers' annual percentage rate of interest (see Chapter 14). FICBs in turn make capital assessments upon PCAs to maintain the equity needed by the bank for operation and expansion.

The legal lending limit to any one PCA borrower is 50 percent of the association's capital and surplus. This percentage increases to 100 percent if an approved loss-sharing agreement is in force with a loan-sharing participant. When FICBs participate with a PCA as a loan maker, the FICB loan limit is 20 percent of the bank's capital and surplus. As with FLB loans, these high loan limits, along with the participation arrangements, make them inconsequential to individual borrowers.

PCAs may also provide leasing or rental services to their members. Financial leasing in particular is being developed by PCAs as an additional method of intermediate-term financing for farmers. The principal incentive is to reduce the farmer's after-tax cost of financing based on the tax savings that PCAs as corporate taxpayers can achieve from depreciation and investment tax credit.

PCAs may also participate with commercial banks or other lenders in agricultural lending. PCA participations have grown substantially, although the total participation volume is only about 1 percent of PCA's total lending activity. Commerical banks wishing to participate with PCAs must fulfill one of the following terms: (1) retain at least 50 percent of the total of each participation loan; (2) retain at least 10 percent of the total of each participated loan, provided the commercial bank does not materially reduce its ratio of agricultural loans to total loans from the ratio maintained during the preceding three years; or (3) retain the maximum amount of the participated loan permitted by banking regulations to which the bank is subject. Banks must also purchase non-voting participation certificates from the PCA, which are analogous to the stock requirement of the association's members.

Other Financing Institutions (OFIs) eligible to borrow from FICBs include commercial banks, trust companies, thrift institutions, credit unions, agricultural credit corporations (ACC), or any other agricultural producer association engaged in extending credit to farmers. OFIs typically have made little use of FICB funds; the volume of FICB loans or discounts to OFIs has been about 3.5 percent of FICB's total loan volume. Nearly all of the OFI activity occurs with commercial banks, their affiliated ACCs, and nonbank ACCs.

For commercial banks or their ACCs to become eligible for funding from FICBs, they must have (1) a significant involvement in lending for agricultural or aquatic purposes, as indicated by having at least 15 percent of their loan volume at the seasonal peak in these types of loans; (2) a continuing need for funds for agricultural and aquatic purposes, as usually indicated by an average loan to deposit ratio of at least 60 percent over the last three years at its seasonal peak; (3) a limited access to national or regional capital markets and full utilization of local funds to finance local needs; and (4) no intention of using FICB funds to expand financing for parties and purposes ineligible for discount with FICBs. These conditions were established by the Farm Credit Act Amendments of 1980, which revised the eligibility conditions for OFIs and put them in essentially the same position as PCAs in using FICB services. Provisions are also specified to assure that the eligible OFIs utilize FICB funds on a continuing basis and to account for bona fide exceptions to the eligibility conditions cited above.

Banks for Cooperatives

The Banks for Cooperatives form a credit system devoted solely to meeting the financing needs of cooperatives engaged in processing, handling, or marketing farm or aquatic products; furnishing products or services to farmers; or furnishing services to eligible cooperatives. These banks provide a major part of the credit used by many farm cooperatives in most states. Thus, they are an important part of the total credit system available to agriculture. A bank for cooperatives is authorized to make both seasonal and term loans. Seasonal loans are normally for up to 18 months. Term loans are normally for financing fixed assets and working capital. The Farm Credit Act Amendments of 1980 provided a new authority for BCs to offer basic financial services to cooperatives for export and import transactions and to engage in international banking activities which facilitate agricultural exports and imports of farmer cooperatives.

Eligible cooperative borrowers from BCs must have 80 percent of their membership comprised of farmers, although this requirement is lowered to 60 percent of voting members for rural electric, telephone, and other utility service and for certain local supply cooperatives. BCs may also finance domestic leasing, including leveraged leasing transactions involving farm or aquatic cooperatives.

An important development among agricultural cooperatives has been their consolidation, through mergers and federations, into large regional and national businesses requiring financing that exceeds the legal limits of individual BCs. The primary purpose of the Central Bank for Cooperatives is to assist in meeting such needs. In addition, a district BC may participate with other district banks or with non-FCS lenders in financing eligible cooperatives whose borrowing needs exceed a BC's legal lending limit.

Life Insurance Companies

In the early 1900s, life insurance companies and commercial

banks were the major institutions making farm real estate loans. While Federal Land Banks and the Farmers Home Administration are now also involved, life insurance companies are still major suppliers of farm real estate debt. Their involvement varies substantially by regions, by company, and with changes in financial market conditions.

Life insurance companies are profit-oriented institutions whose main financial activities are the sale of insurance policies and payments of claims to policy holders. The long-term nature of these activities requires the accumulation and holding of large financial reserves. These reserves are generally invested in a diversified portfolio of low-risk investments.

In total, investments in farm mortgages typically represent about 2 to 3 percent of life insurance companies' total assets, although the proportion is higher for those making farm loans. Thus farm mortgage lending is minor compared to other insurance company investments, although some companies are much more involved in farm lending than others. Life insurance companies' market share of farm real estate debt has declined in recent years due to competing uses for their investment funds, increased demand for loans from policy holders, and usury limits on interest rates in many states, that became effective during periods of tight credit and rising market rates. More liberal lending by Federal Land Banks also depressed insurance companies' market shares.

There are notable exceptions, but most insurance companies tend to make periodic allocations of funds to farm lending and discontinue farm loans for awhile when the allocation is depleted. Life insurance companies prefer lending to larger, low-risk farming operations. The average size of a life insurance company loan is typically greater than an FLB loan or a commercial bank loan. Some insurance companies concentrate their farm lending in selected areas such as the Corn Belt or irrigated farming areas, where production is more stable and weather risks are lower. Laws in some states limit the size of an insurance company's loan to a designated proportion (e.g., 75 percent) of the appraised value of the farm land or other security. Considerable flexibility occurs in the choice of appraisal method. No legal limits are placed on individual loans, although companies may impose their own limits as a matter of policy.

The maturities and repayment schemes for life insurance company loans have changed as these companies seek interest rate protection from the effects of high, volatile inflation. These terms differ considerably, but a typical arrangement in the 1980s may have a loan maturity of from 10 to 20 years, a longer amortization schedule (e.g., 30 years), and a provision for interest rate adjustment every 5 years. Because the loan maturity is shorter than the amortization period, a substantial balloon payment is due at maturity. The borrower either meets the balloon payment with cash or refinances it with the insurance company or another lender.

In recent times, insurance companies have also adopted other innovative methods of responding to borrowers' liquidity problems caused by inflation and swings in farm income. Mortgages with graduated payments, adjustable rates, and shared appreciation are examples. In a shared appreciation mortgage, the borrower agrees to give the lender a percentage of the capital gains on the land in return for a lower interest rate. The lower rate reduces the debt servicing obligation, while the share in prospective capital gains makes up part of the lender's compensation.

Insurance company loans are made to farmers either directly from a company office or indirectly through correspondents, such as mortgage brokers, mortgage companies, real estate companies, and some commercial banks. Coordination between lenders helps both borrower and lender. Insurance companies may, for example, arrange to purchase real estate loans which commercial banks have originated. This arrangement enables banks to offer a full range of loans to their customers and provides low-cost contact and servicing for the insurance company.

Trade Credit

Trade credit represents a significant source of non-real estate financing for farmers. However, this financing source has had a lower share of the farm credit market, as shown in Chapter 15. Aside from direct personal loans, trade credit is perhaps the oldest form of credit known. It has survived competition from specialized, efficient, and responsive lending institutions in widely differing environments around the world.

Trade credit arises from a merchandising transaction. Generally, the originator is the seller of a farm input: feed, fuel, fertilizer, machinery, storage facilities, or buildings. However, firms who buy from farmers through a procurement contract may include financing in the contract package. Trade credit provides a merchant or dealer with a means for facilitating sales and maintaining or increasing sales.

Trade firms use many types of financing arrangements. The *open account* is particularly convenient for the buyer and seller when frequent sales occur. The buyer receives deliveries without requiring immediate payment. An account receivable is generated and held by the seller, based on delivery slips. Billing usually occurs monthly, with prompt payment expected to bring the customer's account up to date.

The *extended open account* extends the open account, with or without interest, until a recognized source of payment becomes available. Again, the only security held by the seller is an account receivable based on delivery slips. Seasonality in farming makes this arrangement attractive to farmers and explains its wide use in acquiring crop and livestock inputs.

Bank credit cards are offered by some trade firms as alternatives to open account and extended open account credit [8]. The trade firm and bank establish a line of credit for the farm customer and prepare appropriate identification cards and sales forms. The farmer may then charge purchases from the trade firm up to the credit limit, with the bank assuming responsibility for billing and collection. When a bank is involved in the credit extension process, lending costs and credit evaluation procedures may be reduced and simplified.

While open accounts and credit cards are attractive and convenient, the limited negotiability of the debt instrument presents trade firms with special liquidity problems. Marketability of the debt instrument is improved with more formal evidence of indebtedness. Three financing methods are commonly used: the unsecured promissory note, the secured promissory note, and the conditional sales contract. The last two are important in capital transactions involving sales of buildings, machinery, and equipment to farmers. The sales contract is frequently used between supply firms and farmers. If an open account or an extended open account is not paid on schedule, the trade firm might have the farmer sign a promissory note and pledge collateral as security.

In installment lending, the trade firm or dealer may transfer the customer's notes to a finance company, a subsidiary credit corporation of a manufacturer, or a local financial institution, such as a commercial bank or PCA. In these cases, the trade firm shifts the credit responsibility to more specialized lenders. Loan documentation is usually more complete, and the borrower's credit worthiness is examined more fully.

The convenience which trade credit offers is an integral part of the merchandising system. Many manufacturers provide credit to their distributors, dealers, and retailers. This credit can be passed to farm customers. However, as credit terms begin to exceed 30 days, the trade credit begins to compete with financing from other lenders. Thus, there must be incentives for trade firms to offer financing and for farmers to accept it.

For the trade firm, the capital used to finance its customers is costly. The cost is direct and visible if the trade firm itself must borrow. It is costly even if the firm does not borrow, because of foregone investment alternatives and opportunity costs incurred in administering sales financing. In addition, loan supervision and collection can be costly for trade firms not specialized in lending. On the other hand, some trade firms become quite familiar with the business and with the financial practices of their customers, based on frequent contacts in merchandising transactions. This familiarity may help support the financing transaction.

Supply firms often attempt to differentiate their products and thus increase their competitive position by offering credit services. However, when pricing of credit services and merchandising transactions are combined, it is difficult to distinguish between their separate effects.

From a farmer's standpoint, trade financing could offer access to larger total credit, although split financing is discouraged by many farm lenders unless it is well planned and justified. Trade credit is also convenient for farmers, and it may be a cheaper means of financing.

In determining the cost of trade credit, the farmer must first be sure that the product is priced competitively. Free trade financing from a dealer who is non-competitive in price or product quality can be a costly source of funds. If a cash discount is not available, and if the quality and product price are acceptable, the farmer can benefit from trade credit if the interest cost is lower than alternative sources and if the farm's primary lender does not respond adversely to the farmer's use of trade credit.

When a cash discount is available, the rate of interest being paid by foregoing the cash discount is based on (1) the size of the cash discount, (2) the maximum time after billing before payment must occur to qualify for a cash discount, and (3) the length of time before an unpaid account becomes delinquent. Most cash discounts range from 1 to 3 percent of the purchase price. Many suppliers allow cash discounts if payment occurs within 10 days of billing and impose penalties if an account is unpaid 30 days after billing. These terms vary among firms. Thus, the buyer should be familiar with a trade firm's credit policy.

For operating inputs, a credit policy might be represented by 3/10, n − 30, which is interpreted as a 3 percent discount if paid within 10 days, with the bill due at face value within 30 days, after which it becomes delinquent. Thus, it costs a buyer 3 percent to finance the account for that extra 20 days between the tenth and thirtieth day after billing. The annual interest rate for these terms is 54.8 percent = 3 ÷ (20/365). This is the buyer's cost for using the trade credit if a cash discount is available. A credit policy of 1/10, n − 30 costs the buyer an annual rate of 18.3 percent = 1 ÷ (20/365), compared to the cash discount.

Interest rates charged on supply accounts vary among suppliers. Where interest is actually assessed and collected, the rates are generally higher than for operating loans from commercial lenders. Thus it is usually less costly to borrow money from a commercial lender and pay the supplier accounts before interest is charged.

Credit terms on installment loans for machinery, equipment, buildings, etc., usually have maturities and repayment patterns comparable to those of commercial lenders. However, interest rates from dealers generally are higher, reflecting the trade firms' higher costs of providing credit services to customers.

Individuals and Seller Financing

Individuals provide about 28 percent—a significant amount—of the total farm real estate debt in the United States. Most of this financing comes from sellers of farm land, who finance a buyer's purchase either through a contract arrangement or through a note secured by a mortgage. Most of these sales are financed with a *land-purchase contract*, also known as a *contract of sale*, a *conditional sales contract*, a *land contract*, or an *installment contract*. It is an agreement to permanently transfer control of the land to the buyer, while land title remains with the seller until the contracted repayment conditions are met. As prices of farm land have risen over time, the purchase contract has become widely used in farm land purchases.

These contracts usually require relatively low downpayments. The terms and rates of interest vary substantially, especially in transactions between close relatives. The term is often rather short—usually no more than 10 to 20 years. Partial amortization may occur, with requirements for a large final or balloon payment (e.g., 30 to 40 percent of the sale price). The repayment schedules can be established through negotiation to meet the needs of the buyer and seller. Most contracts also require the buyer to maintain the property to a specified standard until title is transferred.

The Seller's Viewpoint

Sellers of farm land are interested in contract sales for several reasons. First, these sales can provide a steady, easily manageable flow of returns from an agricultural investment as payments of principal and interest are made. This feature may be important to retiring farmers or other land owners who prefer to withdraw from active management.

Second, tax regulations in the United States permit capital gains from the sale of an asset (land in this case) to be spread over the years of repayment. The only stipulation is that the installment payments include interest at a rate above a threshold level (e.g., 9 percent). Otherwise, interest is recomputed at a higher rate and taxed as ordinary income to the seller.

Sales of most farm land usually involve substantial capital gains; thus, the installment sale is attractive to sellers under either a contract sale or a mortgage sale. Because personal income tax rates are progressive, spreading payments over time results in lower tax obligations over this period. The degree of advantage depends on the current and expected income tax position of both seller and buyer. The seller may, for example, prefer a relatively high sale price and a relatively low interest rate due to the lower tax obligation for capital gains than for ordinary income. The buyer may also prefer price and interest trade-offs, since the sale price establishes the basis for future capital gains and because interest payments are tax deductible. Hence, both price and financing terms are subject to joint negotiation.

Furthermore, in case the buyer defaults, the land purchase contract gives the seller a higher degree of control over the asset than is provided when the buyer receives title and pledges a real estate mortgage. Finally, by reducing the downpayment requirement, the seller may increase the number of potential buyers.

The seller may also incur some disadvantages with a land purchase contract. The buyer's low equity makes the contract a high-risk loan. This financial risk is offset somewhat by the simplified foreclosure procedures on many contracts and by higher land values over time. The contract also has relatively low liquidity, since no formal secondary markets are available. Thus, sellers may have more difficulty selling their interest in the contract without accepting a heavy discount.

The Buyer's Viewpoint

For the buyer, a purchase contract provides the benefits and responsibilities of land ownership with a relatively small downpayment. Hence, the buyer can achieve a high leverage position. If credit is limited from commercial lenders, then seller financing may be the only available source. Moreover, the land contract allows a form of ownership that overcomes the tenure uncertainties of leasing.

Buying on contract also has several disadvantages. The risk of losing the farm by default in payment is typically greater with a purchase contract than with a note secured by a mortgage. The loss could include the downpayment and any equity built up from debt payments and land improvements. In recent years, however, the courts have been tending to support the equity position of the contract buyer during default.

The potential loss of the farm land may hamper short- and intermediate-term financing available from commercial lenders. First, the farmer's balance sheet position deteriorates under a purchase contract, since lenders may not include the accumulation of equity in the land, even though they might include the current year's payment as a liability. Second, if the annual payments on purchase contracts are large, then less cash is available to service non-real estate loans. These factors may make non-real estate lenders more reluctant to finance farmers with contracts compared to mortgage financing.

Before buying land on contract, the buyer should check carefully with other lenders to determine the potential impact on non-real estate credit. If operating credit were curtailed, the total cost of the purchase contract, including loss of liquidity, would be very high. In practice, the buyer often refinances a contract to a real estate mortgage when the contract terminates, or earlier if financial conditions warrant. Legal considerations play an important role in the design of equitable land purchase contracts. These factors need careful study.

Farmers Home Administration

The Farmers Home Administration (FmHA) is a government lending agency operating under the authority of the U.S. Department of Agriculture. The functions now performed by this agency began, for the most part, in the 1930s, though emergency crop and livestock loans had been made earlier. The Farm Security Administration (FSA) was established in 1937 to concentrate on two programs: (1) farm production and subsistence loans and (2) farm establishment loans [14]. In 1946, the FmHA was formally designated to replace the FSA with the purpose of continuing supervised farm credit to U.S. agriculture. Much of this lending has been to young, beginning farmers, or others with limited resources, who have success potential but lack access to sufficient financing from commercial sources. As these farmers become better established, they are expected to use commercial sources of financing.

FmHA's lending activities occur through direct loan programs, guarantees of farm loans made and serviced by commercial lenders, and various emergency loan programs. Much of the rapid increase in FmHA lending in the late 1970s and early 1980s reflected economic emergency loan programs, which were authorized by legislation in 1978 and extended in 1980. This legislation broadened the concept of emergency beyond natural disasters to include adverse economic events as well as unanticipated shortages in credit availability from commercial lenders at reasonable rates.

Direct loans from the FmHA have included those for farm ownership and enlargement, operating expenses, rural housing, water development and soil conservation, business and industrial development, and losses due to natural disasters. Farm borrowers are required to accept supervision and guidance in their farming operations. This supervision is provided through about 1,700 local offices in the United States, which serve all rural counties. The county programs are administered by a county supervisor and a three-person committee comprised of at least two local farmers.

FmHA loans are subsidized in three ways. First, borrowers have access to credit which is not available at commercial sources. Second, interest rates are generally below market rates, although less so in the 1980s than in the past. Rates are now largely based on the federal government's costs of funds. For some emergency loans, however, interest rates are considerably below market levels. Third, the management-guidance program is greater than could be economically undertaken by a commercial lender.

Each farm ownership loan is based on a farm plan designed to yield revenue sufficient for loan repayment and a reasonable standard of living. Loans are extended for up to 40 years, with a legal limit imposed per borrower to assure a wide distribution of loan funds. This limit is adjusted periodically to reflect changes in borrowers' credit needs.

Farm operating loans are available to buy livestock and equipment, pay operating expenses, refinance debts, and make other needed adjustments in farm operations. Loan repayments on operating loans are generally made when products are sold. Intermediate-term loans are also available for durable resources. As with farm ownership loans, a legal limit per borrower is specified.

FmHA's purpose has on occasion been broadened to establish loan programs designed to improve rural communities and alleviate rural poverty. These programs have included loans to individuals, groups of individuals, local businesses, and rural communities for such purposes as housing, community water handling systems, recreational facilities, and loans to low-income rural families and local cooperatives which serve them.

FmHA's loan funds are obtained through the Federal Financing Bank, which is the mechanism the government uses to finance its credit programs and many others. Repayments on these funds in turn replenish a revolving loan fund. Shortages are made up by Congress, which provides the agency's annual budget.

The FmHA also guarantees qualified loans made by commercial banks and other private lenders. Loan terms are negotiated directly between the borrower and the lender, and payments are made directly to the lender. The FmHA guarantees up to 90 percent of the loan against loss. The guarantee may result in more favorable terms for the borrower. Moreover, the program has enabled many agricultural banks to accommodate both large and small farm loans having high risk. Lending risks are reduced, and returns from interest and service fees have been favorable to the commercial lender. The guaranteed portion does not count against a bank's legal lending limit, and it may be sold through brokers in secondary markets.

The FmHA has played an important role in financing high risk borrowers. Moreover, it has often benefited other lenders by assuming the financing of deteriorating loan situations. Commercial lenders also benefit from the managerial skills acquired by graduates from the FmHA.

In the 1980s, however, much concern surfaced about special credit treatment in agriculture, the proper balance between public and private sectors, the degree of subsidy involved, and the tax consequences for the U.S. Government. The administration of President Ronald Reagan sought to reduce the magnitude of, and subsidy in, FmHA programs and largely return the FmHA to its role as a lender of last resort for farmers. Interest rates are now tied more closely to the government's costs of funds. Closer coordination is sought between FmHA and commercial lenders in dealing with income problems in farming, and greater reliance is placed on graduating FmHA borrowers into the commercial credit markets.

Commodity Credit Corporation

Price and income support programs administered by the Commodity Credit Corporation (CCC) in the U.S. Department of Agriculture provide a comprehensive financial control program that combines buffering of price variability for many commodities with provision of inventory financing, added marketing flexibility for farmers, and maintenance of farm incomes. The CCC also administers longer-term storage and commodity reserve programs that extend the inventory financing and shift some of the marketing control to the government. Loans are also available for the purchase, construction, and installation of storage and drying equipment on the farm [15].

The CCC was established by executive order in 1933 as part of a package of emergency farm programs designed to boost farm income and to foster an efficient and orderly marketing system. The CCC is a USDA agency operating through personnel and facilities of the Agricultural Stabilization and Conservation Service and other USDA agencies. The CCC is authorized by charter and statute to buy, sell, make loans, store, transfer, export, and otherwise engage in agricultural commodity operations [15].

A basic justification of CCC loans under the original charter was that they enabled farmers to hold their commodities after harvest until prices rose as a result of production control programs. Although a primary objective of the CCC is to minimize the effects of low commodity prices on farm income, the inventory financing of the marketing of several important farm products has been greatly influenced by CCC lending and other price support activities.

The primary lending feature of the commodity program involves the pledging by eligible farmers of stored crops to CCC as collateral for a loan. The loan amount is equal to the level of price support for the particular commodity multiplied by the quantity of crops in storage. The farmer can then sell the stored crop on the open market and pay off the loan plus interest at a rate based on the government's costs of funds. However, if the commodity price remains below the loan rate, at the end of the loan contract (usually nine months) the commodity pledged as collateral can be transferred to CCC ownership, thus serving as full payment of loan principal and interest. This arrangement is called a *non-recourse loan*. It assures the participating farmer a minimum price for the commodity.

The basic eligibility requirements for a CCC loan are that producers comply with any allotment or acreage set-aside programs authorized by the U.S. Department of Agriculture in a particular crop year and store their crops in CCC-approved facilities. Besides the regular non-recourse loan program described above, a second choice for non-recourse loans has been the farmer-owned grain reserve program for producers of eligible commodities. Under the reserve program, participants have the same minimum price protection as under the regular program, but enter a longer (three-year) contract, agreeing to hold grain in the reserve until the contract matures or until the national average market price reaches pre-determined release or call levels. Upon loan maturity or at a call price currently ranging from 145 to 185 percent of the loan rate (depending on the individual commodity), the participant must either redeem the loan or forfeit the commodity.

Recourse loans for storage facilities, drying, and other grain-handling equipment are also available from the CCC. Loans are limited to 85 percent of the cost of construction and currently cannot exceed $100,000 per farmer. Loan repayments may occur over a period of eight years, with the interest rate based on the government's costs of funds.

CCC loan participation tends to be directly related to the difference between CCC price support levels and commodity market prices. When market prices are near or below the support level, CCC program loan participation increases. The opposite occurs when market prices rise above the support level. Thus producers make greater use of the program when farm prices are declining. However, CCC loan activity is also influenced by other variables, such as interest rates, producers' expectations about variability in seasonal crop prices, and the preferences of commercial lenders. Indeed, many commercial lenders prefer farm borrowers to shift inventory financing to the CCC, using the proceeds of price support loans to pay off production and operating loans.

Topics for Discussion

1. Identify some of the unique features of agricultural banks' involvement in farm lending. Distinguish between unit and branching systems of banking and their relationships to bank holding companies.
2. Identify some of the major regulations affecting commercial banks. How have interest rate controls on deposits and loans influenced banking over time? What effects will the removal of these ceilings have on bank lending to agriculture?
3. Evaluate the various sources and uses of bank funds, and contrast these with the Farm Credit System's sources and uses of funds. What are the implications for portfolio management of these farm lenders?
4. Characterize the loan-to-deposit feedback relationship in banking. How does it arise? What are its implications for bank lending and investment activities?
5. What role do agricultural credit corporations play in agricultural finance? Why are they used by commercial banks? What are their major sources of funds?
6. Explain the role of correspondent relationships in banking, including the arrangements used in loan participations among banks. How do balances and deposit relationships affect pricing policies on loan participations?
7. Explain the organizational structure, ownership, control, and supervision of the Cooperative Farm Credit System. Why did the system develop? What factors explain its growing importance in agricultural finance?
8. What are the Farm Credit System's sources of loan funds? What factors affect its access to the national financial markets? What are the important areas of the system's portfolio management?
9. How does the Farm Credit System generate its equity capital? What procedures are followed? What are the effects on farmers' costs of borrowing? How do income tax obligations of the farm credit banks and associations affect farmers' costs of borrowing?
10. Give a brief synopsis of the lending programs of FLBs, PCAs, and BCs.
11. Why has life insurance companies' involvement in farm real estate lending declined, relative to that of other major farm lenders?

12. Why does trade credit persist as a major source of farm lending, since trade companies do not specialize in farm lending? What types of trade credit are commonly used? How costly is trade credit?

13. What are the advantages and disadvantages of seller financing for farm land—from the seller's viewpoint? From the buyer's viewpoint? How are income tax factors involved?

14. Contrast and critique the role of government credit for farmers as administered through the Farmers Home Administration and the Commodity Credit Corporation. What purposes do these programs serve? For what types of borrowers? What are the credit terms? Sources of funds? Costs of funds? Do these programs compete with or complement lending programs of commercial lenders?

References

1. *Agricultural Banking in the 1980s*, American Bankers Association, Washington, D.C., 1980.

2. Barry, P. J., "Agricultural Lending by Commercial Banks," *Agricultural Finance Review*, 41(1981):28-40.

3. _____, "Impacts of Regulatory Change on Financial Markets for Agriculture," *American Journal of Agricultural Economics*, 63(1981):905-912.

4. _____, "Prospective Trends in Farm Credit and Fund Availability: Implications for Agricultural Banking," *Future Sources of Loanable Funds for Agricultural Banks*, Federal Reserve Bank of Kansas City, 1981.

5. _____, "Rural Banks and Farm Loan Participation," *American Journal of Agricultural Economics*, 60(1978):214-224.

6. Benjamin, G. L., "Problems Facing Agricultural Banks," *Economic Review*, Federal Reserve Bank of Kansas City, March 1980.

7. Board of Governors of the Federal Reserve System, *Improved Fund Availability for Rural Banks*, Washington, D.C., 1975.

8. Boehlje, M. D., "Non-institutional Lenders in the Agricultural Credit Market," *Agricultural Finance Review*, 41(1981):50-57.

9. Brake, J. R., and E. O. Melichar, "Agricultural Finance and Capital Markets," *A Survey of Agricultural Economics Literature*, University of Minnesota Press, Minneapolis, 1977.

10. Farm Credit Administration, *Project 85*, Economic Analysis Division, Washington, D.C., 1980.

11. Fenwick, R. S., C. E. Harshbarger, and G. L. Swackhamer, "The Role of the Farm Credit System in Financing Agriculture," *Agricultural Finance Review*, 41(1981):20-27.

12. *Future Sources of Loanable Funds for Agricultural Banks*, Federal Reserve Bank of Kansas City, 1981.

13. Hardy, W. E., and M. W. Moore, "The Profitability of Agricultural Cus-

tomers for Commercial Banks in the Southeast," *Southern Journal of Agricultural Economics*, 12(1980):57-62.

14. Herr, W. M., and E. LaDue, "The Farmers Home Administration's Changing Role and Mission," *Agricultural Finance Review*, 41 (1981):58-72.

15. Hottel, J. B., "The Commodity Credit Corporation and Agricultural Lending," *Agricultural Finance Review*, 41(1981):73-82.

16. LaDue, E., J. L. Moss, and R. S. Smith, "The Profitability of Agricultural Loans by Commerical Banks," *Journal of the Northeastern Agricultural Economics Council*, 7(1978):1-7.

17. Lee, J. E., S. C. Gabriel, and M. D. Boehlje, "Public Policy Toward Agricultural Credit," *Future Sources of Loanable Funds for Agricultural Banks*, Federal Reserve Bank of Kansas City, 1981.

18. Lee, W. F., et al., *Agricultural Finance*, 7th ed., Iowa State University Press, Ames, 1980.

19. Lins, D. A., "Life Insurance Company Lending to Agriculture," *Agricultural Finance Review*, 41(1981):41-49.

20. Lins, D. A., and T. L. Frey, "Covering Agriculture's Lending Needs," *Agri Finance*, Parts 1-5, selected issues, 1979.

21. Melichar, E. O., "Rural Banking Conditions and Farm Financial Trends," Board of Governors of the Federal Reserve System, April 1980.

22. _____, "Some Current Aspects of Agricultural Finance and Banking in the United States," *American Journal of Agricultural Economics*, 59(1977):967-972.

23. Webb, K., "The Farm Credit System," *Economic Review*, Federal Reserve Bank of Kansas City, June 1980.

Chapter 17

Policy Issues Affecting
Financial Markets
for Agriculture

The two previous chapters have examined the functions of financial intermediation for agriculture. We considered the financial markets for farm securities and then the financial intermediaries from which farmers borrow.

This chapter will summarize the functions of the Federal Reserve System and how monetary and fiscal policies influence financial intermediation in agriculture. We will then consider the effectiveness of financial intermediation for agriculture and some policy issues affecting farm credit markets in the 1980s.

Monetary and Fiscal Policies

Monetary policies refer to actions of the Federal Reserve System that influence the cost and availability of credit in the economy. Fiscal policies involve a government's powers to tax and spend in order to influence overall economic activity. Monetary and fiscal policies are closely related. Since both affect the behavior of financial intermediaries, understanding these policies can assist managers to anticipate possible policy actions and to develop appropriate responses.

The Federal Reserve System

The Federal Reserve System, often called the "Fed," is comprised of 12 district banks and a Board of Governors [4]. Its control over money supplies—defined as the total of currency and bank demand deposits—is achieved primarily through commercial banks, although other depository institutions also are subject to Federal Reserve requirements and other aspects of monetary control. Depository institutions are the focus of monetary control because of their capacity to "create" money. These institutions expand the money supply by making new loans, which, in turn, create new deposits. This linkage between lending and deposits gives new reserves a multiplying effect. Similarly, the withdrawal of reserves from commercial banks and other depository institutions can have a multiple contracting force on the money supply.

The Federal Reserve System was created in 1913 as the nation's central bank in order to make the flow of bank credit and money more elastic, to provide for discounting commercial paper, and to improve the supervision of banking. It was established amid considerable controversy as to its appropriate role and reflected a compromise between the large urban banks' preferences for a stable centralized banking authority and western "frontier" banks' preferences for a decentralized autonomous system of banks. There was a general consensus with the need for a system to manage monetary reserves more flexibly than was possible with the old National Bank System.

Various legislation over the years has clarified the Fed's objectives and modified the system's structure and function. Currently, the Fed's policy objectives include (1) economic stability and growth, (2) high employment, (3) a stable dollar in the domestic economy, and (4) a reasonable balance of international payments. Responsibility for these sometimes competing objectives rests with the Board of Governors of the Fed, although in none of the objectives does it have sole responsibility.

The Fed contributes to national economic goals through its influence on availability of money and the cost of borrowing. Over the longer run, it attempts to ensure sufficient money and credit growth to achieve a rising standard of living. In the short run, its policies may combat inflationary and deflationary pressures and forestall liquidity crises and financial panics. Sometimes its actions on domestic problems interact with international trade and exchange rate considerations. Similarly, the responses to international finance pressures may also influence U.S. financial market conditions. The importance of the interactions has grown markedly in recent years, with the U.S. export sector growing, relative to the total U.S. economy, and with even greater relative growth of U.S. bank lending in international markets.

The Fed's Monetary Tools

The Fed's primary tools for influencing the money supply and the cost of credit are (1) reserve requirements, (2) open-market operations, and (3) the discount rate.

Reserve requirements

All depository institutions in the United States are required to hold a specified percentage of their deposits on reserve (see Chapter 16). In turn, these reserve requirements strongly influence the financial system's capacity to expand the money supply. To illustrate, suppose a bank receives a new deposit for $1,000,000 generated from a depositor's large sale of wheat. If this bank's reserve requirement is 20 percent, its reserves increase by $200,000, leaving excess reserves of $800,000 for loans or investment in securities.

Suppose the bank makes a new loan of $800,000 by depositing this amount in the borrower's checking account. Deposits would immediately increase by $800,000, and reserve requirements would increase by $160,000 = (.20)(800,000). *Excess reserves* now equal $640,000—which could be loaned—and so on. The proceeds of subsequent loans might be deposited in other banks, but the aggregate effects on money supplies are the same. The *limit* of this expansion through the banking system is the *reciprocal of the reserve requirement.* For a 20 percent reserve requirement, the new $1 million deposit could be expanded to $5 million of deposits. Of the $5 million in deposits, $1 million would be held in required reserves, and $4 million would be used for new loans.

Changing the reserve requirements thus affects the power of depository institutions to create money, subject to the demand for loans. The range of reserve requirements for various deposits is specified by law. The Board of Governors must operate within these limits.

Reserve requirements are changed infrequently in practice, usually only when the Fed wants to highlight an emerging financial or economic problem. Such changes have the disadvantages of producing overly pronounced effects on financial markets and relying greatly on loan demand, which is beyond monetary control.

Open-market operations

The Fed's most frequently used and flexible tool is its "open-market" operations. By selling or buying securities—primarily U.S. Government securities—in the open-money market, the board can reduce or increase the reserves of financial institutions and thereby influence the supply of loanable funds. Most transactions occur through dealers who have contact with larger commercial banks, life insurance companies, thrift institutions, and other businesses with large financial reserves. The Federal Open-Market Committee (FOMC) is responsible for implementing monetary policy. This 12-member committee is comprised of the 7 members of the Board of Governors and 5 presidents of district Federal Reserve Banks. They conduct transactions continually and maintain confidentiality about their strategies.

The initial impact of FOMC action is on the availability and cost of reserves in depository institutions. However, these effects soon spread throughout the economy. Suppose the FOMA is concerned over the inflationary effects of a rapidly expanding economy, and its recommended action is to sell a large volume of securities. This action would reduce bank reserves and deposits; the value of bonds and other securities would decline, thus increasing interest rates on loans and other financial assets. The higher-loan rates would discourage investment, alter savings patterns, and cause other secondary effects.

The Fed uses one or more indicators and targets to guide its open-market operations. These targets include the level of bank reserves or, more recently, rates of change in one or more of the money supply measures. Interest rates are considered less effective indicators because they respond to a broader range of factors. As an example, interest rates may increase due to greater demand for loanable funds or slower growth of the money supply. In any case, appropriate monetary policies are needed when the targets are not achieved.

Discount rate

The discount rate is the rate charged depository institutions who borrow from the Fed to meet temporary needs. Control over this rate directly influences interest rates on loans, whereas the other monetary tools affect interest rates indirectly.

. When its policies change market interest rates, the Fed frequently must change the discount rate. In response to heavy open-market sales, for example, short-term interest rates will rise. Banks and other borrowers will then find the Fed discount window (which has not yet changed its discount rate) to be a cheap source of money. To counter overuse of the discount window, the Fed may raise the discount rate. Thus, the discount rate follows rather than leads the market. The discount rate is not considered an effective monetary tool, because it has pronounced effects and because the borrowing initiative lies with the depository institutions.

Minor Policy Tools

The Fed occasionally uses other policy tools to achieve its objectives. These have included: (1) ceilings on interest rates that banks and other depository institutions pay for funds—under authority of Regulation Q—although the rate ceilings are being phased out, and (2) control over the margin or minimum downpayment required for stock purchases. This margin is raised to restrict speculative stock purchases and lowered to revive a sluggish stock market.

In addition, the Fed exerts substantial influence over the financial community through "moral suasion" or "jawbone control." Through its power to close the discount window to potential borrowers or its possible influence over the zealousness of bank examiners, the Fed can strongly "encourage" financial institutions to support its policies and programs.

Fiscal Policy

Fiscal policy refers to the taxation and expenditure policies of government. Although both functions are essential to any government, sufficient flexibility exists in the magnitude and timing of expenditures and in the magnitude and structure of taxation that fiscal policies can materially affect economic activity. In recessions, for example, expansionary monetary policies of the Fed may fail to generate sufficient demand to increase employment and stimulate the economy. In response, the federal government could introduce public expenditures, tax incentives, or both to stimulate capital investment and employment and thereby augment monetary policy. These issues are quite complex. If the government initiates a tax cut, while not reducing its expenditures, then it must finance the expenditures by borrowing in the financial markets. Such borrowing can conflict with the Fed's monetary policies to cope with recession or inflation.

A number of stabilizers are built into the fiscal system. The graduated income tax, for example, immediately reduces tax withholdings at the start of a recession as personal and business incomes fall; this tends to increase disposable income. Similarly, a sudden increase in the rate of general inflation might be dampened by an immediate increase in marginal tax rates. A number of welfare transfers, such as unemployment compensation, also become more effective when a recession starts. These stabilizers serve as a first line of defense in reducing fluctuations but do not remove the need for active fiscal policy.

Among the active fiscal policies used to influence economic activity are:

1. Welfare expenditures that result in transfer payments in specific sets of people. Farmers and rural areas are influenced through such fiscal programs as subsidized FmHA loans, rural-development programs, and emergency-relief programs for officially designated disaster areas resulting from drouth, freeze, or other adverse weather. Payments to farmers under government farm programs are also important.

2. Public works and other government expenditures designed to reduce unemployment.

3. Modification in tax rates and other tax programs. The investment tax credit (see Chapter 3) has been used effectively at times to stimulate investment in new capital equipment. Tax surcharges are sometimes assessed to help curb inflation, and tax rebates or tax cuts may stimulate spending. If the tax cuts successfully stimulate the economy, the resulting higher incomes provide extra tax revenues.

Besides fiscal policies of the federal government, state and local governments frequently influence local economies through taxing and spending programs. In turn, these policies may influence the demand for and supply of loanable funds in the community and the behavior of local financial intermediaries.

Implications for Financial Intermediaries and Agriculture

Both fiscal policies of government and monetary policies of the Fed reflect responses to their perceptions of particular economic conditions. Ideally, these perceptions are similar at any given time so that fiscal and monetary policies are coordinated.

With the relative independence of the Federal Reserve System, however, perceptions of economic problems by the Board of Governors sometimes differ from those of Congress and the president. Moreover, congressional leaders do not always agree with the president on the seriousness of the problem or the appropriate courses of action. Consequently, fiscal policies are not always clearly defined nor consistent with monetary policy. Nonetheless, such actions will influence the availability and cost of loan funds to farmers who borrow from banks, the Farm Credit System, or other intermediaries. Finally, international factors must be considered too, as shown in the following section.

International Factors

The international dimension of financial markets has grown in importance for the total U.S. economy as well as for the farm sector and its sources of financial capital. Included are international trade in commodities and financial assets, the financing activities involved, and exchange rates among countries' currencies. All these factors influence financial flows, interest rates, inflation, and other economic conditions worldwide. Thus, a comprehensive analysis of financial market conditions involves a global perspective on these issues.

Capital flows *to* the United States in exchange for exports and securities sold to non-U.S. buyers. Both are paid for with U.S. dollars. Capital flows *from* the United States in exchange for imports and securities bought from non-U.S. sellers. Both are paid for in the sellers' currency. The magnitude of commodity transactions depends on prices of U.S. commodities relative to prices elsewhere. The securities' transactions depend on the comparative risk-adjusted returns expected on U.S. and other securities.

International transactions also involve the exchange of currencies as well as goods, services, and securities. Their prices are made comparable between the United States and other countries through the exchange value of the currencies involved; for example, the U.S. dollar is expressed in terms of other countries' currencies (the Canadian dollar, the Mexican peso, the German mark, and so on).

Other countries' demands for U.S. exports increase with a decrease in dollar-prices of U.S. exports and with a decrease in the exchange value of the U.S. dollar. In contrast, U,S. demand for imports responds in just the opposite manner to changes in relative prices and in exchange rates for the U.S. dollar. Other countries' demand for U.S. securities increases in response to an increase in dollar-denominated returns (adjusted for risk), but the securities' response to changes in exchange rates is not clear-cut. A lower exchange rate reduces the price of U.S. securities to foreign investors, but the decrease may also reduce the expected earnings rate when it is translated into the investor's currency.

Exchange rates for most currencies are established in well developed international markets, although non-market factors are involved as well. The exchange rates of most minor currencies are defined in terms of one or more of the major currencies. The U.S. dollar is one of these major currencies.

Since the early 1940s, an "International Capital Market" (ICM) has emerged as a major source of international finance. The commercial banks of more developed countries are the dominant institutional lenders in this market. Centrally planned countries also participate, using Eurocurrencies for settling transactions if their own currencies are non-convertible. Banks participating in the ICM borrow from and lend to each other. They also make and administer international loans to private borrowers and governments. Much of the interbank and bank-country lending activity occurs beyond the direct influence of central banks and other regulations that affect in-country banking activity. Examples are reserve requirements, interest rate controls, and deposit insurance. Relatively high rewards have drawn U.S. banks and Eurobanks increasingly into ICM activities. In the 1970s the earnings of large U.S. banks grew far more rapidly from international activity than from domestic activity.

The United States also is linked with other countries through the World Bank and the International Monetary Fund. Both institutions began after World War II as outcomes of the Bretton Woods Agreement. The World Bank finances economic development projects with loans funded by securities sales in capital markets of the more developed economies and from appropriations of donor governments. The former loans occur with commercial terms; the latter have highly concessional terms to developing countries.

The International Monetary Fund (IMF) was established to avert the occasional chaos in international money trade arising from a country's abuse of exchange rates to gain export advantages. It is authorized to monitor exchange rates and to advise on changes in exchange rate practices. It also is authorized to borrow and lend among member countries, which comprise most of the world's sovereign nations. Finally, it can issue "Special Drawing Rights" (SDRs), based upon its own reserves and provided by appropriations of member countries. Allocations of SDRs are used by recipient countries to supplement exchange reserves that may be threatened by temporary trade deficits.

During the 1970s, ICM lending to some borrowers among developing and centrally planned countries grew rapidly and, in retrospect, excessively. For some countries, annual debt service has grown to a large percentage of exports—in a few cases, more than 100 percent. In the absence of sudden and substantial trade improvement, default can be avoided only through debt rescheduling by ICM participants and/or refinancing by IMF. In the process, ICM participants (U.S. banks included) may well have new lending and depository constraints from their respective monetary authorities. And IMF, faced with unprecedented responsibility and challenge, seems necessarily dependent on new capital infusion. In any event, the performance of U.S. agriculture's financial markets is increasingly dependent upon international trade and financial linkages.

Evaluating Financial Intermediation in Agriculture

In general, financial intermediaries have exhibited strong performances in providing credit and related services to agriculture. Loan funds can be made available to farmers in a timely fashion, for various purposes and in amounts, costs, and maturities that compare favorably with other economic sectors. These features of financial intermediaries have strengthened the linkage between farm and nonfarm sectors over time and increased the farm sector's sensitivity to changing conditions in national and international financial markets. However, relatively few studies have comprehensively evaluated the effectiveness of financial intermediation for agriculture in the United States. Most studies have focused on selected intermediaries and specific types of performance. In this section, we will explore various performance criteria and consider some of the findings and judgments.

Efficient Allocation of Loan Funds

Efficiency criteria in economic theory specify that an optimal allocation of capital is characterized by equal marginal productivity of capital for all users in all geographic areas. Under perfect financial intermediation, two farm businesses producing the same products in different regions but having similar operations should have similar access to loan funds and similar interest rates. Imperfections in capital markets can cause differences in financing terms and can account for differences in regional growth.

The nationally federated structure of the Farm Credit System, along with its member banks' sharing in the sale of consolidated Farm Credit Securities, helps to assure that FCS borrowers nationwide have high uniformity in interest rates and other credit terms. Differences in loan rates among PCAs and FLBs primarily reflect differences in these lenders' operating costs, risk reserves, and capitalization policies. While these differences may be high in some cases, in general, the FCS borrowers experience comparable borrowing costs among regions, farm types, and risk classes.

For farm borrowers from commercial banks, differences in bank structure, size, diversity, and funding sources may cause substantial differences in availability and cost of borrowing for farmers. Regional differences in banks' market shares of farm real estate debt and non-real estate debt were shown in Chapter 15. Other differences in lending performance are considered in the following sections, although comprehensive evidence about these factors is not available.

A study by the Federal Reserve Bank of Kansas City in the late 1960s found significant differences among regions in interest rates on farm loans for similar purposes among farms of similar size and for loans of similar risk and secured by similar assets. This study also found other evidence of imperfections in rural banking markets, including differences among banks in (1) their ability to use federal funds and certificates of deposit as sources of funds, (2) the rates paid on time and savings deposits, (3) their ability to finance specific individuals and businesses, and (4) their knowledge of and access to financial market information.

These differences have likely declined over time in response to the deregulation of banking, easing of geographic restrictions on banking, growing competition in financial markets, and continued deinsulation of rural financial markets from national market conditions. Thus regional and other differences in credit terms should be less significant than in the past.

Operational Efficiency

Operational efficiency refers to the costs of producing the products and services of financial intermediation. Minimizing operating costs per dollar of loan volume is a desirable criterion. Some of the variables affecting operational efficiency are (1) loan volume and economies of size, (2) level of technology, and (3) quality of management and personnel. The latter two factors are closely linked to the first. Only the larger banks, for example, can afford to own large computerized systems so important to modern banking. However, most automation services are now available to smaller banks, either through rental arrangements or through micro computers.

Studies indicate that small banks may experience size economies as bank growth occurs, although the gains in size economies diminish rapidly and vary with the organizational structure and product lines. As an example, the potential size economies differ depending on whether larger size results from the addition of branch offices or from growth of existing offices. The evidence is less clear in the middle-sized range of banks, although some studies indicate slight size economies up to about $400 million in total assets. The implications for rural banks are clear. Many rural banks are small enough to have potential for economies of size if growth occurs.

The operating costs incurred by financial intermediaries must be paid from differences in the costs of funds and interest earnings on loans and investments. In general, the costs of financial intermediation relative to interest rates on farm loans have declined over time for both commercial banks and the Farm Credit System. The primary forces causing this decline include (1) the development and use of new technology, including electronic data processing; (2) size economies achieved in the growing volume of farm lending; and (3) increased competition among lenders.

Differences between lenders in the factors that comprise their interest rates are also important. Table 17.1 indicates average costs of money, lending costs, losses or loss provisions, taxes, and earnings per loan dollar for commercial banks and Farm Credit System lenders in 1979. Bank data are from the Federal Reserve's Functional Cost Analysis reports on commercial and agricultural loans of 349 banks with total deposits of less than $50 million. FCS data are from the annual report for 425 PCAs and 12 FLBs. The data are not strictly comparable because of differences in accounting methods, types of

Table 17.1. Interest Rate Composition on Farm Loans: 1979

	Commercial Bank $0 to $50 mill. Deposits	Production Credit Assoc.	Federal Land Banks
Cost Components			
Cost of money (interest, noninterest)	5.90	9.04	7.46
Operating expenses[1]	1.61	1.21	.51
Losses or loss provision[2] and taxes	.32	.62	.20
Net earnings	3.02	.96	.84
Gross yield	10.85	11.83	9.01
Yield Components			
Interest	10.70	10.71	8.65
Other income or adjustments	.15	.38	.36
Patronage refund, FICB		.74	

[1]Operating expenses for individual PCAs ranged from .36 to 3.62.
[2]Net losses for reporting banks; loss provision and federal and other income taxes for PCA and FLB.

loans, loss treatment, tax omissions for banks, omission of stock and deposit balances, and other features of the deposit relationship. Still, they show important differences for these lenders.

Costs of money were a lower proportion of total lending costs in 1979 for banks than for PCAs. These money cost differences would be less in the 1980s. Operating costs per loan dollar were higher on average for banks, although substantial differences occur among some PCAs. The largest difference in rate composition between banks and FCS lenders is in earnings rates. The before-tax return on loan assets for these banks averaged 3.02 percent in 1979. In 1979 banks could sustain these favorable earnings rates while remaining competitive with PCA rates on farm loans because of differences in their costs of money. Sharp increases in the banks' money costs along with their need or desire to keep earnings at earlier levels appear to explain a wider spread in the farm loan rates in the early 1980s.

Interest Rates on Farm Loans

A comparison of interest rates charged on farm loans by commercial banks and Farm Credit System lenders over time is shown in Figure 17.1. Several features are clearly evident. One is the sharp increase in rate levels since the mid-1970s; the second is the greater rate volatility; a third is the wider spread, during this time, between bank rates and FCS rates; and a fourth is the difference in timing and magnitude of rate changes from these lenders. In general, these rate

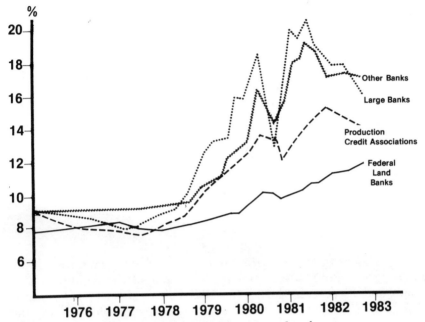

Figure 17.1. Average interest rates on farm loans.

characteristics reflect the continued deinsulation of farm credit from forces in national financial markets, attributed largely to high inflation, financial deregulation, competitive responses of lenders, and a shift in 1979 by the Federal Reserve toward heavier reliance on monetary aggregates as a target in monetary policy, with interest rates fluctuating more widely.

For agricultural banks, the rapid increases and sharp moves in farm loan rates are due to these banks' growing reliance on rate-sensitive sources of funds. As market interest rates change, so will the banks' average costs of funds, and thus their loan rates. As the figure shows, the rate swings are stronger at larger banks but still substantial at smaller banks as well.

The rate spread that favored the FCS rates during the early 1980s in part reflects the FCS practice of pricing loans with floating rates that are adjusted periodically for changes in PCA's and FLB's costs of funds, the average maturity of which exceeds that of commercial banks. This pricing practice moderates the pace and magnitude of rate changes for FCS lenders but still tends to clearly transmit signals to farm borrowers about financial market conditions.

Comparable data from other farm lenders are not available. However, rates on all types of farm loans now follow market interest rates much more closely than in the past. In the future, these rates should continue to follow market rates, with their magnitude and volatility largely determined by the effects of inflation, monetary policies, and other aggregate conditions.

Interest rates in national economies also interact with and thus are influenced by international monetary conditions, as expressed by exchange rates on countries' currencies. Capital that flows to and from the United States responds to interest rate differentials as well as to bank balances. The interest rates paid by foreign borrowers, when translated to borrower currencies, depend on the exchange rate relevant to the calculation.

Volume of Loans

As shown in Chapter 15, farmers' use of debt capital has grown rapidly since 1960—at an average annual rate of 7 percent during the 1960s and 12 percent during the 1970s. Several reasons account for this growth in farm debt. Included are (1) consolidation of farm units into larger sizes and fewer numbers, (2) withdrawal of equity capital by retiring farms, (3) continued mechanization and modernization of farming operations, (4) effects of inflation and other factors on costs of operating inputs and capital items, (5) reduced savings rates from net cash flows by farm families, and (6) public loan programs responding to various kinds of farm risks.

Clearly, the farm credit markets have responded to the strong growth in farm loan demand. Moreover, there are no strong evidence, concerns, or other indications that farm credit markets cannot continue to meet the aggregate of projected credit needs. The more pressing questions involve the relative positions of farm lending groups in meeting these credit needs and how these market shares may respond to various future scenarios and to changes in regulations that influence competitive positions in local financial markets. These factors can significantly affect the financial performance of farm businesses.

Part of the Farm Credit System's steady growth reflects success in its mission to provide financial services to farmers through both good and bad times. As earlier data have shown, commercial banks' market shares have declined, reflecting past difficulties in generating sufficient funds for farm lending, especially from nonlocal sources.

However, as discussed below, the effect of financial deregulation is freeing up these banks' ability to compete for local and nonlocal sources of funds. Still, unit banks tend to experience binding legal lending limits for their largest farm borrowers, which triggers the use of loan participations with correspondent banks or possible loss of the farmers' businesses.

Much of the increase in farm lending from 1978 to 1982 occurred through public credit programs, which softened the impacts of volatile credit markets and variable farm incomes on the farm sector. But credit from government lending will likely be less available in the rest of the 1980s, unless low farm income nationwide persists for several years. Thus, if future patterns resemble those of the past, farmers' credit and the market shares of lenders will rest heavily on regulatory and competitive conditions in farm credit markets, as well as on the financial performance of the farm sector.

Loan Maturities

Another criterion for evaluating financial intermediaries serving agriculture is their capacity and willingness to provide self-liquidating loans. As shown in Chapter 5, whenever loans must be repaid faster than cash is generated by the asset or service being financed, the farmer's liquidity position is reduced.

The application of this criterion varies by type of loan. For short-term loans used to finance operating inputs, loan maturities should coincide with the expected sales of farm products. When receipts are delayed into the following season by a farmer's participation in a marketing cooperative, for example, the loan maturity should be scheduled accordingly. Loans for capital items should have a maturity that matches the asset's economic payoff period. Long-term real estate loans are repaid from net income. Their maturities should be long enough so that annual payments do not heavily burden the firm's cash flow.

There are few legal constraints on a financial intermediary's choice of loan maturities. PCAs cannot make loans with maturities longer than 10 years. This limit is consistent with their designated purpose to make short- and intermediate-term loans. FLBs can make loans up to 40 years in length, which provides a long payoff period. Commercial banks may utilize their own policies and guidelines in setting maturities on short- and intermediate-term loans.

Thus, problems associated with loan maturities are largely those of custom and habit or of inadequate loan analysis. Some lenders' practice of making short-term loans for capital assets with longer payback periods largely results from custom, or as a basis for repricing loans in the rollover of maturities. The best approach is to follow the procedures in Chapter 5 for synchronizing the loan terms with the business's cash flows.

Regulatory Issues and Credit Policies

The development of financial intermediation in agriculture has been a dynamic process characterized by institutional changes, innovations, and improvements in efficiency. Continued changes will occur in the future as well. The beginning of the 1980s, in particular, is a landmark in U.S. financial markets because of the regulatory changes that marked this time. Especially important were passage of the Depository Institutions Deregulation and Monetary Control Act of 1980 (DIDMC) and the Depository Institutions Act of 1982 (DIA). Also under consideration are liberalization of geographic restrictions on banking and other regulatory changes. Other issues specific to agricultural finance include the Farm Credit Act Amendments of 1980 and a more conservative role for government credit programs. In this section we discuss these regulatory and policies issues and consider their implications for agricultural finance.

Financial Deregulation

The changes contained in the 1980 DIDMC and the 1982 DIA represent a significant deregulation of financial markets in the United States that will profoundly affect structural characteristics, levels of performance, and competitive relationships throughout these markets. The acts culminated a lengthy regulatory review by various commissions, congressional debate, and the financial services industry [7]. They were finally passed into law in response to the stringent limitations, high costs, and resulting instabilities placed on depository institutions by the past regulatory environment.

Numerous conditions prompted these regulatory changes. Included were disintermediation problems associated with high inflation and interest rates, increasing competition among financial institutions, new unregulated entrants to the financial services industry, new electronic technologies in funds' flows, strong credit demands, changing methods of implementing monetary policies, attrition of banks from the Federal Reserve System, and disadvantages of small savers. The stresses from these conditions had fallen heavily on smaller banks significantly involved in farm lending and on their farm and agribusiness borrowers.

The 1980 DIDMC established uniform Federal Reserve requirements at all depository institutions, provided for the orderly phase-out by 1986 of interest rate ceilings on deposits, authorized interest-bearing transaction accounts, preempted state usury laws on certain types of loans (including agricultural loans over $1,000), increased federal insurance coverage on deposits and accounts of depository institutions, liberalized investment and lending limits of thrift institutions, and required the Federal Reserve to competitively price its services and make them available to all depository institutions.

The 1982 DIA focused on the problems of ailing thrift institutions, although its provisions affected commercial banks and other institutions as well. Regulatory agencies were granted expanded authority to assist troubled depository institutions and to arrange acquisitions of such institutions across state lines and between banks and thrifts if conditions warranted. Federally chartered thrifts were granted expanded authority to make consumer loans (up to 30 percent of total assets) and commercial and agricultural loans (up to 10 percent of total assets). In addition, the phase-out of rate ceilings on deposits was accelerated, and many other provisions were also included.

For agricultural finance, these acts significantly affected smaller banks which had fund availability problems and less flexibility in balance sheet management, compared to regional and money center banks. The changes in reserve requirements released some additional bank funds to support lending in rural areas. Elimination of interest rate controls on deposits and loans should continue to improve efficiency in local flows of funds; allow more equitable competition by banks for funds; increase variability in interest rates; and bring more market-oriented pricing at the bank, department, and customer levels. However, deregulation may also increase the risk positions of financial intermediaries, leading to greater concerns about their credit worthiness as well as greater merger and bankruptcy activity.

The regulatory changes should further blur the distinction between commercial banks and thrift institutions, allowing them to compete for funds on more equal footings with unregulated institutions that offer money market mutual funds and other financial services. As a result, some of these intermediaries may continue to specialize in selected financial services (farm lending, for example) to better tailor products and services to these market segments and to compete effectively in a dynamic financial services industry. In any case, the costs and availability of farm loans should reflect changing conditions in national and international financial markets much more fully and quickly than in the past.

Structural Changes in Banking

In the 1980s, conditions are favorable for significant changes in the geographic structure of banking. As indicated in Chapter 16, the current setting has resulted in a diverse set of state limitations on branching and holding companies. A presidential task force [15] studied the issues associated with geographic restrictions on banking and, in 1981, recommended a phased liberalization to initially modify holding company restrictions and later branching restrictions.

The findings of the task force indicated that liberalization (1) could improve competition in local markets without significant increase in undue concentration of economic power; (2) would increase the range of financial services in local communities; (3) would improve banking performance through greater actual and potential competition; (4) would not significantly threaten the viability of small banks, the safety and stability of the banking system, or dual chartering at national and state levels; and (5) would create more equitable competition between bank and nonbank institutions. Anti-competitive behavior resulting from geographic liberalization should be offset by greater reliance on anti-trust laws, increased potential competition from other banks, and growing nonbank competition.

The report's research findings indicate that smaller independent banks historically have withstood competition from new bank competitors, albeit with the pro-competitive effects of lower prices for services and lower earnings. Evidence is cited that unit banks in statewide branching states use more of their resources for loans than do similar banks in unit banking states and that average rates of return on total assets decline with increasing bank size, are highest in unit banking states, and are higher for banks in non-metropolitan areas. Factors explaining the survival and prospering of small and medium-sized banks faced with large, branch bank competition include their location in non-metropolitan markets, where earnings are higher and competition apparently less; their competitive pricing of necessary services, often through correspondent arrangements; loyalty of customers; and innovations in operations and policies.

These factors are consistent with past views that rural unit banks have made important use of mechanisms designed to cope with problems in financing farmers [6]. On balance it thus appears that geographic liberalization of banking should positively affect bank performance and enhance credit services for agriculture.

Farm Credit System Issues

Policy issues in the early 1980s affecting the Farm Credit System include the Farm Credit Act Amendments of 1980 and the agency status of FCS securities. Passage of the Farm Credit Act Amendments of 1980 culminated a long legislative process that yielded new insight on the competitive relationships in farm lending. Major provisions in the act, designed to update and improve the operation of FCS, included (1) increased scope for cooperation between FCS, commercial banks, and other lenders; (2) authorization for Banks for Cooperatives to finance agricultural export activities benefiting U.S. cooperatives; (3) reductions in farmer-member eligibility requirements in certain cooperatives financed by BCs; (4) provisions for Federal Land Banks and Production Credit Associations to finance more fully the processing and marketing activities of eligible borrowers; and (5) expanded limits for FLBs on loans guaranteed by a federal or state agency.

Most of these changes should have relatively minor effects on farm financing; however, impacts on nonfarm financing may be greater, depending on FCS responses to some of these provisions. The increased cooperation with commercial banks involves further development of loan participations between banks and PCAs and new authorization for participation between FLBs and banks. Significant revisions also occurred in the authority for Federal Intermediate Credit Banks to loan to or discount loans from other financing institutions, including commercial banks (see Chapter 16).

In a broader context, the debate on the 1980 act brought to light substantial differences in the regulatory environment for commercial banks and the FCS that influence the competitive balance in farm credit markets. Included were differences in income tax obligations, ranges of financial services and borrowing clientele, legal reserve requirements and lending limits, geographic restrictions, stringency of regulation and supervision, and access to financial markets. It is especially difficult, however, to evaluate competitive equality between depository and non-depository institutions when they serve different clientele, provide different services, and thus have different opportunities for acquiring funds and earning revenue.

Periodic concern also arises about the "agency status" accorded FCS securities and the benefits the system has in obtaining loan funds from national and international financial markets at relatively favorable costs and high volume. Possible changes in some factors affecting agency status were under study in the early 1980s as part of the Reagan administration's philosophy of reducing government involvement in the nation's credit markets. If changes do occur, they would clearly increase the cost of obtaining loan funds for farmers and likely alter the volume and channels through which these securities are sold.

Government Credit Programs

The growth in the late 1970s and early 1980s of government's farm lending through the Farmers Home Administration and the Commodity Credit Corporation has clearly softened the impacts of volatile credit markets and variable farm incomes on the farm sector. However, much concern has surfaced about special credit treatment in agriculture, the proper balance between public and private sectors, the degree of subsidy involved, the distributional aspects of various FmHA programs, and the resulting tax burdens. Some observers [10] suggest the past structure of farm credit markets, including the prominence of government programs, has resulted in overfinancing of the farm sector, thus abating the needs for resource adjustment, shifting risk bearing to the government, and capitalizing the effects of concessionary financing terms into higher values of land and other farm assets.

The administration of President Ronald Reagan sought to reduce the magnitude and subsidy in FmHA programs and largely return its role to a lender of last resort. Besides the high taxpayer costs of government programs, these changes were also based on the following conditions: (1) more moderate growth in farm debt than occurred in the 1970s; (2) expanded use of new federal crop insurance programs for disaster protection; (3) more effective coordination of public and private credit programs, tailored to beginning farmers or other target groups; and (4) greater innovation by commercial lenders in acquiring loan funds and in countering business and financial risks in agriculture. The result is a pullback of the public safety net for farm lending and greater concern about problem credit situations where FmHA cannot step in.

Looking Ahead

Besides the regulatory issues just cited, the farm credit market's capacity to meet future credit needs of agriculture is strongly influenced by aggregate farm income, government policy, and national and international economic conditions. Most projections [9] for the 1980s have pointed toward stronger financial performance in farming and more moderate growth rates for farm debt. Greater reliance should be placed on commercial lenders, with less need for government credit programs. These projections are based on stronger economic conditions worldwide, permanent reduction in inflation, and sounder financial policies in government. If, however, monetary and fiscal policies do not produce a healthy economy, the farm financial situation will likely be very weak by 1990.

A major point of the projections by agricultural finance economists in the United States is the strong sensitivity of the farm sector's performance to nonfarm conditions, domestic and international, that are strongly influenced by inflation and transmitted through financial markets and other channels. Hence, farmers have much at stake in the programs to achieve growth and stability in the national economy.

Topics for Discussion

1. What are the primary objectives of the Federal Reserve System? In what ways might these objectives conflict?
2. What tools does the Federal Reserve System use to achieve its monetary objectives? Explain how each one works, and evaluate its relative effectiveness.
3. Distinguish between monetary policy and fiscal policy. Where does each originate? How do these policies, individually and jointly, impact on the ability of farmers to obtain adequate loans?
4. Compare PCAs, commercial banks in a unit banking state, and commercial banks with statewide branching in terms of:
   a. Their response to monetary policy.
   b. Their capacity to attract loanable funds to agriculture from nonlocal sources.

    c. Their ability to make loans of adequate size to meet farmers' needs.

    d. Their ability to make loans of adequate maturities.

5. What factors explain the closer integration between conditions in rural financial markets and national financial markets in the 1980s?

6. Interest rates on farm loans from major farm lenders have increased and become more volatile in recent times, compared to the distant past. Why have these interest rate conditions occurred? Why do they occur among major farm lenders, especially commercial banks and the Farm Credit System?

7. Identify the major components of interest rates on farm loans from commercial banks and Farm Credit System lenders. How do differences in these components affect the level and responsiveness of rates to changes in financial market conditions? Why do the earnings rates differ between these lenders?

8. Summarize the forms of financial deregulation and the major reasons for them in the 1980s. What are their major effects on farm lending by agricultural banks? What impacts will deregulation have on the level and volatility of farm loan rates?

9. What conditions make liberalization of geographic restrictions on banking a current policy issue? What effects would liberalization have on credit services and bank performance in rural areas? What disadvantages might arise from geographic liberalization?

10. Explain some current policy issues affecting the Farm Credit System, its relationships to commercial banks, and its sale of securities in the national financial markets.

11. Identify and evaluate the major issues associated with government credit programs for agriculture. What is the proper balance between public and private sectors in meeting farmers' credit needs? What instruments and programs besides credit programs are possible?

References

1. Barry, P. J., "Impacts of Regulatory Change on Financial Markets for Agriculture," *American Journal of Agricultural Economics*, 63 (1981):905-912.

2. _____, "Prospective Trends in Farm Credit and Fund Availability: Implications for Agricultural Banking," *Future Sources of Loanable Funds for Agricultural Banks*, Federal Reserve Bank of Kansas City, 1981.

3. Baum, E., H. Diesslin, and E. Heady, *Capital and Credit Needs in a Changing Agriculture*, Iowa State University Press, Ames, 1961.

4. Board of Governors, *The Federal Reserve System, Purposes, and Functions*, Federal Reserve System, Washington, D.C., 1974.

5. _____, *Improved Fund Availability at Rural Banks*, Federal Reserve System, Washington, D.C., 1975.

6. Brake, J., and E. O. Melichar, "Agricultural Finance and Capital Markets," *A Survey of Agricultural Economics Literature*, Vol. 1, University of Minnesota Press, Minneapolis, 1976.

7. Federal Reserve Bank of Chicago, "The Depository Institutions Deregulation and Monetary Control Act of 1980," *Economic Perspective*, Federal Reserve Bank, Chicago, January 1981.

8. Gisselquist, D., *The Political Economics of International Bank Lending*, Praeger Publishers, New York, 1981.

9. Hughes, D. W., "An Overview of Farm Sector Capital and Credit Needs in the '80s," *Agricultural Finance Review*, 41(1981):1-19.

10. Lee, J. E., S. C. Gabriel, and M. D. Boehlje, "Public Policy Toward Agricultural Credit," *Future Sources of Loanable Funds for Agricultural Banks*, Federal Reserve Bank of Kansas City, 1981.

11. Melichar, E. O., "Impact of Banking Structure on Farm Lending: An Examination of Aggregate Data for States," *Improved Fund Availability at Rural Banks*, Board of Governors of the Federal Reserve System, Washington, D.C., 1975.

12. Mendelsohn, M. S., *Money on the Move: The Modern International Capital Market*, McGraw-Hill Book Co., New York, 1980.

13. Mundell, R. A., and J. J. Polak, eds., *The New International Monetary System*, Columbia University Press, 1977.

14. Swackhamer, G. L., and R. J. Dahl, *Financing Modern Agriculture: Banking Problems and Challenges*, Federal Reserve Bank of Kansas City, 1969.

15. U.S. Department of the Treasury, *Geographic Restrictions on Banking in the United States*, Washington, D.C., 1981.

16. Wilkinson, D. E., "The Farm Credit System: Another Source of Loanable Funds," *Future Sources of Loanable Funds for Agricultural Banks*, Federal Reserve Bank of Kansas City, 1981.

SECTION VI

Other Topics

Chapter 18

ALTERNATIVES IN BUSINESS
ORGANIZATION

The ultimate financial success of agricultural businesses may be strongly influenced by their legal form of organization. Traditionally, agriculture has been organized primarily as either sole proprietorships or family partnerships. Other business organizations are available, however, and merit serious consideration. In this chapter, we will outline and apply selected criteria for comparing alternative forms of business organization in agriculture. The consequences for estate management are also considered, with the tax implications developed in the appendix.

Evaluative Criteria

In earlier chapters, three criteria—profitability, liquidity, and risk—were used to evaluate management alternatives and to monitor and assess financial success. These criteria also serve to evaluate different business organizations, although expansion and modification are needed to compare their effects on the generation and conservation of the firm's equity capital.

Profitability

An important characteristic of modern agriculture is the high payoff for superior management. The farm business must attract and train effective management and maintain a high level of performance over time. The importance of business continuity is demonstrated in Figure 18.1. Line A reflects the changing performance of management for a single owner-operator family farm over three generations. Each generation, as a rule, passes through the four stages in its life

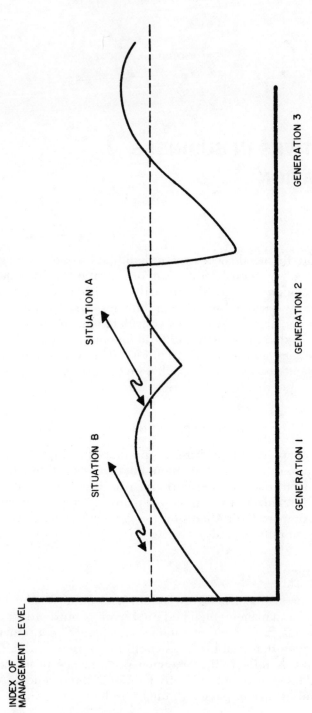

Figure 18.1. A comparison of management level over time under two hypothetical situations.

cycle outlined in Chapter 2—establishment, expansion, consolidation, and transfer. Thus, the first generation might begin at a relatively low level of management, lacking the necessary training, experience, and capital to achieve operational efficiency. As these ingredients are acquired, the level of management rises, reaching a peak before declining, as the manager approaches retirement. Eventually, the business is transferred to the next generation.

The second generation then repeats the process of gaining the necessary management experience and expanding the business. Let's assume the process ends abruptly with the untimely withdrawal of the manager.[1] By the time new management is established, new financing arranged (and perhaps the estate transfer settled through the courts), much of the liquidity and momentum of the business and a sizeable portion of the equity capital are lost. The next generation essentially starts over and completes its own life cycle of management effectiveness. Each generation, in turn, reaches a peak of efficiency during its life but maintains that level for a relatively brief span of its total responsibility.

Line B of Figure 18.1 represents the efficiency of similar resources when combined into a hypothetical firm large enough to provide the necessary training and experience to assure continuity of competent management, labor, and finance over time—even during periods of intergeneration transfer. It might be a large, industrial corporation, or it could be a family-farm business, large enough to involve two or more families *and* organized to provide management competence over time. Under these circumstances, firm B could bid resources away from firm A in an ongoing quest for survival, even if B never reached A's peak levels of efficiency.

Part of the problem in firm A is the small size of business. There are numerous, important economies of size in agriculture, and those associated with intergeneration transfer are especially important. Farms large enough to provide full-time employment and income for two or more operators and their families also provide training experiences in business, financial planning, and decision making. Such experiences better prepare all the parties involved for eventual leadership.

---

[1] A number of reasons might cause such a withdrawal. The manager might be killed or be physically, mentally, or emotionally incapacitated by sickness or accident. Or, his managerial performance might have fallen short of original expectations. These types of occurrences are not unusual in farming. Their seriousness is more apparent when no provision is made to have a replacement trained and sufficiently experienced to provide management continuity.

With some forms of business, continuity is linked directly to the life cycle of an individual operator; with others, business continuity is independent of any particular individuals. The relationship between business continuity and management productivity is an important factor in choice of business organization.

Finally, some forms of business organization are more costly to organize than others. Differences in organization and administration costs should be considered in choosing a business organization.

Conserving Income

The usefulness of farm income depends on the earnings that remain *after taxes.* One aspect of conserving income is to provide as many employee benefits as possible with *before-tax* dollars. Such practices are legal with some types of business organizations and illegal with others.

Business organizations also differ in the total after-tax burden of social security taxes and in the social security payments allowed after retirement. Even more important are the differences in income tax rates experienced by different business organizations.

Generating Equity Capital

Historically, most new equity capital for agriculture has been provided by retained earnings and unrealized capital gains on farm assets. However, with increased capital needs, high risks, and lower per-unit profit margins on farm products, commercial agriculture is hard pressed to generate sufficient equity capital from retained earnings alone. As a result, an increasing number of farmers must find ways of tapping outside equity sources.

To make the investment convenient to prospective investors, business organizations have been developed with ownership divided into minute shares of claims on the undifferentiated total net worth of the business. In contrast, the owners of a traditional family farm claim specific acres of land, head of livestock, kinds and numbers of machinery, and so on. These differences in claims may significantly affect the firm's ability to generate outside equity capital. For example, a potential investor might be interested in owning 100 shares of stock in a successful farming venture rather than owning 1.4 of its tractors or 5.6 of its dairy cows.

Conservation of Equity Capital

The choice of legal form of business organization can significantly influence the farm's effectiveness in conserving equity capital. A farm business can lose its equity capital in several ways. When cash withdrawals from the business exceed farm income, farm equity is reduced. In the traditional family farm, family living withdrawals are often not separated from business expenses, thus increasing the chances for such losses. The loss of business efficiency plus costs associated with intergeneration transfer are also severe drains on agriculture's equity capital.

Equity-capital losses also may arise from the liability of the firm and/or its owners for obligations, damage suits, and other contingent liabilities incurred by management and employees. The extent of this liability varies, depending on the type of firm organization and the effectiveness of risk management.

Equity capital is also lost through a decline in the value of farm assets. However, fluctuations in asset values are independent of the legal form of business organization and need not be considered here. It is worth noting, however, that acquiring capital with equity instruments instead of debt instruments reduces the firm's financial risk.

Organizational Alternatives

A farm business may be organized as a sole proprietorship, a general partnership, a limited partnership, a "regular" or subchapter C corporation, or a subchapter S corporation. In some cases, a land trust may also be used.

Sole Proprietorship

Most farms in the United States are organized as sole proprietorships wherein a single person or family has exclusive title and legal rights to the property of the business and sole responsibility for business conduct. The proprietorship offers a maximum of management control with a minimum of administrative costs. Its simplicity and flexibility make it an attractive form of business organization for a limited period of time. If, for example, the business is to be sold when the father retires, the sole proprietorship is likely the most effective form of business organization. The fact that business performance and managerial control are limited only by the capacity and resources of the proprietor is both its strength and its weakness.

A sole proprietor is self-employed. Therefore, he or she pays social security taxes at a rate (effective January 1, 1983) of 9.35 percent of the first $35,700 of "before-tax" net income (adjusted annually for inflation). Thus, social security taxes are not a deductible expense for income tax purposes for a proprietorship.

The costs of most employee benefits to the proprietor and family are not tax-deductible. Exceptions include the cost of life insurance, when the lender requires insurance as a condition of a business loan, and a limited tax-sheltered retirement-investment program based on self-employment status.

A proprietorship incurs no income tax obligation. Instead, the proprietor is taxed on all farm profits whether or not the income is withdrawn from the farm business. Any salary paid to the proprietor as manager is also taxable to the proprietor. Consequently, both the farm business and the proprietor are indifferent as to whether the money is paid as a salary or as family withdrawals from farm profits.

The proprietorship has serious limitations in estate planning and intergeneration transfer. First, business continuity is linked directly to the life cycle of the proprietor. Consequently, the level of business performance tends to drop off significantly as the sole proprietor approaches an age of about 60, due to limitations in energy and a tendency toward conservatism in planning and investment. Situation A in Figure 18.1 likely represents a sole proprietorship.

Second, the proprietor's wealth in the business is usually transferred to others as titles to specific farm assets—tractors, trucks, buildings, livestock, acres of land. This process becomes so cumbersome that most proprietorships do not transfer either the title to or the control of business assets until the retirement or death of the proprietor. These procedures hamper the incoming generation and provide limited opportunity for minimizing estate taxes at the time of transfer. If the farm business is to continue into the next generation, other business organizations should be considered.

Partnership

A partnership is an association of two or more persons to carry on, as co-owners, a business for profit. Parent-child partnerships, for example, have become a popular form of business organization in U.S. agriculture. Two types of partnerships have a place in agriculture: general partnerships and limited partnerships.

With *general partnerships,* each partner is an integral part of both ownership and management, and each has unlimited liability not only for obligations incurred by the business but also for liabilities incurred by other partners while representing the business. A general partnership can be established and operated under a very informal agreement by the partners. It can be established to achieve any legal purpose. No written agreement is necessary, although a recorded agreement helps to avoid misunderstandings among general partners.

Limited partnerships, on the other hand, are comprised of one or more *limited* partners and one or more *general* partners. They differ from general partnerships in several important ways. First, a more formal legal arrangement is required for organizing and operating a limited partnership. This agreement must meet the requirements of the state in which it is organized and be filed with the appropriate legal body of that state, usually the secretary of state. Second, the liability of limited partners is limited to their investment in the business. This advantage can be important to a prospective investor who wishes to avoid the liability of a general partnership. The burden of general and total liability in a limited partnership rests with the general partners, who are responsible for management.

Either type of partnership may have no more stability over time than a sole proprietorship, since both are generally dissolved on the death or withdrawal of a general partner. If desired, provisions can be made for business continuity by requiring the partnership, or the surviving partners, to purchase the interest of the deceased partner. However, the partnership relationship is usually a personal one and tends to dissolve when a general partner withdraws. This problem is usually less acute with parent-child partnerships, provided proper estate planning occurs. Many limited partnerships outline how limited partners may transfer their interest to other limited partners. Such transfers can usually occur without disrupting the business.

Like proprietorships, a general partnership pays no income taxes. Instead, all profits are allocated to the partners for income tax accounting. Salaries paid to partners are operating expenses to the partnership but are taxable to the partners. Thus, general partners are indifferent as to whether their income occurs as salary or distributed profits.

Limited partnerships may be taxed either as a partnership or as a corporation, depending on the election of the partnership (with concurrence of IRS) or a ruling by IRS. If IRS determines that the partnership is more like a corporation, it will be taxed as a corporation, and the "income pass-through" privilege is lost. Since tax provisions are an important attraction of limited partnerships for many investors, those who draft limited partnership agreements should be sure they resemble a partnership rather than a corporation. The primary criteria on which corporate resemblance is assessed are (1) continuity of life, (2) centralized management, (3) limited liability, and (4) free transferrability of interests.

Limited partners do not receive a management salary, since they cannot participate in management. Instead, they share directly in the profits or losses of the business. The typical limited partnership allocates a percentage of gross receipts to the general partners as a "cost" for management. Such costs are a deductible expense in computing profits for the limited partnership. Profits or losses are then allocated to limited partners, based on their percentage of ownership.

The social security tax for partnerships is similar to that for sole proprietors. It is paid by the partner and is not tax deductible to either the partnership or the partners. Furthermore, there are restrictions on the amount of partnership income a general partner can receive after retirement without disrupting social security benefits. Partnership income to limited partners does not affect social security payments, inasmuch as limited partners do not participate in management. The cost of employee fringe benefits for partners and their families is not tax deductible for either general or limited partnerships.

New equity capital for a partnership can come from (1) partnership profits retained in the business, (2) additional investments by existing partners, or (3) new partners brought into the business. One advantage of limited partnerships is the attraction of outside equity capital from limited partners without diluting management control by general partners.

There are also advantages to the limited partners. They can invest in a business without management responsibility or the unlimited liability of a general partnership or a proprietorship. At the same time they incur any operating losses of the business during a given accounting year, thereby reducing taxes on other income. This feature makes investment in a limited partnership attractive to persons with high incomes, such as doctors, lawyers, etc. (see Chapter 19).

They might also convert ordinary income in a given year to capital gains in later years.

A partnership is not very effective for estate planning and intergeneration transfer. If a partner dies, that partner's property is subject to probate. Moreover, when the partnership is dissolved, the transfer of title to the physical property tends to be cumbersome.

Problems arise in transferring an existing interest in a general partnership to minors. No partner can be forced to accept another person as a general partner, and assigning a partnership interest to a son or daughter might suggest bringing in an additional partner. Such action could lead to the dissolution of the partnership. Some of these disadvantages do not exist in a parent-child partnership that is intended to achieve an intergeneration transfer over a period of time. There are obvious limitations, however, on the ability of many minors to participate in management and assume its responsibilities.

Farm Leases

A business form, in some way unique to agriculture, is the owner-tenant arrangement in a farm lease. Such an arrangement strongly resembles a partnership. Thus we consider it here. Indeed, the lease terms must be properly fixed, lest the arrangement be legally interpreted as a partnership.

As indicated in Chapter 12, the more rapidly growing farm firms have their land resources partly or wholly leased. Such farms often depart dramatically from the popular image of the small-scale tenant farmer trying to become established on the "first rung of a tenure ladder," leading ultimately to full ownership of land resources. Instead, today's typical operation might combine the tracts of several land owners, who are each relatively small contributors to the farm's total resources.

The tenant may be a proprietor in the business (with all the attributes previously listed for sole proprietors) and may acquire the use of land resources without the capital commitments of ownership. In a livestock-share lease, the tenant may acquire the use of other resources as well. Among all types of leases, the land owner frequently participates in furnishing operating inputs, although participation is minimized in most cash leases. In most crop-share and livestock-share leases, the tenant's participation commonly is proportionate to his or her share of farm output and includes participation with the owner in planning fertility, tillage, and crop enterprises.

The Corporation

A corporation is a *legally created* "person" or entity. It can perform any economic function accomplished by a proprietorship: producing, marketing, financing, etc. It can sue or be sued independently of its human associates. It provides a means of separating ownership from management and of insulating both parties from the liabilities associated with the corporation. The liabilities of owners are limited to the owners' individual investment in the business. The liabilities of management, on the other hand, are defined only in terms of prudence and reasonable competence in the performance of management.

Ownership of the corporation is held as small shares or claims on the net worth and profit stream of the business. However, several types of equity claims are possible.

Preferred Stock: a stock having preference over other equity claims on the assets of the business in bankruptcy. That is, the preferred stock is paid out as par value before any value is given to other equity claims. It also has preference over other equity claims on income. Most preferred stock carries a fixed-dividend obligation per share which must be paid whenever the company generates a profit. Only after the dividend claims of preferred stockholders have been met can dividends be paid on other equity claims.

If the corporation does not generate profits in a given year, dividends need not be paid on preferred stock. However, if the stock is *accumulative preferred*, the fixed-dividend obligation accumulates from year to year when not paid and has a priority claim on income if and when the business shows a profit. Voting privileges may be attached to preferred stock, but usually are not.

Common Stock: a stock that has no right or priority over any other stock for dividends or asset distribution, should the corporation be dissolved. It is the ultimate residual claimant on both income and net worth. Each share of common stock usually entitles the holder to one vote on matters coming before the stockholders, such as electing the board of directors and establishing important policy matters. Income allocated to common stockholders is distributed equally per share of common stock. Market values tend to fluctuate more sharply for common stock than for preferred stock.

Warrant: an assigned right to purchase a specific security at an established price. Warrants are often used by established corporations in selling additional stock. The warrants are allocated to existing stockholders, who can then either exercise their warrants themselves or sell them.

Convertible Debenture: a debt instrument carrying the right to be converted into equity claims, usually common stock, at a predetermined price at the option of the holder. The "convertibility" attribute of the debenture usually lowers the interest rate required to make the instrument attractive to buyers. Once issued, however, it constitutes a potential dilution of existing common stock.

Two important types of corporations are the regular corporation and the pseudocorporation. These are called "subchapter C" and "subchapter S" corporations, respectively, because of the related sections of the Internal Revenue Code. The subchapter S corporation was authorized in 1958 to benefit small businesses, including those in agriculture. To qualify, a firm must meet all of the following conditions: (1) have only one class of stock outstanding;[2] (2) have no more than 35 initial stockholders, all of whom must be individuals or estates (i.e., another corporation could not be a stockholder); and (3) have the consent of all shareholders to the choice.

The subchapter S corporation may be terminated if a majority of stockholders voluntarily agree to termination and file such action appropriately with the IRS. Legislation in 1982 also changed the type of income which the business may earn. Any unincorporated business that becomes a subchapter S corporation or any business that has had subchapter S status since it incorporated can now have unlimited "passive" income from such sources as interest, dividends, and rent. However, a regular corporation switching to subchapter S status may earn only up to 25 percent of its income from passive sources.

The subchapter S corporation differs from a regular corporation primarily on two counts. First, it is limited to only one class of stock and to 35 or less stockholders. Second, it is taxed as a partnership rather than as a corporation. Consequently, it pays no income tax.

Corporate income tax obligations were considered in Chapter 3. Dividends from the regular corporation to stockholders are also taxed at each stockholder's marginal tax rate. Thus, the payment of dividends leads to double taxation. Where possible, income to stock-

[2]Legislation passed in 1982 permits common stock in a subchapter S corporation to carry different voting rights. For example, this law will enable company owners to give stock to family members, who are taxed at lower rates, without giving them voting powers. Moreover, an instrument treated as a straight debt instrument is not treated as a second class of stock.

holders should be in the form of salaries, wages, and bonuses, rather than dividends.

With the subchapter S corporation, *all* profits are allocated to the stockholders for income tax accounting, whether or not dividends are distributed; whereas, a general corporate stockholder must pay taxes only on the cash dividends received. Moreover, long-term capital gains and losses are "passed through" (with tax implications) to the stockholders in a subchapter S corporation. In a regular corporation, capital gains taxes are added to the corporation's tax on ordinary income.

Most of the remaining discussion on corporations applies to both types. The corporation offers clear advantages over the sole proprietorship or partnership in generating equity capital. With a corporation, ownership is subdivided into minute fractional claims on the net worth of the business. This procedure makes it easier to redistribute existing-ownership shares. It facilitates raising additional equity capital through selling stock. The fractionalization of shares also simplifies merging two or more businesses. Thus, a corporation provides an alternative to the limited partnership for selling equity claims having limited liability. A farmer who is a general partner would probably lose more management control by incorporating and selling stock, unless it was non-voting stock, than by selling limited-partnership shares.

Studies of farm debt show that corporate-farm borrowers tend to carry heavier debt loads than other forms of business organizations. Several reasons besides differences in business size and levels of management might account for greater debt use by corporate farms. If, by incorporating, the firm can attract outside-equity capital, its credit would be strengthened. Moreover, the record keeping, business analysis, and financial planning required to make appropriate corporate reports may also strengthen a firm's credit.

If, however, the business was incorporated primarily to limit the liability of owners, the financial strength of the corporation likely would be less impressive than that of the proprietorship or family partnership prior to incorporation. In this case, incorporation may reduce the firm's credit. Lenders usually respond by requiring the principal stockholders to personally guarantee any debt. This guarantee nullifies the limited liability condition for that particular debt, but not for third-party claims.

The corporation also facilitates estate planning (see the Appendix to this chapter). It is easier for an owner to give shares of corporate stock to heirs than it is to give title to tractors, buildings, or a small acreage of land. Existing tax laws permit both a husband and his wife to transfer to any individual up to $10,000 of value per year, tax free. Few farm proprietorships take advantage of these gift privileges, partly because transferring titles to small tracts of land to several persons each year becomes very complicated. The corporation overcomes this difficulty.

The regular corporation may also have some distinct advantages over the subchapter S corporation in estate planning. The subchapter S corporation—similar to a proprietorship and a partnership—does not pay income tax. However, this advantage also carries the disadvantage of inflexibility. With a regular corporation, money can flow from the business to the employee-owners either as salaries, which are tax deductible to the business, or as dividends, which are not tax deductible. With this flexibility, a good tax accountant may achieve a tax-minimizing balance between salaries, corporate profits, and dividends.

Social security taxes are assessed to corporations at the current rate (1983) of 6.7 percent on the first $35,700 of each employee's salary. This cost is tax deductible to the corporation. The employee pays an equal amount, but it is not tax-deductible to either the corporation or the employee. Thus, the total cost of social security taxes, including both corporate and individual assessments, is higher for corporations than for proprietorships or partnerships. The corporation's payment of the social security assessment with "before-tax" dollars reduces the cost somewhat. But even on an "after-tax" basis, the total assessment is higher through a corporation.

The costs of many employee benefits are deductible expenses for corporations, even though the employee-recipients are the owners or family members of owners. Tax-sheltered investment plans, medical and hospital insurance, group life insurance, health and accident insurance, sick-pay benefits, tax-free gifts on the death of an employee, and costs of certain employee recreational facilities might all be considered as "legitimate" and "reasonable" operating expenses of a corporation. Most of these are subject to legal limits, however.

The costs of administration are likely higher for the corporation than for other business organizations, although differences between the corporation and the limited partnership are small in many states. The costs of establishing a corporation—including legal fees for drafting the articles of incorporation and for obtaining and registering the charter—are usually more costly than for other types of business organizations. Furthermore, most states require chartered corporations to file an annual report and may levy various types of taxes on the corporation.

Since the corporation is a legally created entity, it is only eliminated by legal action. Its continuity is not dependent on any person's life cycle. This does not assure that management competence will continue at a high level over time. However, it does provide the legal and organizational setting for achieving such continuity. If a corporation is to be terminated, then the tax consequences of the alternatives for distributing assets, some of which may have experienced capital gains or losses, need careful consideration.

Table 18.1 summarizes each business organization (sole proprietorship, general partnership, limited partnership, regular corporation, and subchapter S corporation) with respect to several selected characteristics. Not all of the characteristics can be conveniently reduced to tabular form; however, the summary indicates the important features associated with each alternative. The farm lease is not included in this summary. It falls partly in the proprietor category and partly in the partnership category.

Land Trusts

By means of trusts, legal title to designated properties can be transferred to a trustee, who then becomes responsible for managing the beneficiaries' properties. The objectives and constraints in management can be spelled out in the trust agreement. The *land trust* is an organizational alternative by which ownership of a farm business can be—but does not have to be—separate from management. Its uses tend to be restricted to farming businesses in which land ownership is an important business activity.

The land trust gives to the trustee the legal and equitable title to the real estate placed in trust and charges him or her with responsibility of dealing with such title according to the trust agreement; however, the beneficiaries have the rights to: (1) possession and control, (2) income generated, and (3) funds from the sale of the real estate. Even so, the interest of the beneficiaries is considered personal property rather than title to real estate.

The land trust is not available in all states. Most states have not established statutes specifically authorizing and regulating land trusts. In such states, some uncertainty always exists concerning the

Table 18.1. A Comparison of Selected Organizational Alternatives for the Agricultural Business Firm

Characteristics	Sole Proprietor	Partnerships		Corporations	
		General	Limited	Regular	Subchapter S
1. Source of Equity Capital.	Limited to proprietor's equity: primarily new capital from retained earnings.	Limited to equity capital of partners: new capital from retained earnings *and* from equity of new partners brought into partnership.	Specifically designed to attract equity capital from limited partners who do not have management responsibility.	From selling equity securities and from retained corporate earnings.	From selling preferred *or* common stock (not both) to 35 or less persons and from retained earnings.
2. Liability to Owners.	Liability extends to the total assets of the proprietor for obligations of the firm.	Liability extends to total assets of all partners for obligations of the firm and for actions of partners.	Liability of limited partners limited to amount they invest in partnership. General partners assume major liability.	Liability limited to the assets of the corporation. Liability of stockholders limited to their individual investments in corporation.	
3. Continuity of Owners.	Linked directly to the life cycle of proprietor.	Can be dissolved by any partner. Tends to be associated with life cycle of partners, but need not be.	Can be dissolved by a general partner, but is usually not affected by withdrawal of a limited partner.	Continuity through law is not associated with life cycle of any one person. Instead, the organization is created by law and is terminated by legal action.	
4. Management and Control.	Limited only by the capacity and resources of the proprietor.	Typically, partners share management equally. Each partner has power to bind the partnership, thus requiring high level of confidence.	General partners share management, and each has power to bind the partnership. Limited partners cannot obligate the partnership.	Ultimate power rests with stockholders, who elect board of directors that appoints management.	With fewer stockholders, there usually is a close link between stockholders, directors, and management.
5. Income Taxation.	All farm profits are taxable to proprietor. Any salary paid to proprietor as manager is taxable by proprietor.	Partnerships pay no income taxes. All profits as well as losses are allocated directly to partners (both general and limited) for tax accounting. Salaries paid to general partners are taxable to the recipients and are a deductible expense to partnership.		Corporation pays tax on corporate profits. Salaries to employees are tax deductible to corporation and taxable to employees. Stockholders pay tax on dividends.	Taxed as a partnership, i.e., all profits are allocated to stockholders for tax reporting (stockholder *could* have taxable profits and no dividends with which to pay taxes).

(Continued)

Table 18.1. (Continued)

Characteristics	Sole Proprietor	Partnerships		Corporations	
		General	Limited	Regular	Subchapter S
6. Employee Status.	Social security tax stipulated by law on earnings. Restrictions on amount of farm income proprietors can receive without disrupting social security payments after retirement. Cost of employee benefits to proprietor and family not tax deductible to business.	Partnership itself pays no social security tax. Restrictions on amount of partnership income a general partner can receive without disrupting social security benefits. Limitations do not apply to limited partners. Cost of employee benefits to partners and families not tax deductible to business.		Social security tax stipulated by law for salary to each employee, paid by corporation as tax deductible expense. An equal amount paid by each employee is not tax deductible. Only salaries and *not dividends* diminish social security payments to stockholders. Costs of many employee benefits to the owner-employees and families are tax deductible as expenses to the corporation.	
7. Formalization and Cost of Organization.	No organizational cost. No minimum required records and reports except for income tax, employee withholdings, and workmen's compensation reports.	Can be organized with or without written agreement or contract. Records become more vital than for sole proprietorship.	Must be formally organized with written agreement. Requires official reports to limited partners.	Organization, legal, and filing fees more costly than for partnerships. Franchise tax varies by states.	
8. Intergeneration Transfer and Estate Planning.	Title to actual resources must be transferred on death of proprietor.	Usually difficult to plan for continuity of partnership business beyond first generation. Title to actual resources of partners must be transferred.		At death of stockholder, only the corporation stock owned by decedent is subject to probate (not the underlying assets of that stock). Fractionalization of ownership in undifferentiated assets of firm makes easier transfer possible using tax-exempt gift privileges. 49% of voting stock may be given away without losing control. Regular corporations can have two classes of stock, giving some advantages in estate planning.	

legality of the land trust. In states where the "Statute of Uses" is operative and where courts have given force to the concept that the "holder of the use" becomes the "holder of the legal estate," it is questionable whether land trusts are legally valid.

Where the legality of land trusts is clearly established, they appear to be an effective form for holding title to real estate properties, including farm and ranch holdings.

On balance, where title to land is an important part of the farm business, the land trust appears to offer a promising organizational alternative. Because the legal basis and constraints of the land trust are not clearly defined, however, one should seek experienced legal counsel when considering the use of land trusts for the farm business.

Finance Implications of Interfirm Coordination

Commercial agriculture has experienced strong trends toward increasing specialization in production, and a separation of the control of the various stages of production. New technology has created possibilities for significant economic gains from specialization—resulting in the creation of markets outside the farm for many products and services formerly produced on the farm. Increased specialization, then, is giving rise to new economic stages of production.

A *stage* of production is an operating process which starts with marketable inputs and ends with a saleable product. For example, most dairy farmers a few generations ago sold their products directly to consumers and produced essentially all of their inputs (feed, fertilizer, power, etc.) on the farm. Today, the milk industry is comprised of many economic stages, including commercial fertilizer production and marketing, hay production and marketing, commercial feed manufacturing and distribution, equipment manufacturing and distribution, commercial production of dairy heifers, artificial breeding, milk production, milk transportation, dairy processing, and dairy retailing.

Changes in marketing have also increased the payoff from closer coordination of successive stages of production in order to assure that products meet market specifications at each successive stage. Products which do not meet such specifications are either sold at lower prices or, in extreme cases, denied a market at any price.

Successive stages of production are coordinated in several ways. In a market-oriented economy, coordination is largely guided by prices and other terms of exchange generated *external* to the firm. Coordination may be (1) vertical—the coordination of successive stages in production and distribution—or (2) horizontal—coordination of two or more units of production within the same economic stage. The latter may achieve scale economies in production or marketing or reduce business risks through geographic diversification.

Types of Vertical Coordination

Vertical coordination may range from forward contracting to complete vertical integration. *Forward contracting* usually involves a relatively low level of interfirm coordination, yet achieves some degree of interstage coordination. Various types of contracts have varying degrees of market coordination and management control:

1. The most prevalent is the *market-specification contract* often used with dairymen producing market milk or farmers producing chipper potatoes. Under such a contract, the farmer has substantial latitude in production decisions so long as the product meets the timing, quality, and quantity specifications of the processor or shipper.

2. The *production-management contract* reflects a higher level of interfirm involvement. Here, the buyer specifies certain resource inputs and management practices for producers to follow to assure that the product meets the specifications of the market.

3. The *resource-providing contract* involves a higher level of interfirm involvement. Here, the coordinating firm supplies inputs of a particular specification (a patented variety of seed, a patented type of baby chick, a specified feed, etc.). These inputs are usually financed by the coordinating firm. Sometimes the coordinating firm becomes the farmer's major supplier of operating capital.

Varying arrangements of product pricing are used with these forward contracts. In some instances, the contract guarantees a particular price for specified amounts of products meeting the quality specifications of the contract. In other situations, the price applies to the total output from a specified acreage. In still other cases, the contract guarantees a market outlet for the product and outlines a procedure for price determinations.

At a still higher level of vertical coordination, the successive stages are combined into one decision-making unit by means of *total vertical integration*. It could represent the merger of a farm supply or farm-marketing firm with a farm operation or a large farming operation integrating forward into processing or distribution. Vertical integration also occurs when groups of farms combine to perform their own cooperative processing and distribution functions.

There have been significant examples in recent years of cooperating grain growers entering into commercial cattle-feeding and hog-feeding activities, and dairy farmers forming cooperative milk processing and marketing businesses. Similarly, soybean growers have combined to provide their own crusher and oil-mill cooperatives, cotton growers have provided their own cooperative cotton-ginning and oil-processing facilities, and many other types of producers have formed cooperative associations through which to process and/or market their products.

Some Possible Advantages of Vertical Integration

There are several reasons why an individual farmer might consider some form of vertical coordination.

1. To closely ally with a particular market outlet to assure future market access.
2. To become tied more closely with a particular source of raw product, such as a patented seed or special breeding stock that is not available on the open market but that might improve profitability.
3. To acquire marketing and supervisory skills in order to better coordinate production to market specifications.
4. To reduce or shift risks arising from production or price uncertainties.
5. To obtain better financing through vertical coordination. Farmers producing fruits or vegetables for the open market (either for the fresh market or for processing) face such a high degree of price uncertainty that lenders may refuse to finance them until they have a market contract. More favorable in-

come prospects from contracting could also favorably affect
financing terms. In addition, direct financing from a supply or
market firm might be available.

Vertical coordination—either through a contractual arrangement
or through total merger—may provide more alternatives in resource
control and management. If so, a farmer should carefully consider the
potential economic gains and compare the possible disadvantages—
usually appearing in the form of management constraints imposed by
the coordinating firm. However, a farmer who cannot obtain adequate financing because of (1) a relatively small, inefficient operation; (2) shortages in managerial skills; or (3) market uncertainties
might sacrifice little real economic freedom for the benefits of vertical coordination.

The degree and type of vertical coordination vary greatly within
agriculture. Nearly all dairy production and most commercial fruit
and vegetable production in the United States operate under some
form of contract. The poultry industry generally and broiler production in particular have moved rapidly toward total vertical integration. The last decade has witnessed substantial vertical coordination
in the beef industry. More recently, the swine industry has experienced similar developments.

Vertical coordination might affect different farmers to different
degrees. In a multiproduct firm where one product is "integrated,"
only part of the operator's business is affected. The effect may be
much greater, however, in firms where one product dominates.

Through vertical coordination, a farmer may shift price and yield
uncertainties to the integrating firm; however, a new uncertainty associated with continuation of the contract may be incurred. Thus, the
farmer's strategies will include efforts to preserve the new contractual relationship.

Topics for Discussion

1. What attributes of the corporate form of business organization might explain the difference over time in the "Index of Management Level" reflected in Figure 18.1?
2. Under what conditions is a subchapter S corporation more appropriate
   than the regular corporation?
3. Some have argued that to incorporate a farm firm is likely to *reduce* the
   amount of capital that can be attracted to the firm rather than to *increase*
   it. How could this be true?

4. What are the principal advantages and disadvantages of incorporating the farm business?
5. The firm can grow "horizontally" or "vertically," in terms of production stages and interstage markets. Which type of growth is induced by size economies? By economies of complementarities in production?
6. Contrast and compare the corporate and limited partnership organizations of business.
7. The taxable estate of a farm business is $1 million, comprised mostly of farm land. Identify and evaluate several ways in which the estate tax obligation could be reduced by prior planning.

References

1. Coffman, George W., *Corporations with Farming Operations*, Agricultural Economics Report 209, ERS, USDA, Washington, D.C., June 1971.
2. Garrett, Wm. B., *Land Trusts*, Chicago Title and Trust Company, Chicago, 1971.
3. Goldberg, R. A., *Agribusiness Coordination: A Systems Approach to the Wheat, Soybean, and Florida Orange Economies*, Graduate School of Business, Harvard University, Boston, 1968.
4. Harl, N. E., *Agricultural Law*, Matthew Bender & Company, Inc., New York, 1980.
5. _____, *Farm Estate and Business Planning*, Century Communications, Inc., Skokie, Illinois, 1981.
6. Harris, Marshall, and Dean T. Massey, *Vertical Coordination via Contract Farming*, Miscellaneous Publication 1073, ERS, USDA, Washington, D.C., 1968.
7. Hopkin, John A., "Conglomerate Growth in Agriculture," *Agricultural Finance Review*, Vol. 33, ERS, USDA, Washington, D.C., July 1972.
8. Kenoe, Henry W., *Land Trust Practice, 1974 Edition*, Illinois Institute of Continuing Education, Chicago.
9. Krausz, N. G. P., *Corporations in the Farm Business*, Rev., Agricultural Extension Service Circular 797, University of Illinois at Urbana–Champaign, 1975.
10. Matthews, S. F., and V. J. Rhodes, *The Use of Public Limited Partnership Financing in Agriculture for Income Tax Shelter*, North Central Regional Research Publication 223, July 1975.
11. Mighell, R. L., and L. A. Jones, *Vertical Coordination in Agriculture*, Agricultural Economics Report 19, USDA, Washington, D.C., 1963.
12. Scofield, W. H., and G. W. Coffman, *Corporations Having Agricultural Operations*, a preliminary report, Agricultural Economics Report 142, ERS, USDA, Washington, D.C., August 1968.
13. Thomas, K. H., and M. D. Boehlje, *Farm Business Arrangements: Which One for You?* North Central Publication 50, College of Agriculture, Iowa State University, Ames, 1982.

14. Uchtmann, D. L., et al., *Agricultural Law: Principles and Cases,* McGraw-Hill Book Company, New York, 1981.

Appendix to Chapter 18

Estate Taxes: Implications for Farmers

In this appendix we briefly review the effects of federal estate and gift taxes in the United States that are levied on transfers of property by donors at death, or during their lifetime, and discuss some of the alternatives available to farmers in dealing with the tax obligations. The effects of these tax obligations on farmers have increased over time, because many farm estates have grown in value to levels where they are subject to large transfer taxes and other costs but have limited capacity for generating easily the funds to pay such costs. In response to the high burden of transfer costs at death, federal tax legislation passed in 1976 and in 1981 have eased these burdens and provided some special options for farm estates. Future changes will occur as well, so that this discussion only illustrates some of the issues involved.

Estate management is a pervasive, long-term process. It includes all of the activities that go into building an estate, generating retirement income, planning an equitable distribution of property among heirs, and minimizing the cost of transferring assets. The costs involved in transferring assets are numerous. They include transfer taxes levied on the estate by the U.S. Government, inheritance taxes levied on heirs by the respective state governments, transactions costs in liquidating assets, legal fees, costs of funeral and burial, payments of debts, and others. If not well planned, these costs can be very high and may substantially reduce the value of an estate. Moreover, inadequate planning can substantially lengthen the time involved in transferring a decedent's estate to heirs. These effects may adversely influence the operation and ownership of an on-going farm business whose owner has died as well as impacting on the financial position and management choices of heirs for many years.

Among the many transfer costs, the federal estate and gift tax obligation is a substantial one. It is levied on transfers of property as gifts during one's life or as bequests at death. For transfers at death, the tax is basically levied on the decedent's net worth. However, special rules apply in determining the level of net worth. In filing a federal estate tax return, the *taxable estate* is found by deducting allowable *deductions* from the decedent's *gross estate*. The gross estate includes the fair market value of all property owned outright by the deceased, all property in joint tenancy (unless the surviving joint tenant can prove his or her original contribution), plus half the value of property owned by the decedent and another person as equal tenants in common, plus the proceeds of life insurance and life estates in which the deceased retained any incidence of ownership. Recent gifts are also included in the gross estate, although they are offset in the deductions for arriving at the taxable estate.

The taxable estate is essentially found by reducing the gross estate for (1) claims against the estate, including those of creditors; (2) funeral expenses and other administrative costs; (3) charitable deductions; and (4) an unlimited marital deduction for bequests or gifts to a spouse. Federal estate taxes are then figured on the taxable estate, based on the unified transfer tax rate schedule, and an allowable tax credit is applied to reduce the tax liability to yield the amount of tax actually owed.

Table 18.2 indicates the Unified Transfer Tax Rate Schedule that will be in effect during 1985 and beyond. Prior to 1985, the marginal tax rates on transfers over $2,500,000 are higher. Table 18.3 indicates the unified credit that is subtracted from the taxpayer's estate or gift tax liability in the respective years in determining the level of taxes actually paid. As the table indicates, the unified credit of $192,800 in

Table 18.2. Unified Transfer Tax Rate Schedule, 1985

If the amount is		tentative tax is			
over	but not over	tax	+	%	on excess over
0	10,000	0		18	0
10,000	20,000	1,800		20	10,000
20,000	40,000	3,800		22	20,000
40,000	60,000	8,200		24	40,000
60,000	80,000	13,000		26	60,000
80,000	100,000	18,200		28	80,000
100,000	150,000	23,800		30	100,000
150,000	250,000	38,800		32	150,000
250,000	500,000	70,800		34	250,000
500,000	750,000	155,800		37	500,000
750,000	1,000,000	248,300		39	750,000
1,000,000	1,250,000	345,800		41	1,000,000
1,250,000	1,500,000	448,300		43	1,250,000
1,500,000	2,000,000	555,800		45	1,500,000
2,000,000	2,500,000	780,800		49	2,000,000
2,500,000 and over	. . .	1,025,800		50	2,500,000

Table 18.3. Unified Federal Estate and Gift Tax Credit

Year	Unified Credit	Estate Exemption Equivalent
1983	$ 79,300	$275,000
1984	96,300	325,000
1985	121,800	400,000
1986	155,800	500,000
1987 and thereafter	192,800	600,000

1987 completely exempts taxable estates of up to $600,000 from taxation.

The unified credit protects many estates from federal taxation. However, the estates of many farmers may still exceed these levels due to the importance of farm land and other non-real estate assets. Thus, the tax obligation on estates could be significant.

To illustrate, consider the estate tax obligation on Farmer X, who might die under 1985 conditions. Farmer X is a surviving spouse who owns 400 acres of farm land valued at $3,000 per acre and has $140,000 of nonfarm assets. Thus, Farmer X's gross estate is projected to be $1,340,000. Assuming deductions of $40,000 and no previous gift transfers, the taxable estate is $1,300,000. Using Table 18.2, the gross estate tax is projected as $469,800. Subtracting the 1985 unified credit of $121,800 leaves a net estate tax of $348,000—a sizeable amount. Because Farmer X's estate is dominated by farm land, the funds to meet the tax obligation must come from partial liquidation of the estate, from borrowing sources, or by qualifying for special valuation or installment payment privileges allowed by the tax laws. In addition, Farmer X might consider other alternatives in estate management in order to reduce the tax burden or increase the estate's liquidity position. We now consider some of these alternatives.

Gifts

Making tax-free gifts prior to death is one way to reduce the size of an estate and assure that continued growth in asset values will rest with the recipient of the gift. Federal estate tax laws, in general, allow a 100 percent marital deduction on qualifying property passing to a donor's spouse. In addition, a donor may exclude up to $10,000 annually per donee from the value of total gifts subject to tax. For a husband and wife making gifts, the annual exclusion becomes, in ef-

fect, $20,000 per donee per year. Gifts above these levels are subject
to the transfer tax, although the unified credit applies.

Trusts and Life Estates

The trust is a contractual instrument by which title to property is
transferred to a trustee to hold and manage for the benefit of other
persons designated as beneficiaries. The trust agreement specifies
the objectives and terms of the contract.

A trust created and operated during the lifetime of the grantor is
called a living trust. If the grantor retains the right to change or terminate the trust, it is revocable and thus subject to estate taxes at the
grantor's death. If the power to control the property or the income
from it is given up, the trust is irrevocable and essentially a gift.

A testamentary trust is created by a will at death. The property in
such a trust is part of the grantor's estate for tax purposes. The trust
can be used to (1) relieve a spouse or other beneficiary of management burdens, while assuring the beneficiary of income benefits
from the property; (2) provide income and care for an incompetent
person; (3) prevent a beneficiary from unwisely spending an inheritance; (4) provide interim management for minors or temporarily incapacitated beneficiaries; and (5) provide an income for life to a
spouse or children with the remainder going to the children, grandchildren, or others.

The life estate arrangement, in which the holder of a current
interest receives the income for his or her life, while the holder of
the remainder interest acquires a future ownership claim, has the
advantage of removing the property's value from the estate of the
holder of the current interest. If, for example, Farmer X leaves his
estate with a remainder interest to his grandchildren and a current
interest in the estate's income to his children, then the property only
enters the estate of Farmer X and his grandchildren. Since the children's current interest terminates at their death, it does not enter
their estate and is not subject to tax.

Life Insurance

Life insurance on the grantor's life is one way to provide the
liquidity needed by the estate or by the beneficiaries in transfer at
death. Either the estate or some persons may be designated as beneficiary. If the grantor assigns all benefits to a beneficiary and relin-

quishes control rights over the policy, the life insurance proceeds likely will be excluded from the estate, with obvious tax benefits. If the grantor does not want the benefits paid directly to the beneficiary, they could be paid to a trust set up for the beneficiary, as designated by the grantor. In any case, life insurance provides an effective source of liquidity to meet an estate's financial obligations.

Incorporation

The corporation has distinct advantages over proprietorships and partnerships in transferring assets. Thus it offers a high degree of flexibility in estate management and may aid in reducing transfer costs. Moreover, a corporation can effectively maintain business control while still transferring assets to heirs or other parties.

One of the corporation's advantages in estate management is that of having more than one class of stock. A farmer can maintain managerial control over the business while transferring substantial ownership to heirs by transferring non-voting shares and maintaining voting shares. For example, a relatively young but successful farmer, with farm assets valued at say $1 million, could incorporate with 499,000 shares of common stock at par value of $1 and 501,000 shares of preferred stock at par value of $1 and paying a fixed dividend per share. Both classes could be made voting stock.

The common stock could be transferred to heirs either directly or through a trust, depending on the circumstances and preferences. It could be transferred all at once, subject to the transfer tax, or it could be transferred over several years to take advantage of the annual gift exclusions.

Alternatively, the stock could be sold to heirs in exchange for their debt, thus fixing the value of the wealth being transferred. The father could then make gifts to the heirs over the years by cancelling a portion of the debt each year. As the firm continues to expand, the increased net worth would accrue to the common stock held by the heirs. By holding the preferred stock, the parent maintains control of the business and assures a flow of income so long as the business is profitable. In this fashion, the growth in wealth accrues directly to the holders of common stock—the heirs—without costs of estate transfer.

Of course, numerous other factors associated with incorporation need to be considered. However, incorporation does offer additional flexibility in estate management.

Use Valuation of Farm Land

The Tax Reform Act of 1976 provides that property in a gross estate be valued at fair market value. However, the act, along with subsequent amendments, allows qualifying farm land to be valued on an "actual-use" basis at the election of the executor or administrator of an estate. On an actual-use basis, the value is determined by capitalizing the fair rental value of the property. Where relevant information is available, net cash rent on land, averaged for the past five years, is capitalized at the interest rate charged on new Federal Land Bank loans, also averaged over the past five years. Thus, for net cash rent of $100 per acre and interest of 10 percent, the actual-use value would be $1,000. In contrast, the land's market value might be in the $2,000 to $3,000 per acre range. In times of rapidly inflating land values, this procedure will produce a value substantially less than could be obtained by selling the property. Thus, it is an attractive tax alternative for farmers.

However, there are several conditions on using actual-use values: (1) qualifying conditions, (2) limiting conditions (the "maximum benefit rule"), and (3) recapture provisions. To qualify, at least half the value of the gross estate, net of indebtedness, must be comprised of assets used in farming and must pass to one or more family members; at least 25 percent of the value of the gross estate must be comprised of real property used in farming; and the deceased, or a member of the deceased's family, must have owned the real property for five of the eight years preceding death and, in like period, must have participated materially in the farming operation involving the real property.

The maximum benefit rule limits to $750,000 the amount by which the value of the estate can be reduced by actual-use valuation. Finally, if within 10 years (15 years for deaths prior to 1982) after the death of the deceased, the family recipient disposes of the qualifying real property to a nonfarm buyer, or converts it to a nonfarming use, any savings in estate taxes are subject to recapture. Thus, while the savings may be substantial, restrictions on subsequent use or disposition also may have substantial financial consequences.

Installment Payment of Federal Estate Tax

Farm estates frequently are plagued by excessive illiquidity, creating disruptive cash flow problems for transfer recipients who are confronted with large tax obligations. Tax laws have allowed for this problem by providing for a deferment of tax payments attributable to a farm, or other closely held business, if the interest in the closely held business or farm exceeds 35 percent (65 percent before 1982) of the decedent's adjusted gross estate. Installment payments may occur over a 15-year period at a favorable interest rate.

Chapter 19

Outside Equity Capital
in Agriculture

This chapter will focus on the use of outside equity capital in agriculture. We will consider the role of outside equity, methods of obtaining it, and the agricultural operations that can use these methods. The impacts of tax obligations are a crucial factor affecting the availability of new equity capital. The chapter concludes with discussions of private versus public investment offerings and the process of going public.

The Role of Outside Equity Capital

Financial management in agriculture has focused on the management of debt capital under the assumption that farmers could generate sufficient equity capital from retained earnings, capital gains, inheritances, and gifts. This assumption has been consistent with the structural characteristics of agriculture, in which farming operations are largely controlled by individual farmers and farm families. However, these features are subject to change, as illustrated by the substantial leasing of farm land, which separates land ownership and control, and by the production of some commodities by non-proprietorship business organizations relying heavily on outside equity capital. Even growth-oriented proprietorship firms or partnerships may be under pressure to expand faster than they can generate equity capital from within the business. Alternatively, some highly leveraged operations may wish to attract additional equity in order to reduce leverage and thus high financial risks.

Within agriculture, farmers and ranchers often pool resources for a larger, more efficient operation. Some of these arrangements involve leasing; others occur as joint ventures, partnerships, mergers, or family corporations. Intergeneration arrangements are especially common within families. Pooling of family equity has often resulted from estate planning to minimize intergenerational transfer costs and maintain farms as integral units. While these consolidations of resource control cause structural changes among farms, the total equity position of the participating parties remains largely unaffected.

Outside equity capital enters agriculture through informal and formal market arrangements. Informal market transactions occur when outside investors buy land directly from farmers, for example. The investor generally arranges for labor, management, and other capital services through leasing contracts or direct hiring. The result is part-owner tenancy, although often with professional management services playing an important role.

Outside equity entering through formal market arrangements represents the specialized efforts of agricultural entrepreneurs to attract equity through limited partnerships, common stock, and agency services. These ventures have been commonly used in financing growth of large cattle feeding operations, as well as cattle breeding, citrus, and vineyard operations. Newer channels are associated with pension funds, life insurance companies, foreign investors, and equity participation loans considered by some lenders.

Outside equity may come from many sources, including individuals, associations, trusts, nonfarm corporations, or other organized groups with investable funds. Considerable interest is also developing in packaging outside equity capital for farm investments from people in nearby communities who have the savings and know the local farming industry. Most outside investors prefer not to participate in management. They generally have strong financial incentives for making the investment and prefer limited liability, reasonable liquidity, and undifferentiated ownership shares in the business. Proprietorships and general partnerships are poorly adapted to these investors.

Many prospective outside investors are strongly motivated to shelter high nonfarm incomes from tax obligations. Tax shelters provided by farming generally rest on the availability of cash accounting, current deductions of some capital expenditures for developing orchards and ranches, potentials for converting ordinary income to capital gains, and the pass-through of income losses to the investor, as with limited partnerships or subchapter S corporations. However, changes in tax laws over time have modified the ability of nonfarm and farm investors to benefit from these tax provisions. An example is the Tax Reform Act of 1976, which, among its many provisions, stipulated the following: (1) large corporate businesses were required to use accrual accounting to figure their tax liabilities from farm operations, (2) loss deductions from farm operations were limited to the amount the investor actually has at risk in the operation, (3) cash basis taxpayers were prohibited from deducting prepaid interest, and (4) syndicates (including partnerships) were required to capitalize certain expenses.

Because changes in tax laws are difficult to predict and may occur relatively frequently, it is difficult and inappropriate to establish definitive guidelines about their use in attracting outside equity into agriculture. Moreover, the impacts of changes in tax laws are difficult to project. One expert, for example, observed that in response to the 1976 Act "... the incentives which have motivated outside investors in the past still exist, and although the means by which they can be tapped have changed, they will continue to attract risk capital to agriculture" [10].

Equity Capital and Limited Partnerships

With a limited partnership, the financial liability of each partner is limited to each one's investment in the partnership, the limited partner does not participate in management, and profits and losses are passed directly to the partners for income tax purposes.

Investment Characteristics and Limited Partnerships

Raising equity capital in U.S. agriculture through limited partnerships has been used most in cattle feeding. Also involved are cow-calf operations and orchard development. The development of large-scale commercial cattle feeding illustrates the process. Federal income tax policies clearly interacted with economies of size, new technologies, and profit potential to result in the development of very large-scale, capital-intensive cattle feeding operations, and a shift from small farm feedlots in the Midwest to the southern high plains of Texas, Oklahoma, Colorado, and Kansas. When rapid expansion of cattle feedlots occurred in the mid- to late 1960s, an important source of equity capital was the sale of limited partnerships in the national financial markets. Millions of dollars were raised in this manner between 1965 and the early 1970s. Much of these flows, in turn, was attributed to tax savings for their investors. These funds, when leveraged with debt capital at rates of up to 4 to 1, furnished the capital needed to buy millions of head of cattle and the necessary feed for this industry each year during this period.

Use of outside equity capital in cattle feeding also added to financial instability. Declining beef prices in 1972 to 1973 caused capital to be withdrawn from existing cattle limited partnerships, and few new partnerships were formed. In turn, cow-calf operators experienced short-term cash flow problems, as they had to finance the placement of their calves in commercial feedlots, rather than through sales to other custom feeders. The 1976 tax changes cited above also dampened the attraction of limited partnerships in cattle operations.

Nonetheless, several characteristics of large-scale cattle feeding made limited partnerships attractive for raising equity capital. New technologies provided significant economies of size in cattle feeding and high capital needs to meet the related financing requirements. Innovative methods of attracting capital were needed. The deferral of near-term tax obligations was attractive to high-income nonfarm investors. Cattle feeding is also a relatively high-risk, high-return venture. High risk itself does not make a limited partnership attractive, but this type of business organization generally does offer some risk-reducing advantages.

A risk to the investor, in addition to the usual business risks, is the limited opportunity to resell limited partnership interests. Two courses of action may help reduce this risk. First, limited partnerships may provide the investor an opportunity to liquidate the investment within a specified number of years, with provision for earlier withdrawal under a penalty. Second, some limited partnership offerings are designed to appeal to high-income investors, for whom short-term liquidity is not a problem. Frequently, the prospectus will stipulate a minimum salary and net worth for prospective investors.

Steps in Creating a Limited Partnership

One basic requirement for creating and selling limited partnership interests is the presence of at least one general partner who is responsible for management and liability. Since limited partners have limited liability, the general partner(s) must assume unlimited liability for the partnership. Hence, the general partner(s) must demonstrate financial responsibility to the limited partners.

The general partner may be an individual, a general partnership, an informal association, or a corporation. Having a corporation as the general partner introduces the limited-liability provision of the corporation as well. However, providing limited liability to the general partner increases the possibility of having the business classified by the U.S. Internal Revenue Service as a corporation for tax purposes.

The limited partnership must also be registered in its home state. If interstate offerings of partnership shares are anticipated, the registration must be filed and cleared with the Securities and Exchange Commission (SEC) in the U.S. Department of Commerce. The general partner(s) may then offer limited partnership shares to the public.

Equity Capital and Corporations

Incorporation for attracting outside equity capital has not been widespread in agriculture. Those firms that have publicly sold common stock generally cite high administrative costs and lengthy review of their prospectus by state and federal regulatory agencies. Liquidity of corporate shares can be high, but variability of earnings and difficulty in attracting high-quality management dampens income prospects for investors. The more successful corporate arrangements often arise when well managed agricultural enterprises are combined with other enterprises in vertical sequence (input supplier, processor) or in conglomerate arrangements.

Nonetheless, the corporation offers several advantages over a proprietorship and a general partnership in tapping outside sources of equity capital. The regular corporation permits the use of two classes of stock. This provides unique advantages over the subchapter S corporation and the limited partnership in long-term tax planning and flexibility for channeling current returns and capital gains to investors.

The process of forming a corporation is relatively simple, although it varies among states. The articles of incorporation must be cleared by and registered with the appropriate state agency. An experienced attorney can help in deciding in which state to register and in obtaining clearance and registration. One argument offered against incorporating a farm business without public stock offerings is the limited marketability of the stock. This creates liquidity problems for stockholders who desire to withdraw from the business. This problem is not unique to corporations, however. It can be even more severe for proprietorships and partnerships with multiple owners. A market must be found for an undivided interest in the business, or some assets must be sold.

The marketability problem often depends on provisions in the articles of incorporation that control the trading of ownership interests. If the business is large enough to warrant selling stock to outsiders, the issues and suggestions which follow are applicable. If the business is not large enough to establish a market price, the stockholders can meet to establish the price for redeeming a member's stock during the following year.

In the following discussion the central focus will be on problems and processes of obtaining new equity capital by selling corporate stock. However, the discussion is also generally applicable to limited partnerships. Moreover, the issues and techniques apply to farm firms and to many farm-related businesses which are family oriented.

Why Sell Corporate Stock?

One of the first questions the owner and manager should answer for himself, and for possible investors, is why sell stock in a successful business to outside investors?

To increase the corporation's equity capital

One obvious reason is to obtain outside equity capital. Once the business is leveraged to a level that the manager and lender feel is optimal, further growth is limited by the rate of equity accumulation. Unless new stock is sold, additional equity is limited to retained earnings and unrealized capital gains.

Equity capital may be needed for other reasons too. If large debt obligations are severely straining the firm's cash position, the owner-manager might seek relief through a stock offering, using the proceeds to pay off debts. Substituting equity for debt reduces the heavy drain on cash to service principal and interest. However, prospective investors would likely need to be convinced that the adverse cash flow problem did not result from operational inefficiencies and poor management.

To reduce private holdings of corporate stock

A successful farmer with a sizeable estate, completely tied up in a farming corporation, may prefer to sell corporate stock in order to diversify a personal investment. It is important to distinguish between stock offered by a corporate officer as an individual and stock offered by the firm itself. With many family corporations, the major investment holding of one parent is his or her stock in the corporation.

There are several reasons why the parent might diversify under these circumstances. One reason is to protect the business against potential sale for payment of estate and inheritance taxes. Although life insurance reduces this risk, there may be merit in selling corporate stock and investing the proceeds in non-corporate assets so that future income is not solely dependent on the farm business.

Second, a parent's sale of corporate stock that has appreciated in value might generate a higher after-tax value than would receipt of dividends or salary from the business. Dividends and salary are taxed as ordinary income, while capital gains from the sale of stock are taxed at a lower rate.

Third, outside sales could establish a stock price for purposes of estate planning, settling estates, or making income and holding adjustments within a family. Sales of stock are always difficult in a closely held family corporation, and a sale to outside buyers might establish a base price for settlements.

Another reason for selling stock is that it allows an individual to withdraw from the business. The withdrawal of a valuable manager will clearly affect the business's income-generating capacity. Thus, if a father who successfully built up the business is planning to withdraw, he should assure that strong management will continue in his absence. Otherwise, the stock's sale price would be adversely affected.

Several disadvantages of outside stock sales should also be considered. First, selling common stock dilutes the relative claims of existing owners on the business's stream of income and net worth. Management must choose between a total claim to a smaller cash flow and net worth and a partial claim to potentially larger sums.

Second, selling common stock extends voting rights and business control to new stockholders. Owner-managers of farm corporations are often reluctant to share control with outsiders. It is not uncommon to read of "outsiders" gaining control of a business, pushing the original management out, draining the firm's liquidity, and then selling for a "tax" profit. Maintaining majority control of the stock, combined with effective management, will insure against such a take-over.

Third, when a privately held corporation becomes a public corporation, its annual report (including balance sheet and income statement) is more readily available to outside parties. However, in most instances, the extent and advantages for secrecy are overestimated.

Fourth, the transactions costs of obtaining outside-equity capital are higher than those of debt capital—sometimes much higher. Examples are the costs of underwriting and distribution for common stock. Common stock typically must be sold at a higher expected yield than debt instruments because of its higher risk for the investor. Also, dividends are not tax deductible, while interest paid on debt is tax deductible.

Assume, for example, that a term loan is negotiated at 15 percent interest. For a corporation in the 46 percent tax bracket, this represents an after-tax equivalent of 8.10 percent. The sale of preferred stock to cover this investment likely would have to pay a dividend yielding at least 16 percent to the purchaser, unless, of course, part of the return occurs as capital gains. Thus, a $100 preferred stock would carry an annual dividend of $16. If it costs $10 per share to market the preferred stock, the selling firm would pay $16 per year on $90 realized capital, or a minimum annual rate of 17.7 percent. Since stock dividends are not tax deductible, the after-tax cost of the capital through preferred stock is more than double the cost of borrowed funds. The cost for common stock would likely be higher still, since it carries greater uncertainty for the investor.

A *Private Placement Versus a Public Stock Offering*

Once a farm corporation has decided to obtain new equity capital, it must make either a private placement of stock or a public offering. For a corporation seeking less than, say, $500,000 in equity capital, the public sale would be too costly. Otherwise, for any but very large firms, this is a crucial decision.

There may be a few close personal contacts who are interested in buying stock in the farm business. Where the capital needs are not too great, such a sale may be attractive to all parties. Even the small farm proprietorship might persuade a local lawyer, a physician, or other person of means to invest in the farming operation.

Registration with the Securities Exchange Commission (SEC) is not required for a private sale, thus saving important costs. The cost of an investment banker's services may even be saved. In most instances, however, a sizeable private offering can be more successful (and certainly smoother) through the services of an investment banker. The investment banker has important contacts with individuals and firms seeking investments in private stock offerings.

In recent years a number of mutual funds, insurance companies, and some pension funds have been attracted to private offerings of common stock or other forms of equity participation in successful small companies, including those in agriculture and related industries. Investment-banker fees are generally less for arranging a private sale than for underwriting a public offering. Furthermore, if a farm corporation has unusual financial problems that are being resolved, or unrealized potential, these circumstances can often be explained to, and better understood by, a few investors than by many small investors who must be reached through a prospectus.

Private offerings have possible disadvantages, however. Unless the buyers know and have enthusiasm for the company and its management, they might insist on imposing tight control. They likely will follow management actions far more closely than would public investors and will probably respond more vigorously if not fully satisfied.

The regulations determining whether an issue can qualify as a private sale or must be registered with the SEC as a public sale are spelled out in the Securities Act of 1933. In broad terms, public offerings of $300,000 or more that will be offered in interstate sales must be registered. However, the number of offerees (and their intentions toward resale), the uniqueness of the offering, and other factors must also be considered. Qualified legal counsel, along with economic analysis, is essential in determining whether or not to go public.

The best counselor for choosing between a private versus a public sale is likely an investment banker who is experienced in placing agricultural securities. Whether to use a regional or national firm depends on the ultimate objectives and characteristics of the business. If the farm corporation is primarily local in its resource base and market, a local company likely could best handle the underwriting.

More than one investment banking firm should be contacted. Some large companies prefer not to handle sales under $1 million; whereas a local company might accept a smaller offering with enthusiasm. Contacting one large national firm and one relatively local firm gives a good basis for choosing an investment banker. Such discussions should also provide a clearer idea of whether to make a private or a public offering. One probably should not contact more than two firms, however, if the confidential nature of the undertaking is an important issue.

Timing Problems

Two important timing questions must be resolved with a public issue. First, is the company ready for the market? If it has management, financial, or marketing problems which are being resolved or is on the threshold of a profit breakthrough, a public issue might be delayed until these situations are resolved. If delay is not possible, a private sale likely would be preferred. A private sale can proceed immediately; whereas a public sale is subject to SEC approval and possible time delays.

In determining whether or not the company is ready for the market, one should honestly evaluate the business from the standpoint of both the underwriter (who might have to sell the stock) and the prospective investor. In doing so, one should consider the information in the prospectus. Realistically, one might ask, "Given the alternatives available in the market, would I, as a detached outsider, be attracted to invest in this company? If so, why? Is it in a 'growth' industry? Is it recession proof? And what is this firm's position within the industry in terms of earnings ratios, growth rates, liquidity, and risk?"

The second timing element relates to the market. Is the market ready for this type of new offering? Is the market "bearish," generally, and toward new issues, in particular? How will this market attitude affect price? Competent investment bankers are a good source of advice on timing.

If it seems wise to delay the public offering, interim sources for long-term funds likely will be needed. Perhaps a term loan with a bank or insurance company is possible, with the agreement that the loan will be repaid when stock is sold. The investment banker may be able to sell debentures. However, if bank or PCA financing is already large, this lender may require that any long-term financing be subordinated to his debt.

Basic Steps in Going Public

After the decision to go public, the next step is to secure the services of three competent professionals—an investment banker, an attorney, and an accountant. The investment banker will advise on the marketability of a new stock offering, suggest the procedures to follow in preparing for the stock offering, and recommend the price. The banker's function in underwriting and syndicating the stock issues will depend on the method of underwriting, whether under a *fixed-commitment* basis or a *best-effort* basis.

Under the fixed-commitment basis—the method most used by reputable investment banking firms—the underwriter agrees to purchase the stock offering at a mutually specified price, and a check for this amount, net of the underwriter's commission, is received immediately, once SEC clearance and all the registrations have been accomplished. Aside from certain *escape* clauses, the underwriter assumes the full risk of marketing the stock. The escape clauses should be studied carefully, for they outline the conditions under which the underwriter can cancel the agreement.

For more speculative issues, underwriters might prefer to enter agreements on a best-effort basis, whereby they exert their best efforts to sell the stock offering but do not agree to purchase unsold stock. Most of the cattle feeding limited partnership subscriptions were offered to the general public on a best-effort basis. Some general partners also reserved the right to sell directly to the general public at the commission rate charged by underwriters. Under most circumstances, however, one should be wary of best-effort contracts. They could reflect either a financially weak underwriter or a market situation judged weak or hazardous by the underwriter.

Investment bankers can also serve as agents in arranging private financing through private sale of stock, sale of debentures, purchase and lease-back, or mergers. As investment counselors, they have contact with many types of investors and other investment bankers. Consequently, they are in a strategic position to help evaluate the market for a particular company.

The selected attorney should be experienced in securities registration. The outcome success depends on a smooth and judicious process. If the registration proceedings are mishandled, one can be subject to civil suit and penalties. It may be necessary to contact a regional financial center to find experienced legal counsel. Although the attorney must work closely with the underwriter's counsel, he or she should represent the client's interest in preparing the corporate documents, the prospectus and the registration statement, and in negotiating the details of the underwriting agreement. The attorney is also responsible for obtaining SEC clearance and registration and for getting registration in each state where stock might be sold. An accountant will assist in preparing the prospectus, financial statements, and registration statement. Since these documents must be cleared by SEC, an accountant familiar with SEC procedures can greatly facilitate the process.

The accountant, attorney, and underwriter must work jointly to cover the basic steps of (1) assembling the necessary information about the business to satisfy SEC regulations, (2) preparing the prospectus, (3) reorganizing the firm to its new capital and organizational structure after the stock offering, (4) taking care of all regulations, (5) printing stock certificates, and (6) arranging to sell the stock.

Costs of Going Public

The total costs of underwriting will vary substantially with the size of the issue, the strength of the firm selling the stock, the amount of legal and accounting detail required, the market conditions, and the way the underwriter views the marketability of the stock. Included in the total expenses, in addition to the underwriter's commission, are legal and accounting fees; state and federal taxes, fees, and registrations; costs of printing the preliminary and final prospecti, stock certificates, and other documents needed in volume; and travel and miscellaneous expenses. The total expenses, including the underwriter's commission, could vary from less than 8 percent to 20 percent or more of the gross revenue from the public sale. Naturally, these costs must be included in any budgeting analysis of the profitability of public stock offerings.

Equity Capital and Mergers

A merger is the process of combining two or more existing businesses into a single-business entity. The firms being merged may be proprietary, partnership, or corporate, and the merging process may be any of various methods. Similarly, the business established through merger may have any legal form. This section will present three merger situations and the benefits involved.

1. Many small businesses—including farm businesses—have solved pressing financial and marketing problems by merging with a larger, established firm through some form of vertical

integration. In some instances farmers have merged with a processing or marketing firm (referred to as integrating forward), or they have merged with a supply firm (integrating backward). Both pricing and tax advantages may arise in the exchange of equity (either proprietor's equity or corporate stock) in a privately held business for stock in a publicly held corporation. Moreover, the transaction is far less costly than a public offering. However, when a relatively small farm operation merges into a large corporation, management control may be lost to the large corporation.

2. A merger might be particularly attractive to a farmer approaching retirement. An example is a producer of quality tree fruits, who was approaching retirement and whose children did not want to operate the orchard of 100+ acres. The food-processing firm which had purchased the fruit for many years offered to exchange corporate stock for the farmer's equity in the orchard. This firm's stock was listed on the New York Stock Exchange.

The processing firm was anxious to acquire control over orchards in the area to ensure access to raw products. Moreover, acquiring the farm through stock exchange rather than cash strengthened the firm's liquidity. Hence, it offered the farmer a price somewhat above the going market price for quality orchards. The canner also offered the farmer a two-year management contract to help get the farm's operation fully integrated into the corporate business.

By exchanging acres of land, irrigation equipment, sets of buildings, and machinery items for shares of stock in the food-processing corporation, the seller secured a flow of income that was more reliable than was the income from the orchard. The stock also provided considerably more flexibility in transferring the producer's wealth to heirs.

3. Merging might provide a way for two or more farmers to combine operations to achieve economies of size and specialization in management. However, the merging parties need not relinquish title to their real estate in order to achieve the desired benefits so long as the *use* of resources is pooled. A newly created firm might operate informally as a general partnership or might be incorporated.

To illustrate, consider an actual case of four young farmers, each of whom owned and operated approximately 300 acres of corn-soybean land in central Illinois. In each case, the operator felt that his operation was too small to achieve efficient use of machinery, labor, and management. Moreover, none of them felt that he had sufficient equity capital and credit to expand. Hence, these four farmers decided to merge as a general partnership providing a single operation of over 1,100 acres within an acceptable radius under an arrangement in which each retained title to his own land.

The merger allowed each operator to specialize in one phase of management. One assumed responsibility for budgeting, financing, and fiscal control. Another took on the planning, operation, and maintenance of the production and harvesting equipment. As an extension of this specialization, he supervised the machinery and crews in performing custom operations for other farmers. Another planned and supervised the cropping program, including the fertilizer and other farm chemical applications. Soon, he was also selling fertilizers and farm chemicals, including applications. The remaining partner specialized in marketing, including programs for forward contracting and futures contracts.

While this operation is not representative of what most "average" farmers are doing, it represents what can happen when farmers identify the nature of their problems, inventory their resources, and exercise imagination and initiative in resolving the problems.

Topics for Discussion

1. Discuss agriculture's need for outside-equity capital.
2. Identify the types of financial criteria a prospective outside investor might use in evaluating a farm investment.
3. Why are some types of agricultural enterprises better suited than others for attracting outside-equity capital?
4. Explain the concept of a tax shelter. What role does it play in attracting outside-equity capital in agriculture?
5. Compare proprietorships, general partnerships, limited partnerships, subchapter S corporations, and regular corporations in terms of their adaptability for raising outside-equity capital.
6. Why might a "private offering" be more advantageous to most agricultural firms than a "public sale" as a means of raising equity capital? Does it have any disadvantages?

7. Consider a farm business typical of your geographic area. In what ways might mergers help resolve some of the existing capital and management constraints?

References

1. Davenport, C., M. D. Boehlje, and D. Martin, *The Effects of Tax Policy on American Agriculture*, Agricultural Economics Report 480, ERS, USDA, Washington, D.C., 1982.

2. Friend, Irwin, *Investment Banking and the New Issues Market: Summary*, Vol. 3, Wharton School of Finance and Commerce, University of Pennsylvania, Philadelphia, 1965.

3. Hopkin, John A., *Cattle Feeding in California: A Study of Feedlot Finishing*, Bank of America, San Francisco, February 1957.

4. _____, "Conglomerate Growth in Agriculture," *Agricultural Finance Review*, 33(1972):15-21.

5. Krause, K. R., and H. Shapiro, "Tax Induced Investment in Agriculture: Gaps in Research," *Agricultural Economics Research*, 26:1(1974):13-21.

6. Matthews, S. F., and V. J. Rhodes, *The Use of Public Limited Partnership Financing in Agriculture for Income Tax Shelter*, North Central Regional Research Publication 223, July 1975.

7. Moore, C. V., "External Equity Capital in Production Agriculture," *Agricultural Finance Review*, 39(1979):72-82.

8. Scofield, W. H., "Nonfarm Equity Capital in Agriculture," *Agricultural Finance Review*, 33(1972):36-41.

9. *Securities Exchange Commission, Form S-1 Registration Statement Under the Securities Act of 1933*, U.S. Department of Commerce, Washington, D.C., 1958.

10. Sisson, C. A., "Tax Reform Act of 1976 and Its Effects on Farm Financial Structure," *Agricultural Finance Review*, 39(1979):83-90.

11. Solomon, Martin, Jr., *Investment Decisions in Small Business*, University of Kentucky, Lexington, 1963.

12. Thomas, K. H., and M. D. Boehlje, *Farm Business Arrangements: Which One for You?*, North Central Regional Extension Publication 50, College of Agriculture, Iowa State University, Ames, 1982.

13. Winter, Elmer L., *A Complete Guide to Making a Public Stock Offering*, Prentice-Hall, Inc., Englewood Cliffs, New Jersey, 1971.

14. Zwick, Jack, *A Handbook of Small Business Finance*, SBA 15, Washington, D.C., 1965.

Appendix

APPENDIX TABLE I
Future Value of $1.00
$V_n = \$1(1+i)^n$

n	.5%	.75%	1.0%	1.5%	2%	3%	4%	5%	6%	7%
1	1.0050	1.0075	1.0100	1.0150	1.0200	1.0300	1.0400	1.0500	1.0600	1.0700
2	1.0100	1.0151	1.0201	1.0302	1.0404	1.0609	1.0816	1.1025	1.1236	1.1449
3	1.0151	1.0227	1.0303	1.0457	1.0612	1.0927	1.1249	1.1576	1.1910	1.2250
4	1.0202	1.0303	1.0406	1.0614	1.0824	1.1255	1.1699	1.2155	1.2625	1.3108
5	1.0253	1.0381	1.0510	1.0773	1.1041	1.1593	1.2167	1.2763	1.3382	1.4026
6	1.0304	1.0459	1.0615	1.0934	1.1262	1.1941	1.2653	1.3401	1.4185	1.5007
7	1.0355	1.0537	1.0721	1.1098	1.1487	1.2299	1.3159	1.4071	1.5036	1.6058
8	1.0407	1.0616	1.0829	1.1265	1.1717	1.2668	1.3686	1.4775	1.5938	1.7182
9	1.0459	1.0696	1.0937	1.1434	1.1951	1.3048	1.4233	1.5513	1.6895	1.8385
10	1.0511	1.0776	1.1046	1.1605	1.2190	1.3439	1.4802	1.6289	1.7908	1.9672
11	1.0564	1.0857	1.1157	1.1779	1.2434	1.3842	1.5395	1.7103	1.8983	2.1049
12	1.0617	1.0938	1.1268	1.1956	1.2682	1.4258	1.6010	1.7959	2.0122	2.2522
13	1.0670	1.1020	1.1381	1.2136	1.2936	1.4685	1.6651	1.8856	2.1329	2.4098
14	1.0723	1.1103	1.1495	1.2318	1.3195	1.5126	1.7317	1.9799	2.2609	2.5785
15	1.0777	1.1186	1.1610	1.2502	1.3459	1.5580	1.8009	2.0789	2.3967	2.7590
16	1.0831	1.1270	1.1726	1.2690	1.3728	1.6047	1.8730	2.1829	2.5404	2.9522
17	1.0885	1.1354	1.1843	1.2880	1.4002	1.6528	1.9479	2.2920	2.6928	3.1588
18	1.0939	1.1440	1.1961	1.3073	1.4282	1.7024	2.0258	2.4066	2.8543	3.3799
19	1.0994	1.1525	1.2081	1.3270	1.4568	1.7535	2.1068	2.5269	3.0256	3.6165
20	1.1049	1.1612	1.2202	1.3469	1.4859	1.8061	2.1911	2.6533	3.2071	3.8697
24	1.1272	1.1964	1.2697	1.4295	1.6084	2.0328	2.5633	3.2251	4.0489	5.0724
25	1.1328	1.2054	1.2824	1.4509	1.6406	2.0938	2.6658	3.3864	4.2919	5.4274
30	1.1614	1.2513	1.3478	1.5631	1.8114	2.4273	3.2434	4.3219	5.7435	7.6123
36	1.1967	1.3086	1.4308	1.7091	2.0399	2.8983	4.1039	5.7918	8.1473	11.4239
40	1.2208	1.3483	1.4889	1.8140	2.2080	3.2620	4.8010	7.0400	10.2857	14.9745
48	1.2705	1.4314	1.6122	2.0435	2.5871	4.1323	6.5705	10.4013	16.3939	25.7289
50	1.2832	1.4530	1.6446	2.1052	2.6916	4.3839	7.1067	11.4674	18.4201	29.4570
60	1.3489	1.5657	1.8167	2.4432	3.2810	5.8916	10.5196	18.6792	32.9877	57.9464

(Continued)

APPENDIX TABLE I (Continued)

n	8%	9%	10%	11%	12%	13%	14%	15%	16%
1	1.0800	1.0900	1.1000	1.1100	1.1200	1.1300	1.1400	1.1500	1.1600
2	1.1664	1.1881	1.2100	1.2321	1.2544	1.2769	1.2996	1.3225	1.3456
3	1.2597	1.2950	1.3310	1.3676	1.4049	1.4429	1.4815	1.5209	1.5609
4	1.3605	1.4116	1.4641	1.5181	1.5735	1.6305	1.6890	1.7490	1.8106
5	1.4693	1.5386	1.6105	1.6851	1.7623	1.8424	1.9254	2.0114	2.1003
6	1.5869	1.6771	1.7716	1.8704	1.9738	2.0820	2.1950	2.3131	2.4364
7	1.7138	1.8280	1.9487	2.0762	2.2107	2.3526	2.5023	2.6600	2.8262
8	1.8509	1.9926	2.1436	2.3045	2.4760	2.6584	2.8526	3.0590	3.2784
9	1.9990	2.1719	2.3579	2.5580	2.7731	3.0040	3.2519	3.5179	3.8030
10	2.1589	2.3674	2.5937	2.8394	3.1058	3.3946	3.7072	4.0456	4.4114
11	2.3316	2.5804	2.8531	3.1518	3.4785	3.8359	4.2262	4.6524	5.1173
12	2.5182	2.8127	3.1384	3.4984	3.8960	4.3345	4.8179	5.3503	5.9360
13	2.7196	3.0658	3.4523	3.8833	4.3635	4.8980	5.4924	6.1528	6.8858
14	2.9372	3.3417	3.7975	4.3109	4.8871	5.5348	6.2613	7.0757	7.9875
15	3.1722	3.6425	4.1772	4.7846	5.4736	6.2543	7.1379	8.1371	9.2655
16	3.4259	3.9703	4.5950	5.3109	6.1304	7.0673	8.1372	9.3576	10.7480
17	3.7000	4.3276	5.0545	5.8951	6.8660	7.9861	9.2765	10.7613	12.4677
18	3.9960	4.7171	5.5599	6.5436	7.6900	9.0243	10.5752	12.3755	14.4625
19	4.3157	5.1417	6.1159	7.2633	8.6128	10.1974	12.0557	14.2318	16.7765
20	4.6610	5.6044	6.7275	8.0623	9.6463	11.5231	13.7435	16.3665	19.4608
24	6.3412	7.9111	9.8479	12.2391	15.1786	18.7881	23.2122	28.6252	35.2364
25	6.8485	8.6231	10.8347	13.5855	17.0000	21.2305	26.4619	32.9190	40.8742
30	10.0627	13.2677	17.4494	22.8923	29.9599	39.1159	50.9502	66.2118	85.8499
36	15.9682	22.2512	30.9127	42.8181	59.1356	81.4374	111.8342	153.1519	209.1643
40	21.7245	31.4094	45.2592	65.0008	93.0508	132.7816	188.8835	267.8635	378.7212
48	40.2106	62.5852	97.0172	149.7970	230.3908	352.9923	538.8065	819.4007	1241.6051
50	46.9016	74.3575	117.3908	184.5645	289.0015	450.7359	700.2330	1083.6574	1670.7038
60	101.2570	176.0312	304.4812	524.0562	897.5950	1530.0535	2595.9187	4383.9987	7370.2014

(Continued)

APPENDIX TABLE I (Continued)

n	17%	18%	19%	20%	21%	22%	23%	24%	25%
1	1.1700	1.1800	1.1900	1.2000	1.2100	1.2200	1.2300	1.2400	1.2500
2	1.3689	1.3924	1.4161	1.4400	1.4641	1.4884	1.5129	1.5376	1.5625
3	1.6016	1.6430	1.6852	1.7280	1.7716	1.8158	1.8609	1.9066	1.9531
4	1.8739	1.9388	2.0053	2.0736	2.1436	2.2153	2.2889	2.3642	2.4414
5	2.1920	2.2878	2.3864	2.4883	2.5937	2.7027	2.8153	2.9316	3.0518
6	2.5652	2.6996	2.8398	2.9860	3.1384	3.2973	3.4628	3.6352	3.8147
7	3.0012	3.1855	3.3793	3.5832	3.7975	4.0227	4.2593	4.5077	4.7684
8	3.5115	3.7589	4.0214	4.2998	4.5950	4.9077	5.2389	5.5895	5.9605
9	4.1084	4.4355	4.7854	5.1598	5.5599	5.9874	6.4439	6.9310	7.4506
10	4.8068	5.2338	5.6947	6.1917	6.7275	7.3046	7.9259	8.5944	9.3132
11	5.6240	6.1759	6.7767	7.4301	8.1403	8.9117	9.7489	10.6571	11.6415
12	6.5801	7.2876	8.0642	8.9161	9.8497	10.8722	11.9912	13.2148	14.5519
13	7.6987	8.5994	9.5964	10.6993	11.9182	13.2641	14.7491	16.3863	18.1899
14	9.0075	10.1472	11.4198	12.8392	14.4210	16.1822	18.1414	20.3191	22.7374
15	10.5387	11.9737	13.5895	15.4070	17.4494	19.7423	22.3140	25.1956	28.4217
16	12.3303	14.1290	16.1715	18.4884	21.1138	24.0856	27.4462	31.2426	35.5271
17	14.4265	16.6722	19.2441	22.1861	25.5477	29.3844	33.7588	38.7408	44.4089
18	16.8790	19.6733	22.9005	26.6233	30.9127	35.8490	41.5233	48.0386	55.5112
19	19.7484	23.2144	27.2516	31.9480	37.4043	43.7358	51.0737	59.5679	69.3889
20	23.1056	27.3930	32.4294	38.3376	45.2593	53.3576	62.8206	73.8641	86.7362
24	43.2973	53.1090	65.0320	79.4968	97.0172	118.2050	143.7880	174.6306	211.7582
25	50.6578	62.6686	77.3881	95.3962	117.3909	144.2101	176.8593	216.5420	264.6978
30	111.0647	143.3706	184.6753	273.3763	304.4816	389.7579	494.9129	634.8199	807.7936
36	284.8991	387.0368	524.4337	708.8019	955.5938	1285.1502	1724.1856	2307.7070	3081.4879
40	533.8687	750.3783	1051.6675	1469.7716	2048.4002	2847.0378	3946.4305	5455.9126	7523.1638
48	1874.6550	2820.5665	4229.1603	6319.7487	9412.3437	13972.4277	20674.9920	30495.8602	44841.5509
50	2566.2153	3927.3559	5988.9139	9100.4382	13780.6123	20796.5615	31279.1953	46890.4346	70064.9232
60	12335.3565	20555.1400	34104.9709	56347.5144	92709.0688	151911.2161	247917.2160	40.2996.3472	652530.4468

APPENDIX TABLE II
Present Value of $1.00
$$V_0 = \$1(1 + i)^{-n}$$

n	.5%	.75%	1%	1.5%	2%	3%	4%	5%	6%	7%
1	.9950	.9926	.9901	.9852	.9804	.9709	.9615	.9524	.9434	.9346
2	.9901	.9852	.9803	.9707	.9612	.9426	.9246	.9070	.8900	.8734
3	.9851	.9778	.9706	.9563	.9423	.9151	.8890	.8638	.8396	.8163
4	.9802	.9706	.9610	.9422	.9238	.8885	.8548	.8227	.7921	.7629
5	.9754	.9633	.9515	.9283	.9057	.8626	.8219	.7835	.7473	.7130
6	.9705	.9562	.9420	.9145	.8880	.8375	.7903	.7462	.7050	.6663
7	.9657	.9490	.9327	.9010	.8706	.8131	.7599	.7107	.6651	.6227
8	.9609	.9420	.9235	.8877	.8535	.7894	.7307	.6768	.6274	.5820
9	.9561	.9350	.9143	.8746	.8368	.7664	.7026	.6446	.5919	.5439
10	.9513	.9280	.9053	.8617	.8203	.7441	.6756	.6139	.5584	.5083
11	.9466	.9211	.8963	.8489	.8043	.7224	.6496	.5847	.5268	.4751
12	.9419	.9142	.8874	.8364	.7885	.7014	.6246	.5568	.4970	.4440
13	.9372	.9074	.8787	.8240	.7730	.6810	.6006	.5303	.4688	.4150
14	.9326	.9007	.8700	.8118	.7579	.6611	.5775	.5051	.4423	.3878
15	.9279	.8940	.8613	.7999	.7430	.6419	.5553	.4810	.4173	.3624
16	.9233	.8873	.8528	.7880	.7284	.6232	.5339	.4581	.3936	.3387
17	.9187	.8807	.8444	.7764	.7142	.6050	.5134	.4363	.3714	.3166
18	.9141	.8742	.8360	.7649	.7002	.5874	.4936	.4155	.3503	.2959
19	.9096	.8676	.8277	.7536	.6863	.5703	.4746	.3957	.3305	.2765
20	.9051	.8612	.8195	.7425	.6730	.5537	.4564	.3769	.3118	.2584
24	.8872	.8358	.7876	.6995	.6217	.4919	.3901	.3101	.2470	.1971
25	.8828	.8296	.7798	.6892	.6095	.4776	.3751	.2953	.2330	.1842
30	.8610	.7992	.7419	.6398	.5521	.4120	.3083	.2314	.1741	.1314
36	.8356	.7641	.6989	.5851	.4902	.3450	.2437	.1727	.1227	.0875
40	.8191	.7416	.6717	.5513	.4529	.3066	.2083	.1420	.0972	.0668
48	.7871	.6986	.6203	.4894	.3865	.2420	.1522	.0961	.0610	.0389
50	.7793	.6883	.6080	.4750	.3715	.2281	.1407	.0872	.0543	.0339
60	.7414	.6387	.5504	.4093	.3048	.1697	.0951	.0535	.0303	.0173

(Continued)

APPENDIX TABLE II (Continued)

n	8%	9%	10%	11%	12%	13%	14%	15%	16%
1	.9259	.9174	.9091	.9009	.8929	.8850	.8772	.8696	.8621
2	.8573	.8417	.8264	.8116	.7972	.7831	.7695	.7561	.7432
3	.7938	.7722	.7513	.7312	.7118	.6931	.6750	.6575	.6407
4	.7350	.7084	.6830	.6587	.6355	.6133	.5921	.5718	.5523
5	.6806	.6499	.6209	.5935	.5674	.5428	.5194	.4972	.4761
6	.6302	.5963	.5645	.5346	.5066	.4803	.4556	.4323	.4104
7	.5835	.5470	.5132	.4817	.4523	.4251	.3996	.3759	.3538
8	.5403	.5019	.4665	.4339	.4039	.3762	.3506	.3269	.3050
9	.5002	.4604	.4241	.3909	.3606	.3329	.3075	.2843	.2630
10	.4632	.4224	.3855	.3522	.3220	.2946	.2697	.2472	.2267
11	.4289	.3875	.3505	.3173	.2875	.2607	.2366	.2149	.1954
12	.3971	.3555	.3186	.2858	.2567	.2307	.2076	.1869	.1685
13	.3677	.3262	.2897	.2575	.2292	.2042	.1821	.1625	.1452
14	.3405	.2992	.2633	.2320	.2046	.1807	.1597	.1413	.1252
15	.3152	.2745	.2394	.2090	.1827	.1599	.1401	.1229	.1079
16	.2919	.2519	.2176	.1883	.1631	.1415	.1229	.1069	.0930
17	.2703	.2311	.1978	.1696	.1456	.1252	.1078	.0929	.0802
18	.2502	.2120	.1799	.1528	.1300	.1108	.0946	.0808	.0691
19	.2317	.1945	.1635	.1377	.1161	.0981	.0829	.0703	.0596
20	.2145	.1784	.1486	.1240	.1037	.0868	.0728	.0611	.0514
24	.1577	.1264	.1015	.0817	.0659	.0532	.0431	.0349	.0284
25	.1460	.1160	.0923	.0736	.0588	.0471	.0378	.0304	.0245
30	.0994	.0754	.0573	.0437	.0334	.0256	.0196	.0151	.0116
36	.0626	.0449	.0323	.0234	.0169	.0123	.0089	.0065	.0048
40	.0460	.0318	.0221	.0154	.0107	.0075	.0053	.0037	.0026
48	.0249	.0160	.0103	.0067	.0043	.0028	.0019	.0012	.0008
50	.0213	.0134	.0085	.0054	.0035	.0022	.0014	.0009	.0006
60	.0099	.0057	.0033	.0019	.0011	.0007	.0004	.0002	.0001

(Continued)

APPENDIX TABLE II (Continued)

n	17%	18%	19%	20%	21%	22%	23%	24%	25%
1	.8547	.8475	.8403	.8333	.8264	.8197	.8130	.8065	.8000
2	.7305	.7182	.7062	.6944	.6830	.6719	.6610	.6504	.6400
3	.6244	.6086	.5934	.5787	.5645	.5507	.5374	.5245	.5120
4	.5337	.5158	.4987	.4823	.4665	.4514	.4369	.4230	.4096
5	.4561	.4371	.4190	.4019	.3855	.3700	.3552	.3411	.3277
6	.3898	.3704	.3521	.3349	.3186	.3033	.2888	.2751	.2621
7	.3332	.3139	.2959	.2791	.2633	.2486	.2348	.2218	.2097
8	.2848	.2660	.2487	.2326	.2176	.2039	.1909	.1789	.1678
9	.2434	.2255	.2090	.1938	.1799	.1670	.1552	.1443	.1342
10	.2080	.1911	.1756	.1615	.1486	.1369	.1262	.1164	.1074
11	.1778	.1619	.1476	.1346	.1228	.1122	.1026	.0938	.0859
12	.1520	.1372	.1240	.1122	.1015	.0920	.0834	.0757	.0687
13	.1299	.1163	.1042	.0935	.0839	.0754	.0678	.0610	.0550
14	.1110	.0985	.0876	.0779	.0693	.0618	.0551	.0492	.0440
15	.0949	.0835	.0736	.0649	.0573	.0507	.0448	.0397	.0352
16	.0811	.0708	.0618	.0541	.0474	.0415	.0364	.0320	.0281
17	.0693	.0600	.0520	.0451	.0391	.0340	.0296	.0258	.0225
18	.0592	.0508	.0437	.0376	.0323	.0279	.0241	.0208	.0180
19	.0506	.0431	.0367	.0313	.0267	.0229	.0196	.0168	.0144
20	.0433	.0365	.0308	.0261	.0221	.0187	.0159	.0135	.0115
24	.0231	.0188	.0154	.0126	.0103	.0085	.0070	.0057	.0047
25	.0197	.0160	.0129	.0105	.0085	.0069	.0057	.0046	.0038
30	.0090	.0070	.0054	.0042	.0033	.0026	.0020	.0016	.0012
36	.0035	.0026	.0019	.0014	.0010	.0008	.0006	.0004	.0001
40	.0019	.0013	.0010	.0007	.0005	.0004	.0003	.0002	.0000
48	.0005	.0004	.0002	.0002	.0001	.0001	.0000	.0000	.0000
50	.0004	.0003	.0002	.0001	.0001	.0000	.0000	.0000	.0000
60	.0001	.0000	.0000	.0000	.0000	.0000	.0000	.0000	.0000

APPENDIX TABLE III
Future Values of a Uniform Series

$$V_n = \$1\left[\frac{(1+i)^n - 1}{i}\right]$$

n	.5%	.75%	1%	1.5%	2%	3%	4%	5%	6%	7%
1	1.0000	1.0000	1.0000	1.0000	1.0000	1.0000	1.0000	1.0000	1.0000	1.0000
2	2.0050	2.0075	2.0100	2.0150	2.0200	2.0300	2.0400	2.0500	2.0600	2.0700
3	3.0150	3.0226	3.0301	3.0452	3.0604	3.0909	3.1216	3.1525	3.1836	3.2149
4	4.0301	4.0452	4.0604	4.0909	4.1216	4.1836	4.2465	4.3101	4.3746	4.4399
5	5.0503	5.0755	5.1010	5.1523	5.2040	5.3091	5.4163	5.5276	5.6371	5.7507
6	6.0755	6.1136	6.1520	6.2295	6.3081	6.4684	6.6330	6.8019	6.9753	7.1533
7	7.1059	7.1595	7.2135	7.3230	7.4343	7.6625	7.8983	8.1420	8.3938	8.6540
8	8.1414	8.2132	8.2857	8.4328	8.5830	8.8923	9.2142	9.5491	9.9975	10.2598
9	9.1821	9.2748	9.3605	9.5593	9.7546	10.1591	10.5828	11.0266	11.4913	11.9780
10	10.2280	10.3443	10.4622	10.7027	10.9497	11.4639	12.0061	12.5779	13.1808	13.8164
11	11.2792	11.4219	11.5668	11.8633	12.1687	12.8078	13.4864	14.2068	14.9716	15.7836
12	12.3356	12.5075	12.6825	13.0412	13.4121	14.1920	15.0258	15.9171	16.8699	17.8885
13	13.3972	13.6014	13.8093	14.2368	14.6803	15.6178	16.6268	17.7130	18.8821	20.1406
14	14.4642	14.7034	14.9474	15.4504	15.9739	17.0863	18.2918	19.5986	21.0151	22.5505
15	15.5365	15.8137	16.0969	16.6821	17.2934	18.5989	20.0236	21.5786	23.2760	25.1290
16	16.6142	16.9323	17.2579	17.9324	18.6393	20.1569	21.8245	23.6575	25.6725	27.8881
17	17.6973	18.0593	18.4304	19.2041	20.0121	21.7616	23.6975	25.8404	28.2129	30.8402
18	18.7858	19.1947	19.6147	20.4894	21.4123	23.4144	25.6454	28.1324	30.9057	33.9990
19	19.8797	20.3387	20.8109	21.7967	22.8406	25.1169	27.6712	30.5390	33.7600	37.3790
20	20.9791	21.4912	22.0190	23.1237	24.2974	26.8704	29.7781	33.0660	36.7856	40.9955
24	25.4320	26.1885	26.9735	28.6335	30.4219	34.4265	39.0826	44.5020	50.8156	58.1767
25	26.5591	27.3848	28.2432	30.0630	32.0303	36.4593	41.6459	47.7271	54.8645	63.2490
30	32.2800	33.5029	34.7849	37.5387	40.5681	47.5754	56.0849	66.4388	79.0582	74.4608
36	39.3361	41.1527	43.0769	47.2760	51.9944	63.2759	77.5983	95.8363	119.1209	148.9135
40	44.1588	46.4465	48.8864	54.2679	60.4020	75.4013	95.0255	120.7998	154.7620	199.6351
48	54.0978	57.5207	61.2226	69.5652	79.3535	104.4084	139.2632	188.0254	256.5645	353.2701
50	56.6452	60.3943	64.4632	73.6828	84.5794	112.7969	152.6671	209.3480	290.3359	406.5289
60	69.7700	75.4241	81.6697	96.2147	114.0515	163.0534	237.9907	353.5837	533.1282	613.5204

(Continued)

APPENDIX TABLE III (Continued)

n	8%	9%	10%	11%	12%	13%	14%	15%	16%
1	1.0000	1.0000	1.0000	1.0000	1.0000	1.0000	1.0000	1.0000	1.0000
2	2.0800	2.0900	2.1000	2.1100	2.1200	2.1300	2.1400	2.1500	2.1600
3	3.2464	3.2781	3.3100	3.3421	3.3744	3.4069	3.4396	3.4725	3.5056
4	4.5061	4.5731	4.6410	4.7097	4.7793	4.8498	4.9211	4.9934	5.0665
5	5.8666	5.9847	6.1051	6.2278	6.3528	6.4803	6.6101	6.7424	6.8771
6	7.3359	7.5233	7.7156	7.9129	8.1152	8.3227	8.5355	8.7537	8.9775
7	8.9228	9.2004	9.4872	9.7833	10.0890	10.4047	10.7305	11.0668	11.4139
8	10.6366	11.0285	11.4359	11.8594	12.2997	12.7573	13.2328	13.7268	14.2401
9	12.4876	13.0210	13.5795	14.1640	14.7757	15.4157	16.0853	16.7858	17.5185
10	14.4866	15.1929	15.9374	16.7220	17.5487	18.4197	19.3373	20.3037	21.3215
11	16.6455	17.5603	18.5312	19.5614	20.6546	21.8143	23.0445	24.3493	25.7329
12	18.9771	20.1407	21.3843	22.7132	24.1331	25.6502	27.2707	29.0017	30.8502
13	21.4953	22.9534	24.5227	26.2116	28.0291	29.9847	32.0887	34.3519	36.7562
14	24.2149	26.0192	27.9750	30.0949	32.3926	34.8827	37.5811	40.5047	43.6720
15	27.1521	29.3609	31.7725	34.4054	37.2797	40.4175	43.8424	47.5804	51.6595
16	30.3243	33.0034	35.9497	39.1899	42.7533	46.6717	50.9804	55.7175	60.9250
17	33.7502	36.9737	40.5447	44.5008	48.8837	53.7391	59.1176	65.0751	71.6730
18	37.4502	41.3013	45.5992	50.3959	55.7497	61.7251	68.3941	75.8364	84.1407
19	41.4463	46.0185	51.1591	56.9395	63.4397	70.7494	78.9692	88.2118	98.6032
20	45.7620	51.1601	57.2750	64.2028	72.0524	80.9468	91.0249	102.4436	115.3797
24	66.7648	76.7898	88.4973	102.1742	118.1552	136.8315	158.6586	184.1678	213.9776
25	73.1059	84.7009	98.3471	114.4133	133.3339	155.6196	181.8708	212.7930	249.2140
30	113.2832	136.3075	164.4940	199.0209	241.3327	293.1992	356.7868	434.7451	530.3117
36	187.1021	236.1247	299.1268	380.1644	484.4631	618.7493	791.6729	1014.3457	1301.0270
40	259.0565	337.8824	442.5926	581.8261	767.0914	1013.7042	1342.0251	1779.0903	2360.7572
48	490.1322	684.2804	960.1723	1352.6996	1911.898	2707.6334	3841.4753	5456.0047	7753.7817
50	573.7702	815.0836	1163.9085	1668.7712	2400.0182	3459.5071	4994.5213	7217.7163	10435.6488
60	1235.2133	1944.7921	3034.8164	4755.0658	7471.6411	11761.9498	18535.1333	29219.9916	46057.5085

(Continued)

APPENDIX TABLE III (Continued)

n	17%	18%	19%	20%	21%	22%	23%	24%	25%
1	1.0000	1.0000	1.0000	1.0000	1.0000	1.0000	1.0000	1.0000	1.0000
2	2.1700	2.1800	2.1900	2.2000	2.2100	2.2000	2.2300	2.2400	2.2500
3	3.5389	3.5724	3.6061	3.6400	3.6741	3.7084	3.7429	3.7776	3.8125
4	5.1405	5.2154	5.2913	5.3680	5.4457	5.5242	5.6038	5.6842	5.7656
5	7.0144	7.1542	7.2966	7.4416	7.5892	7.7396	7.8926	8.0484	8.2070
6	9.2068	9.4420	9.6830	9.9299	10.1830	10.4423	10.7079	10.9801	11.2588
7	11.7720	12.1415	12.5227	12.9159	13.3214	13.7396	14.1708	14.6153	15.0735
8	14.7733	15.3270	15.9020	16.4991	17.1189	17.7623	18.4300	19.1229	19.8419
9	18.2847	19.0859	19.9234	20.7989	21.7139	22.6700	23.6690	24.7125	25.8023
10	22.3931	23.5213	24.7089	25.9587	27.2738	28.6574	30.1128	31.6434	'33.2529
11	27.1999	28.7551	30.4035	32.1504	34.0013	35.9620	38.0388	40.2379	42.5661
12	32.8239	34.9311	37.1802	39.5805	42.1416	44.4737	47.7877	50.8950	54.2077
13	39.4040	42.2187	45.2445	48.4966	51.9913	55.7459	59.7788	64.1097	68.7596
14	47.1027	50.8180	54.8409	59.1959	63.9095	69.0100	74.5280	80.4961	86.9495
15	56.1101	60.9653	66.2607	72.0351	78.3305	85.1922	92.6694	100.8151	109.6868
16	66.6488	72.9390	79.8502	87.4421	95.7799	104.9345	114.9834	126.0108	138.1085
17	78.9792	87.0680	96.0218	105.9306	116.8937	129.0201	142.4295	157.2534	173.6357
18	93.4056	103.7403	115.2659	128.1167	142.4413	158.4045	176.1883	195.9942	218.0446
19	110.2846	123.4135	138.1664	154.7400	173.3540	194.2535	217.7116	244.0328	273.5558
20	130.0329	146.6280	165.4180	186.6880	210.7584	237.9893	268.7853	303.6006	342.9447
24	248.8076	289.4945	337.0105	392.4842	457.2249	532.7501	620.8174	723.4610	843.0329
25	292.1049	342.6035	402.0425	471.9811	554.2422	650.9551	764.6054	898.0916	1054.7912
30	647.4391	790.9480	966.7122	1181.8816	1445.1507	1767.0813	2160.4907	2640.9164	3227.1743
36	1669.9945	2144.6459	2754.9143	3539.0094	4545.6848	5837.0466	7492.1113	9611.2791	12321.9516
40	3134.5218	4163.2130	5529.8299	7343.8578	9749.5248	12936.5353	17154.0456	22728.8026	30088.6554
48	11021.5002	15664.2586	22253.4753	31593.7436	44815.9222	63506.4897	89886.9215	127061.9174	179362.2034
50	15089.5017	21813.0937	31515.3363	45497.1908	65617.2016	94525.2793	135992.1536	195372.6442	280255.6929
60	72555.0381	114189.6664	179494.5838	281732.5718	441466.9943	690500.9823	1077896.5910	1679147.2800	2610117.7870

APPENDIX TABLE IV
Present Value of a Uniform Series

$$V_0 = \$1\left[\frac{1-(1+i)^{-n}}{i}\right]$$

n	.5%	.75%	1%	1.5%	2%	3%	4%	5%	6%	7%
1	.9950	.9926	.9901	.9852	.9804	.9709	.9615	.9524	.9434	.9346
2	1.9851	1.9777	1.9704	1.9559	1.9416	1.9135	1.8861	1.8594	1.8334	1.8080
3	2.9702	2.9556	2.9410	2.9122	2.8839	2.8286	2.7751	2.7232	2.6730	2.6243
4	3.9505	3.9261	3.9020	3.8544	3.8077	3.7171	3.6299	3.5460	3.4651	3.3872
5	4.9259	4.8894	4.8534	4.7826	4.7135	4.5797	4.4518	4.3295	4.2124	4.1002
6	5.8964	5.8456	5.7955	5.6972	5.6014	5.4172	5.2421	5.0757	4.9173	4.7665
7	6.8621	6.7946	6.7282	6.5982	6.4720	6.2303	6.0021	5.7864	5.5824	5.3893
8	7.8230	7.7366	7.6517	7.4859	7.3255	7.0197	6.7327	6.4632	6.2098	5.9713
9	8.7791	8.6716	8.5660	8.3605	8.1622	7.7861	7.4353	7.1078	6.8017	6.5152
10	9.7304	9.5996	9.4713	9.2222	8.8926	8.5302	8.1109	7.7217	7.3601	7.0236
11	10.6770	10.5207	10.3676	10.0711	9.7868	9.2526	8.7605	8.3064	7.8869	7.4987
12	11.6189	11.4349	11.2551	10.9075	10.5753	9.9540	9.3851	8.8633	8.3838	7.9427
13	12.5562	12.3423	12.1337	11.7315	11.3484	10.6350	9.9856	9.3936	8.8527	8.3577
14	13.4887	13.2430	13.0037	12.5434	12.1062	11.2961	10.5631	9.8986	9.2950	8.7455
15	14.4166	14.1370	13.8651	13.3432	12.8493	11.9379	11.1184	10.3797	9.7122	9.1079
16	15.3399	15.0243	14.7179	14.1313	13.5777	12.5611	11.6523	10.8378	10.1059	9.4466
17	16.2586	15.9050	15.5623	14.9076	14.2919	13.1661	12.1657	11.2741	10.4773	9.7632
18	17.1728	16.7792	16.3983	15.6726	14.9920	13.7535	12.6593	11.6896	10.8276	10.0591
19	18.0824	17.6468	17.2260	16.4262	15.6785	14.3238	13.1339	12.0853	11.1581	10.3356
20	18.9874	18.5080	18.0456	17.1686	16.3514	14.8775	13.5903	12.4622	11.4699	10.5940
24	22.5629	21.8891	21.2434	20.0304	18.9139	16.9355	15.2470	13.7986	12.5504	11.4693
25	23.4456	22.7188	22.0232	20.7196	19.5235	17.4131	15.6221	14.0939	12.7834	11.6536
30	27.7941	26.7751	25.8077	24.0158	22.3965	19.6004	17.2920	15.3725	13.7648	12.4090
36	32.8710	31.4468	30.1075	27.6607	25.4888	21.8323	18.9083	16.5469	14.6210	13.0352
40	36.1722	34.4469	32.8347	29.9158	27.3555	23.1148	19.7928	17.1591	15.0463	13.3317
48	42.5803	40.1848	37.9740	34.0426	30.6731	25.2667	21.1951	18.0772	15.6500	13.7305
50	44.1428	41.5664	39.1961	35.9997	31.4236	25.7298	21.4822	18.2559	15.7619	13.8007
60	51.7256	48.1734	44.9550	39.3803	34.7609	27.6756	22.6235	18.9293	16.1614	14.0392

(Continued)

APPENDIX TABLE IV (Continued)

n	8%	9%	10%	11%	12%	13%	14%	15%	16%
1	.9259	.9174	.9091	.9009	.8929	.8850	.8772	.8696	.8621
2	1.7833	1.7591	1.7355	1.7125	1.6901	1.6681	1.6467	1.6257	1.6052
3	2.5771	2.5313	2.4869	2.4437	2.4018	2.3612	2.3216	2.2832	2.2459
4	3.3121	3.2397	3.1699	3.1024	3.0373	2.9745	2.9137	2.8550	2.7982
5	3.9927	3.8897	3.7908	3.6959	3.6048	3.5172	3.4331	3.3522	3.2743
6	4.6229	4.4859	4.3553	4.2305	4.1114	3.9975	3.8889	3.7845	3.6847
7	5.2064	5.0330	4.8684	4.7122	4.5638	4.4226	4.2883	4.1604	4.0386
8	5.7466	5.5348	5.3349	5.1461	4.9676	4.7988	4.6389	4.4873	4.3436
9	6.2469	5.9952	5.7590	5.5370	5.3282	5.1317	4.9464	4.7716	4.6065
10	6.7101	6.4177	6.1446	5.8892	5.6502	5.4262	5.2161	5.0188	4.8332
11	7.1390	6.8052	6.4951	6.2065	5.9377	5.6868	5.4527	5.2337	5.0286
12	7.5361	7.1607	6.8137	6.4924	6.1944	5.9176	5.6603	5.4206	5.1971
13	7.9038	7.4869	7.1034	6.7499	6.4235	6.1218	5.8424	5.5831	5.3423
14	8.2442	7.7862	7.3667	6.9819	6.6282	6.3025	6.0021	5.7245	5.4675
15	8.5595	8.0607	7.6061	7.1909	6.8109	6.4624	6.1422	5.8474	5.5755
16	8.8514	8.3126	7.8237	7.3792	6.9740	6.6039	6.2651	5.9542	5.6685
17	9.1216	8.5436	8.0216	7.5488	7.1196	6.7291	6.3729	6.0472	5.7487
18	9.3719	8.7556	8.2014	7.7016	7.2497	6.8399	6.4674	6.1280	5.8178
19	9.6036	8.9501	8.3649	7.8393	7.3658	6.9380	6.5504	6.1982	5.8775
20	9.8181	9.1285	8.5136	7.9633	7.4694	7.0248	6.6231	6.2593	5.9288
24	10.5288	9.7066	8.9847	8.3481	7.7843	7.2829	6.8351	6.4338	6.0726
25	10.6748	9.8226	9.0770	8.4217	7.8431	7.3300	6.8729	6.4641	6.0971
30	11.2578	10.2737	9.4269	8.6938	8.0552	7.4959	7.0027	6.5660	6.1772
36	11.7172	10.6118	9.6765	8.8786	8.1924	7.5979	7.0790	6.6231	6.2201
40	11.9246	10.7574	9.7791	8.9511	8.2438	7.6344	7.1050	6.6418	6.2335
48	12.1891	10.9336	9.8969	9.0302	8.2972	7.6705	7.1296	6.6585	6.2450
50	12.2335	10.9617	9.9148	9.0417	8.3045	7.6752	7.1327	6.6605	6.2463
60	12.3766	11.0480	9.9672	9.0736	8.3240	7.6873	7.1401	6.6651	6.2492

(Continued)

APPENDIX TABLE IV (Continued)

n	17%	18%	19%	20%	21%	22%	23%	24%	25%
1	.8547	.8475	.8402	.8333	.8264	.8197	.8130	.8065	.8000
2	1.5852	1.5656	1.5465	1.5278	1.5095	1.4915	1.4740	1.4568	1.4400
3	2.2096	2.1743	2.1399	2.1065	2.0739	2.0422	2.0114	1.9813	1.9520
4	2.7432	2.6901	2.6386	2.5887	2.5404	2.4936	2.4483	2.4043	2.3616
5	3.1993	3.1272	3.0576	2.9906	2.9260	2.8636	2.8035	2.7454	2.6893
6	3.5892	3.4976	3.4098	3.3255	3.2446	3.1669	3.0923	3.0205	2.9514
7	3.9224	3.8115	3.7057	3.6046	3.5079	3.4155	3.3270	3.2423	3.1611
8	4.2072	4.0776	3.9544	3.8372	3.7256	3.6193	3.5179	3.4212	3.3289
9	4.4506	4.3030	4.1633	4.0310	3.9054	3.7863	3.6731	3.5655	3.4631
10	4.6586	4.4941	4.3389	4.1925	4.0541	3.9232	3.7993	3.6819	3.5705
11	4.8364	4.6560	4.4865	4.3271	4.1769	4.0354	3.9018	3.7757	3.6564
12	4.9884	4.7932	4.6105	4.4392	4.2784	4.1274	3.9852	3.8514	3.7251
13	5.1183	4.9095	4.7147	4.5327	4.3624	4.2028	4.0530	3.9124	3.7801
14	5.2293	5.0081	4.8023	4.6106	4.4317	4.2646	4.1082	3.9616	3.8241
15	5.3242	5.0916	4.8759	4.6755	4.4890	4.3152	4.1530	4.0013	3.8593
16	5.4053	5.1624	4.9377	4.7296	4.5364	4.3567	4.1894	4.0333	3.8874
17	5.4746	5.2223	4.9897	4.7746	4.5755	4.3908	4.2190	4.0591	3.9099
18	5.5339	5.2732	5.0333	4.8122	4.6079	4.4187	4.2431	4.0799	3.9279
19	5.5845	5.3162	5.0700	4.8435	4.6346	4.4415	4.2627	4.0967	3.9424
20	5.6278	5.3527	5.1009	4.8696	4.6567	4.4603	4.2786	4.1103	3.9539
24	5.7465	5.4509	5.1822	4.9371	4.7128	4.5070	4.3176	4.1428	3.9811
25	5.7662	5.4669	5.1951	4.9476	4.7213	4.5139	4.3232	4.1474	3.9849
30	5.8294	5.5168	5.2347	4.9789	4.7463	4.5338	4.3391	4.1601	3.9950
36	5.8617	5.5412	5.2531	4.9929	4.7569	4.5419	4.3453	4.1649	3.9987
40	5.8713	5.5482	5.2582	4.9966	4.7596	4.5439	4.3467	4.1659	3.9995
48	5.8792	5.5536	5.2619	4.9992	4.7614	4.5451	4.3476	4.1665	3.9999
50	5.8801	5.5541	5.2623	4.9995	4.7616	4.5452	4.3477	4.1666	3.9999
60	5.8819	5.5553	5.2630	4.9999	4.7619	4.5454	4.3478	4.1667	4.0000

Indexes

NAME INDEX

SUBJECT INDEX